The Dark Reign of Gothic Rock

In The Reptile House
With
The Sisters of Mercy
Bauhaus, and The Cure

Rock'n'roll put into practise the fermenting liberation of post-war teenaged exuberance and proved that kids were no longer merely objects awaiting the protracted death of adulthood.

Glam liberated sex, in all its manifold permutations.

Punk crystallised the frustrations that came with freedom and rubbed the establishment's nose into all its foul failures.

And Gothic unchained the spirit and freed the soul.

All that Gothic Rock would ever become is captured on The Sisters of Mercy's REPTILE HOUSE EP; all that a hundred, a thousand, bands have tried to recapture in their own variations was blueprinted across those five (six if you count the reprise of 'Kiss The Carpet') songs. It is to the Sisters' own enduring credit that they would not be counted among that number.

First edition published in 2002 by Helter Skelter Publishing
4 Denmark Street, London

Copyright 2002 © Dave Thompson

A CIP record for this book is available from the British Library

ISBN 1-900924-48-X

The authors would like to give special thanks for help beyond the call of duty to Bleddyn Butcher and Mick Mercer. For anyone interested in discovering more about goth and, in particular, anyone who would like to see more photos of goth bands, check out Mick's excellent website at www.mickmercer.com
Thanks also for special help with visual material go to
Richard Strange http://www.richardstrange.com and
Stephen Wilkin http://www.dharmajester.com

The Dark Reign of Gothic Rock

In The Reptile House With The Sisters of Mercy Bauhaus and The Cure

By Dave Thompson

Helter Skelter Publishing

Contents

Acknowledgements

Any book this size necessarily demands the help and dedication of an army of people – I'd like to thank everybody who threw something into the pot, but most especially Jo-Ann Greene, for providing access to her own redoubtable Gothic archive; Amy Hanson, for donating her 1998 Love & Rockets interview, and remembering so much that I'd forgotten; Brian Perera and Barbara Mitchell, for their enthusiasm and energy; and editor Sean Body for some great ideas and more besides.

And then there's the musicians who spent so much time over the years, reflecting upon their own contributions to the cabinet – Craig Adams, Daniel Ash, Ian Astbury, Jay and Michael Aston, Kirk Brandon, Budgie, Pete Burns, Nick Cave, Billy Duffy, Nik Fiend, Simon Gallup, Kevin Haskins, Peter Hook, Wayne Hussey, David J, Brian James, Nick Marsh, Stephen Morris, Peter Murphy, Iggy Pop, Dave Roberts, Rocco, Steve Severin, Siouxsie Sioux, Robert Smith, James Stevenson, Colin Stoner, Richard Strange, Bernard Sumner, Dave Vanian, Rozz Williams, Steve Wilkins, Ollie Wisdom – and anyone/everyone else.

Finally, thanks to everybody else who helped bring the beast to life – Anchorite Man; Bateerz and family; Blind Pew; Barb East; Ella and Sprocket; Gef the Talking Mongoose; the Gremlins who live in the furnace; K-Mart (not the store); Geoff Monmouth; Nutkin; Snarleyyowl The Cat Fiend; Sonny; Squidge and Grabby; a lot of Thompsons and Neville Viking.

Introduction
'The Bracket of Goth'

Wherein the author discusses the nature of Gothic, or Dark, Rock and, in questioning some of its restrictive definitions, sets out his stall for what is to come.

"To be credited among the founding fathers of the movement is to be rated within a hierarchy that includes Elvis Presley and the Beatles, Pink Floyd and David Bowie, the Sex Pistols and Nirvana."

 **hat** is Dark Rock?

A good question. It isn't, after all, one of those familiar terms forever bandied around by rock historians – it isn't Punk or Glam or Rockabilly or Psychedelia, although there are elements of all four in there. Neither is it Gothic, Industrial, Ethereal or Horror Rock, although those movements, too, have a part to play in the story.

Rather, Dark Rock is more-or-less an umbrella term beneath which we can place great swathes of that generation of British rock bands that grew out of the first fires of Punk in the late 1970s, but who drew their impetus and inspiration from far further afield, and then spread them even wider.

Who would have thought, watching Bauhaus' twisted vision of glam-from-beyond-the-grave, that, one day, Marilyn Manson would be taking much of the same vision to the portals of America's heart? That Southern Death Cult's gestating mutation from tribal intensity to hard rock insanity would morph into the calculated hedonism of Guns n'Roses? That the Sisters of Mercy's twice-removed Suicide sonics would spawn the nihilistic cacophony of Nine Inch Nails? Or, that more than 20 years after it rose, peaked and was ostensibly buried, the musical form that those bands pioneered would remain such a vibrant art form that it is all but unrecognisable to its forefathers themselves.

Today's Goths, the black-clad, white-faced, ghoulishly grave individuals for whom Bela remains undead, have little to do with the Gothic Rock that was created and christened in the first frightened years of Thatcher's Britain. Neither do the Industrial noise merchants who still clatter on the furthest extremes of the mainstream; neither do the Brit Pop bands that flourished in the mid-1990s, and who now labour as uncomfortably beneath that term as Bauhaus and co did beneath theirs.

They share little, though they owe a lot. By refusing to admit to (or even acknowledge) that debt, they perpetuate the creative impulse that fired those earlier bands in the first place, a need to continue pressing forward and never look back.

There was always more Bauhaus than Bowie about Suede, which might well be why Brett Anderson always decried the media's insistence on christening him an even thinner White Duke. Gene clearly have as much in common with Joy Division as they do the more frequently cited Smiths and/or Morrissey; and, as for Pulp, their Dark Rock credentials reach back to the height of the music in its original form. Their debut album, *It*, that ranks among the most off-kilter treats of the entire era. And that is before you recall that one of their earliest members, the young Simon Hinkler, later turned up in the Mission.

Dark rock is everywhere, then, and in almost everything. But this book is not about where it is today; it is not even, always, about what led up to today. Rather, it is an examination of what transpired when one specific tentacle of the post-Punk British rock octopus stopped flailing around in the wastes above its head, and burrowed instead into its blackest cave, there to contemplate… whatever.

Some of its thoughts were indeed of a distinctly Gothic bent. Mrs Radcliffe, Edgar Allen Poe, Mary Shelley, Alice Cooper and Sir Francis Dashwood, Gothic archetypes one and all, each plays their part in the pantomime. But others ricocheted off at a myriad other tangents – warped sex, dada-damaged art, sick humour, philosophical literature, Andy Warhol, Agatha Christie, *Dr Who* and Vincent Price; and that's just for starters.

It was an age… a decade… that began with Punk unchaining the shackles of expression and purpose; that brooded in the shadow of Siouxsie and the Banshees, Joy Division and the Doctors of Madness; that shuddered into daylight with Bauhaus, the Cure and the Sisters Of Mercy; that exploded into hyper-cult prominence via Specimen, Alien Sex Fiend and the Sex Gang Children before attaining its ultimate destiny in the arenas of America with the Cult, the Mission and Love and Rockets, direct descendents of, respectively, the tribally inclined Southern Death Cult, the 'classic' sundered Sisters and, with circular purity, Bela's boys in Bauhaus.

But it was an age, too, when a lot of bands discovered that, sometimes, it didn't matter what they said or did – audiences were going to make up their own minds regardless. As early as 1982, what we here call Dark Rock was already being dubbed Gothic Rock, and Siouxsie and the Banshees' bassist Steve Severin speaks for almost all of those bands when he states, 'All the time the Gothic thing was growing up alongside us, we were doing something completely different to what the audience imagined we were doing.'

That something, of course, would swiftly be sublimated beneath this new audience's demands, with oft-times fatal results. 'The Gothic tag was always there,' Bauhaus' Peter Murphy has mourned, 'and, of course, we eventually found ourselves playing to our reputation. That's really why Bauhaus didn't have a longevity. We were just clicking with energy but, when it came down to thinking about what we were doing, we realized that we were pandering to the audience, to what we thought the audience would like.' The Gothic audience.

Popular musical histories – that is, those weighty tomes that line the bookshop shelves with phrases like 'encyclopaedia of rock' prominent in their titles – describe Gothic as a style of dress characterised by an abundance of black, lace and pancake make-up, and Gothic Rock as a musical movement which developed in Britain towards the end of the 1970s, one of the half dozen or so viable life forms to be spawned by the exploding consciousness of Punk.

Read on and you will learn how it flourished flirtatiously on the fringes of the mainstream for perhaps three years, until a new thrill came along to replace it, then slunk underground, until its absorption, in the early 1990s, into the Industrial noise revolution then making itself heard in the United States.

Delve further and you will discover how, again, it flourished for a few years, only to be axed down once more by the countrywide hysteria that followed a succession of highly publicised, over-analysed American High School shootings later in the decade. The killers wore black and didn't get on with the jocks. Their websites quoted from Crowley and Manson (Charlie, not Marilyn), and they rehearsed in their garage with bands called the Cryptic Corpsefuckers. In the eyes of an hysterical tabloid media (is there any other kind?), 'Goth' became synonymous with 'Psychopathic Son Of A Bitch,' and the nation's true Goths were painting smiley faces on their crypts before the first headlines had even hit the streets.

All of this is probably true and, if that satisfies you, our job here is done. Like Glam before it, and Baggy thereafter, Gothic Rock was simply another of the uniformed convolutions that the British pop scene is so adept at producing… running parallel with that original Gothic heyday, after all, were such three-minute wonders as Power Pop, 2-Tone, Mod, Oi! and the Futurists, and where are any of those today?

Propping up the Needless Reissue racks, as another record shop owner opens a boxful of remastered Leyton Buzzards CDs and wonders, what on earth possessed him to stock them? Replace, in your mind, the Buzzards with any of Goth's great survivors – Sex Gang Children, Fields of the Nephilim, Ghost Dance, Alien Sex Fiend – and the same scenario replays every time.

Yet Gothic, as befits a genre born of the fascinations it espouses, has never submitted itself to such pat autopsy. There are, after all, two very distinct forms of musical movement: those that are created, by the media, by the music, by sheer force of personality; and those that have existed all along, simply awaiting the moment when the zeitgeist zaps and history catches up with ambition.

Into the first category, one can place any of the movements that shared Gothic Rock's original limelight, and most of those on either side of it. Into the second, one can place perhaps four.

The rock'n'roll of Elvis and Bill Haley, which put into practise the fermenting liberation of post-war teenaged exuberance, and proved that kids were no longer merely objects awaiting the protracted death of adulthood.

Punk, which crystallised the frustrations which that freedom itself thrust to the fore, and rubbed the establishment's nose into all its foul failures.

Glam, which liberated sex, in all its manifold permutations, from behind the bike shed and the graffiti-strewn public lavatory, and forced society to finally take the 'X' out of experimentation.

And Gothic, which unchained the spirit and freed the soul.

Attempting to trace the musical antecedents of the first three of those movements is relatively straightforward. Glibly, rock'n'roll grew from R&B, which in turn sprang from the blues. Glam is younger, but only just. Its founding principles were certainly formulating in the music halls of Victorian Britain, and taking shape in the cabarets of Weimar Germany. Punk is more youthful still, but was certainly in the air a full decade before the Sex Pistols fired their first shots, in the urban squall of the Velvet Underground, and the nihilistic slobber of the Stooges. And, along each of those lines of descent, one can isolate the records, the groups, and the events that ultimately shaped the things to come.

Gothic, however, is more subjective, depending upon whether one approaches it in terms of performance, mood or simple aesthetic. Artistically, one could begin one's excavations with the grim, decay-etched works of 17th century Italian landscape artist Salvator Rosa, but that is to complicate and over-intellectualise matters far more than is necessary. Musically, too, there are moments in the classical catalogue that are supremely Gothic – and have provided the soundtrack for more horror movies than one would even want to begin calculating.

In terms of popular song, however, the options are less open to interpretation. One begins with Leonard Cohen, the original Duke of Despair, oozing razor blades and crucifixes from every sonorous lyric and, besides that, gifting one of his finest song titles to one of the greatest of all the so-called Gothic bands.

Producer Joe Meek, whose own deep-held superstitions were flavouring his work even before he linked with Screaming Lord Sutch – the archetypal British rock ghoul – certainly contributed a few Gothic archetypes. As performed by TV soap star John Leyton in 1960, 'Johnny, Remember Me' was a deeply melodramatic romantic drama that tapped both the contemporary mood for death songs and the spiritualist beliefs which Meek and lyricist Geoff Goddard shared, a sonic milestone drenched in echo and stormy FX.

There should be room to consider King Crimson, whose magnificently titled and sublimely textured debut album, 1969's *The Court Of The Crimson King*, arrived bearing an on-sleeve comparison to shards of light in a Gothic cathedral and which, once past the mutant miasma of '21st Century Schizoid Man,' actually lived up to that billing. And, of course, there's should be time for Nick Drake, the brilliant young singer-songwriter who set to music a veil of tears that even Ian Curtis was hard-pressed to mop, and passed away after just three albums of beautiful decay, too sad to live, too willing to die.

Peter Hammill, the former Van Der Graaf Generator frontman whose 30+-year career is both infuriatingly patchy and horrifyingly prone to didactic, nevertheless represents one of the most consistent figures in the development of what we might term the proto-Gothic musical stream of the 1970s.

The four solo albums he cut prior to the reformation of Van Der Graaf in 1975 – that is, *Chameleon In The Shadow Of Night* (1972), *The Silent Corner And The Empty Stage, In Camera* (both 1974) and the prescient Punk *Nadir's Big Chance* (1975) – abound with textures, concepts and themes that would resonate through the later era, with only Hammill's own growing conviction that his fears were man-made, not Godlike, lessening his impact – ironically at a time when it should have been at its greatest.

If any art form that is obsessed with the harshest reality of life (namely, death) can simultaneously be accused of escapism, it is Gothic. Hammill's increasing reliance upon nuclear/chemical disaster to set up his scenarios, be it via the twisted liturgy of 'Mediaevil' ('God lives in underground silos'), the bio-political commentary of 'Porton Down,' or the science-friction 'Fogwalking' ('... through what used to be Whitechapel'), isolated him from the very children he had been nurturing for the past decade. He remains significant, though he has apparently done his damnedest not to.

There is space, too, for the young Kate Bush, and her 1978 debut single 'Wuthering Heights.' Even without the advantages derived from lifting its theme wholesale from Emily Bronte's spellbinding saga of love, death and betrayal in the barren moorland of a Yorkshire winter (crashing casements, howling winds and spectral visitations all inclusive), 'Wuthering Heights' is as unquestionable a Gothic masterpiece as it is an unlikely one.

Period reviews of the 19-year-old's first waxing, after all, dwelt not on the otherworldly lyrics, so luminously exaggerated by Bush's own preternatural vocal presence. They concerned themselves with the gnawing novelty of a record that only dogs and dolphins could listen to, and the noble nubility of its maker's teenaged form. Neither did the record's success – a month at #1 – hush the harshest critics; indeed, it took the arrival of Bush's second album, *Lionheart*, to confirm the arrival of a genuine, as opposed to merely precocious, songwriting talent. Only then could her detractors track back and work out what they'd missed.

To Bush and, more specifically, 'Wuthering Heights's most ardent admirers, of course, such considerations were utterly irrelevant. Not since television's Monty Python restaged *Wuthering Heights* in semaphore, some half a decade previous, had such a classic been so soundly and memorably reappraised. The fact that the bulk of the lyric was phrased to near-incomprehensibility only furthered the air of moorland mystery pervading the performance, as the wind swept the words from the speaker's mouth, leaving mere fragments of syllables hanging in their stead.

Ironically, a decade later, Bush rerecorded the vocals for her *The Whole Story* hits collection and did, indeed, reveal them to be the work of a very young, and very unformed writer. In its original form, her naive desire to simply tell her story equals that which powered Bronte herself to write and publish the only novel of her life. Revised, it says nothing.

We are fortunate, then, that the same guileless child who penned 'Wuthering Heights' also composed 'Hammer Horror,' a tribute – or, at least, an elegy – to the famed movie studios whose once-shocking schlock was now a staple of Friday night television. Written around 1976, for inclusion on the audition tape that Bushdom now refers to as *The Cathy Demos*, 'Hammer Horror' resurfaced both on *Lionheart* and as Bush's third single.

Opening with reference to one of the three film versions of *The Hunchback Of Notre Dame* then in circulation (Lon Chaney, 1923; Charles Laughton, 1939; and Anthony Quinn, 1957) – none of which was even English, let alone a Hammer production – 'Hammer Horror' nevertheless conjures a very enjoyable air of menace simply by invoking the name of that most legendary of studios. By the mid-1970s, after all, the term had itself become all but a cinematic sub-genre, pertaining to any horror film whose tongue (together with any other pointed instruments which might come to hand) seemed firmly stuck in cheek.

For the first time, Bush rues, she has to sleep with the lights on and, if it was a long time since any connoisseur of the studio's output had suffered that particular inconvenience, still it was a sentiment everyone could identify with, as Peter Murphy once admitted. 'Before I was old enough to not be so silly, I always thought Hammer Horror films were a terrifying prospect.' Later, of course, 'having seen them,' he found them 'laughable.'

But the fact remains, he continued watching them. We all do.

By the early 1980s, then, 'Gothic' was already a familiar face in the rock critic's lexicon. But, it is important to remember that, though so many acts (and factors) were Gothic, they were *not* Goths.

Indeed, even with such weighty precedents lurking in the closet, there never was a single moment when the world awoke and found Gothic Rock waiting at the bottom of the bed; just as, with the best will in the world, nobody can sit down and pinpoint the day – even the week or month – when a clutch of bands operating within roughly the same musical and/or visual parameters were suddenly thrust together in the vanguard of a new cultural movement/phenomenon/bandwagon.

It would be 1982, some four years after the prescribed figureheads of Joy Division and Siouxsie and the Banshees made their vinyl debuts, before any bands purposefully opted to play along with the Gothic Rock movement, as groups like Specimen, Alien Sex Fiend and the Sex Gang Children, the contingent that made London's Batcave club their home, were either formed or forged specifically to follow the form to its logical conclusions.

Of those bands that had already established themselves beforehand, some simply shrugged and went about their business, confident that they could ride out the storm – 'the day it got latched onto as a label, and became a uniform of black dresses for everybody… that was a sad day for me,' shrugged Siouxsie and the Banshees' bassist Steve Severin.

Other bands, a little more nervously, began going out of their way to escape the new label's adhesion; others still, if one really wants to get into the pigeon-holing game, might be better served by such obvious manufactures as Death Rock, Doom Rock, Post-Glam Apocalyptic Decadence Punk, *whatever*.

In fact, if you take every band ever to be saddled with the Gothic Rock epithet, the only thing any of them had in common was a refusal to adhere to the general tenets of the mainstream (even when those tenets became the mainstream).

Even the general assumption that their parameters were rooted in morbidity ('miserable fuckers,' in the vernacular of the time) collapses under the vaguest scrutiny. Indeed, the best of them were, in fact, as humourous as they were horrifying, as daft as they were dramatic, and as informed by T Rex as they were by Thanatos.

Nevertheless, from Alien Sex Fiend to X-Mal Deutschland; from Bauhaus to the Virgin Prunes; from the Cult and the Cure to, fleetingly, Ultravox and (for one impossibly brief but immortally delicious) moment, the youthful U2, Gothic remains the quickest and easiest way of summing up an entire school of musical thought, no matter how far from those original precepts the musicians themselves have strayed. Nor how belligerently they now defend that departure.

'I think you're living in a bit of a small community if you think Peter Murphy is still a Goth,' the former Bauhaus frontman snapped in an American interview in 1995. 'Obviously, I can assume you are a Goth, but it's been a long time since then and my albums sell to many more people than so-called Goths. I think you're wrong, actually. When an artist has got a background and has a pedigree if you like, a past which does involve such a definition, it's difficult for a journalist not to be lazy and to actually come to realise that that's a distant record, it has a distant relevance.

'Because I'm a bit of a sucker and I don't say 'I will not talk about Bauhaus,' I leave myself open to that to some extent. But I'm very well known for my three albums, not my first one, which wasn't released here, but my three American albums. I've toured here extensively and I've been adopted as Peter Murphy.'

And he has. But forget lazy journalism, what about lazy fans? Even today, touring to support his magnificent *Dust* solo album in May 2002, Murphy's audience contains as many black clad, white faced, be-fanged and cloaked denizens of death as it does suburban couples and MTV teens.

Fully on the offensive, Murphy continued, 'The Sisters probably were the consummate Goth band, and you could probably lump the Cure in with that, except the Cure were going pre-Goth. They were an indie band that continued down an indie path. But they did help formulate the sound that became an integral part of what was called Gothic.'

That, too, is true. But Robert Smith also has serious reservations as to whether his most visible fans are the most numerous. Well into the 1990s and beyond, the Cure ranked among the most popular bands in America – 1992's *Wish* peaked on the chart at #2, 1996's *Wild Mood Swings* entered at #12, 2000's *Bloodflowers* at #16. And there aren't enough Goths in the whole wide world to account for those statistics. So, when the *New Musical Express* described the band as 'quintessentially Goth with pop overtones,' Smith was deeply unimpressed.

'We're not a true Goth band, we fail the audience in too many ways,' he mused, with bassist Simon Gallup continuing, 'The bracket of Goth – there was a name, "Goth," and then certain groups went into it, the Mission – God bless 'em – the Sisters, Fields of the Nephilim. But you couldn't say *Faith* sounds like *First And Last And Always*.'

Could you?

That is what is at issue here: the 'bracket of Goth,' with the narrow musical confines that that implies, as opposed to the actual aesthetics of a Gothic mentality, within which Dark Rock as a whole tends to function.

In much the same way as early Punk observers and chroniclers were as ready to embrace Ian Dury and Nick Lowe as they were the Adverts and the Sex Pistols, so the original Gothic mindset was a remarkably egalitarian beast, happy to wrap its cloak around any number of willing sinners. However, whereas the development of a distinct 'punk' discipline ultimately excluded virtually every band that had initially played beneath its banner (no-one calls Costello a New Wave Dylan today), Goth never did lose touch with its parents. Which means, whereas Punk's stylistic outcasts simply got on with their careers and were seldom reminded of their roots again, the so-called Goths have never been able to shake off the shroud. And that, in turn, goes a long way towards explaining the hostility with which many of them view the categorisation.

If a master chef flipped burgers at Wimpy when he first left school, would you still say he worked in the fast food trade? No.

If the author of *Oliver Twist* once worked the court beat for a newspaper, would you still call him a crime reporter? No.

So why, if the 45-year-old Ankara-based master of a captivating Trance-Worldbeat hybrid once wrote a song about a Hollywood vampire, would you still call him a Goth?

That is one of the questions that this book intends to answer – or, perhaps more accurately, it is one of the answers that this book intends to put into its proper perspective.

Gothic Rock's connotations are pejorative; its confines are restrictive; its very existence, at least among the artists who spawned it, is pedomorphic. But, used in its full and fullest (Dark Rock) context, it is neither insulting, narrow nor childish. Rather, to be credited among the founding fathers of the movement is to be rated within a hierarchy that includes Elvis Presley and the Beatles, Pink Floyd and David Bowie, the Sex Pistols and Nirvana, the so-select and painfully exclusive ranks of musicians who not only founded a musical dynasty (fleeting or otherwise), but also imbued it with enough of their own personality and being that one simply cannot be mentioned without construing the other, nor judged within criteria that exclude their presence.

Maybe Gothic Rock did get a little silly, a little clichéd, and awfully distorted somewhere down the line. But what do you think happened to Glam, Punk and Rock'n'Roll itself? They hardly remained pure and pristine, either. But they survived, not simply to continue resonating within the world of modern rock, but to form the physical building blocks of everything that passes for rock music today. Gothic Rock is as vital a part of that construct as any of those others.

This is its story.

Part One:

Dostoevsky's

Children

Kid Strange of Doctors of Madness live at Friars Club Aylesbury, 1976

Chapter One
Dum Dum Boys…
And Girls

In which Iggy the Idiot returns from the brink of the abyss to illuminate the future for all who care to see it. The Doctors discover where the rats come to die, the Last Days of Earth are caught on record, and a movement begins to merge with the night.

'When The Idiot came out, it stayed on my turntable for a whole month.' Pete Murphy

e'll start with a guy named Dave. Just Dave, partly because it's an easy name to remember but, more importantly, it's not really a name you need to remember at all. And he lives in Leeds but, again, it could be anywhere. Somehow, though, Leeds seems pertinent to a lot of what comes later, and not only for musically historical reasons.

Leeds is an awkward town, full of complexes and insecurities, but packed with dynamism and confidence, too. Perched on the sunny side of the Pennines, it can be a gruelling place, but it has a grandiosity anyway, one that allows it to lord it over the other cities congregating around its skirts – the Bradfords and Sheffields and so on – and look further afield for its rivals and peers.

Sometimes, it gazes wistfully in the direction of Manchester, with her Olympic dreams and Himalayan accomplishments; others, it stares intently towards the sprawling Yorkshire moors with their hauntings and Heathcliffs and the charabancs full of American tourists come to catch some wuthering culture to show the folk back home. And other times, it looks inward, to the clusters of ambition and art that have always made their home on its streets.

Dave used to be a student there, as were so many other future musical movers and shakers – Andy Gill, Hugo Burnham and Jon King of Gang of Four, Green Gartside of Scritti Politti, Frank Tovey *aka* Fad Gadget, Marc Almond and Dave Ball of Soft Cell, Andrew Eldritch of the Sisters Of Mercy, Simon Denbigh, who formed the March Violets. Most of them even followed their academic ambitions through. Dave, on the other hand, got out before his final year, to fulfil the grander strategy of working in a record shop. See, you know him already. And, in the spring of 1977, you know exactly what music he used to play on the days when he had the shop to himself – Punk Rock, of course.

But he went past Punk. Way past it. He was blasting out Akron's Bizarros and Devo, a full 18 months before Stiff began hyping Rubber City USA. He used to frighten passing schoolkids with San Francisco's Residents, when *Third Reich'n'Roll* was still something that elitist critics alone seemed to know about. And he positively worshipped Iggy Pop and the Stooges at a time when only the swank London import stores carried their albums.

You have to remember, this was in the days of vinyl; the days, too, when vinyl was still in the process of recovering from the oil embargo and the shortages that shook the entire western music industry to its manufacturing core.

Today, you only have to wish hard enough and some Major Label Tinkerbelle will free another forgotten treasure from a cold and dusty vault, remastered and annotated and usually attended by a clutch of unknown bonus tracks as well. Twenty-five years ago, you had to work for the music you most needed to hear; more than that, you had to scrape and scratch and scour at the door of every record shop you could find, in the hope that someone, somewhere, someday…

Dave was that someone. He couldn't find everything, of course, but he had an uncanny knack of turning up weird things in unexpected places, anyway. He travelled down to London for Peter Gabriel's first solo concert and came home with Peter Hammill's autograph. He took a customer order for the Velvets' *White Light*

White Heat album, and turned up a copy in brain-charring mono at a car boot sale in Pontefract.

He wasn't cool, he wasn't hip and he certainly wasn't a Punk Rocker, in the sense that the rest of the pack pictured themselves to be. But he knew music and he understood things that other people simply listened to. Which brings us back to Iggy Pop.

In early 1977, Iggy Pop was a creature of legend. Close to four years had passed since his last 'new' LP, the David Bowie produced *Raw Power* – four years during which Pop had dived into the gutter and then kept digging, with only a deeply posthumous, lo-fi rendering of the Stooges' riot-torn finale, *Metallic KO*, to break his fall.

Time moved a lot slower in those days. An album a year was the norm; two wasn't at all unusual. Even the superstars of the day, the Stones and ex-Beatles, Zeppelin and Genesis, adhered to a timetable of annual pronouncements – to do anything else was tantamount to suicide. True, Emerson, Lake & Palmer took three years off between albums, but they were touring through one of them and released a couple of much-fanfared solo singles in the others. A far cry from the pampered layabouts of today, stony, cold-hearted silence was the exclusive province of the dead and the demented alone. And, in the bosom of popular legend, Iggy could have been either.

But then things began to happen. Scour the musician credits on David Bowie's *Low*, released in January 1977 to unexpected delirium, and observe that Iggy is listed on backing vocals on one track. Then Bowie himself spoke, of how he'd hauled his old friend out of a mental hospital, intending to cut a one-off single, only for the sessions to turn into a full-blown album. It was called *The Idiot*, and it would be released on 12th March, one week after the duo completed Iggy's first-ever tour of Britain.

We can gloss over the shows themselves. They were, of course, magical. But reputation is a hard act to follow, all the more so when it's wrapped up in the clothes that you expect it to be wearing.

To anyone who had procured those first three legendary Stooges albums (or even if they hadn't, but knew the hits from the Damned and Sex Pistols' covers), great swathes of the set were already familiar, and the tracks from the new album were just that, surprise sandwich fillings between 'Raw Power' and 'TV Eye.' Except it wasn't a surprise because Iggy was the Godfather of Punk and he'd patented that sound eight long years before. Now the rest of the world had caught up with him, and the new songs churned and burned and riffed and rocked, just like everybody knew they would.

The first suggestion that maybe there was something else on the wind arrived in the form of a single, a week or so ahead of the album. And it was a weird one. 'China Girl' had already been headlined in the music press because of one line about Iggy having swastikas in his head and 'plans for everyone' – the National Front was gearing up for its first major offensive of the year, taking to the London streets to confront a growing Anti-Nazi League movement and, though nobody ever called Iggy a Fascist, producer/co-writer Bowie was another kettle of commandants altogether.

Only twelve months earlier, he'd arrived at Victoria Station in a brown shirt and a Mercedes, and regaled the waiting crowd with a Heil Hitler salute. Of course it was all a misunderstanding – he'd simply been waving when the camera's eye clicked, and he was only joking when he said he was writing a musical about Josef Goebbels, Hitler's wartime propaganda chief. And most of the dirt washed away. Some didn't, however, and now here was 'China Girl' turning the spotlight back onto that most contentious of moments. Which was good in a way, because the more time you spent dissecting the language, the less attention you paid to the soundtrack around it, the droning, malevolent, doom-laden edifice that had less in common with safety-pins than it did the machines that made them, big clunking machines working relentlessly into the night. No, with all the fuss about the swastikas, nobody even noticed them.

The Idiot offered no such reprieve and no room for manoeuvre either. Dave's workmates in the record shop let him play precisely three songs from side one on the in-store hi-fi before replacing Iggy with RCA labelmates Hall & Oates. When the lunchtime rush of schoolboys descended, he was eating lunch in the backroom with the headphones on. And when he finally emerged, about half an hour later, he looked like Scrooge on Xmas Eve, expecting Christmas Past on the strength of Christmas Present – expecting the Stooges on the strength of the show. Instead, he got Christmas Future, eight songs in a row.

'You need to buy this record now,' he said, 'and play it non-stop for a week. Because if you don't, a lot of other people will. And, if you want to have even half a hope of understanding where things are going to go once Punk has run its course, you're going to need to know where it came from. This album is going to change everything.'

And he was right. On every count.

We look back on 1977 today and think of it as one long breathless roar, punk from start to finish. Marking Punk's Silver Jubilee in mid-2002, the UK music press gleefully gloated of all the horrors that the new music swept away. 'In the week that ended 12 April 1975,' *Q*'s *Never Mind The Jubilee* Punk Rock special shuddered, 'the British singles chart was in a funny old state. At number one sat… the Bay City Rollers. The Sweet were immediately below them. Then came… Guys And Dolls… the Goodies… Kenny… Mike Reid. [And] it was hardly an atypical rundown."

Then Punk came along and we all lived happily ever after. Or did we? Precisely (give or take a day or three) two years later, ABBA sat at number one. American cop show icon David Soul was number two, and after him – Manhattan Transfer… Boney M… Billy Ocean… Elvis Presley…. And that was hardly an atypical rundown, either.

Throughout the first four months of 1977, Punk bands were forming and gigging relentlessly. But, if you wanted to take them home to hear, your options were viciously limited. The Clash's first single, the 'White Riot' call-to-arms, had just been released; the Sex Pistols' 'Anarchy In The UK' had just been deleted; the Stranglers were scraping the Top 50 with 'Grip'; the Buzzcocks were initiating the DIY boom with *Spiral Scratch*.

True, the Damned and the Vibrators were onto their second singles, and you could always look towards America for further kicks. But even Don Letts, Rastaman house DJ at the Punk Mecca Roxy Club, spent most of his evenings blasting reggae and dub at the assembled hordes and, once you got out of London, half the bands forming in the spirit of the age were making music *not* in emulation of the bands they'd heard, but those that they'd read about – because, the truth was, in a lot of cases, they hadn't heard them.

They played what they imagined those other bands sounded like and, if there is any single explanation for the sheer variety and vivaciousness of all that we now look back on as the first storms of Punk Rock, that is it. Music made in a half-informed vacuum, then thrown at the wall in the hope that they'd got it right.

Iggy haunted that vacuum like a predatory bat. He'd been a key component within the British pop psyche for so long that, even without the Bowie connection, his past appetite for self-destruction would have become part of the language. Before *The Idiot* was even released, The Damned were jamming the Stooges' 'I Feel Alright,' the Pistols were playing 'No Fun,' and Gaye Advert was gumming his photo to her bass. And Iggy happily bestowed his approval upon them all. 'I love what the Sex Pistols have done with "No Fun",' he once mused. 'It's like looking at a pile of rubbish and knowing you made it rubbish.'

But his days as a dustman were over. It was only through David Bowie's involvement and influence that he'd even been given a new record deal, from RCA in late 1976 – a second chance that most observers had despaired of him ever receiving. Now he had to prove he was worth it. The way to do that was not by competing in the same field as the burgeoning army of little Iggies out there, but by giving them something new. Something that they could never have expected, something that was as dramatic, as dangerous and, overall, as alienating as the music he'd made the first time around.

The first song cut for what became *The Idiot*, the oedipal plod of 'Sister Midnight,' was a relentless mutant funk piece based around a riff that Bowie's guitarist, the brilliant Carlos Alomar, happened upon one day. Bowie himself had completed just one verse of the song when he showed it to Iggy – the speed with which the singer completed the lyric, then reeled off enough material for a half dozen more, convinced Bowie that they should set their sights on an album.

They began shaping the monolith at the Chateau D'Heuroville, outside Paris, where Bowie was recording his own *Low* album; from there, the party moved to Munich, and finally Berlin, to Hansa-by-the-Wall. It was the perfect match.

'I've always wanted to come to Germany,' Iggy enthused. 'Even when I was a kid, I read everything about it. I always knew I wanted to come here, just like some guys always knew they wanted to wear a dress. Berlin is a green and pleasant city. I love the air, I love the streets, I love the people. I aspire to be German some day, quite completely.'

Now he was there, he threw himself into the nation's artistic *uber*-life. The motorik pulse of disco master Giorgio Moroder, the computerised precision of electronic mavens Kraftwerk, and an isolating Wall of Sound erected from sonic bricks and mortar that owed as much to a construction site or a demolition yard, as they did to Phil Spector and Joe Meek.

Like Bowie's *Low* (with which it would inevitably be compared), *The Idiot* divided neatly down the middle, one side of shorter songs, one of longer epics, and it's an indication of the album's intent that only Bowie's own subsequent revisions of two of its songs ("Sister Midnight" became the lacklustre "Red Money," "China Girl" became a lightweight radio staple) has at all diminished its impact.

On headphones, an implausibly dense mix places the bass and drums somewhere down around your solar plexus, the half-growled, half robotic vocal smack between your eyes, and the squalling, flailing, agonised guitars simply wriggle into whichever empty corners they can find.

The *New Musical Express* called the record disturbing and coined the term "Mekanik Rock." But, even if you thought you understood what they were talking about, there was no respite from a barrage that lurched with such painstaking deliberation that, even as you reeled from one blow – the murderous thud of 'Nightclubbing,' where the favourite dance is the Nuclear Bomb – you were sucker-punched by the next – the brooding, metronomic threat of 'Funtime,' where the listener can only imagine precisely what the 'fun' might entail. And, from the dreadful, drawling, eight-plus minute beauty of 'Mass Production,' to the betrayed nostalgia of 'Dum Dum Boys,' with Bowie's guitar all but screaming his own name, even Iggy seemed astonished at how it all turned out.

'When David plays guitar, he gets nuts. You know that little part on "Dum Dum Boys"? That "boweeeewaaaaah"? That's his part. That's David doing that. He struggles with that thing – UH! Struggles to the C chord. His fingers start cramping after a while and we have to stop halfway through and he's yelling, "I don't know why the fuck I'm doing this for you, you jerk!" We have a very abrasive relationship.'

When Eno, one of Bowie's other collaborators of the era, was asked what he thought of *The Idiot*, he described it as 'an experience akin to being encased in a block of concrete.' Iggy himself, contemplating the sheer, unrelenting weight of the record, openly wondered, 'how can two friends make an album sound like that?' But, all across the UK, as *The Idiot* marched towards an absolutely undreamed-of Top 30 chart placing, other friends wondered whether they could make the same sounds themselves.

When Siouxsie and the Banshees went into the studio to cut their debut album, a little over one year later, they told producer Steve Lillywhite to make it sound like *The Idiot*. When what Peter Hook affectionately describes as "four knobheads from Manchester" first formulated what would become Joy Division, around the same time, *The Idiot* was constantly spinning in the background – and would still be playing two years later when singer Ian Curtis hanged himself in his kitchen. 18-year-old Gary Numan went to see Iggy at the London Rainbow, and pronounced the album "brilliant"; and, one year his senior, Peter Murphy admits, 'when *The Idiot* came out, it stayed on my turntable for a whole month.'

The point is, *The Idiot* wasn't simply a new record. It was an entire new way of thinking. Watchful eyes were not slow to pinpoint its impact. Months before the vinyl emergence of Siouxsie and the Banshees and Joy Division set about reshaping great swathes of the British rock underground, in an issue dated 26th November 1977, the weekly newsprint *Sounds* was postulating the emergence of a maverick new musical force, called – for want of a more quantified term – New Musick.

It was a scattershot branding, encompassing everything from the electronics of Eno, Kraftwerk and Throbbing Gristle to the dub techniques bleeding in from Jamaica; from the structured subversion of European (primarily German, and most singularly, Moroder) disco to the aural terrorism of the American art-pack – Devo, the Residents, Suicide and Pere Ubu; and, central to the argument whether the writers spotted it or not, the tide of bands arising from closer to home, nurtured in the all-encompassing grasp of Punk, but positively refusing to pay anything but vague lip-service to the fast-constricting aural uniforms that the genre now demanded.

The Banshees, Wire, XTC, the Only Ones, the Fall, the glowering promise of the as-yet unheard Magazine, the brutal thud of the still-maligned Stranglers. In the space of just one twelve-month stretch – and that's a generous chronological span – Punk Rock had flourished, flowered and then splintered completely, shrugging aside the genre's supposed notions of simplicity spelled out in as few chords as possible to embrace the limitless pastures of experimentation. And the fact that the best of the groups could (or, at least, would) fulfil that brief from within the confines of a 7-inch single only amplified their achievement.

Peter Murphy: 'During the summer of 1977, I was staying in Aylesbury at my sister's house, and people would notice me and think I was a very interesting new Punk Rocker. But I wasn't one at all, I was completely… I was like a pre-romantic Romantic, and the only person who walked around looking like a misfit without knowing it.

'I personally didn't like the Sex Pistols back then, I saw through it. It needed more, there was something missing. I thought it was just snotty-nose, my mate from school, a snotty-nosed little fucker who was just making music. It was okay, it served a purpose. But it didn't really offer anything other than the catalyst for something which *was* important.'

Punk – even by the Sex Pistols' definition of the term – was never about being "a Punk" – a leather jacketed, spiky green haired, safety-pinned dustbin liner with its legs bondaged together. Of course that was part of it, and the tabloid press never tired of publishing its own garish guides on how to identify these menacing mutants. But "Punk" was also an attitude, a mindset and an inner fidelity, a belief in oneself and one's vision that didn't simply ignore the dictates of the immediate surroundings, it eschewed them altogether. Punk was about being true to your self, and the further removed that truth was from the norm, the closer you were to the ideals of Punk. Anybody could dress up like the kids on the King's Road, then get a gig at the Vortex and scream the odds to a buzzsaw. Finding your own route to self-expression was a little harder.

Sex Pistol Johnny Rotten himself said as much when he appeared on London's Capital Radio on 16th July 1977 to play through a couple of dozen of the records that meant the most to him. Anybody expecting a blitzkrieg of mach two guitars and sneering nihilism was in for a shock. Rotten made it immediately apparent that it wasn't the Boring Old Farts of past renown who were to blame for all that Punk had set out to eliminate. Complacency, lethargy and gullibility were equally culpable and those were sins that had always had their enemies.

Cut through the library of reggae odds and teenaged obsessions that constituted the bulk of Rotten's selections, and a handful of names chimed with prescient rage – Captain Beefheart, Tim Buckley, Can, Kevin Coyne and Peter Hammill all pre-dated Punk's firestorm nativity, some by upwards of a decade. But all, too, had existed utterly beneath the mainstream radar, carving out niches of such specialised interest that, when their detractors labelled them "cults," no weightier damnation was necessary.

'It was interesting that Van Der Graaf were never frowned on by Punks as old dinosaurs: "die, you horrible long-haired people",' Hammill's bandmate Nic Potter told *Mojo* 25 years later. 'We weren't in any way affected by the Punk world.' And that, in a way, was the secret of their acceptance – theirs, the other acts singled out by Rotten, and a select clutch of other names besides: the Velvet Underground, Kraftwerk, the Residents, the Deviants, Syd Barrett, the Mothers Of Invention, Alex Harvey, Roky Erickson's 13th Floor Elevators, the Modern Lovers, Joe Meek, Scott Walker, Hawkwind, Amon Duul II, the Doctors of Madness… Iggy Pop!!!

Deliberately or otherwise, willingly or perforcedly, all simply went their own sweet way, unheeding of what might be happening around them, impervious to critical acclaim or commercial demand, oblivious to the marketing forces of their day and age. Punks in everything but time, place and hairstyle, they espoused freedoms that their more successful contemporaries could never contemplate, and ideals that had no place in the marketplace.

Hindsight can glibly say that the marketplace was changing, that what was once unmarketable was now halfway to gold dust and, in a way, that'd be true. In 1976, Iggy Pop looked as likely to have a British hit record as he was to walk on the moon. Maybe even less. By the end of 1977, he'd racked up three, as *The Idiot* was pursued to glory by a reissued *Raw Power* and Iggy's own next album, *Lust For Life*. The Modern Lovers scored three more, Roky Erickson landed a major label deal. Labels, critics and audiences alike rushed to embrace the eccentrics of the past, anxious to repair all those years of past neglect.

But it was *only* the eccentrics of the past who were being so lovingly rehabilitated. It would be another couple of years before a band could actually be strange and make a decent living at the same time – by which time, the boundaries of strangeness had shifted so far that normalcy itself was a far more out-of-synch gesture.

Deep into 1977, and on into the new year, the lessons of *The Idiot* were still being learned and, no matter how many groups would eventually emerge that could pinpoint their own genesis to the first time they heard that record, those that were already in circulation did not suddenly find all those once-locked doors opening. If anything, they remained locked even tighter, a predicament proven by the fate of perhaps the one band that could have foretold much of what *The Idiot* delivered. Instead, they were swept aside by it, and it would be a new decade before the Doctors of Madness could again stand up and tell the world 'I told you so' – by which time, they had long since perished.

The Doctors of Madness emerged in 1975, just as Glam Rock limped towards its final resting place. Discovered playing an already hard-hitting combination of paranoiac originals and maggot-encrusted covers of Dylan, Reed and William Burroughs at a pub in Putney, the Doctors were unveiled in early 1975 under the aegis of veteran rock manager Bryan Morrison and former Twiggy svengali Justin DeVilleneuve. It was the latter, introducing the group to the world, who referred to them as 'a reflection in the '70s, of the decadence of Berlin in the '30s' – an adequate description, but by no means the most accurate.

The Doctors had already been through a handful of line-up changes before they arrived at the final, suitably pseudonymed quartet of Kid Strange, Urban Blitz, Pete Di Lemma and Stoner ('just Stoner') and, having done so, they now spent their time, as Stoner put it, 'plotting these absurd ideas, this really outrageous image that we wanted to create to match the type of songs [Strange] was writing.'

'We are concerned with a kind of cinematographic style, where images come in and out,' Strange confirmed, 'not making much sense on a rational level, more on a sensory one. Our music, our show, has got this cold, sleazy feeling to it, of those old street corners. We are much more nasty than Alice Cooper.' They were also, Stoner proudly observed, 'one of the few bands who get booed before we play a note. Not many others can get that reaction.'

The group's make-up further reflected their nature, with the Frankensteinian Stoner especially offering an immediate foothold for anybody seeking the cinematic inspirations that the band admitted to. Hammer horror, indeed.

The Doctors' public unveiling arrived in early 1976, as special guests on television's *Twiggy Show* – at that time, contrarily, one of the most musically adventurous programmes around. But even its audience was not quite ready for Strange's bright blue hair and kinky knee-high boots, nor for a band whose first album would be footnoted with the notation: TO BE PLAYED WITH THE GAS FULL ON.

Late Night Movies, All Night Brainstorms (1976) is a singularly uncompromising record, the logical conclusion to that school of vicariously gruesome thought which sweeps from the paranoia of the Velvet Underground to the paradise of Roxy Music and on to the paradox of the original (pre-'Make Me Smile') Cockney Rebel.

So, a pop group which sings of death and decay? How decadent. Except the Doctors weren't decadent. They were dangerous and, in a pre-Punk age when the rock epic ruled, *Late Night Movies, All Night Brainstorms* tore the rulebook to shreds by taking it to its furthest extremes – then kept going from there. As Punk began squeezing out of glam rock's urethra, this was the sound that drowned out the screams.

On plastic, *Brainstorms* was sensibly divided between one sidelong suite, two comparative vignettes, and a veritable marathon – sensibly, because it was not an easy album to sit through in one sitting. Both sides conjured peaks of painful intensity: the concerto for earthquake bass, nerve-end violin, and fall-out siren which introduced 'The Noises Of The Evening,' toward the conclusion of side one; the shattered verbals and scratching fiddle which punctured the epic 'Mainlines' at the end of side two. Taken individually, the effect was the musical equivalent of bungee jumping. Taken together, you suddenly realized that someone had just cut the cord. Never had an album been so aptly titled.

True to the group's stated intentions, Strange's lyrics were never less than cinematic and, if flashes of Bowie's similarly widescreen *Diamond Dogs* came to mind, that may have been an intention. But unlike *Dogs*, or Lou Reed's *Berlin*, or any of those other period charmers that are routinely described as depressing or doomy, the Doctors' vision had no escape hatch. The easy options of death or surrender were not available to *Brainstorm*'s protagonists, and guilt was a luxury they could never afford. The most hopeful line on the entire album was, 'We just have to sit back and hope for the best.' The most chilling was, 'The doctors know best.'

The album bombed. Few people looked beyond the band's make-up, and fewer still cared to actually play their record. People really did not like the Doctors of Madness, but the group marched on regardless, gigging through the fall of 1976 with the End Of The World tour, a wild extravaganza featuring exploding dummies and great swathes of the band's rush-released second album, *Figments Of Emancipation*. Again, it was monumental. Again, it bombed.

Although they continued to gig fairly regularly, and issued their first-ever single, the raw anti-media rant 'Bulletin,' the Doctors remained silent throughout much of 1977. But their desolate dreamscapes did not remain uninhabited, nor their position among the media's favourite whipping boys. Very early in the year, Ultravox! emerged to try on both dubious crowns.

The roots of Ultravox lay in vocalist John Foxx and bassist Chris Cross confirming a shared preoccupation with Roxy Music, after Foxx placed an ad in *Melody Maker*, calling for just such obsessives. The pair 'must have auditioned every floater in London,' Foxx recalled, before they were finally joined by Billy Curry, Warren Cann and Steven Shears, and stepped out in mid-1975 as Tiger Lily.

Tiger Lily cut just one single, a darkly camp version of Fats Waller's 'Ain't Misbehavin'' that was universally ignored despite being taken up as the title song to a 1975 porn movie. Mildly chastened, the band followed through with a string of gigs, mainly at King's Cross's less-than-salubrious Doll's House, at the same time as furiously writing the songs with which they would shake off the Tiger Lily taint.

According to legend, they changed their name to Ultravox!, because everybody they suggested it to reacted with absolute disdain. 'Everyone disliked it, so we thought it must have some virtue,' said Fox, before acknowledging that very few people admired their music, either. Every post seemed to bring another major label rejection letter, but a set of summer 1976 demos recorded with the then-unknown Steve Lillywhite did intrigue Island Records – as it had been intended to. Unashamedly, Ultravox!'s influences were drawn from cream of the recent Island catalogue – Roxy Music, Sparks, John Cale, Eno – and, by the year's end, the band was in the studio with the latter, working on their debut album.

Bearing in mind that few of the comparisons favoured by latter-day critics even existed at the time that *Ultravox!* was recorded, the album emerged a spellbinding concoction. 'It's not like anything I've ever known before,' John Foxx sings on the first single, 'Dangerous Rhythms,' and he's right… almost.

Eno's influence surely allowed strains of Bowie and Iggy's forthcoming exertions to intrude, while the band's own preconceived notions of Roxy Music's legacy certainly colour in the wider spaces. Longer memories will even detect hints of William R Strickland's 'Computer Love' fidgeting around a few of the edges and one wonders whether any of the band ever owned the late 1960s Decca sampler *Wowie Zowie! The World Of Progressive Music*, wherein that gem was most readily available?

But the imminence of Kraftwerk's then-unheard *Trans-Europe Express* is predicted with an edgy naivety, while the occasional flash of assaultive fury proves that the band wasn't blind to the spiky tumult taking place all around them. As 1976 slipped into the New Year, many of Ultravox's live shows took place in the full glare of the formative foam of Punk, and the experience was readily absorbed into their sound. Even at its most abandoned, *Ultravox!* was never going to be another *The Idiot* (or even an earlier one – it was, after all, released a full fortnight before Iggy's album). But at least it had a few mutual friends, and it wasn't about to be shocked by the Pop record's disclosures.

Slammed by the music press, the first shots in a broadside that would ultimately spell the end of the Foxx-led incarnation of the band (and pave the way, of course, for the more resilient Midge Ure-powered version) *Ultravox!* nevertheless found a few ears that were interested. Gary Numan, again, speaks glowingly of it, readily acknowledging its guiding role in his own embrace of electronics, then pinpointing another mad messiah without whom the world might well have been a very different place.

Emerging just a couple of months too late to be termed strictly prescient in their understanding of their own portents, Rikki and the Last Days of Earth were nevertheless the first band to truly harness both the capabilities of electronics and the soundscapes of *The Idiot* (which was made, perhaps surprisingly, without a synth in sight), and actually get the results down on solid wax.

That is, as an aside, an important distinction to make. As far back as 1974, boss Buzzcock Pete Shelley had made sufficient experiments with an oscillator to record an hour-plus tape titled *Sky Yen* but, in 1977, it existed only in rumour. The Future (soon to become the Human League), Cabaret Voltaire, Thomas Leer and more were all stepping out in one form or another and looking, too, towards an icy electronic future. But they, too, were more theory than practise, and certainly hadn't been heard beyond their own immediate confines.

Rikki and the Last Days of Earth, on the other hand, were actively gigging by mid-summer 1977, opening the first ever Audition Night at the Roxy Club on 29th June, and headlining the same hallowed premises six weeks later.

A black and leather-clad five piece, Rikki and the Last Days of Earth immediately set themselves apart from the pack with their synth-heavy sound and frontman Rikki Sylvan's unmistakeably Bryan Ferry-esque vocals. It was an uncompromising melange – so much so that today, whenever old Punk rock fans gather to chew over the detritus of their youth, sooner or later one inevitably mentions Rikki & The Last Days Of Earth. And the others all laugh. Even among people who've never heard the group, they are generally remembered (and universally derided) for having released one of the most reviled albums of the entire late 1970s Punk explosion – indeed, as one critic put it, when your best song is a cover of an old Rolling Stones song, you know you're in trouble.

In fact, 'Street Fighting Man' wasn't even close to being the group's best number

– they themselves buried it away on a b-side. But still, it was only a few years later, when Sylvan's name surfaced alongside Gary Numan's in the small print of the latter's *Replicas* album, that many people even remembered what he'd been doing in 1977, while any fame that attends the singer today owes more to his groundbreaking work alongside the young William Orbit than to his own career.

Nevertheless, across an opening single in late 1977, the brutally belligerent 'City Of The Damned,' and onto a self-titled album early in the New Year, the group knew precisely what they were doing. The world was about to fall apart, and they were here to orchestrate Armageddon.

Dave Vanian

Chapter Two
Do You Remember Rudolph Hess?

How New Musick placed its finger on the pulse of the things that really upset people. We see the Ice Queen crowned, and the Magazine opened, while Warsaw starts to erect some dark walls of their own.

'Dave's whole thing, right from the start, had been that he was a kind of vampire bloke. It wasn't something he put on just before he went onstage, it was the way he was when he got up in the morning, went to bed, working on the car. He was committed to that look... and that's why we stuck with him because people would say, 'ah, look at him, he's funny'; but he really wasn't. He was probably the most genuine person [in the band].' Rat Scabies

Rikki Sylvan's vicious vision of decadence, darkness and destruction was painted in mile high neon. The end of the world, after all, is no time for understatement or allegory and, occasionally, the Last Days sounded as desperate as the last days they were describing, a bleakness so profound that they weren't even convinced that they'd live long enough to actually finish the record.

The best of the album, however, was nothing less than an adrenalined rush of futuristic noise. The instrumentals 'For The Last Days' and 'No Wave' indisputably determined the course that the new wave would take at decade's end; while 'City Of The Damned,' 'Outcast,' 'Twilight Jack' and 'Victimized' documented the kind of people it would find when it got there, a demented land of deranged loners who straddled society like a chainsaw-wielding colossus.

'Aleister Crowley,' named for the self-styled Beast whose teachings were numbered among Sylvan's own proudest influences, put a name to the shadowy faces that flitted in the featureless grey at the edge of eyesight, while 'Loaded,' the album's most blatant concession to humour, set the listener's teeth on edge as Sylvan played the role of the ultimate Nouveau Rich Kid – and prophesied Eighties' yuppiedom with way too much accuracy.

Of course, *Four Minute Warning*'s antecedents bleed all over the floor. To the obvious names, one can add possibly everyone who has ever prophesied disaster from atop a spiky, raunchy roar built on the shifting sands of angst, anger and alienation. The Last Days' downfall lay in doing it without the safety net of subtlety. Because, when the world didn't end – or even come particularly close to it – it all sounded very silly indeed.

By mid-1978, Rikki and the Last Days of Earth had, indeed, lived out their last days, bowing to the inevitable at around the same time, coincidentally, as the Doctors of Madness acknowledged that their license to practise, too, was not likely to be renewed.

The Doctors' third and final album, the icily monochromatic *Sons Of Survival*, arrived in early 1978 and, if they didn't know they were dying as they recorded it, they didn't let their ignorance show. Re-emerging over a year after the sophomore *Figments Of Emancipation*, but still far out on a limb of their own devising, the Doctors reflected upon the first 12 months of Punk Rock with an album that mourned the members' own apparent old age ('here we are the '50s kids, on collision course with 30'), then let fly with more fire than rebels half their age.

It was peculiar, at the time, to realize just how violent an electric violin could sound. Of course, that was always the instrument's role in the Doctors but, on past albums, Urban Blitz had couched his psychoses in a chilling darkness, the barely audible promise that 'I'll scare you, but I won't hurt you' – interestingly, Ultravox offered the same paradigm with similar icy charm. *Sons Of Survival*, however, stripped away all such pretence and pretensions and, only when the record was complete, did it become apparent that the effort was too much for the Doctors' beleaguered frame to bear. The departure of Blitz inevitably spelled the end of the group but, stubbornly bucking expectations once again, the band girded its loins for one last hurrah.

Blitz was replaced, numerically if not instrumentally, by the supremely vespertine Dave Vanian, vocalist with the recently sundered Damned, first generation Punk rockers whose own frustration with the crash'n'bash tenets of the genre had seen their second album swoop off into seriously progressive rock territory (it was produced by Pink Floyd's Nick Mason!). It was an unlikely partnership, but it made sense. The Doctors truly were the only other functioning band of the age in which a vampire could pass unnoticed, if only because the rest of the group looked just as horrific.

A former gravedigger who had long since undertaken no longer to undertake for a living, the erstwhile David Letts was the fourth and final member to join the Damned, the band formed by guitarist Brian James and drummer Chris 'Rat Scabies' Miller as they fled the legendarily under-achieving London SS in August, 1976. Indeed, with the founding duo joined by bassist Ray 'Captain Sensible' Burns, the Damned had already played a couple of gigs by the time Letts was recruited, backing journalist Nick Kent as the Subterraneans.

With Letts renaming himself in tribute to his perceived country of origin – dressed like he was, he had to be Transyl-*vanian*, the Damned immediately found themselves sliding in alongside the Sex Pistols as harbingers of the then-unnamed Punk movement, a role that their music – direct, brash, high octane three-chord mayhem – certainly did not contradict.

In Vanian, however, the Damned possessed a frontman who would never allow them to be sucked permanently into the vortex of Punk, even if the sheer dexterity of his persona would not fully manifest itself until the pressures of the group's early standing had already caused the 'classic' line-up to splinter, in early 1978.

Offstage and on, he dressed the part – and the part was Christopher Lee, in any one of the seemingly dozens of vampire films he made from the age of 36, in 1958, in Hammer's first *Dracula*. In the years since that memorable debut, Lee's characterisation of Count Dracula had become immutably engrained in the consciousness of the British filmgoer. It is testament to Vanian's own gift for self-perpetuation that, after more than a quarter of a century in a similar role, he is as much of an icon as his idol.

Through the 18 month comet ride of the Damned's original incarnation, however, Vanian didn't quite keep his interests to himself – full, and full-time, vampire drag was hardly the most inconspicuous look of the day. But he didn't allow them to take centre-stage either. Little of Vanian's night-stalker persona was echoed in the Damned's music. True, 'Feel The Pain,' a cut from their maiden *Damned Damned Damned* album in early 1977, pays sonic tribute to vintage Alice Cooper. Elsewhere across that seminal debut, however, and into its doomed, but dementedly heroic successor, *Music For Pleasure*, later in 1977, the Damned offered no further clues as to what lay behind Vanian's visage, a disappointing development for the vicarious onlooker but, with hindsight, an extraordinarily wise one.

To obsess on Vanian's appearance, after all, would have been to flag it as something that the band themselves found remarkable, like pinning a placard to the village idiot. To the Damned, as Brian James recalled, 'what would have been the point of dwelling on it? It was just who Dave was. We might as well have written a song about my leather jacket.' And the fact that half of the Damned's audience was indeed wearing leather jackets only backs up his remarks. Because the other half was dressed up like Vanian.

'Long before there was a recognized Gothic look,' James continued, 'there were fans turning up at shows dressed like Dave, which was brilliant at the time, because it lifted us right out of the typical Punk Rock Band thing. Other groups had the safety pins and the spitting and the bondage trousers, but you went to a Damned show, and half the local cemetery would be propped up against the stage.'

Rat Scabies continued, 'Dave's whole thing, right from the start, had been that he was a kind of vampire bloke. It wasn't something he put on just before he went onstage, it was the way he was when he got up in the morning, went to bed, working on the car. He was committed to that look... and that's why we stuck with him because people would say, 'ah, look at him, he's funny'; but he really wasn't. He was probably the most genuine person [in the band].'

The roll-call of the Damned's achievements has been reiterated so often it is a cliché. The first of the Punk groups to release a single, 'New Rose' in November, 1976, the Damned were also the first to issue an album, the first to appear on children's TV, the first to visit America and the first to record a second LP.

But poor press and worse relations did much to derail the group. It was during the Damned's headlining performance at the 100 Club Punk Festival in London in September 1976 that a girl lost an eye, hit by flying glass when a thrown bottle shattered on a nearby column. Two months later, visiting Americans the Flaming Groovies publicly bemoaned the Damned's lack of what they construed as musical ability. In December, a highly publicised dispute with the Sex Pistols, when the two groups toured together, further soured the Damned's relationship with the Punk *cognoscenti*.

With the music press leaping aboard that same bandwagon, the Damned's drive for credibility was always going to be an uphill battle. Their records never charted and seldom got good reviews; their attempts to explain their behaviour simply aroused further hostility; and the good-natured buffoonery that was the band members' natural form of defence simply fell on humourless ears. Beset on all sides, the Damned commenced their collapse.

In September 1977, drummer Scabies faked a suicide bid and quit the band (he was replaced by future Culture Club icon Jon Moss). In October, that second album was released to unrelentingly hostile reviews; by December, both management and record label had dispensed with their services; in February, the group broke up. They reunited in April for a farewell London concert but, by early spring, the Damned were strictly dead and buried.

Vanian was the first to be reincarnated, but his latest life was to be supremely short-lived. A new Doctors of Madness single was announced, composed by Adverts frontman (and occasional Strange writing partner) TV Smith, but 'Don't Panic, England,' like the rebirth it heralded, was doomed from the outset. The band's label, Polydor, rejected the single even as audiences rejected the new-look band. They already had Frankenstein onstage; what did they need Dracula for? Particularly when his only function appeared to involve skulking around the edge of the stage, while Kid Strange continued to sing all the songs.

Within weeks, Vanian had departed, rejoining sundry Damned pals in the near-reunion Doomed; the Doctors themselves broke up, after one final show at the Music Machine in London that October that – even in the rudely abridged form in which it was released in 2001 – stands as a celebration of all that they never achieved. What they could not have realised as they left the stage for the final time was that their day was still to dawn.

Within two years, with Strange reborn as a solo artist, and Stoner now a member of TV Smith's Explorers, the Doctors of Madness were suddenly deemed to have been right all along, a point that Strange himself would gleefully reiterate in an interview in 1980. 'While I would never be so presumptuous as to say we were responsible totally for the direction [music] did take in the late 1970s, I think we were very influential, and that influence is becoming more apparent in the bands that have emerged in the past few years, people like Joy Division, the Skids and Simple Minds – who acknowledged their own debt when they introduced a cover of the Velvet Underground's 'Waiting For The Man' as a song written by Richard Strange.

Strange's claims, and the Doctors' profound influence notwithstanding, the New Music movement that *Sounds* so boldly prophesied in November 1977 was slow in making itself heard and even slower in coalescing. In fact, if the newspaper's intentions in even running the story involved actually fermenting a "movement" from so many disparate elements, it was a signal failure – at least in the short term.

The key ingredients were all in place, to be sure, and the success of *The Idiot* proved that they were workable. But even Iggy himself shied away from following through on that album's predictions, slamming the rocking *Lust For Life* into circulation just six months after *The Idiot* was released, while few of the aspiring musicians most affected by the record were in any state to actually give voice to their feelings.

While the Doctors, Sylvan and Ultravox! continued screaming in the wilderness of public apathy and critical disdain, neither Siouxsie and the Banshees (cover stars of the New Musick issue) nor Joy Division (then thrashing around under the name of Warsaw) would truly find their metier until mid-1978 at the earliest. Bauhaus were close to a year away from forming, and the composite parts of other future legends – Theatre Of Hate, Specimen, Alien Sex Fiend, Southern Death Cult – were still finding their feet in sundry renta-Punk Rock bands.

Only Magazine, the band formed by vocalist Howard Devoto following his departure from The Buzzcocks, had broken through the general uncertainty surrounding Punk's development as it moved into its second year of existence, and even he was responding more to a disdain for what Punk was than a vision of what it might become.

In February 1977, Devoto told the *New Musical Express*, 'I'm tired of noise and short of breath,' and pledged that there would be no further musical activity until he had formulated a vision that didn't rely on speed and shouting to get its message across. He found it, like so many others were finding it, in *The Idiot*. By the end of March 1977, Devoto had ignited a new songwriting partnership with guitarist John McGeoch.

Placing postcards calling for musicians on the notice board at the Newton Street, Manchester branch of the Virgin record store – WANTED, MUSICIANS TO PLAY FAST AND SLOW MUSIC – Devoto and McGeoch completed the band line-up in late August. Bassist Barry Adamson, keyboard player Bob Dickinson and drummer Martin Jackson were duly unveiled when Magazine made their live debut on 2nd October, 1977, at the final night of the Electric Circus.

Utilising equipment borrowed from the headlining Buzzcocks, Magazine played three songs, their own 'Shot By Both Sides' and 'The Light Pours Out Of Me,' plus a cover of Captain Beefheart's 'I Love You, You Big Dummy,' a song Devoto had been nursing since his Buzzcock days. A month later, on 28th October 1977, the band played their first full gig at Rafters, at a benefit for the *Manchester Review* news magazine; by year's end, Magazine were signing to Virgin.

'Shot By Both Sides,' Magazine's monumental debut single, arrived in mid-January 1978. A Devoto lyric married to a snarling Pete Shelley guitar line, it was an instantly confrontational number, but an oddly vulnerable one as well. The title came from a conversation Devoto once had with a socialist friend, discussing a contentious course of action and being warned, in no uncertain terms, that he was going to get it in both ears… shot by both sides.

Not that Devoto's own period utterances allowed for any explanation so mundane as that. Even the record company, addressing the song's subject matter in Magazine's first press release, had no alternative but to repeat his cryptic insistence, that it concerned the moment 'when the Kray brothers meet the Buddha in the marketplace.' Clearly, this was one Magazine that was not going to be a quick read in the bathroom.

As Magazine took their first steps into the public consciousness at that Electric Circus show, Warsaw were playing one of their final shows as they inched towards the more emotive name of Joy Division.

Like Magazine, they were a Mancunian concern; like Magazine, their musical impetus was drawn at least in part from *The Idiot* – when RCA professed interest in signing the band towards the end of 1977, simply being on the same label as Iggy Pop was enough to send vocalist Ian Curtis in raptures. And, like Magazine, they were prone to the occasional confrontational comment.

'Do you remember Rudolph Hess?' demanded Curtis at the Electric Circus that evening, a remark guaranteed to provoke attention for an act that had hitherto spent the majority of its short life in the shadows not only of Manchester's heavier hitting acts (the Buzzcocks, the Fall, the Drones, the Distractions and Slaughter and the Dogs), but also their own insecurities. As it turned out, Joy Division were to receive more attention than they knew what to do with.

Having been in the (future) star-studded audience present when the Sex Pistols played Manchester's Lesser Free Trade Hall on 20th July, 1976, to watch their own musical ambitions unfold before their own eyes, bassist Peter Hook and guitarist Bernard Sumner pieced together their own band in early 1977. Vocalist Ian Curtis and drummer John Tobac joined them, the latter arriving just days before the Stiff Kittens (as Buzzcocks frontman Pete Shelley suggested the new quartet call themselves) changed their name to Warsaw, from a track on the unlistenable ha-ha side of David Bowie's *Low*.

Warsaw made their live debut at the bottom of the bill when the Buzzcocks and Penetration played the Electric Circus on 20th May 1977. It was a tentative showing but it caught the eye of producer Martin Hannett, then part of a booking agency called Music Force – he was able to land Warsaw a solid run of further shows, including a few vaguely prestigious support slots. When they were finally ready to record, of course Hannett was at the controls.

Curtis' own interests and influences ran from the conventional godheads of Iggy Pop and the Velvet Underground, through to the harsher realities of Throbbing Gristle. Curtis and Gristle's Genesis P-Orridge became friends during 1977, after Curtis heard the Industrial progenitors' *Second Annual Report* album; the following year, even as Warsaw honed their own sound, Curtis fell in love with the suicide note 'Weeping,' from Gristle's *DOA* album.

The emergence of Magazine exerted further musical pressure on Warsaw, but the band were more than capable of living up to it. Like Magazine, their output was as much mood as melody, imbibed with a melancholia that Curtis' naturally sonorous voice could not help but convey. But, overlaid with jarring splinters of guitar, the tones never sank into any form of conformity – long before they got to grips with the intricacies of song *structure*, Warsaw had already sussed out dynamics, and their earliest studio recordings, cut as demos for the vaguely interested RCA in late 1977, reveal almost all the trademarks of the later band to be in place. Almost.

Joined by their third drummer in as many months, Stephen Morris, Warsaw became Joy Division following the sudden emergence of a more immediately headline-worthy London based band, Warsaw Pakt, that fall. Taking Punk's purported penchant for speed to its extreme limit, Warsaw Pakt's moment of fame revolves around the release of their debut album, recorded, mastered, pressed, packaged and shipped to the stores within one record-breaking 24 hour period. Warsaw/Joy Division, on the other hand, sounded like they spent that long contemplating a single minor chord.

The new name, Curtis' suggestion, was taken from a trashy Holocaust novel, *House Of Dolls* – there, the 'joy division' was the area within the concentration camp where the more attractive female prisoners were sent to work as unpaid prostitutes.

Like the Hess crack at the Electric Circus (and, presumably, his own interpretation of Iggy's swastika visions), Curtis was in no doubt as to the effect the new name would have. At a time when British street politics were being utterly riven by the rise of the racist National Front, and Punk had already made it clear that its own internal beliefs were in direction opposition to the Front's, any invocation of Nazi sympathy was a dangerous move. Journalist Mick Middles, attending the Electric Circus gig, sniffily recalled 'feeling extremely irritated at this foolish remark', living proof that some topics are simply too weighty to be subjected to even ironic revision. Especially when it isn't quite apparent just how ironic the intention is.

Joy Division, however, not only remained unrepentant, they deliberately set about raising the temperature even further. Their debut EP, June 1978's *An Ideal For*

Living, arrived draped in a picture sleeve splashed with the Hitler Youth. But, beyond the hysterical response that such material would naturally (and was deliberately intended to) provoke, the group's fascination with wartime imagery can be looped back to any number of sources. Guitarist Bernard Sumner remembers spending school holidays with grandparents whose attic was a treasure-trove of World War Two-era memorabilia, and he readily points out, 'that kind of stuff does make an impression. You do become fascinated by the era.'

Another point of reference was Curtis' now well-publicised love of Throbbing Gristle, themselves no fainthearts when it came to devising fresh shock tactics. And a third is maybe deducible from an offstage comment made at one of Joy Division's first-ever London shows, at the Moonlight Club in West Hampstead.

At a table near the bar, before the gig got started, an onlooker was leafing through a pile of second-hand albums he'd purchased that afternoon. Nico's *The End* was among them: the sight of it prompted a passer by to stop and run a finger down the track listing. '"Deutschland Uber Alles",' he said, as he jabbed at the final track. 'You know, if more people understood what society is trying to hide, a lot less people would be inclined to try and recreate it.' Half an hour later, that same passer-by was onstage, the lead singer with Joy Division.

Through the spring and summer of 1978, Joy Division gigged regularly around Manchester, although they seldom put on the kind of show that their growing band of supporters believed they were capable of – in April, they famously bombed at the Stiff Test/Chiswick Challenge travelling talent show, and similar disappointments became part and parcel of the Joy Division experience.

By summer, however, *New Musical Express* reporter Paul Morley was comparing Joy Division to Siouxsie and the Banshees, and *not* because of any misunderstood imagery – that band, too, had had their brush with the emotive whack of Nazi symbolism. Back at their debut concert, at the 100 Club Punk Festival in 1976, the Clash reneged on an offer to lend their gear to the newly formed band after Siouxsie turned up at the gig with a swastika armband, mortifying her would-be benefactors with the taint of Nazi sympathy. The performance finally went ahead using the Sex Pistols equipment.

The stigma remained. When Siouxsie and the Banshees lifted one of Herman Goering's speeches for the song 'Metal Postcard', you could cut the condemnation with a knife – *not*, however, because the words themselves were any more inflammatory than most of the obese transvestite's other utterances, but because everyone knew who (and what) Goering was, and simply knee-jerked their way to the obvious conclusion. The song's real inspiration, John Hartfield, was as obscure in the complainants' minds as any 1930s-era anti-Nazi propagandist-in-exile could be.

The group would never truly place such controversies behind them, but they would turn its ramifications to their own advantage. Across the bleak, windswept tracts of their debut album, *The Scream*, Siouxsie and the Banshees had perfected the same melange of atmosphere and energy that Joy Division were still experimenting with. Indeed, where the Manchester band was already capable of sending shivers down the most warmly insulated spine, the Banshees had learned how to switch the heating off altogether. 'Polar region rock,' shivered *Sounds*, wherein journalist Jane Suck recommended that the band confront their audience – and 'freeze their souls to death with [their] music.'

Siouxsie and the Banshees formed, as Siouxsie herself put it, 'to fill a gap at the 100 Club Punk Festival. We entered into the pure spirit of it, on the spur of the moment, forming a band to fill this slot then disbanding after it, one night only, taking the Andy Warhol idea to its extreme, and also the idea that now is now, and it's important – no future, no past.' Twenty years of 'one night only's later, riding on the back of their finest album in a decade, *The Rapture*, Siouxsie & the Banshees finally broke up (at least for a few years – they reformed in 2002), the last survivors of the original Punk bands, and one of the precious few who retained their original vision (if not their intentions!) all the way through.

The original group line-up – Siouxsie and bassist Steve Severin, future Adam & The Ants guitarist Marco Pirroni and eventual martyr Sid Vicious on drums – debuted on the first night of the 100 Club Punk Festival. The group played just one piece, a storming, hypnotic (and all but incomprehensibly amateurish) medley of 'Knocking On Heaven's Door,' 'Twist And Shout' and a loosely blasphemous rendering of 'The Lord's Prayer,' improvised by musicians who'd never even appeared on stage before, let alone actually played together.

Neither would they do so again. The band members went their separate ways the moment the show was over; only Sioux, Severin and manager Nils Stevenson remained together, vaguely scheming the creation of a new line-up that they hoped would be ready in time to join the Sex Pistols' 'Anarchy' tour in December. In the event, it would be July 1977, before a stable line-up finally emerged, the founding duo joined by John McKay (guitar) and Kenny Morris (drums).

Siouxsie herself revelled in the controversies that pursued the group. Bathed in make-up, barking songs like orders to the serried ranks of Punk, she came across like a cross between the Ice Queen of Narnia and Charlotte Rampling in *The Night Porter*, a skinny black fantasy given its own sleepless voice in the nightmares of the listener. 'Love In A Void,' 'Bad Shape,' 'Overground': nightly the band's frost-encrusted apocalypse took shape and, for everyone who was thrown to the lions by the riffs like switchblades and Antarctic attitudes, there was another who knew exactly what the Banshees were all about.

'We just like to get people's backs up,' Siouxsie mused. 'It's like laughing at spastics. We've got a morbid sense of humour. I think that everyone finds sick things funny if they're honest about it – when I was young, the only books I used to read were those cheap horror paperbacks, the ones by Herbert Van Thal. My favourite films were Hammer films, especially ones with Vincent Price. The way he acts is so corny and obvious, but still he's amazingly effective. You should never be afraid to be corny.'

And they weren't. They referenced *Devil's Rain* in song ('Make Up To Break Up'), the schlocking mid-1970s Ernest Borgnine, William Shatner, Ida Lupino flick in which Satan plagues earth with an acid-like downpour that melts people's faces and makes their eyeballs pop full of pus.

A version of the Beatles' 'Helter Skelter' reinforced all the messages that Charles Manson thought he had detected in the original, and made the Family's creepy-crawl antics look like an end-of-term hippy school panto. The *sturm und drang* clatter of 'Metal Postcard' raised hackles wherever anti-Nazi leaguers congregated to dripfeed their consciences; and 'Carcass,' as Siouxsie gleefully related to *Zig Zag*, was the story of 'a butcher's assistant who can't get girls, so he falls in love with a lump of meat on the slab and, so he can be like the object of his affections, he cuts off his own arms and legs.' *You should never be afraid to be corny.*

So far, so Alice Cooper, then. What raised the Banshees above the usual horror rock circus was their refusal to play it by the book. Early Banshees songs – 'Make Up To Break Up' included – were little more than a renta-Punk blur. But, as the songs developed and the band's own ideas crystallised, the riffs, the rhythms, the lyrics started to separate, the tunings twisted, the chords coalesced. Before your eyes, as the Banshees gigged through the first half of 1978, the pace slowed, the atmosphere deepened, the colours were muted, the emotions grew older.

It was an impressive metamorphosis and, like so many of rock's most potent icons, it was little more than a happy coincidence. Steve Severin acknowledged, 'a lot of it was just sort of accident, attempting to find something of our own. Our influences were the Roxy Musics, David Bowies, T Rexs, a twisted sexuality, a black humour that was different. With the guitar we'd say to John, "make it a cross between the Velvet Underground and the shower scene from *Psycho*"; we didn't say, "oh, you have to play an A sharp minor there and it'll be really spooky." Plus, we weren't very good musicians, so we didn't have anything else to fall back on.'

For all the critical support that the Banshees were now receiving, few record companies showed any interest. Even a graffiti campaign couldn't force the labels' hands, a night of concerted paintwork that spraypainted half of the London music industry with the words SIGN THE BANSHEES NOW! At one point, DJ John Peel was even trying to persuade the BBC to place the band on its own label, hitherto the preserve of TV soundtrack music, simply to give them an outlet. The BBC were unmoved by his entreaties. By early 1978, Siouxsie and the Banshees had recorded two sessions for Peel's late night show and, leafing through the material on offer, there was little which would not have grated horribly against the Beeb's traditional output.

But the group persevered and finally, Polydor stepped in where no other had dared to read, signing Siouxsie and the Banshees within weeks of dropping the Doctors of Madness – perhaps the one band in the land that had already intruded upon the Banshees' own turf.

The irony of that change-over is inescapable, but so is its significance. For all their scathing modernity, the Doctors were widely viewed as a hold-over from an earlier time, unlikely survivors of the changing-of-the-guard that so rudely bisected the British rock scene with the nativity of Punk. The Banshees, on the other hand, represented the future and, in the studio with producer Steve Lillywhite, they knew precisely how it should look.

At a time when the media referred to them as Punks, the Banshees leaned towards metal motorik. Manager Nils Stevenson recalled, 'The group and I went out for a pizza with Steve and talked [it] over... gave him a list of records to listen to.' *The Idiot*, of course, was at the top of the list, Bowie's *Low* and *Heroes*, Eno and

Roxy Music lay behind it, and every one of them another grey concrete slab of malnourished feedback, burning insects, screaming wires and tortured twilight. The result, *The Scream*, slipped effortlessly into that same sanctified company. But it would also slide into an arena of its own.

It was the spaces in the songs that stunned, the wide-open gaps that hung haunting between every note, awaiting the banshee wail of Siouxsie's first vocal ('Pure') or last cry. A couple of reminders of the group's Punk club rawness were still in evidence – 'Carcass' and 'Nicotine Stain' were the ugliest offenders. But, with Lillywhite's crystalline production isolating every nuance of sound, even they took on a new, eternally menacing aura.

Neither did it end with the album. In fact, it only got better. Flip the group's uncharacteristically pop-toned 'Hong Kong Garden' debut single, and 'Voices' delivers some six minutes of calculated malice, its effects-laden guitars and hypnotic staccato bespeaking a menace that was all the more palpable for Siouxsie's own, deeply phased, apparent uncertainty – *something* is whispering at the window, *something* is scratching on the inside....

There was a distinct hint of Hitchcock (*Rebecca* comes to mind) in the atmosphere, and a trembling taste of Cathy and Heathcliff, freed by Kate Bush to haunt other quarters. But most of all, there was the sense that something new was happening; that some day all music was going to sound like this. All worthwhile music, anyway. The swooping 'Voices,' the pounding 'Metal Postcard,' the desperate 'Suburban Relapse' and the desolate 'Switch' were more than a band's sonic reinvention. They were the moment when the phrase 'post Punk' finally took on a valid meaning – and then commenced its relentless shift towards even more descriptive terms.

It would be misleading, of course, to portray the vague stylistic union of Siouxsie and the Banshees, Joy Division (and, to what swiftly transpired to be an ever-diminishing extent, Magazine) as the sole purveyors of any emergent genre, although in terms of press coverage – at that time, the crucial focus of any up-and-coming band's profile – it was an easy mistake to make.

By the time the Banshees began work on *The Scream* in June 1978, XTC and Wire were already recording regularly, Punishment Of Luxury were preparing to unleash the stygian magnificence of 'The Puppet,' and Cabaret Voltaire (from Sheffield), the Pop Group (from Bristol), the Gang of Four (Leeds), Durutti Column (Manchester) and Simple Minds (Glasgow) were all taking their first tentative steps out of the Punk orthodoxy, casting ever darkening shadows over such historical notions as melody, verse and recognisable structure.

The nature of the music industry itself, too, had changed beyond recognition. Prior to 1976, it was a leviathan dominated by major labels, many of which had been in place since before the birth of rock'n'roll – EMI, Pye, Decca, Warners, RCA, CBS, Polydor.

'Independents,' as we know them today, existed either in the history books (Joe Meek's short-lived Triumph, Andrew Loog Oldham's slightly longer-lived Immediate), or in the fevered imaginations of back street folkies and progressive rock retentives who pressed up a few records to sell at their gigs. Now, however, it was the major labels that dreamed of success, and the Indies that were making the music that mattered.

Peter Murphy – who would spend the first 25 years of his own career with one of the most tenacious of the first wave of Punk-era indies, Beggars' Banquet – explained: 'Suddenly, there was this whole new culture where we could all get up and make a statement, make art, without having to go through any bureaucratic or artistic agency, institution or process. It was complete liberation on a very street level, loads of bands around, loads of people. People were willing to listen to new music, there was an audience that identified with the "Indy" culture, there were Indy promoters, Indy labels, Indy shops, it was just brilliant.'

A lot was happening, then, and there were a lot of names being bandied around to sum up what it was. Whether in the eyes of the individual bands themselves or simply within the fevered imaginations of over-enthusiastic critics, cliques were forming, movements were stirring. With the Banshees and Joy Division at its heart, however, a tiny dark ball had coalesced in the soul of all that was going on elsewhere, one whose requirements Paul Morley, in the *New Musical Express*, delineated within another of his Joy Division reviews.

'They were a dry, doomy group,' he proclaimed, 'who depend promisingly on the possibility of repetition, sudden stripping away. With deceptive dynamics...' Though those other bands certainly aspired towards such levels, only a precious few were able to sustain the mood for longer than it took them or their audience to begin tiring of it.

Magazine's debut album, *Real Life*, described by one passing commentator as the marriage of Kraftwerk and Kafka, was dark and doomy to be sure, but it nevertheless flung the curtains aside occasionally – 'The Light Pours Out Of Me' remains the best Gary Glitter record that Gary himself never made. XTC and Wire were simply too quick and convoluted to remain rooted to the spot while the darkness slowly cloaked around them; other bands had other needs.

The Banshees themselves constantly, and expertly, sidestepped attempts to bracket their sound alongside any other act; fought furiously against the critical inclination to label other bands as showing any kind of Banshees influence. 'A lot of what we were doing,' mused Severin, 'if you have to put a name to it, was intended to be resonant, rather than innovative. We read a lot, we watched a lot of movies and we tried to interest people in the same kind of things.' And it swiftly became apparent that their efforts were not in vain. 'When Joy Division came out,' Severin continued, 'that's when I thought "ah." For the first time, you felt that something was going on."

Pete Murphy

Chapter Three
I Won't Watch
A Band Wearing
Make-Up

Wherein the Factory opens it doors, and undivided joy spills over the land. Meanwhile, reports of Bela Lugosi's death seem more than a trifle premature. Or do they?

'We were living in the murder Mecca of the midlands, Northampton. It was a blank, the grey, hopeless, hopeless dank British island mentality. Non-culture. We were in the middle of that, and "In The Flat Field" was, literally, about living up in this godless flat field, this linear non-ascending consciousness, the result of what Nietzsche prophesied, the death of God.' Pete Murphy

In August 1978, Roger Eagle, owner of Liverpool's Eric's club, contacted Tony Wilson, *So It Goes* TV host, Joy Division manager and the self-styled guru of the Manchester scene, to discuss a joint venture, a record label that would pinpoint both the best of the two cities' musical output, and highlight their bitterly earned independence from the London scene that still, in the pages of the press and the ears of radio, dominated British rock.

The projected label broke down before its first release was even finalised – indeed, that is why it broke down. Eagle's vision was of a budget-priced LP length compilation, introducing a clutch of bands in the spirit of the legendary record label samplers of years gone by – Island's *You Can All Join In*, CBS's *Fill Your Head With Rock* and so forth. Wilson, on the other hand, imagined a pair of 7-inch singles with grandiose packaging that, in itself, was an event before you even heard the music.

When they realised that they couldn't even agree on this issue, the pair knew they were unlikely to see eye to eye on anything else. Eagle returned to his own Eric's label; Wilson inaugurated Factory, soon to become one of the dominant independents of the age and, even in its infancy, a remarkable venture. That much was certain from the moment the label debuted, in December 1978 with, indeed, a double 7-inch. A *Factory Sample* featured two tracks apiece by Joy Division, Durutti Column and Cabaret Voltaire, and three from John Dowie. All four acts would become Factory staples. But only Joy Division would become a landmark, not only for the label but, as their reputation spread and their sound began filtering into even a limited consciousness, for the post-Punk scene in general.

Recorded with Martin Hannett in April, 1979, Joy Division's debut album, *Unknown Pleasures*, was unquestionably a direct descendent of *The Scream*, albeit (and so appropriately) a deeply introverted one.

It seems peculiar now to recall that, though the album was released to a hail of critical astonishment, sales were poor. It would be two years before the record actually charted, and no wonder. With chilling irony, *Unknown Pleasures* was held up by *Sounds* as the last record you'd play before committing suicide, beneath a headline howling 'Death Disco' – John Lydon's Public Image Ltd would later turn that title into an extraordinarily unlikely hit single. *Melody Maker* compared the album to a tour of Manchester, 'endless sodium lights and semis seen from a speeding car, vacant industrial sites… gaping like teeth from an orange bus.'

All, however, were in agreement over one thing: that Joy Division were, quite simply, the most depressing band ever to walk the earth. 'It was very unsettling,' bassist Peter Hook reflected two decades later. 'To go from being nothing, to being lauded as one of the darkest groups known to man was a trifle confusing.' He never understood, he continued, 'why people thought we were so miserable, because I thought it was quite exciting.'

So did Curtis. Seated with his bandmates, all he would say, in the same soft-spoken monotone he always adopted for interviews, was that things were not always what they seemed. 'Some people have said [our music] is all about death and destruction. But it isn't really. There are other things. None of the songs are about death and doom; it's such a Heavy Metal thing, that.' And Joy Division were anything but heavy metal.

Nevertheless, doom and gloom remained an easy mantel to wrap around Joy Division's shoulders. The group's greatest strength was Curtis' lyricism, and the band's ability to ally those lyrics to the power of their music. There, names like Peter Hammill, Richard Strange and, in later critical retrospectives, Nick Drake, could, and would, be dropped as potent forebears, distinctly English romantics who understood the emotional equation that gave them that distinction in the first place.

Like them, Joy Division's music possessed an innate changeless timelessness; like Drake in particular, Curtis operated from a position of absolute isolation. Six years earlier, reviewing Drake's *Pink Moon* swansong, *Zig Zag* magazine remarked, 'The album makes no concession to the theory that music should be escapist. It's simply one musician's view of life at the time, and you can't ask for more than that.' That same observation was echoed time and time again as *Unknown Pleasures* made its presence felt.

'It's funny, isn't it,' mused Peter Hook. 'Americans have this thing where they can sing about what a beautiful day it is. Whereas with the English, its always a really rotten day.' John Cale, discussing the commercial failure of Nico's *Marble Index* album, once opined, 'It's an artefact. You can't package suicide.' Joy Division and Siouxsie and the Banshees, it seemed, suddenly proved that you could. You just needed to be very selective about the kind of wrapping paper you used.

'To a large extent,' Psychic TV frontman Genesis P-Orridge remarked in 1982, 'Joy Division evolved a unique sound of their own, a new sound amongst the sort-of progression of musical sound. They had their own recognizable, individual style. And then suddenly there's 50 other groups who, because they like Joy Division, use the same style [but] can't have the content because they're not Ian Curtis.'

• • •

At school in Northampton, Daniel Ash and Peter Murphy were widely – and wisely – regarded as the weird kids, 'Peter had bright orange hair, all sticking up,' Ash recalled. 'He was the first person I knew who did the Bowie hairstyle. All the soccer players wanted to beat him up, and all the girls thought he was weird, but I thought it was great.'

Murphy reciprocated his best friend's enthusiasm. 'I loved him at school. He was a great mate, and he was really enigmatic. I really admired him a lot and he knew that I had something as well.' The pair were, Murphy readily admits, 'Bowie casualties' – as an impressionable 15-year-old in 1972, Murphy would gaze for hours at photographs of the man, enraptured by all that Bowie appeared to be promising.

'Pictures of Bowie appearing with the Lindsay Kemp mime troupe. It was very erotic, but asexual, this beautiful spaceman – at least, that's what I picked up from them. Of course, the reality that was really happening in the Bowie mind was nothing like what I was creating in mine, but that didn't matter.' That early, that young, Murphy had comprehended his first lesson in image-making.

51

Another school friend, David John Haskins – soon to become David Jay and, today, simply David J – was equally out of step with his Led Zeppelin-loving schoolfriends. He and his younger brother Kevin spent hours perfecting their own versions of Gary Glitter and T Rex hits, David on a cheap guitar, Kevin on a tiny drum kit. A couple of years later, turning onto reggae and dub, David progressed to playing bass and applied those techniques to the same basic repertoire.

Emboldened, he and Haskins swiftly established themselves as a rhythm section to be reckoned with, conjuring a sibling sound that would pass through a myriad of barely remembered bands, playing occasional gigs at local working men's clubs. It was inevitable that their paths would eventually cross with Ash's. He, too, had a series of area bands to his credit and, by mid-1978, the three were playing together for the first time, in the immortally titled Jackplug and The Sockets.

Murphy, now working at a printing firm and only daydreaming of pursuing some form of musical career, caught Jackplug performing at a Northampton pub, but was far from impressed by their repertoire of warmed-up Rolling Stones covers. Neither did things improve after the band changed its name to the Craze – a little less beholden to Punk rock's penchant for silly band names, perhaps, but still a bashing, crashing noise. By autumn 1978, the Craze had broken up and Ash began casting around for further challenges.

Re-enter Peter Murphy. 'I wasn't doing anything creative at all. I was really suppressed. And then Daniel rang me up, he'd just split up from a band, like his sixth attempt. And he said, "I really want to do something different, can you sing?" I said yes. "Can you write?" Yes. "Okay, so let's meet up and see what happens." And I knew I could. Ever since I was a kid, whenever I saw a band, a cabaret act, I knew I could do that better. I sang all the time. We rehearsed, he said, "You've got a really good voice." And two weeks later we had a gig! It was unreal. A dream, and a total accident.'

In fact, that first session was blindingly creative. Ash himself had not written anything yet – he simply played the first thing that came into his head and let Murphy, his voice cloaked in echo, handle lyrics that he extemporised from a newspaper he'd brought with him. It did the trick. 'As soon as I heard him sing, I knew within five minutes,' Ash recalled.

'There was this energy,' Murphy marvelled. 'We met up for a weekend and I'd never opened my mouth in front of a microphone before. But we wrote 70% of "In The Flat Field" that afternoon... just me and him with a guitar, on the first afternoon that we met up. We just started banging it out.'

'In The Flat Field,' a song destined to become the title track of this tentative union's debut album, in many ways stands as a manifesto for the entire post-Punk movement. It is dedicated, in no uncertain terms, to the uniformity that still surrounded the youth of the age; the grey drabness that Punk had promised to tear down but had, ultimately, only redesigned.

'We were living in the murder Mecca of the midlands, Northampton,' Murphy explains. 'It was a blank, the grey, hopeless, hopeless dank British island mentality. Non-culture. We were in the middle of that, and "In The Flat Field" was, literally, about living up in this godless flat field, this linear non-ascending consciousness, the Nietzschien... the result of what Nietzsche prophesied, the death of God. Scary stuff, almost like limbo. That really scared me as a child, "How can I live here?"'

Now, for the first time in his life, he was sensing an escape. Awakened by Ash's enthusiasm, discovering that it aroused feelings within that he'd scarcely ever paid attention to, Murphy vowed to make a go of it.

Murphy: 'I think the whole reason why I started writing is because it was out of an insulated area. I was never involved with music other than listening to it. I used to sing on my own, without ambition. Out of that negative insularity, suddenly you're thrust into this creative machine. It was like a break, I was free and really happy. I left my job. The change was amazing.'

Looking to complete the line-up, Ash promptly recruited one-half of the old Craze rhythm section, drummer Kevin Haskins. On bass, however, another friend stepped in, Chris Barber. David J would not be invited to partake for another couple of months, although he wasn't quite relegated to watching from the sidelines. On at least one occasion, at a Northampton Teachers Training College show, he actually shared the bill with the still-unnamed quartet, coincidentally enough reading cut-ups from his own supply of newspapers. The rest of the time, he was preparing for the next step in his own career, playing bass in a band touring the American airbases in Germany, spending every waking hour studiously learning the 60-odd classic soul and R&B numbers that made up the band's basic repertoire. He'd just nailed the last one and was packing to leave when Ash dropped by to play a tape of his own new group. The bassist took one listen, and quit the touring band on the spot, to replace Chris Barber on bass.

Murphy continued, 'It was the others' second or third bands, but they were into making music. Once Danny [Ash] and I started working, it was nothing like that, which is why David begged to be in the band. He said at the time, "I've got to unlearn everything I know".'

J immediately gelled with his new bandmates, not only introducing a bass style that had long since learned all the right places to play in, but also suggesting a name for the outfit. Bauhaus 1919 was named for the German Weimar-era school of design, selected both for its stylistic implications and for the arty exclusivity it transplanted upon what was otherwise a somewhat roughshod repertoire. At their first-ever show, at the Cromwell pub on December 31st, the group played Iggy Pop's 'Raw Power' four times, and hoped the party revellers wouldn't notice.

Through their first months together, Bauhaus 1919 opened for anyone who would let them – usually without giving them any choice in the matter. Rather, they'd simply turn up at other peoples' shows and set up their equipment. More often that not, they got away with it but, if anyone did ever challenge them, J remembers, 'Our gear was already set up, so they'd just let us get on and play! We supported loads of bands like that!'

The group was also composing material at a furious pace – so much so that, within a month of their live debut, Bauhaus 1919 were ready to begin touting their first demos around the London record companies. But no ordinary demos were these. Rather, a band friend, Graham Bentley, had got his hands on a portable colour video recorder. Bauhaus 1919 would make their entrance into the music industry in style.

Unfortunately, they were also making it a couple of years ahead of their time. Few of the labels Bentley visited with his tape had video playback equipment, even fewer knew how to operate it. Soon, he was reduced to lugging his own player around the offices, only to find another problem. Nobody seemed to like what they saw, with Murphy in particular a major sticking point. Awkward, ungainly, nervous as hell, he was the kind of performer that you either loved on the spot, or loathed with a passion. It was certainly unlike anything anyone had ever seen before – and that, just two years after Punk tore down every barrier, was one hell of an accomplishment. It just wasn't necessarily one to be proud of.

Retracing their footsteps, the group decided to abandon the video project and take a more traditional route. They booked themselves into the tiny Beck Studios in nearby Wellingborough to record a conventional demo tape, five songs drawn from their self-composed repertoire: 'Boys,' 'Dark Entries,' 'Some Faces,' 'Harry' and, to make sure people were paying attention, an opening opus that was quite unlike anything else on the tape, 'Bela Lugosi's Dead.'

They recorded it live (none of them knew their way round the studio sufficiently to do anything else) and they produced themselves as well. Studio owner Derek Tompkins admitted that, for what they were trying to do, the band alone could judge whether or not it was working. So, he sorted out the best sound he possibly could, helped Ash and J set up the echo and effects, and then left them to get on with it. A shade under ten minutes of clicking, scratching, scraping and keening later, it was finished. And it was brilliant.

Daniel Ash and David J took the credit for creating the song in the first place, Ash by slowing down an old Gary Glitter riff, then messing with the chords; J for hatching a chorus toying with the idea of whether Hollywood's greatest vampire could ever really be dead. It all seems so simple and self-explanatory today. But Murphy's response, when he was first told of the gestating gem, was one of absolute mystification. 'I received a telephoned "Hey Pete! Dave's got this lyric to this song and it's called 'Bela Lugosi's Dead'." And I said, "What? Bela Luigi Who?" And he was "no, no, Bela *Lugosi*."

Even on paper, without any lyric beyond J's tentative chorus, 'Bela Lugosi's Dead' was unique. It crackled in on percussion alone, a tapping, rattling rhythm into which a three-note bass line eventually intruded itself, before Ash's treated guitar slid in, echoed and echoing the most atmospheric dub.

The ingredients merged, but the curtain was still only slowly rising. Even after he'd penned a suitably bat and blood-letting lyric, it took an age before Murphy, his voice a deep, sepulchral rumble, was finally cued to take the stage; and minutes more before there was even a hint of relieving the tension, as the song – such an inappropriate word – moved towards its melody.

It was relentless, one of those scarce moments when performer, performance, mood and music are so expertly blended that the actual components of the piece became absolutely inextricable. Guitars became coffin lids, creakingly opening, the bass became footfalls in a deserted corridor overhead, the drum was the flapping of a myriad bat wings and Murphy? Murphy was the Count, dead, undead.

The roots of the lyric that the swiftly enlightened Murphy dashed off lay in a conversation the band had often drifted into, discussing what Murphy recalled as 'the erotic quality of vampire movies, even if they were the Hammer horror type. There was this conversation about the sexuality and eroticism of Dracula, and how that was very, very powerful for a pubescent male... or female. Never mind the form of what we look at now as being kitsch Hammer Horror movies, to our minds, relatively, they were *real* horror movies. But they have this underlying immorality and twisted religiosity and, therefore, really related well with a pubescent glamorous eroticism.' The rest, as they say in the movies, is history.

Bela Lugosi himself was born on 20th October 1882, in the Hungarian town of Lugos – Bela Blasko adopted a variation on his hometown's name as his own following his arrival in America in 1921, by which time the youth who had apprenticed as a coal miner, following the early death of his father, had already made a string of movies in both Hungary and Germany.

His impact on his adopted homeland was negligible. Having made his Hollywood debut in 1923's *The Silent Command*, Lugosi's meagre command of the English language saw him confined to bit parts. Even there he struggled. Any lines he was given, he learned phonetically, but worse was to come. Having been hired to direct a drama, *The Right To Dream*, Lugosi was then dismissed when it became apparent that he was incapable of communicating with his cast. He sued for wrongful dismissal but the court could make no more sense of his complaint than the actors could of his direction. He lost the case and was forced to auction off his own possessions to pay the legal fees.

Undeterred, Lugosi remained on the fringes of the acting world and, in 1927, he was finally offered a role in which his heavily accented, beguilingly faltering English would play to his advantage, the title role in a Broadway adaptation of *Dracula*. An immediate hit, Lugosi remained in the role for three years, then returned to Hollywood in triumph, to repeat the feat on film.

The vampire legend that originated in the Balkan regions of south-eastern Europe was, of course, already established among mankind's most enduring bogeymen. Greek playwright Aristophanes' *Women In Parliament* includes a reference to 'some kind of vampire, all swollen with its victims' blood,' while the same culture's legends of the Lamia and the Empusa, creatures which survive by devouring some crucial element of their victims' being, be it blood or soul, can (and have) both been allied with traditional vampirism.

Imperial Rome believed that owls possessed vampiric tendencies, although their *modus operandi* remained unaltered – Ovid's *Fasti* cautions, 'they fly by night and attack nurseless children and defile them, their throats gorging with blood.' The best defence against these nocturnal visitors was running water, a tradition that has survived to this day.

Vampire legends appear in most European cultures. Not until 1800, however, did they impact again on the arts, when German romance writer Johann Ludwig Tieck published a short story titled *Wake Not The Dead*. Well-read at the time, *Wake Not The Dead* was still percolating in the collective subconscious two decades later. Genevan theologian Dr John Polidori's *The Vampyre*, however, lifted it to centre stage.

Bringing to fruition a project which Polidori's former friend (but now avowed foe) Lord Byron had toyed with during the same haunted holiday that spawned Mary Shelley's *Frankenstein*, *The Vampyre* (1819) established many of the criteria by which all subsequent vampires have been chained, and spawned a line of undead descent that reaches from JM Ryner's *Varney The Vampyre*, *Or The Feast Of Blood* (1845) a masterpiece of Penny Dread so popular that it stretched to 109 weekly parts before it was bound into one volume, to Le Fanu's *Carmilla* (1872) and on to Mary Elizabeth Braddon's *Good Lady Ducayne* (1896). All that before Bram Stoker's *Dracula* (1897) swept in from Transylvania.

Balkan-born, but certainly schooled in the very best British manners and mores, Stoker's vampire was woven not only from the author's own researches but from his own experiences, too. In August 1888, Stoker was employed as business manager to Henry Irving, then owner of the Lyceum Theatre in London, and rejoicing in one of the most successful stage plays of the season, an imported American adaptation of Robert Louis Stevenson's *The Strange Case of Dr Jekyll & Mr Hyde*.

From the moment it opened on 4th August, *Jekyll & Hyde* created a sensation, not only for its gripping presentation, but also for the sickening realism of the murder scenes. When, less than four weeks later, London awoke to news of the first of the five brutal murders that criminal history now attributes to Jack The Ripper, actor Richard Mansfield, so convincing in the Lyceum play's title role(s), was among the first innocents to come under suspicion. Then, when his guiltlessness was declared, the play itself came under the spotlight, for inspiring the killer in the first place.

Like a Whodunit with the final chapter torn out, the Ripper was never apprehended – over a century after the fact, he has not even been identified, though painter Walter Sickert has recently become a prime suspect. But his reign of terror, brief though it appears by modern standards (just ten weeks, from start to finish), continues to haunt the national psyche, not only for the sake of the mystery, but also because of the unparalleled brutality of the executions.

In choosing to transplant his Transylvanian Count to the same streets as had been so recently haunted by the Ripper, Bram Stoker ruthlessly (and, one presumes, deliberately) rekindled fears that the killer's continued liberty had ensured were never laid to rest – indeed, those souls who blamed the Rippings themselves on some unknown supernatural entity could have taken no comfort whatsoever from the knowledge that the city was again under attack from a being whose bloodlust knew no limits.

Stoker's *Dracula* was not an immediate success. Indeed, when the author died in 1912, he still had no idea that the sixth of the 12 fictional works he published was to take on such a life of its own; nor the form that life would take.

As early as 1920, Hungarian director Karoly Lajthay had adapted *Dracula* for a moving picture – tragically, his *Drakula* is long lost, but its success can be gauged from the fact that just two years elapsed before Friedrich Murnau recast the story (and rewrote elements of the action, after failing to secure the necessary permissions) as *Nosferatu*. Six years later, Broadway was thrilling to the vampire's embrace; now, Hollywood was preparing to succumb to the same savage seduction.

Universal Studios, the movie's backers, originally had no intention whatsoever of casting Bela Lugosi in the movie role, much preferring Lon Chaney Jr. He, however, was battling cancer at the time and was too ill to work. Other possibilities fell through. Finally, Lugosi was the only name left in the frame, and neither studio nor director Tod Browning were left with any choice. Lugosi became Dracula – in every sense of the phrase.

It is impossible today to recapture the sheer power of *Dracula*. Vampire movies themselves were new to American eyes and ears – *Nosferatu* had enjoyed only very limited showings outside of Germany and other efforts had scarcely caught even a cultish imagination. *Dracula*, however, rode the renown of the stage-show to the top of the box office, then rode its own moody atmosphere and unparalleled scenes of horror and ugliness even further.

Overnight, Lugosi was transformed from a litigious mumbler who once had an affair with Clara Bow to the hottest property in Hollywood, an international star who suddenly found he could take – or turn down – any role he chose.

It was a freedom that he enacted to the full, although not necessarily to his own advantage. Among the offerings he rejected was the title role in director James Whale's forthcoming *Frankenstein*; Lugosi's eyes were set on another European masterpiece, a remake of *The Hunchback Of Notre Dame*, titled for its main character, *Quasimodo*.

Unfortunately, while *Frankenstein* rocketed to peaks approaching *Dracula*'s own, *Quasimodo* was never made and Lugosi – who had seen that role as essential to proving he was more than a simple stereotype monster – would never really recover. Although he remained constantly in demand, he was indeed stereotyped, if not as Dracula, then at least as a mysteriously sinister eastern European, and few of the movies he made throughout the remainder of his career allowed him to break out of that cliché. By 1948, he was reduced to caricaturing his finest moment in the comedy *Abbott & Costello Meet Frankenstein*, a depth that apparently horrified him so much that he would not return to the screen for another four years.

He resurfaced in 1952, finally resigned to his fate by an appetite for drugs that demanded he take all the employment he was offered. Indeed, he embraced the role with such relish that his every subsequent public appearance found him clad in full costume, while the films he now made were calculated to play on his reputation: *Bela Lugosi Meets A Brooklyn Gorilla*, *My Son The Vampire*, *Old Mother Riley Meets The Vampire* and a pair of films with the eccentric Ed Wood, *Glen Or Glenda?* And *Bride Of The Monster*.

In 1955, Lugosi voluntarily committed himself in the hope of shaking off his dope habit. He succeeded, but at dreadful cost. Having shot just a handful of his scenes for another Wood spectacular, *Plan 9 From Outer Space*, Lugosi was felled by a massive heart attack. On 15th August, 1956, the world learned that Bela Lugosi was dead. Twenty three years later, almost to the day, it was reminded that he still was.

Lugosi's genius, albeit one that led directly to his downfall, was that, in that one crucial role, he was eminently believable. No matter that the Count, as played by the Hungarian, was subsequently to become punishingly parodied, not only by

Lugosi himself but by countless other would-be bloodsuckers too – the respective Grandpas in the Addams Family and The Munsters, are only the first to spring to mind; Christopher Lee and the Damned's Dave Vanian only the most apparent. Throughout the 1930s, when a nervously isolationist America was spotting beasties under every bed, Lugosi's Dracula was flesh-eater made flesh.

From the moment he first materialises in Dracula, to that in which he is vanquished at the end, Lugosi not only overcame any incredulity that his own audience might have felt towards the entire concept of Transylvanian bloodsuckers, he also vanquishes that of any modern viewer, too. He was, quite simply, too damned brilliant for his own good. How ironic that, 50 years later, a song about him should meet the same fate.

Bauhaus' triumph was not simply musical, however. 'Bela Lugosi's Dead' flourishes, too, as a cultural watershed, the moment when themes that had long flourished within the realms of rock'n'roll gimmickry were enabled to step out of precocious cultdom, and into something approaching the mainstream. That the band was simply the latest in a long line of vampiric contenders, any of whom could have sparked the ensuing fascination, is beside the point. Any of them could have. But Bauhaus did.

Their secret was sex. Other rockers, again, had played with Dracula, but they did so purely from the comic horror angle. Bauhaus' approach was considerably more seductive, a deep eroticism that fed into a cultural perception that had itself taken years to break into the mainstream consciousness.

Although it was unquestionably there, the eroticism that is today implicit in vampire stories in general, and Stoker's Dracula in particular, was barely even suggested in the earliest productions. The revelation, in 1936, that there was a Dracula's Daughter was the medium's first overt suggestion that sex played any part whatsoever in a vampire's lifestyle; while 1957's Blood Of Dracula (UK title Blood Is My Heritage) pandered more to its audience's libido than its subject's: the action is set in an all-girl's school, with all the connotations which that surely spells.

It was with the advent of the British Hammer studios' move into full-blooded horror productions, and a return to the girl's school scenario for 1960's Brides Of Dracula, that the old Count was finally revealed for the sexual allegory that learned commentators now insist that he is – the possibility that the studio was simply combining two eternally saleable items into one pulsating package apparently escapes such enquiries. By the late 1960s, in both film and book, physical desire was as much a part of the vampire legend as blood lust and, by the time Anne Rice's spellbinding novel Interview With The Vampire came along in 1976, to completely revitalise what was now becoming an increasingly weary genre, the book's candid overtones of sexuality were probably the least surprising element in the entire tale.

Anxious to maintain the saga's popularity, Rice herself subsequently, and hopelessly, devalued it with a series of sequels, including one – 1986's The Vampire Lestat – that recast its hero as a 1980s rock star. The result was as hokey as it sounds; the impact of the original story, however, remained inviolate. Indeed, though one would dearly love to postulate otherwise, it is no coincidence that the most pervasive and, in terms of longevity, successful vampire images in rock'n'roll also debuted in 1976, although

Rice's work can scarcely be credited with the emergence of Dave Vanian. He had, after all, been dressing as a vampire for years at that point, furthering his own private fantasy by finding work as a grave-digger long before he ever joined a band.

Rice did, however, reacquaint society with a primeval thrill and terror it had long since lost sight of, and Bauhaus grasped the moment with pure and deliberate artifice, a point that was hammered home, again, by its absolute dissimilarity to anything else in Bauhaus' songbook.

Shortly after completing 'Bela Lugosi's Dead,' Bauhaus returned to the studio to record a hefty slice of their current set, imminent classics such as 'In The Night,' 'A God In An Alcove,' 'Dark Entries' and their so-stylised version of T Rex's 'Telegram Sam.'

But none had anything in common with 'Bela Lugosi's Dead'; none really deviated from a frenetic post-Punk thrash that was possessed of nothing more remarkable than a certain intellectual darkness. *Live In The Studio, 1979*, the title under which this session would eventually (1997) be released, is simply the sound of a band. 'Bela Lugosi's Dead,' on the other hand, is the sound of a lifestyle.

By May 1979, Bauhaus (the 1919 had now been abandoned) had arranged for their masterpiece to appear as a one-off single release through the Walthamstow, north London, based Small Wonder Indy; by August, the 12-inch-only waxing was in the stores, and preparing to reign on the Independent chart for the next two years. It will probably be wrapped around its makers' necks for the rest of their lives.

Peter Murphy: '"Bela Lugosi's Dead" was a very tongue-in-cheek song, which sounds extremely serious, very heavyweight and quite dark. But the essence of the song, if you peel back the first layer, is very tongue-in-cheek, 'Bela Lugosi's dead, undead' – it's hilarious.'

Unfortunately, nobody got the joke. From the first reviews to the last stake in the heart, 'Bela Lugosi's Dead' wasn't simply taken at face value. It was swallowed hook, line and sinker. 'Monochromatic repetition... undead alienation... moody intensity... mysterious vocals....' *Melody Maker* caught Bauhaus live at the Music Machine before they'd brought a second record out and was already observing, 'the audience [take them] so seriously'. As if that was a crime! As if the writer himself knew where the punchline fell! As if.

Murphy continues. 'Look at the cover of "Bela," which is a still from pure Gothic cinema, *The Cabinet Of Dr Caligari*. That was the aesthetic we identified with a lot, although it wasn't on an academic level, it was that relativity of the songs and also what we looked like. I looked at stills of *Dr Caligari*, having never seen the film, and I said, "That's me, that's what I look like." After the fact. I looked like this somnambulant character without knowing he existed, so it wasn't a mask or an emulation or anything, that's what we were.

'The mistake we made is that we performed the song with such naive seriousness! That's what pushed the audience into seeing it as a much more serious thing. The intense intention going into the performance actually overshadowed the humour of it.' Bauhaus created a monster. And then the monster recreated them.

Peter Murphy: 'What became Gothic Rock, with the ingredients that comprised it, was a cartoon, almost a tongue-in-cheek kitsch angle on what would be called traditional Gothic – black-and-white films of the '20s and so on. It was a pop mutation, a reinvention of the most superficial, kitsch aspects of Gothic, a visuality. Did it have anything to do with romanticism? No. But "Bela" does fit into that category, because the intense intention going into the performance of the song actually overshadowed the tongue-in-cheek elements of it.

'Plus, the fact we pushed it in a very heavy way. My part... I played it out in a way that was very serious. It was a way of getting attention. I basically became the clown at the front... or the Count. It was pretty perverse, but it was what it was, and because of that, the Gothic tag was always going to be there.'

Between July 1979 and the end of the year, Bauhaus played just 16 live shows, nine of them in London. And, as their onstage confidence grew, so the audience's awareness of what the group portended – or could be construed to portend – developed apace.

Early shows caught Bauhaus themselves utterly unprepared for the theatricality that their performance was destined to embrace. But they learned very quickly. On 7th September 1979, Bauhaus opened at the Marquee for Gloria Mundi, an oddly misshapen band whose post-glam apocalyptic demeanour had pushed them towards much the same brink – musical, commercial and critical – as had already devoured the Doctors of Madness.

Ploughing on with their peculiar vision regardless, Gloria Mundi retained the make-up and costumes that had always raised a roar of their own and Bauhaus, whose jeans and T-shirted shapes had prompted nothing more than a bored glance from the crowd, surely learned something from the experience. Back at the Marquee two months later, with Bauhaus headlining this time, their street clothes were firmly locked back in the dressing room. The Count was born. And, returning to that same venue a few days before Christmas, for the first time you saw that the look was contagious. Either that or, as one witness to the queue on the street outside remarked, there was a Dave Vanian convention going on up the road.

Even this early, Bauhaus put on a staggering show, a visual extravaganza that simply exploded into life – and then kept on exploding. Murphy: 'We had make-up, lights, dynamics, and it was all ours. It was a baroque manifestation that was tinged with a real sense of theatre and occasion and not a lot of bands had that or have that. You can manufacture that, you can buy all the sets you want, you can put on all the costumes you want – hence later Gothic music – but nothing equates with the moment of pure theatre.'

Joy Division's Ian Curtis apparently agreed with him. Murphy continued, 'Even though we were completely different acts, people were telling us about them and them about us, they were preparing us on the street.' He remembered one evening in January 1980, during Bauhaus' residency at Billy's, a semi-exclusive club in London's Dean Street. 'Tony Wilson and Ian came to see us, and it was very much like a terror campaign; the audience were completely whammy, the moment we walked on it was complete confrontation, almost scary – "wait a minute, do I want to be in this room?" And the moment we walked on, Tony said, "Ooh, I won't watch a band wearing make up!" But Ian said, "I'm not going." He stayed and watched the show, and he really liked us. This is what we hear afterwards.'

Neither was the theatre restricted exclusively to play-acting. In Manchester, during one of Bauhaus' first trips north, Murphy was charged with Grievous Bodily Harm after attacking a member of the audience, an onlooker whose unerring aim had landed a glob of spittle in Murphy's open mouth. Enraged and disgusted, the singer leaped off stage to physically deal with the perpetrator, then he continued with the performance, incident forgotten. His victim, however, was not so lenient.

After the show, Bauhaus returned to the low rent (and certainly low morals) hotel where they were staying. Still clad in his on-stage outfit of black leotard and not-much-else, Murphy was in his room when the police arrived to arrest him for assaulting the phlegm flinger. He wasn't even given time to change his clothes, or grab an overcoat. Instead, he spent an uncomfortable night in a gaol cell, then appeared in court the following morning, still dressed for the show. The muffled laughter from the public gallery, where the band's manager and some friends were waiting, only added to his discomfort; so did the discovery that the rest of the band had already left for the next gig.

Murphy was finally released after paying a fine. Bauhaus, however, would never escape the cell that such intensity constructed around them.

Siouxsie

Chapter Four
Are You The Singer
That Has Fits?

Showing how Robert Smith finds the cure, the Banshees lose their rhythm and Joy Division get closer to some unknown pleasures. We visit Futurama, and then we watch a film.

"The movie over, Curtis placed his well-worn copy of The Idiot on the turntable, and waited for Deborah to arrive…"

iouxsie and the Banshees commenced the gargantuan task of following up *The Scream* in March 1979, with the release of the grinding 'Staircase (Mystery)', a plausibly uncompromising second single. 'Playground Twist', in June, ushered in a malevolent third, a taut delight contemplating the notion that the innocence of children disguises untapped powers of evil, little beings unencumbered by the learned taboos of civilised society (or reverting them when left unattended – *Lord of the Flies* in suburbia). Musically and lyrically, both offered a tantalising trailer for the band's second album, even as they ensured that all expectations were to be turned on their head.

Released in August 1979, *Join Hands* was dense where *The Scream* was brittle, swampily blurred where its predecessor was abattoir sharp. Indeed, it is the wilful wandering that characterised these two albums that ensured the Banshees' ultimate longevity. You never knew what to expect them to do, and they'd never have done it if you did.

Even within a single album, the group would slip and slide, referring to their past even as they looked to the future, and forever confirming their position on the furthest fringes of rock sensibility – a position they would never relinquish.

There was a moment, however, in late 1979 when their very survival appeared touch and go.

On 6th September, 1979, just one week into the *Join Hands* UK tour, Siouxsie and the Banshees were hosting a meet 'n'greet at an Aberdeen record shop when guitarist John McKay and drummer Kenny Morris simply walked out of the door and out on the band, without a word of warning or a note of notice.

Later, it transpired that tensions had been building for weeks beforehand, simply waiting for a spark to ignite them. Misunderstandings over the nature of the in-store appearance provided that spark – and, once lit, there was no extinguishing it.

Shocked and shattered, Siouxsie and Severin initially considered abandoning the band altogether – the tour, of course, was out of the question. But calmness followed the calamity and, in the event, no more than four subsequent shows were canned. On 18th September, less than two weeks after the split, the Banshees were back to full strength and on the road again. Former Slits drummer Peter "Budgie" Clark slid into the back line, and remains there today; guitar duties, meanwhile, were temporarily handed over to a certain Robert Smith, still hot and sweaty from support band The Cure's own opening slot. For future analysts, it was truly a case of Goth meet Goth. And the only thing that ruins that scenario is, not only was that term still utterly meaningless in a generic rock sense, the Cure wouldn't have fit it even if it wasn't. Not back then, anyway.

Discussing David Bowie, at whose 1997 50th birthday concert he was a special guest, trading off verses of a heartfelt 'Quicksand', Robert Smith acknowledged, 'despite the fact I've said I don't like a lot of what he's been doing, particularly things like Tin Machine, he is the only living artist involved in music who's ever had a real impact on me.'

For a great many people, particularly (but not only) the generation that came of age in the 1980s, as the Cure themselves came of age on the worldwide stage, Smith maintains the same hold on their hearts as Bowie exerts on his. 'Trust in me through closing years,' sang Smith midway through the title track of the Cure's third album, *Faith*; more than two decades later, trust remains the bond which cements the Cure to one of the most loyal audiences in rock'n'roll. That and a healthy dose of what even Smith acknowledges to be sheer bloody-mindedness. *His* bloody-mindedness.

It was that bloody-mindedness that transformed the Cure from a likeable pop group, the 'southern Buzzcocks' of late 1970s' British press clippings, into the dark, depressed monolith whose shadow still hangs over their music today; that forced the band to keep going even after it had all but split up; and that has seen the Cure moodily swing from some wild highs to some mighty lows, album by album – sometimes track by track. Smith says it himself: he works to please himself and, if anybody else happens to like it as well, 'that's their tough luck.'

Born in the northern seaside paradise of Blackpool but raised in Crawley, deep in the London commuter belt, Robert Smith was 13 when he formed his first band. The Obelisks lined up with two other future Cure members aboard, Michael Dempsey and Lol Tolhurst, and were, in Smith's own words, 'horrible.' It took them two years even to stage their first proper rehearsal, by which time half the members had already quit, the other half had swapped instruments, and the band itself had changed its name to Malice. With a repertoire of old Bowie, Alice and Alex Harvey songs, they played their first live show at nearby Worth Abbey in December 1976, and pretty much invented the concept of 'Unplugged' performances at the same time. 'The only way they'd book us was if we were a folk band, so that's what we said we were,' Tolhurst later admitted. 'We even rearranged our set for acoustic instruments.'

Chip Taylor's 'Wild Thing', Bowie's 'Suffragette City', Hendrix's 'Foxy Lady', Thin Lizzy's 'Jailbreak', Smith's 'A Night Like This' and Tolhurst's 'Easy Cure' all filtered through the group's set, as did a succession of vocalists and a few more name-changes. By January 1977, the group had rechristened itself Easy Cure after the song; by March, they had a vocalist named Peter O'Toole (of course it wasn't the actor chap); and, by April, they had an indefinable 'something special' that immediately attracted the German record label, Ariola-Hansa.

That month, the label placed an ad in the British music press calling for young, unsigned bands to enter a special talent contest – first prize, a Hansa record contract. Recording their entry in Smith's front room, Easy Cure entered, and out of 1,400 entrants, were one of just 60 bands invited up to London for a first-hand inspection. On 13th May, the band trooped up to Morgan Studios to record a couple of songs; five days later, they signed a 1,000-pound contract.

Throughout the fall of 1977, Easy Cure worked towards what they dreamed would be their first album. Overriding the departure of O'Toole by simply promoting guitarist Smith to lead vocals, the band recorded ten songs for the label's inspection: seven originals ('Meathook', 'See The Children', 'I Just Need Myself', 'I Want To be Old', 'Pillbox Tales', 'I'm Cold' and 'Killing An Arab') and three covers ('I Saw Her Standing There', 'Little Girl' and 'Rebel Rebel').

The label rejected them all, fuelling Smith's growing conviction that they had chosen the band on the strength of its photograph and never once listened to their original tape. It was the year of Punk and, without ever purposefully leaping aboard that particular gravy train, Easy Cure were very much a child of their times. Hansa, on the other hand, had built their reputation on the back of good-looking teen fodder and catchily-clad disco performers. Punk never once entered the label's calculations.

Looking for some kind of saleable compromise, Hansa despatched the band back to the studio to record some rock'n'roll covers, à la Showaddywaddy. Easy Cure returned with fresh versions of 'Rebel Rebel' and 'I Just Need Myself', plus two more new songs, 'Smashed Up' and 'Plastic Passion'. Hansa turned them down on the spot.

The relationship was doomed, and it was only going to get worse. Discussing their now imminent debut single with the label heads, Easy Cure had already made up their mind what they wanted to release: 'Killing An Arab', a captivating few minutes based loosely on Albert Camus' novel, *The Stranger*. Hansa were horrified: by the suggestion, by the title, by the song itself. Deadlock ensued and, a year after winning the talent contest, Easy Cure were dropped from the label's roster. They celebrated by writing a new song about their experiences, 'Do The Hansa', and by abbreviating their name to the Cure. 'Killing An Arab', however, remained their first choice for a single.

Nevertheless, it was absent from the Cure's next demo, a four song tape which instead highlighted 'Boys Don't Cry', '10.15 Saturday Night', 'Fire In Cairo' and 'It's Not You,' and it was this clutch which brought the band to the attention of Polydor A&R man Chris Parry, just as he was preparing to uncork his own record label, Fiction. He invited the group to meet with him at his London office and, over the next few months, it was apparent to all that the Cure would become Fiction's debut signing. Work began on the band's debut album a week later.

Gigging regularly through the remainder of 1978, the Cure intended releasing their first single immediately before Christmas – it would, of course, be 'Killing An Arab'. Fiction's distributors Polydor, however, steadfastly refused to go along with the proposed December 22 release date, prompting Fiction to work out an alternative deal with Small Wonder. They would issue the first 15,000 copies from the label's shopfront headquarters in Walthamstow, after which the regular Fiction release would be unleashed. It finally appeared in February, 1979.

The single was an immediate critical success; its makers, however, left many observers scratching their heads as they tried to pigeonhole this apparently image-free and rootless band. When they failed, they coined the term 'anti-image', and let that serve the same purpose. Smith still remembers his mother reading some of the band's early press, then turning round and asking, 'what *is* an anti-image anyway?' Smith had to confess he didn't have a clue.

The Cure's debut album did not alleviate the confusion. In place of a band photograph, *Three Imaginary Boys* depicted three household appliances instead: a lampstand, a vacuum cleaner and a fridge. But if the artwork was obscure, the music within was anything but.

Songs were short and tight. Sometimes, the Cure's music verged on the same pointed minimalism as characterized early Talking Heads and Wire; other times, it echoed the melodic purity and catchiness of the Buzzcocks, the Pleasers and the Boyfriends, the power pop hordes whom, if you believed what you read in that spring's music press, were set to become the Next Big Thing. The Cure, it was generally predicted, would be in the forefront of that charge.

Built around many of the same songs that Hansa so hated, *Three Imaginary Boys* has held up a lot better than many of its spring 1979 contemporaries – the Members' *At The Chelsea Nightclub*, the Undertones' self-titled debut, Devo's *Duty Now For The Future*, Nick Lowe's *Labour Of Lust*. It is only with the benefit of liberal hindsight, however, that the future direction of the Cure can be gauged from its contents, with such once-sparkling jewels as 'Fire In Cairo' now revealed to be a virtual dead end, at least in terms of style and intent.

'The songs on *Three Imaginary Boys* were really embryonic,' Smith would later condemn. 'They were just put down. There were so many songs on that record only because they were drawn from two years before we recorded it.' The songs the band themselves preferred were those in which a darker edge loomed unexpectedly out of the diamond mine: the cloying claustrophobia of '10.15 Saturday Night', with its vision of the tap incessantly 'drip… drip… drip… drip… dripping' (Massive Attack later co-opted the moment for their impossibly foreboding 'Man Next Door'); the unstated, understated, menace of 'Another Day' and, most powerful of all, the fear-tinged nostalgia of 'Three Imaginary Boys' itself. Everything that the Cure were to become over the next few years was hinted at in those earliest manifestations of Robert Smith's unique songwriting.

'I've always written things down, ever since I can remember. I've got a really bad temper, but it's not physical. I don't throw tantrums or anything like that, so I go off somewhere and, rather than smash the room, I write things down. It's a release. I worry that my words aren't going to interest people because they're mainly about me. They're not just about world situations or alternatives.'

That, however, was the reason why people were interested. The late 1970s saw the maniacal sneering energy which had been unleashed by Punk Rock commence its gradual decline into dissipation, a condition which was only exaggerated, on the one hand, by an increasingly desperate drift towards politicising and on the other, by a total absorption in emotional and personal selfishness (an absorption that Smith understood, but was always able to haul himself away from just as it seemed he must crash).

That was the band's true blueprint; not, though it certainly seemed that way at the time, those first unforgettably incandescent singles: 'Killing An Arab', of course, 'Boys Don't Cry' in June, and the bandwagon-berating 'Jumping Someone Else's Train' in October. Smith himself agreed that, 'in a perfect world, "Boys Don't Cry" would have been a #1 hit,' but he was also profoundly grateful that it wasn't. 'Imagine having to rewrite that song again and again, just to maintain the success,' he shivered.

'Jumping Someone Else's Train', on the other hand, was also to influence the group's immediate future. For the past 14 months, the Cure had been a trio of Smith, Tolhurst and Dempsey, but the latter was growing increasingly uncomfortable with what he perceived to be the darkening direction of Smith's songs. 'Train', apparently, was one of the final straws. The bassist had already made up his mind to quit as the Cure commenced their first major British tour in September 1979, opening for Siouxsie & The Banshees.

There, Dempsey's – and the Cure's – problems were immediately put in humbling perspective by the catastrophe that now tore the headliners apart.

The night of the actual split, in Aberdeen, an audience of 2,000 sat for two hours waiting for the headliners to appear. The opening Scars had played, so had the Cure. Now it was down to Siouxsie and Severin to explain to the audience what had happened. Severin recalled, 'when the manager of the hall announced that we wouldn't be playing, they were pretty incensed. All that Siouxsie and I could do was go out and say sorry; that we were there and were willing to play, but that the other two had gone. [The crowd] took it well and started shouting for the Cure to come back, which they did. That was really good of them. Siouxsie and I then asked the Cure if they knew 'The Lord's Prayer,' so we went back on and played it for about ten minutes.'

Do you know 'the Lord's Prayer'? There can't be many rock'n'roll musicians who've been asked that question.

'It's a noisy joke,' Severin explained, when *Sounds* suggested that the closing track on *Join Hands* might be construed as somewhat sacrilegious. 'We're making this horrendous noise and Sioux's singing "Claire De Lune". I have to laugh.' On vinyl, it could have been even grander – manager Nils Stevenson's original vision was for 'The Lord's Prayer' to devour one entire side of the album, the band's blur accompanied by a choir and an orchestra. That never happened, for a variety of reasons. In concert, however, the prayer became a mass in its own right and, with Smith more than willing to repeat the experience on a nightly basis, the Banshees' immediate problem was solved.

Nils Stevenson: 'Robert Smith was suggested by Siouxsie and Steve as a temporary replacement. Surprisingly, he went for it. He did two sets a night, one with the Cure and one as a Banshee, and he didn't come off stage and collapse afterwards. He did get the band into bad habits, though, drinking and being silly every single night.'

Smith shrugged. Silliness came easy to him, he admitted following the final night of the tour, in London on 15th October 1979, 'because we all get so excited about things. Sometimes I smile. When Budgie and I make mistakes, we look at each other and grin, we can't help it. But that's not the Banshees' image, is it? They're supposed to be all dark and brooding.' How swiftly he would learn just how tightly that particular straitjacket could fit.

The Banshees tour finally over, Michael Dempsey left the Cure in November 1979; bassist Simon Gallup replaced him, with keyboard player Matthieu Hartley coming on board at the same time. This line-up debuted just weeks later, at the start of another tour, this one a Fiction label package designed to showcase all three of the label's principle signings – the Associates and the Passions opened the bill. (A fourth act, the Cult Heroes, was essentially a Cure spin-off.)

The first gleaming of what would become the Cure's second album began creeping into the Cure's live set as early as August 1979, although it took Dempsey's outspoken departure to truly alert most outsiders to the directions in which the Cure's music was flowing; that, and the skeletal symphonics with which Hartley's keyboards and Gallup's liquid bass sketched the new album's bedrock. And still *Seventeen Seconds* shattered expectations.

'We had ten days to make that record, because we couldn't afford to be in the studio for eleven,' Smith recalled. 'And I'm glad I had that experience, going in, knocking out an album quickly, "the good old days." But I also remember the downside, the lack of time, the lack of money, the lack of belief. The intense frustration I used to feel. But it still seemed like forever.'

Which is about how long the record lasted, according to many of the album's original critics. Smith himself insisted that the general mood of *Seventeen Seconds* was more important than the actual songs, and that the generally damning reviews it received were the direct consequence of critics completely bypassing the album's obvious emotional content. Yet one can hardly blame them. Even witnesses to the Cure's most recent live shows could not have been prepared for the sheer intensity of an album that opened with a wintry instrumental based around the Banshees' 'Pure'; which was bisected amidships by an almost tuneless 52 seconds titled 'The Final Sound'; and whose first single was, as Smith himself has reflected, universally regarded as an atrocious choice. Today, 'A Forest' is lauded among the classic 45s of the early Eighties. In April, 1980, it was as maliciously impenetrable as anything else on the album, and even Smith's facial approximation of a sombre Pete Shelley in the accompanying video scarcely lightened the vista.

An overwhelmingly sobering record, *Seventeen Seconds* grew out of the songs which Smith, who composed them all on a Hammond organ, himself had pinpointed as the most representative compositions on *Three Imaginary Boys*. 'I knew what I wanted [the album] to sound like, the general mood,' he explained. 'There's no point in trying to intellectualise about it, because it's a genuine emotion that's on the LP' – an emotion which Smith was only able to verbalize as the product of what he called 'a black period', during which he was unable to shake depression, felt anti-social, found even songwriting to be a chore.

The penultimate 'At Night', for example, was written at the end of the Banshees tour, 'when there were so many emotional wrecks walking around. It was lifted from a Kafka story piecemeal, very Thin White Duke style, things that resonated in our lives. I just lifted a few phrases, put them together and it made sense. And that was because I couldn't be bothered to write a song.' He described his state of mind as being 'like looking down on myself. I was being two separate people…. One day I'd wake up wanting to kill somebody, the next day I wouldn't even bother getting up. It was awful, I was letting myself slip in order to write songs. I wasn't fighting it, whereas in everyday life you have to control those feelings. All the things I went through, it was a really demented two weeks.'

Reviews of the album were tentative at best. 'For anyone expecting *Seventeen Seconds* to be a collection of great pop music,' the *New Musical Express* warned its readers, 'the joke is definitely on them. Indeed, *Seventeen Seconds* is far more oblique in its arrangements and construction than *Three Imaginary Boys* could ever have been. The sleeve is littered with blurred, out-of-focus shots, while the record itself makes no concessions to alerting the listener to the Cure's current pitch.' What such commentary did not appreciate, and what the Cure themselves could never have planned, was how accurately *Seventeen Seconds* fed into the mood that was seemingly prevalent across 1980 – musical and otherwise.

Seventeen Seconds was released in April 1980, almost precisely one year into Margaret Thatcher's decade-long domination of British politics, with her vision of Conservatism still fresh enough that every new pronouncement took on the portents of darkest repression and fear.

As unemployment edged towards a record three million, the first tentative suggestion of a return to National Service was voiced. In Bristol, the racial powderkeg of St Paul's exploded in flames, an all-too-easily ignored warning of the rioting that would wrack the entire country the following summer; in Lewisham, south London, the Anti-Nazi League locked horns with the National Front. From half a world away, the earth-tremors of Iran's fundamentalist revolution reached London as the Iranian Embassy was taken over by gunmen, precipitating a week-long siege of violence and murder.

From any vantage point you chose, Britain was slipping into a trough of beleaguerment and despair. And, when pop radio's only response was to blare Liquid Gold, Captain and Tennille and the increasingly muddle-headed escapism of the Mod revival, *Seventeen Seconds* took on a pitch of reality that was unbearable to contemplate – but unwise to ignore. *Record Mirror*'s review posited the image of 'a reclusive, disturbed Cure, sitting in cold, dark, empty rooms, watching clocks.' As far as much of their audience was concerned, that was probably the smartest thing they could be doing.

Regardless of the stylistic and cultural connotations that the term would later take on, *Seventeen Seconds* was Gothic in the truest sense of the word, bleak and desolate, chilled and chilling.

It's an important point to make, bearing in mind the band's subsequent reputation; however, as with Bauhaus (whose own next single was the decidedly angst-free clattering aggression of 'Dark Entries') any other connotations lay purely in the eye of the beholder. In the weeks immediately before *Seventeen Seconds'* release, however, a clutch of new bands emerged for whom the assimilation of a prevalent zeitgeist was not, perhaps, so serendipitous.

Early January 1980 brought the first full single by UK Decay, a better-than-many second wave Punk band out of Luton, whose local live schedule had brought them into contact with Bauhaus. The latter had recorded, but not yet released, 'Bela Lugosi's Dead' at the time and, driving home after a show in Northampton, UK Decay listened in absolute awe to a tape of the song that the band had given them. Not quite overnight, but certainly faster than the outside world realised, UK Decay evolved from the hopeful one chord wonders of their debut, two tracks ('UK Decay' and 'Carcrash') on a split EP with Pneumania, to the more moodily propulsive, edgy aggression of the *Black 45* EP.

Similar energies powered Killing Joke, a group that erupted, likewise, from the remains of Punk, and who had spent most of their formative months purposefully setting out to agitate viewers. The Sex Pistols' 'Bodies' was a live favourite for some time, partly for its still-palpable lyrical shock value, but also for the constantly evolving rhythmic holocaust that the band was able to graft onto it.

An utterly disquieting John Peel session in October 1979 marked Killing Joke's entry into the wider world; their self-released debut EP, *Almost Red*, followed that same month and, by the New Year, Killing Joke were on the verge of major labeldom, as they were picked up by Island Records. The relationship survived just one single, a reissue of the EP, but the impact was felt regardless. Returning to their own Malicious Damage label, Killing Joke's next single, 'Wardance', was released in March 1980, and crashed to #4 on the Independent chart.

The third and, possibly, the most significant of these new arrivals hailed not from the hype-strewn streets of London, nor the kicks-starved hell of suburbia. The Virgin Prunes arrived from Dublin, a city that offered the worst of both worlds, but whose most overt horrors they diluted by first squeezing them through the kaleidoscopic fantasy of Lypton Village, a mythical community populated, explained vocalist Fionan 'Gavin Friday' Hanvey, by people 'who are called ugly, but [with] a character that's strong.' Those people were called Virgin Prunes.

Much to the bemusement of subsequent chroniclers, Lypton Village was also home to members of another local band, U2 – singer Paul 'Bono Vox' Hewson and guitarist Dave 'The Edge' Evans; indeed, the Prunes' own guitarist, Dick 'Dik' Evans, was Mr Edge's brother and had been a member of the nascent U2 during their days spent plying the Dublin covers circuit under such names as Feedback and the Hype. The two bands' swiftly diverging destinies, of course, suggest that the Prunes' understanding of Lypton's local characteristics extended further than mere physiognomy.

Following their live debut at a private party in Glasneven, the group made its first moves into Dublin at large. With Friday and Evans joined by further vocalists Dave-Id (aka David Busaras Scott) and Derek 'Guggi' Rowen, bassist Trevor 'Strongman' Rowan and drummer Anthony 'Pod' Murphy, the early Prunes found regular gigs hard to come by, with the experimental Project Arts Center proving the band's most reliable host. However, news of their activities had percolated across the Irish Sea and, in March 1980, the band played their first London show, opening for U2 and Berlin at Acklam Hall. (The U2 connection would continue to deepen: Guggi's brother, Peter, later appeared on the sleeve of U2's *Boy* and *War* albums; while Pod would occasionally roadie for the group.)

There, they were sighted by Dave McCullough of *Sounds*, whose review described them as 'part glam-rock, part Punk-shock, part pure innovatory outrage… a swathing, scything music form that is Banshees-like but less staid, less self-consciously new and stylistically uninhibited.'

Homo-eroticism and transvestisms played a part in the stageshow, banshee wails and disjointed tribalisms made their presence felt in the music. Whichever way you chose to look at it, it was a disconcerting brew and, when the Virgin Prunes departed for Ireland at the end of the month, promising to return as soon as they could, this latest savage addition to the burgeoning post-punk tribe could not help but whet the appetite for whatever other treats might be in store. Nobody could have imagined just how precious little time remained during which such intellectualisms could remain a guilt-free pleasure.

The critical response to *Unknown Pleasures* turned heads dramatically, among musicians and fans alike. For any band that emerged in the wake of that record, Joy Division comparisons were as much an honour to be treasured, as a mean-hearted put-down, even when the latter was the only intent to be offered. People took the group desperately seriously – reviewing Bauhaus' 'Dark Entries', *Sounds* worried, 'do these new Joy Division bands have a social conscience? Where does the pose end and real art begin?'

Four months later, however, that question had been rather dramatically revised. Now it seemed more pertinent to ask, where did the art end and real life begin?

On the evening of Saturday, May 18, 1980, Ian Curtis left his parents' house, and headed round to the home he had recently been sharing with his estranged wife, Deborah, standing empty following the couple's break-up. He wanted to watch Werner Herzog's *Stroszek*, without disturbing his parents – they'd never showed much interest in subtitled art house movie classics, particularly those whose culminating horror, as an artist tries to choose between two women in his life and can't, found an uncanny echo in Ian Curtis' own affairs. He and Deborah married young, just 19 when they tied the knot, but after four years together, Curtis fell in love with Annik Honore, who worked for Joy Division's Belgian record label.

Curtis' bandmates tried to stay out of the triangle. Friendly with Deborah and uncertain how important Honore really was to Curtis, they watched from afar. It was only later, rereading the lyrics Curtis was writing, that they understood just how deeply the conflict was affecting him. But it was Deborah Curtis herself, writing a decade later in her *Touching From A Distance* autobiography, who most publicly noted that 'Ian's personal life was disintegrating, as his professional life was flourishing.' Because it was not only his love life that was falling apart.

Eighteen months earlier, as Joy Division struggled to escape the cult confines that early notices had erected around them, Curtis discovered he suffered from epilepsy. Travelling home from Joy Division's first-ever London gig, trying to sleep in the back of the band's van, guitarist Bernard Sumner suddenly became aware of Curtis tugging at his sleeping bag. He tugged back and the two began to struggle, with Curtis, all the while, wrapping the sleeping bag around his own head.

Drummer Stephen Morris pulled the van over to the side of the road, watching in bemusement as Curtis, still encased in the sleeping bag, began lashing out with his fists, slamming them against the windows with increasing fury and then, just as suddenly, diminishing strength. Finally, as he calmed, Morris restarted the van, and drove to the nearest hospital.

Back home, Curtis' own doctor placed him on a waiting list to see a specialist; meanwhile, the fits continued. One day, he returned home from walking the dog, looking as though he had been beaten up. On another occasion, he slipped into a zombie-like silence from which he could not be aroused. Both events were seizures, extremities that matched the wild mood swings that his newly prescribed medication could so easily set off. 'The whole thing about epilepsy,' Peter Hook reflected years later, 'they can treat it so much more easily these days. Back then, it's amazing the guy didn't rattle, he was taking that many pills.'

Curtis adapted to his illness, just as Joy Division adapted to their reputation of harbingers of a doominess darker than death itself, subconsciously, but nevertheless effectively, incorporating his seizures (or at least, their appearance) into his stage act. 'During the set's many "peaks", *Sounds* journalist Mick Middles wrote, 'Curtis often loses control. He'll suddenly jerk sideways and, head in hands, he'll transform into a twitching, epileptic-type mass of flesh and bone.' And just as suddenly, he would recover again. It was an unsettling display, all the more so since his comrades were never certain exactly what was going on. Was he simply dancing? Or was this the real thing?

Nobody could be sure. When Joy Division appeared on BBC TV's *Something Else* in September 1979, the station switchboard was swamped by viewers complaining about Curtis' appearance, with opinion divided over what they were offended by – the fact that he looked so stoned? (He wasn't.) Or his tasteless impersonation of an epileptic fit? But, even as the band tried to keep Curtis' condition to themselves, the singer's onstage behaviour continued to attract attention. Years later, Bernard Sumner detailed one evening when some fans approached Curtis with one simple question: 'Are you the singer that has fits?' 'I felt like fucking killing them,' he admitted.

At the same time, however, Hook acknowledged that the true extent of Curtis' illness remained an abstract thing to his friends. 'I couldn't see his illness, to be honest with you. We were so young, and so caught up in what we were doing. Now you could stop that; it would be the easiest thing in the world to stop someone who was that unhappy, and that unwell. But at that time, it's just all down to experience.'

He counselled, however, that the group were not alone in the darkness. 'It wasn't as if it was just us four beer-swilling knobheads from Salford who couldn't see what was going on. There was a lot of professional people who didn't spot it either, and he was being treated by doctors and psychiatrists and they didn't seem to spot it either. And you can sit there now, and say "fucking hell, how did you miss that, you dozy bastards?" But I think there's a lot more education these days, about depression and mental illness.'

As Deborah Curtis noted, even as Curtis' private life collapsed, his public appeal sky-rocketed, as Joy Division cemented their status at the forefront of the post-Punk underground with headline appearances at two festivals in late summer 1979.

First, on 27th August, the northern twin towers of Factory and Zoo Records pooled the cream of their individual rosters for the Leigh Festival, a gathering of the black-raincoated clans that featured Joy Division, Echo and the Bunnymen, The Teardrop Explodes, Orchestral Manoeuvres In The Dark, A Certain Ratio, the Distractions and Elti Fits, and was intended – of course and as usual – to spotlight the north-western corridor's independence from the London industry.

Two weekends later, Joy Division co-headlined the Futurama Festival at Leeds' 5,500 capacity Queen's Hall and, there, the brief was somewhat less parochial.

The brainchild of local promoter and F Club owner John Keenan, Futurama was custom-designed as the first national event specifically to acknowledge the widening schism in the Punk/New Wave consciousness, the fact that a vast aesthetic difference had developed within the musical culture, and a massive audience wanted to hear all it had to offer.

Setting the pattern for four future events, Futurama was spread over two days, 8th/9th September 1979. Joy Division closed the first night; space rock veterans Hawkwind, enjoying a new lease of life as parents of a neo-psychedelic strand of Punkoid offspring, headlined the second; lurking elsewhere on the billing were Cabaret Voltaire, the Expelaires (featuring future Sisters Of Mercy/Mission bassist Craig Adams, and Red Lorry Yellow Lorry's Dave Wolfenden), the Fall, Orchestral Manoeuvres In The Dark and Public Image Ltd, playing only their fifth live show. Joy Division triumphed over them all.

The group's inexorable rise continued. At Genesis P-Orridge's prompting, Joy Division's next release was the Martin Hannett-produced 'Atmosphere', released as a limited edition single through the Sordide Sentimental label. A November tour supporting the Buzzcocks introduced the band to its widest audience yet and, in January 1980, Joy Division's latest single, 'Transmission' came close to making the national chart.

By the spring of 1980, it was as if the entire nation was awaiting their second album, *Closer*, and, with it, a new single, 'Love Will Tear Us Apart'. An American tour was imminent, and a European one after that. Had Joy Division wanted, they could have started filling up their diaries well into the next year.

To friends and family, however, it was also apparent that there was a chilling finality creeping into Curtis' life.

Two decades later, Peter Hook outlined one facet of the singer's dilemma. 'The thing was, he desperately, desperately wanted to do the things he wasn't meant to do. He wanted to play in a group, he wanted to push himself that much, and that made him ill, the exertion. The flashing lights made him ill. He liked the touring around – that made him ill, because he was always tired. He wasn't supposed to drink, he wasn't supposed to stay up late. He wanted that life, and his illness wouldn't allow him to do it. It was obvious, really, that something had to give.'

Joy Division were scheduled to play two shows on the night of April 4, 1980. The first, at the Finsbury Park Rainbow, saw them opening for the Stranglers; the second, across north London at the Moonlight Club, placed them top of the bill at a record company showcase. Looking back, everybody concerned agreed that they shouldn't have played either concert. Instead, they did them both.

Curtis suffered one fit at the Rainbow, spinning uncontrollably around until he slammed into the drum kit. The other musicians carried him offstage, still convulsing, and locked themselves away with him until the seizure was over. Then they drove to the Moonlight Club. Five songs into the set, Curtis suffered a second episode.

The seizures were coming faster. On 8th April, at a show in Bury; a week later in Derby; two weeks later in Birmingham. The group was collapsing around an illness which medical science could not control, and which was pushing Curtis to the edge of despair. He'd already attempted suicide, the night before the Bury concert, overdosing on Phenobarbitone, one of the drugs that was doing such a poor job of controlling his seizures.

But he told Deborah what he had done; she called an ambulance, and he was rushed to hospital to have his stomach pumped. A few nights later, spending time at Sumner's house, he talked about what happened.

The guitarist thought he understood. Echoing one of Curtis' own recent lyrics, the opening line of the new album's 'Colony', he suggested that it was a cry for help. Curtis' response would remain with him always. 'No, it wasn't. It wasn't a cry for help. I knew exactly what I was doing when I took the tablets. But when I'd taken them, I realized that I didn't have as many as I thought.' He'd summoned help because he didn't want to risk brain damage. But he never explained why he tried to kill himself, and Sumner admitted that they never really found out why he did it again, six weeks later.

First, however, he had a movie to watch.

The artist, *Stroszek's* hero, is in America when he finally makes up his mind about his two lovers. He decides that he cannot, and will not, decide between them. Then he kills himself. Curtis, for whom the looming US tour was itself a source of considerable dread, knew precisely how he felt – and agreed with his solution.

The movie over, Curtis placed his well-worn copy of *The Idiot* on the turntable, and waited for Deborah to arrive. Their marriage had broken down completely since his overdose; she was staying with her parents now and, when he called and asked to see her, she thought he wanted to try talking things through. She'd be there later that evening, after she got out of work.

Ignoring his insistence that she bring their baby daughter, Natalie, with her, Deborah got to the house in the early hours of the morning. She left again when it became apparent that there hadn't actually been that much left to say.

Curtis drank some coffee, then finished off the whiskey he found in a cupboard. He wrote a letter to Deborah, talking about their old life together, and the love he still held for her, despite Annik, despite everything. By the time she received the note, he continued, he'd be away; he was meeting up with the rest of Joy Division at 10 the following morning, and the day after that, they'd be boarding their plane for New York. He just wanted to say goodbye before he went.

It was Sunday lunchtime when Deborah arrived back at the house, and saw the note on the mantelpiece. Her first thought was one of gratitude, how nice that he'd thought to write to her before heading off. Then, out of the corner of one eye, she saw him still in the kitchen.

'What are you doing now?' she snapped, but something about his stance made her uneasy, even before she'd completed her sentence. 'His head was bowed, his hands resting on the washing machine. I stared at him, he was so still. Then the rope – I hadn't noticed the rope. The rope from the clothes rack was around his neck.' Behind her on the turntable, *The Idiot* was still spinning around.

As the days passed, so further details began to emerge. The night before his death, Curtis had telephoned Genesis P-Orridge, leaving his friend seriously concerned about his state of mind. 'I phoned various people in Manchester and told them I really thought Ian was planning to kill himself,' P-Orridge later said. 'They basically ridiculed me and said, "Ian's always depressed and suicidal, that's how he is." They persuaded me everything would be fine... that I was just panicking.' (After a decade of silence on the subject, P-Orridge finally wrote Psychic TV's "IC Tears" about Curtis' death.)

Bernard Sumner, too, has been haunted by the might-have-beens. 'I've thought about Ian's death countless times. It could have been his epilepsy, that he didn't want to go on with it. It could have been that he couldn't face his relationships crumbling. It could be that the tablets he was on for epilepsy affected his moods so much – and they really did. It could be the fact… that he was a suicidal personality.

'But I tend to think it was a combination of those things coming together at the same time. The one thing I would say about Ian Curtis is that his ambition wasn't – as many singers' ambition is today – to get on *Top Of The Pops* and be famous. That wasn't it. He had something to express. It wasn't a show, it wasn't an act. He wasn't seeking attention. Ian Curtis was the real thing.'

'Ian's death was a pivotal moment,' agreed Peter Murphy. 'I was really upset. It underlined and fixed the idea that depression was real, the illness was real. Joy Division were never poseurs, and I don't think Ian ever was. He was a sweetheart, a good guy. I can imagine he was like a poet. I saw in his eyes that he was obviously unhappy in some areas, but he also had a genuine authenticity about him. He was just a really sensitive soul in the best sense of the word. When he performed he was not entertaining.'

A respectful period of mourning finally over, *Closer*, the second Joy Division album, was released in July 1980, topping the Independent chart and reaching #6 on the national listing. At the same time, the band's final single, the now desperately prophetic (but, oddly, a lot jollier-sounding than history insists) 'Love Will Tear us Apart' took them to #13. Joy Division themselves, however, broke up immediately upon Curtis' death, only regrouping as New Order some months later, and releasing their debut single, 'Ceremony', almost exactly one year after Curtis' death.

The song was one of two recorded at Joy Division's last ever session, two weeks before Curtis' death. Ensconced at the so-ironically named Graveyard Studios in Prestwich with producer Martin Hannett, they chipped away at the two most recent songs they'd written. One was 'Ceremony', the other was 'In A Lonely Place', a melancholy piece, and foreboding as well, as Ian Curtis ad-libbed one of the most haunting lyrics he would ever create, one which would certainly haunt his colleagues as they faced a new life without him. It depicted a waiting hangman, and the moment of death as the cord pulls tight.

Nick Cave

Chapter Five
The Velvets Gone Holy? Or The Sweet Gone Mouldy?

In which Australia throws a birthday party in London, and London almost throws it back. Bauhaus scour parts other poisons cannot reach, and Dave Vanian discovers salvation in further, eternal damnation.

'On the one hand, we had an audience which we had created through our own efforts. But, on the other hand, we were a little perturbed, curious, and nicely confused – why does our audience look like this?' Pete Murphy

The immediate aftermath of Ian Curtis' death was nearly as sobering as the events leading up to it. Throughout the British music press, vague recriminations echoed as critics pondered their own part in precipitating the tragedy ('where does the pose end…?'), ruminations that may have dwelled on utterly unrelated themes, but that manifested themselves with remarkable consistency.

Where once, artistic commitment had been encouraged, now bands were taken to task for taking themselves too seriously. Where once, unscalable heights of personal expression were demanded, now a backlash awaited anyone who dared strive above their station.

In spring 1980, the cerebral mindfucking of the Pop Group, Killing Joke and Public Image Ltd, not to mention the Psychedelic Furs, Echo and the Bunnymen and so many more, were the answer to a maiden's prayers, and a band like U2, fresh on the record racks with their bullish debut single, another Martin Hannett production (albeit of a very different complexion), were but a gaggle of uncouth rabble-rousers. Six months later, the rankings were completely reversed. U2 were the standard bearers of raw honesty and naked integrity, keeping it simple, keeping it thick; and the earlier heroes were art snobs and outcasts.

All of which means it was probably the perfect time to unleash a beast whose hatred of those art snobs was as intense as any rock critic's; and which was only amplified by the fact that the haters themselves were even artier, and even snobbier, than any of those whom they loathed with such passion.

The Birthday Party were an Australian group that flew into London in early 1980 in search of the Promised Land they'd read about in the music papers, only to find themselves filled with such disgust that they spent the next year regurgitating their fury. Actively enjoying a Birthday Party performance was not a matter of musical taste. It was an act of cultural guerrilla-ism.

The precocious son of an English teacher father and a librarian mother, the young Nick Cave spent much of his time reading, writing and painting. He sang in the youth choir of the Wangaratta Cathedral – it was there that he gained his first hands-on experience of the religious iconography and ritual that have threaded through all his work; there, too, that he made his recorded debut, on the choir's own rendering of 'Silent Night' and 'Oh, Little Town Of Bethlehem.'

A less than harmonious spell at the local school where his parents worked ended when Cave was 14; he was then enrolled at Caulfield Grammar School, where the mischievous seeds of his first band were planted among a handful of like-minded fellows – Tracy Pew, Phill Calvert and Mick Harvey shared Cave's love of the Sensational Alex Harvey Band and Alice Cooper, bolstered with an appreciation of Johnny Cash and Hank Williams, the darkness that lies at the edge of all great Americana.

By 1976, the newly-named Boys Next Door were poised to push themselves forward among Australia's prime (and most primal) exponents of Punk Rock, as it was introduced to the country via imported singles and newspapers, then shot through with a healthy sense of post-colonial disdain. Cave mused, '[Punk] was for the people who really knew what was going on. We knew, and were huge fans of, the Stooges and the MC5. We were aware of how cool it was to go onstage and be obnoxious, because of Iggy Pop, basically. And that sort of titillated our schoolboy sensibility.'

Boys Next Door's percolating precocity was not wholly their own creation. Cave continued, 'There was a band in Australia called The Saints, who were a massive influence over us. They would come down to Melbourne from Brisbane and play these concerts that were the most alarming things you've ever seen. I mean, just such anti-rock kind of shows. It was so misanthropic. They were so loud. They played the greatest Punk music. That was already there for us.'

Their awareness also permitted the new band to look at the imports with discretion. 'We had things to compare it to. The Pistols we thought were a great band, and the Ramones we thought were a great band. But we thought the Dammed were shit. We weren't swept along by the whole Punk thing. We were also listening to a lot of country music, and other stuff, like blues. So there was all that kind of mixed in together.'

Early Boys Next Door gigs continued to illustrate this dexterity. 'We were still playing Alex Harvey cover songs, seventy five percent of our music was Alex Harvey songs. I mean, we'd played concerts before the Punk thing happened and we could play reasonably well. But we were playing kind of raucous noisy gigs anyway. And it didn't take that much to change our sound in order that we were a Punk rock group.'

Cave was already writing his own songs at this time, but now regards his early efforts with utter disdain – 'it was really dreadful stuff, I was a late developer.' So, when Boys Next Door hit the college circuit, it was with a set that now included such stock covers as 'My Generation', 'I Put A Spell On You' and 'These Boots Are Made For Walking', while their earliest originals, 'World Panic' and 'Masturbation Generation', really merited no more attention than their titles imply.

Nevertheless, the group's now-fashionable, nihilistic tendencies wasted no time in securing admirers – the Indy Suicide label featured three Boys Next Door performances ('Masturbation Generation', 'Boy Hero' and 'These Boots') on the March 1978 compilation, *Lethal Weapons*, while the Sinatra song made it out as a simultaneous single. The ball was rolling.

Mushroom, Suicide's parent label, had already shown interest in the Boys Next Door; that spring of 1978, they offered the band a burst of studio time, sessions for an album that the band were scarcely even aware they were making. It was not a pleasant experience. Cave explained, 'We had all of our dealings with the rotten evil corrupt side of management and record company bullshit very early, we learned a lot of lessons right from the start.

'We were given a producer… this fucking idiot from this band called Skyhooks, who didn't have a clue about anything. We had a manager who took us into the office one day and said, "Listen, boys, I've been on to the phone to London, Punk's out, Power Pop's in," and he had these diagrams of clothes he wanted us to wear. And we had a record company who had absolutely no idea about anything.'

The band responded in the only way they could, taking out their frustrations onstage and spinning out of control so gracelessly that they soon found themselves banned from virtually every prestigious venue in town. By early 1979, the Boys

Next Door – now joined by guitarist Rowland Howard – were persevering as much out of spite as any sense of shared destiny.

The Boys Next Door's debut album *Door Door*, compiled from both new material and the hated earlier sessions, was released in May 1979. The band itself wanted nothing to do with it. 'We were able to do decent concerts, but the record is absolutely no indication of what we were like as a band,' Cave complained. 'It was produced by this guy who was told to produce us in a Power Pop way. At that stage, we were just kids. We just had to let this guy go ahead and do it. I had to double track all of my vocals. Say "Masturbation Generation" – I had to go in and double-track them. This was [the producer's] idea. Singing each line exactly the same twice so that it would thicken my voice up a bit.'

Desperate to escape Mushroom's grasp, but contractually bound to the label, the Boys Next Door swerved underground. Their next release, a single split with fellow Melbourne-ites the Models, was recorded on a four track in Phill Calvert's bedroom and credited to Torn Ox Bodies; it was the end of the year before they were able to resurface under their own name, signing with Missing Link and unleashing the tremulous *Hee Haw* EP. But still the band knew that further Australian endeavours were a waste of time.

They were still reading the English papers, consumed with envy as they read of the scene bubbling furiously on every street corner. Even the band names sounded impossibly grand – Echo and the Bunnymen, Joy Division, Siouxsie and the Banshees, the Psychedelic Furs, The Teardrop Explodes, Orchestral Manoeuvres In The Dark, Dalek I Love You. They resolved that some day, soon, they would depart Australia to join this portentous coterie.

On 16th February 1980, the Boys Next Door played their final Australian show at the Crystal Ballroom in Melbourne, at the same time as unveiling their chosen new name via one final single – 'Mr Clarinet' by the Birthday Party. Little more than a month later, on 23rd March, they were stalking *en masse* into London's Lyceum Ballroom, where a century before, Bram Stoker and *Jekyll And Hyde* had haunted the corridors, to check out four of the most feted of the groups they'd read about, a monster showcase featuring the Furs, the Bunnymen, Teardrop Explodes and A Certain Ratio. They hated it.

'They all just stood there and played their guitars and sang,' complained guitarist Rowland Howard later. 'It was lame, bland.' But, as Cave acknowledged years later, it was better than the world that they'd left behind, the big, bad corporate piranhas of the Australian record industry. 'We had a manager that ripped us off blind. All the Birthday Party money that was ever made still goes to him... well, it's stopped now, but this went on for ten years. Right from the early stage, we were met with all of these things, so very early on we made the decision – we will never use a producer, no matter what. We got rid of the manager. We changed the record company, and we knew what to look for in a record company. We'd gone through all our lessons before we actually came to England, so we knew what it was all about.'

Or did they? Crammed into a hotel off the Gloucester Road, the Birthday Party spent their first few days in London wandering around the tourist traps, while Cave managed to pay a flying visit to Paris. But their money was running out and, even after the entire band moved into a single room bedsitter in Earls Court, times were hard. Rowland Howard found work as a dish-washer; Mick Harvey got a job with the Lyons food chain; and Keith Glass, their *de facto* manager, was out every day, trying to find just one record label that might show an interest in five displaced and increasingly disconsolate Australian musicians.

It was an uphill battle. Rough Trade nibbled a little, picking up distribution for the newly imported 'Mr Clarinet' single, but so far as the rest of the British industry was concerned, the homefront music scene had not felt so vibrant in years. Why would they need to start importing talent, when any night of the week, you could pick up the gig guide and be first to catch the Next Big Thing?

Seven days in London, the week before Ian Curtis died, were as typical as any. Saturday, the Only Ones at the Electric Ballroom; Sunday, the Cure at the Rainbow; Monday, Brian James' latest band, the Hellions, at the Nashville; Tuesday, Any Trouble at the Hope & Anchor; Wednesday, Elvis Costello was there as well; Thursday was the opening night of the Pistols' *Great Rock'n'Roll Swindle* movie – catch an early showing and you'd just make it for Bauhaus at the Moonlight Club; and Friday was the second ever gig by TV Smith's Explorers, at the Music Machine. With all that going on in your backyard, Australia might as well have been on the other side of the world.

Maybe it was persistence, maybe it was just blind luck. Slowly, however, things did begin to turn around for the Birthday Party and, oddly enough, the transformation began immediately after Ian Curtis died.

First, the Birthday Party encountered the Pop Group, a band who – if we apply conventional ears to unconventional music – were even more discordant than Cave and co. Then, John Peel picked up on the copy of *Hee Haw* that Calvert managed to pass on to him and started to give it regular airings – a year earlier, he'd been similarly impressed by *Door Door*, and was thrilled to discover its makers were now in town. Everywhere the Birthday Party turned, it was as though a vast curtain had finally been flung open on the city and, for the first time in a long time, new ideas were being invited to enter. The group did not need to be asked twice.

On 29th June 1980, six weeks after Ian Curtis' death, and almost six months to the day after they arrived in the city, the Birthday Party played their first ever London show at the Rock Garden opening for the now long-forgotten Temporary Title. Eleven days later, they supported the Mo-Dettes at the Moonlight Club. In September, they recorded their first John Peel session. The waiting was over.

Bauhaus' third single (and second for new label 4AD), the jarring 'Terror Couple Kill Colonel', was released at the end of July 1980, as the band approached the end of a sequence of live shows that had kept them on the road since January.

Their early reliance on the London circuit had long passed; in February, Bauhaus played their first ever northern show at Liverpool's Eric's; in March, they travelled to Europe; in April, they launched a major British tour. And they divided the critics as completely as if they'd sliced them in two with a breadknife.

Some journalists professed nothing but love. From *Zig Zag*, curious readers would learn, 'witnessing Bauhaus live for the first time can be an unsettling experience for any God-fearin' suburban boy. I didn't know which way to turn, as long as I didn't let that man with the microphone out of my sight.'

Other authors, however, had nothing but hatred, as Peter Murphy later recalled. 'I remember a review which said, "Bauhaus thought they were the Velvets gone holy; in fact they were the Sweet gone mouldy".'

Indeed, throughout the group's first year, critics seemed to be actively battling to create the most unappetising margin for the band to flail within. They were, bemoaned *Melody Maker*, 'one of the growing number of foolhardy bands who believe that creating a weird, disorientating sound actually contributes something of well-being to either us, them or music in general.' They were 'firmly entrenched in the New Musik rut,' they were 'reheated Banshees left-overs,' they were every name under the sun. But the little ghouls understood. 'Visually, Bauhaus couldn't be faulted,' said *Sounds*. 'Dramatic Hammer horror lightning flashes, air-raid spotlights, hand-held strobes, black threads, make-up and haircut problems… [and] the mob welcomed them like conquering heroes.'

'Terror Couple Kill Colonel', its title taken from a newspaper headline reporting the murder of a retired British military officer in West Germany, reached #5 on the Independent chart, Bauhaus' biggest hit yet (the chart-topping run of 'Bela Lugosi's Dead', alas, ended shortly before the official inauguration of a truly national listing). It was also a trailer for what was widely regarded among the most anticipated albums of the year, Bauhaus' debut *In The Flat Field*. Anticipated, that is, if you didn't believe what you read in the inkies.

Within those confines, *In The Flat Field* was flattened, backed-up on, and then flattened again. 'Nine meaningless moans and flails bereft of even the most cursory contour of interest,' grumbled the *New Musical Express*. 'Their singles showed Bauhaus weren't devoid of an idea or two; this album shows they've used them both up.' *Sounds* was no more understanding: "It features a lead singer who writes bad poetry… and a band behind him who combine to mistake the youth-club version of Joy Division for Mountain". It was only when you actually listened to the object of so much scorn and rancour that you realised just what utter bollocks Bauhaus inspired – and the fact that they could arouse such hatred surely said more in their favour than even the most slavering review ever could.

In The Flat Field remains one of the most courageous albums of the age. Opening on ARP guitar and sonar blips, the curtain raising 'Double Dare' trod where even the Banshees dared not go, a chaotic jumble of ominous bass lines, military tattoo and a screaming challenge that the band, unable to improve on their initial rendering of the song, lifted wholesale from their first ever John Peel session, recorded back in early January.

David J still recalls the first time he heard the session, standing on the street in Soho with a hand-held transistor blaring full blast. 'They broadcast it just before we were due to play at Billy's. We were running down the street, completely overjoyed, psyched up by it.' Nine months later, that same fission remained electric and today, more than twenty years later, 'Double Dare' is still one of the most *exciting* sounding records ever made, the musical equivalent of having sex in a Stuka.

Elsewhere, the album's title track – that long-serving relic of Murphy and Ash's first-ever rehearsal together – was a sublime encapsulation of *Scream*-era Banshees schizoid pop, riveted into place by the overpowering thunder of drums and bass; 'God In An Alcove' epitomized the slash-and-burn tactics of the earliest Bauhaus, shattered guitars scything into a trance-inducing bass, while the vocals encircled the lyric like a noose; 'St. Vitus Dance' pranced and spun as disjointedly as the disease itself; and 'Stigmata Martyr' simply blazed with persistent rhythm and searing guitar.

It was a devastating album, sparking with creativity, beholden to nothing, unlike anything. Even the absence of what was still the group's best-known number, 'Bela Lugosi's Dead', could not dim the record's sheen – forever grateful to Small Wonder for giving them a chance, Bauhaus allowed the label to maintain exclusive ownership of the song for the next 20 years. *In The Flat Field* swiftly topped the Independent chart, and even made it into the nationals for a week, there to duel with the best that the mainstream could throw at it.

In a world that was rapidly going Insect crazy, as Adam and the Ants completed their own turnaround from press pariahs in a post-Punk flux, Bauhaus' success was complete – more than that, it was flavoured by their own apparent contributions to the kingdom of the wild frontier. Released the month after *In The Flat Field*, the Ants' 'Ant Invasion' ricocheted off a repetitive guitar pattern that could have been lifted wholesale from a Bauhaus composition, and a vocal stretching to peaks that were pure Peter Murphy – so pure that Bauhaus' own next single piloted itself straight into primal Ants territory with a cover of T Rex's 'Telegram Sam', a relic of their earliest strivings that had hatched a dense, threatening life of its own.

For the first time since those abortive demos in the distant past, Bauhaus stepped into the realm of video for the occasion, hooking up with the Don Letts/Mick Calvert directorial team, then decamping to the boiler room of Fulham Swimming Baths, just round the corner from the 4AD offices, to film amid the steam and water pipes.

From such unprepossessing surroundings, a remarkably effective vision was conjured: arguably, 'Telegram Sam' didn't simply recapture the stifling claustrophobia that was Bauhaus' stock-in-trade, it amplified it as well, layering another cloak of imagery over a band that was already pulsating with other peoples' perceptions... so many perceptions. Flip the single over, then, and 'Crowds' dissected the group's dilemma with ruthless precision. 'What do you want of me?' Murphy asked so entreatingly. 'What do you want of me... you fickle shits?'

The paradox was inescapable, as Murphy – looking back from the mid-1990s – explained. 'On the one hand, we had an audience which we had created through our own efforts. But, on the other hand, we were a little perturbed, curious, and nicely confused – why does our audience look like this?' Of course the answer was staring back from every dressing room mirror, but the band themselves had long since stopped looking. 'We just weren't conscious of how we looked. After a while, you become immune to the garishness of the way you look, it becomes the norm.'

One evening, however, Murphy was walking through Camden Town with Bauhaus' lighting engineer, Plug, on their way to the band's show at the Electric Ballroom. They were watching the audience flit towards the venue, and Murphy recalled, 'I turned around to him and said, "God, people really do look strange these days." And he just laughed – "YOU'RE saying OTHER people look strange?"'

While Bauhaus celebrated their first LP release, the revitalised Damned were preparing for their fourth, and revelling in the devotion of much the same audience that was causing Bauhaus so many quizzically-raised eyebrows.

Since the original line-up combusted in early 1978, and Dave Vanian's flirtation with the Doctors of Madness aside, only guitarist Brian James had landed on his feet, forming Tanz Der Youth in devout stylistic tribute to Roman Polanski's off-the-wall horror epic of almost the same name. James: 'I had a poster for *Tanz Der Vampires... Dance Of The Vampires...* and I'd always loved the way it sounded. So I took the *Tanz Der...*' – and left the vampire to its own devices.

Tanz Der Youth never got the breaks they deserved, finally bowing out after just one single and a miserably mismatched time supporting Black Sabbath on tour. James' Damned partners, too, were very much foundering throughout 1978. Rat Scabies' White Cats and Captain Sensible's King went nowhere and, by September, the pair had reunited with Vanian (with Motorhead's Lemmy guesting on bass) for a one-off gig at the Electric Ballroom, London, under the name Les Punks.

Enjoying the experience, the trio opted to remain together, recruiting first, Henry Badowski, then ex-Saint Alistair Ward, as a full-time bassist and, while they negotiated with James for legal rights to the original Damned name, playing a handful of shows as the Doomed. They then returned as the Damned on 7th January, 1979, at the Greyhound pub in Croydon.

The first year of the reborn Damned was tentative but successful. Three singles, 'Love Song', 'Smash It Up' and 'I Just Can't Be Happy Today' made the British Top 50; an album, *Machine Gun Etiquette*, just missed the Top 30.

Little of the album reflected any concerns beyond those that the Damned naturally espoused, a knockabout Punk Rock band with a heightened sense of the absurd. Occasionally, an element leaps out that, were one so inclined, could induce a brief spasm of professorial beard-stroking – the instrumental 'Smash It Up (Part One)', with its odd sonic harbingers of a future Cure riff; an irreverent lyric or two in 'I Just Can't Be Happy Today' and 'Anti-Pope'; and 'Machine Gun Etiquette' itself, with its fearless lift from Gary Glitter's 'Rock'n' Roll' acknowledging the blend of Punk mayhem and Glam affectation that was, itself, an integral element in the less po-faced quarters of the post-Punk sound.

Vanian's eternal vampire notwithstanding, however, the Damned in 1979 were still very much a band in search of a direction. But, as 1980 progressed, the quartet were constantly aware and continually reminded that Bauhaus' crowd of dedicated bloodsuckers were only the tip of the visual circus that was coalescing around a select handful of bands. As the Damned worked towards their latest album – to be suitably untitled *The Black Album* (corollary, of course, to the Beatles' similarly unnamed *White Album*) – their destiny lay, literally, in their own hands. History insists that they succeeded on every count.

Henrik Poulsen, long-time Damned associate and editor of the long-running *Neat Damned Noise* fanzine, describes *The Black Album* as 'the godfather of Goth albums' and he is not alone in that opinion... strangely. The novice spending an evening with the record will certainly be wondering what the fuss is all about, as 'Drinking About My Baby', 'Lively Arts', the drunken Beach Boys pastiche 'Silly Kids Games' and even the promisingly titled 'Wait For The Blackout' speed past with nary a sepulchral chord nor tolling bell in earshot.

But the mysterious 'Twisted Nerve' fits a comic-book definition of what Gothic *could* be, foreboding lyrics flowed over a nagging bass and a ghostly sax; the excellent '13th Floor Vendetta' conjured spectres in delivery ('the organ plays till midnight...' – what an image!), even as the piano line flirted with *Aladdin Sane*-era Bowie; and 'Dr Jekyll And Mr Hyde' at least tells the story you'd expect it to do.

So far, so quixotic and, looking back 15 years, on a mid-1990s GLR Radio appearance, Vanian reflected, 'It was all pretty experimental after [*Machine Gun Etiquette*], every track was viewed on whatever we could do really. There were four people or whatever working on the stuff, so you never knew where it was going to go.' Which means the band were as surprised as their audience when they came up with 'Curtain Call', a 17-minute opus that consumed one entire side of the ensuing double album, a grandiose soundscape of spooky organ, atmospheric guitar and one of Vanian's most impressive vocals ever. In any band's hands, 'Curtain Call' would have been an impressive escapade; coming from the Damned, a group whose past reputation scarcely placed them in the sort of league renowned for such *guignol* gestures, it was staggering.

It was also the point of entry for a host of Gothic fantasies that might never have been entertained had Vanian not induced their devotion in the first place – then retained it with the growing conviction that, as his bandmates had already discovered, what you saw was what he was.

Poulsen: 'So many interviewers have asked Dave about his appearance, and each and every time he avoids it with a brief answer, basically saying nothing. I have never come across a quote from him commenting on this directly – his standard reply is that he has always been like that and it's not part of some image thing, it's just how he is, 24 hours a day. Whenever he gets questions like, "Is it true that you sleep in a coffin", etc., he just glides off or starts talking about something else. But, needless to say, he has been a huge influence, mainly visually, on many Goths.'

Musically, the Damned have paid no more than nudge-and-a-wink lip service to their Gothic audience – song titles like 'Grimly Fiendish' and album names like *Grave Disorder* play to the peanut gallery, but even they never give in to its basest demands. The same band, after all, are also responsible for 'Edward the Bear' and *Strawberries*.

Nevertheless, further fuel for these blossoming fires was provided by the tales surrounding the actual creation of *The Black Album*. It was recorded in just three weeks following the Damned's latest European tour, in what the band themselves quickly discovered was a haunted studio, Rockfield, Monmouthshire.

Bassist Paul Gray, recruited to the band following *Machine Gun Etiquette*, later detailed some of the odder happenstances. 'It was a weird place. We were all walking up the hill to the old house one hot Sunday afternoon. Rat had his dog with him and it started howling horribly and trembling, tail between its legs. It was dragged on up the hill much against its will and, once inside, we settled down to watch a video with all the doors and windows open.

'Suddenly, everything slammed shut at once and went cold, and the dog went mental. It was very spooky. Later that night, I got up about 3am to have a pee, the door creaked shut behind and I couldn't get back in – strange because there was no lock, only a latch. I thought someone was playing silly buggers, the door felt like it was being pushed from behind, but there was only me in the room. All of a sudden it gave way – weird. The studio told us later that Black Sabbath had held séances there years ago and they had fled as things went flying round the rooms....'

Whatever elementals may have been present while the Damned recorded, they certainly had no ill effect on *The Black Album*. Building on the success of its predecessor, the LP became the Damned's first UK Top 30 entry (it would also, following the Chiswick label's decision to abandon major label sponsorship and reclaim its original Indy status, belatedly storm the Independent chart, reaching #13 in 1982).

Equally importantly, however, it confirmed the Gothic equation that literary and artistic history had known all along, but which the music press continued unwilling to acknowledge in the bands that they were cementing into those illustrious footsteps. Death, doom and darkness don't have to be gloomy all the time. And, while the Damned were not the first band to be saddled with the epithet Gothic, they were the first to purposefully point their energies towards the slowly fermenting musical movement that would eventually be titled thus.

Humour, or at least a jovial light-heartedness, was also in evidence at Futurama II, again staged in Leeds over the weekend of 13th/14th September 1980. There, alongside the expected gloom of Siouxsie and the Banshees, the Psychedelic Furs, Echo and the Bunnymen, Clock DVA and Durutti Column, Wasted Youth swaggered out of a post-gynandromorphic approximation of Keith Richard's glammiest cast-offs to utterly divide the raincoated brigades; Altered Images' skip-dancing hybrid of Siouxsie Sioux and Violet Elizabeth Bott subsumed the survivors with idiot glee; U2 huffed and puffed with becoming bellicosity; and, finally, at around 3 in the morning, Gary Glitter himself emerged to confirm his (admittedly surprising and possibly inexplicable) role within the post-Punk universe. It is still extraordinarily difficult to reconcile the media portrait of several thousand deeply serious mopers gathered in the gloom with the sight of an entire building swaying wildly to 'Remember Me This Way', shedding unashamed tears of absolute joy and fighting for the roses that Glitter tossed into the audience

On a more cerebral level, and even more than its predecessor twelve months earlier, Futurama II was a timely intervention. Leeds itself had suddenly exploded with post-Punk idealism, its pulsebeat spreading across the country as the city disgorged wave upon wave of *outré* electronically minded talent onto the streets.

In commercial terms, the Gang of Four and the Mekons were already streets ahead. Within the confines of the Leeds scene itself, however, the self-appointed leaders of the pack were two former art students, Marc Almond and Kris Neate, the brains behind the latest club venture to illuminate the local nightlife. It was staged every Monday night at the Warehouse, a self-styled super-disco launched by one Mike Wyen. According to Almond, the Warehouse already boasted the best sound and lights in the north of England, and played host, too, to the region's most beautiful style-setters, 'glitterati, who came from far and wide to experience its soon-to-be-legendary hedonism.' What Almond and Neate did was open that hedonism to (almost) all-comers.

The Monday night events were initally designed as Leeds' own answer to the sudden insurgence of fashionable new London niteries that the pair had been reading about in the music press. 'Clubs like Blitz, Hell and Le Beat Route were all the rage,' Almond recalled, 'with people dressing outlandishly in make-up and bizarre outfits. There was a new movement afoot, with its own music, entrepreneurs, designers, and bands like Spandau Ballet, Visage and Landscape.'

But London was a long way to travel for a single night of sashaying, so 'we pitched the idea that we would start our own electronic alternative music night, with an emphasis on new electronic dance sounds mixed in with alternative funk, industrial, post-punk and disco. We would encourage all the Leeds alternative freaks to come out of the woodwork and dress up.'

Not only Leeds. Soon the Warehouse was drawing its denizens from as far afield as Sheffield, Bradford and even Manchester and Liverpool – those cities' scenes, after all, were dominated by grey raincoats and dark visions. The Warehouse, however, offered glam and glamour. For as long as the spotlight remained on the new music, it couldn't fail.

Almond's own band, the Soft Cell duo he formed with Dave Ball earlier in the year, played their first ever live show at the Warehouse, very early on into the Monday club's lifetime, interrupting the DJ's routine of Bowie, Throbbing Gristle and Donna Summer with a set that already included future Soft Cell favourites 'Facility Girls' and 'Metro Mr X', plus the showstopping 'Martin', inspired by the George Romero teenaged vampire flick. Just weeks later, they were a natural homegrown attraction for Futurama II. And less than twelve months after that, they were top of the UK chart, kings of the same New Romantic scene that the Warehouse nights had once so impertinently gatecrashed. The Leeds scene had delivered up its first New Musik superstars. Now it was time for Crawley.

The Cure's Robert Smith

Chapter Six
It Was Quite
Good Fun Being So
Po-Faced

Wherein Bauhaus don masks and the Party grows more popular, the Cure determine that there's nothing left but faith, and the lunatics take control of the convent.

'But I was always really upset that the Gothic name got perverted the way it did because, certainly going as far back as 1979, on our second album, we were talking about Edgar Allen Poe and talking about Gothic things, even though what became a trademark Goth look wasn't even around at the time.' Steve Severin

'Faith was going to be a very positive record,' Robert Smith insisted of the Cure's third album, shortly after a January 1981, Peel session made it very clear that it wasn't anything of the sort. Indeed, on the strength of that single, shattering performance, he barely even needed add, 'it turned out to be a very morbid one.'

He was right, however. Things did start out very brightly. But circumstance swiftly twisted its arm. A set of demos recorded in late September 1980 were scrapped when it became apparent that the songs were going nowhere; as the group began working afresh, Lol Tolhurst's mother fell terminally ill and Smith's grandmother passed away.

Reflecting years later on the album's genesis, Smith acknowledged that, circumstantially, *Faith* was taking control of him, long before he realized he needed to take control of it.

Raised as a Catholic, Smith saw that his own sense of religious belief had long since slipped away from his waking mind. It was a numbing irony, then, that he himself was being elevated to iconic status in a lot of listeners' eyes. And that *Faith*, the album with which he attempted to exorcise his own spiritual demons, was to be the vehicle by which he attained his own demagoguery.

'It's worrying that people have built a need in themselves for someone like me,' he reflected. But even worse was the realisation of what they needed him for. 'I hate the idea that you'd die for your audience, [but] I was rapidly becoming enmeshed in that... the idea that Ian Curtis had gone first and I was soon to follow.' *Faith*, an album of unforgiving power, would not alter that perception.

In hindsight, everything about *Faith* seemed pre-ordained; seemed, also, to hinge around the ghostly sleeve photograph of Bolton Abbey, near Shipworth in Yorkshire. The spectral, skeletal sound of the band echoes bleakly across just such a landscape, and the fading voice with which the record closes remains long after the disc has finished playing. There is nothing left but faith, it insists. But what happens when you have none to begin with? The title track itself remains so affecting that when the Cure finally dragged it out of mothballs in 1987, performing it live for the first time in five years, Smith found himself crying uncontrollably. Two years later, as the world learned the truth about the Tianemen Square massacre in Beijing, he unleashed a 15-minute version dedicated to the dead. And today, the Cure perform it only when a show has gone particularly well.

Looking back, Smith acknowledged, 'It was quite good fun being seen to be so po-faced, because we could get away with an intensity which would otherwise have seemed manufactured.' The flipside of that fun, however, was the grim reality that it then engendered, as the Cure found themselves having to live with *Faith* for the next twelve months. 'We toured with it, and it was the one record we shouldn't have done that with. For one year, we lived with this doomy, semi-religious record, we sort of wore it everywhere we went, it was like sackcloth and ashes. It wasn't a very enjoyable year really.'

The state of isolation into which the Cure had crushed themselves was only intensified by their decision to espouse the traditional rock'n'roll practice of touring with a support band. Going out in April 1981, they instead commissioned a movie to open for them. *Carnage Visors* was a 30 minute animated film made by Simon Gallup's brother Richard and, accompanied by a lengthy instrumental recorded by the Cure themselves, a soundtrack whose sheer moody intensity set the stage for *Faith* even before the band came out on stage to deliver it.

'At their best,' the *New Musical Express* would agree, '[the Cure]'s religious devotional care and slow stately pace takes over with a precision and a discipline that is breathtaking and, yes, religious.' It is that precision and discipline that has ensured *Faith* remains the Cure's purest album, their masterpiece and the consummation not only of all they had promised in the past but, also, of all that they have accomplished since then. Arguably, every subsequent Cure album has simply taken a different nuance from *Faith* and expanded upon it, drawn it out to its most logical conclusion.

It is, also, certainly their darkest, and most atmospheric collection. Smith explained, 'I've always tried to make records that are of one piece, that explain a certain kind of atmosphere to the fullest. If you're going to fully explore something, you need more than one song to do it. That's why I've always liked Nick Drake's albums, or Pink Floyd's *Ummagumma*. I like a lot of music that is built around repetition. Benedictine chants and Indian mantras. These musics are built around slow changes, they allow you to draw things out.'

And so, little about *Faith* adheres to even the loosest notions of commerciality, even those that were current in an age when groups like Bauhaus, Siouxsie and the Banshees and the Birthday Party were, despite themselves, conforming to the latest convolution within the Positive Punk axis. *Faith* loomed over them all, a vast, dark cathedral of sound into which only the remotest glimmers of illumination could fall. And, compared to *Faith*, other bands were simply rooting around in the cellar, with all the lights turned on.

Not that they weren't unearthing some fascinating artefacts as they did so. Transferred to 4AD's parent label, Beggars Banquet, when it became apparent that their renown was too vast for that tiny concern, Bauhaus scored their first national hit, 'Kick In The Eye', in March 1981, just as *Faith* arrived to kick everyone else in the teeth. It was, for a band that the music press now roundly despised, an astonishing achievement – and it was no fluke, either. By summer, Bauhaus' next single, 'The Passion Of Lovers' had followed it into the Top 60 and by year's end, their sophomore *Mask* album was on the Top 30.

After the occasionally tentative and certainly inexperienced delights of *In The Flat Field*, *Mask* fully captured Bauhaus' true potential, not only evoking their live presence in all its angular depth, but also summarising the frightening sweep of their musical styles, from machine gun percussion to catacomb atmospheres, from switchback glam to timeless horror – 'Hollow Hills', based around the old Cornish legends of hobgoblins, is as ageless as a Brothers Grimm fairy tale and as deathless as one of those hobgoblins' own victims. As Murphy related, 'The people believe that in these hills are large caverns, where the underworld hold banquets. If you stumble upon one of those, you will be forever reduced to being an immortal.'

Occasionally, the band's ambition did overwhelm not so much their abilities as their creativity. Both 'Muscle In Plastic' and 'Mask' itself revolved more around artiness than atmosphere, although the latter was certainly redeemed by a spectacular video, a bizarre slice of surrealistic horror filmed across the road from Northampton police station by directors Chris Collins and Ken Lawrence. The fact that 'Mask' itself was never considered as a single rendered the exercise redundant from a commercial point of view – increasingly, the primary reason for actually making videos. But posterity views it indulgently, as perhaps the most instantly accessible point of entry to the world of Bauhaus' own influences and imaginings there is.

Having opened the year performing to largely curious, but generally sympathetic audiences in America, Bauhaus spent much of 1981 grinding their way around the UK and Europe, a succession of shows that saw them hit the 'sheer brilliance' button every night. In terms of future legend, however, one sequence of nine gigs that June stands out like a beacon, as the Birthday Party joined the touring party.

Their self-contained arrogance barely masking their own substantial debt to the headliners, the Birthday Party were themselves promoting their official debut album, *Prayers On Fire*. Signed to 4AD in September 1980 as heirs-in-waiting to Bauhaus themselves, the Birthday Party had already paved the way for the album's release by reissuing, first, a single of 'The Friend Catcher', then a self-titled compilation of Australian recordings. Both kept the pot boiling while the band returned to Australia over Christmas; they returned to London in March and, when the 'Nick The Stripper' 45 arrived in April, a definite mood was coalescing around the band.

The Birthday Party's early British coverage was divided firmly into two camps – on the one hand, they were treated with absolute disdain, cast as calculated adherents to the same post-Joy Division banner that Bauhaus were flying; to other observers, however, Birthday Party represented something far more cerebral, far more *meaningful*, than the home-grown run-of-the-mill noise-makers. Confronted by the mass of massive black hair and pointy boots poised on long, lean bodies that was one's first impression of the gangly quintet, *Melody Maker* set the scene for all subsequent eulogies with gushing poetry: 'Five insane souls bravely hurling themselves into a whirl of sonic intensity that approached the sound of a World War Three being fought in a bunker.' Indeed.

The Birthday Party, for their own part, seemed not to care how they were perceived. Attempts to praise them to their face were met with disdain, scorn and rudeness; attempts to condemn them were greeted with ridicule. Calculated indeed was the group's decision to include in their second Peel session in April 1981, a cataclysm (and subsequent single) titled 'Release The Bats'. Of course it sounded like something Bela Lugosi would say. Listen closely, and it sounded a bit like 'Bela Lugosi's Dead' as well. Such was the band's aura, however, that very few people bothered slowing it down sufficiently to note that.

The Birthday Party's comparatively exotic origins, of course, played a part in their deification. With the likes of the Triffids, the Go-Betweens and Midnight Oil yet to descend upon British shores, and with whatever was left of the Saints having long-since been assimilated, an Australian rock band was still something of a novelty at the time. Having once been despised as mere colonial interlopers, then,

Birthday Party had managed to turn their Antipodean roots into a genuine advantage, arguing that their roots in such an isolated culture gave them insights into the human condition that the average suburban bred Brit band could never comprehend. How trusting that people should believe them.

Cave's natural lyricism, too, impressed the impressionable. Wordy and weird, sometimes barely clinging by its fingertips to the maelstrom evolving around it, Cave intrigued with his poetry even as his bandmates seemingly sought to silence it. It was a chillingly effective cocktail but, again, it was divisive. To the band's admirers, Cave's words were tablets of stone. To their detractors – well, it was certainly no sin for rock to strive to be meaningful. But did it always have to try quite so hard?

The Bauhaus tour was the Birthday Party's first significant voyage out of the capital and, quickly, the group learned that the audience extremes they had grown accustomed to in London, half the crowd adoring them while the rest hurled insults into the onstage melee, were by no means common currency out in the provinces.

Kicking off on 17th June 1981 in Newcastle, then moving on to Liverpool, Nottingham, Aylesbury, Brighton, Leeds, Reading, Cambridge the tour played to Bauhaus' crowd through and through, with the support bands – Birthday Party were joined on the bill by lounge punks Subway Sect – at best a curiosity they'd read about in the inkies, at worst an unconscionable delay to be dispensed with as fast as possible. Surly onlookers glared from all corners, daring the Birthday Party to impress them, but refusing to allow them to do so. For every convert convinced that he'd seen the second coming, there were three more who watched for a while then returned to the bar, smugly convinced that the band's supporters in the London media simply didn't know what they were talking about. As usual.

The Birthday Party's task, of course, was made even more difficult by the peculiar lighting arrangements that marked out the tour. As headliners, Bauhaus brought their own light show with them; unusually, it was one that neither support band would be able to employ – or would even, particularly, have wanted to. To heighten the shadows, the Bauhaus rig comprised just five bright spotlights, two for Murphy, one each for his bandmates. Their hapless support acts had no alternative but to leave the house lights on as they played, the harsh illumination killing any last chance the Birthday Party may have had of conjuring a smidgeon of atmosphere from their performance.

In Cambridge on 27th June 1981, it was even worse – it was still daylight outside when the Birthday Party took the stage and the Corn Exchange's windows were tall and wide. It was like watching madmen rehearse in the school gymnasium.

But it was a memorable show regardless, the final night of the tour (London fell two evenings previous) and a trigger for some wild celebrations, first as the Birthday Party raced onstage towards the end of Bauhaus' set to pin Murphy down and draw a giant penis on his chest; then as both bands combined to mutilate an unrehearsed encore of the old Peggy Lee standard, 'Fever'. With Murphy and Cave trading off vocals while the musicians duelled with untrammelled ferocity, only one question remains: Did *no-one* attending the show that night have the foresight to smuggle in a tape recorder?

Where were Siouxsie and the Banshees through all this? Watching, ruminating and waiting for the optimum moment to strike, of course. Recruiting guitarist John McGeoch from Magazine, to replace Robert Smith at the end of the *Join Hands* tour, the group headed immediately into *Kaleidoscope*, their third album and, after the stark terrors of its predecessors, their most open yet. But, when asked to take responsibility for all that had been wrought in their wake, Steve Severin has consistently proven good-naturedly unco-operative.

'I never really spot [our sound] in anything, I'm always surprised when people compare other people to us, I never really think of it. Unless it's a carbon-copy, it's really hard to pull elements of what we do into other things.

'For our own part, we only became aware of it when Joy Division came out. Then Echo and the Bunnymen were very quick after that, and you felt that something was going on there.'

And Bauhaus?

'One would assume so, although it was more Bowie and Lindsay Kemp.'

History justifies his stance. The personnel changes ensured that *Kaleidoscope* emerged the Banshees' own most disparate record yet, the singles 'Happy House' and (to a lesser extent) 'Christine' the last solid reminders of their earlier sound. Gone, as Ray Stevenson's 1986 *Siouxsie & The Banshees Photo Book* pointed out, were 'the thick slabs of guitar, and Morris's heavy-handed thuds were replaced by Budgie's intricate and ingenious percussion. The lyrical content hadn't brightened up [but] the Banshees were using melodies to carry the album and enliven the songs.'

Severin himself agreed. 'With *Kaleidoscope*, we were trying to psychedelic things, in an early Pink Floyd way. We got into those kind of sounds.' But, as 1981 oozed through the hourglass, the Banshees realised that they weren't quite prepared to give up their original mantel of ice and evil just yet.

Part of it was the sudden preponderance of little Siouxsies on the streets of Britain. The shock of black hair, the belligerent panda eye make-up, a regiment of Sues adding 'Zee's to their name, everywhere you turned they were peeping out at you. 'It's only one look out of many that she's had,' Severin mused. 'But it stuck in everyone's head as the definitive one.' Faced, in 1981, with the first wave of all these fossilised hers running around (she waxes and wanes between it being flattering and disgusting), the original decided it was time to remind people where it all started.

Siouxsie and the Banshees previewed their forthcoming fourth album, the monumental *JuJu*, on a John Peel session in February 1981, serving up four songs ('Halloween', 'Voodoo Dolly', 'Into The Light' and 'But Not Them') amid a density that utterly reaffirmed the group's grasp on what Severin jokingly refers to as 'spooky imagery.' It remained tongue-in-cheek, he swore, but there was an underlying conviction to it as well, a sense that, no matter where their musical travels might take them, the soul of the Banshees remained entwined with the tomb.

Severin: 'Every so often, there was a conscious attempt to get away from it. We'd try to think up different labels for ourselves each month, like Glamabilly. All along, throughout our career, whenever anyone tried to categorise us too much, we deliberately moved away from it, to twist people's preconceptions a bit, because it all seemed a bit ludicrous really.

'But I was always really upset that the Gothic name got perverted the way it did because, certainly going as far back as 1979, on our second album, we were talking about Edgar Allen Poe and talking about Gothic things, even though what became a trademark Goth look wasn't even around at the time.' *Juju*, then, was the group's attempt to restate the purity that had once surrounded the Gothic tag, before it became too late, and 'Monitor', closing side one, sums up precisely what the Banshees were thinking – 'sit back and enjoy the Real McCoy.'

Of course Siouxsie and the Banshees would never return to such overt pastures again. Rather, the decade-and-a-half that would elapse between *Juju* and the band's 1995 break-up, would see them swerve as vigorously as their imaginations would allow.

From the revisionist artistry of the *Through The Looking Glass* covers album to the camp post-cabaret of *Peek-A-Boo* (a nadir that came close to blowing their credibility altogether), from the isolationist heartlessness of *Superstition* to the glorious resurrection of the valedictory *The Rapture*, the Banshees not only refused to play to their reputation, they refused to acknowledge that the reputation even existed, with Siouxsie herself undergoing more stylistic reinventions than Margaret Hamilton – the wicked witch in *The Wizard Of Oz*, but an established Hollywood star for many more movies than that. No, the Banshees never went Gothic again. But, like the Damned and their *Black Album*, they never needed to. *Juju* remains an unimpeachable archetype regardless.

Severin's dismissal of all that developing around the Banshees' self-proclaimed miserable sentinels finds ready allies among all of his period peers – Robert Smith and Nick Cave have both echoed Severin's condemnation of the looming shift. Peter Murphy puts it most succinctly: 'There were bands that were identified later with a movement called Gothic Rock. But, at the time, we were simply people who were led into it, who were making a really wonderful noise and enjoying it, and living out our fantasies of – whatever.'

Severin continued, 'I think the thing that really surprises me about the Gothic thing is that a lot of people tend to get so po-faced about it. They're just completely humourless, and that's why I can't feel associated with it at all. It's got nothing to do with the Banshees.'

The Banshees, however, had everything to do with *it* and Severin was not necessarily being condemnatory when he concluded, 'We weren't going to play ball and the fans realised that. So they started doing it themselves. And, when the Sisters of Mercy came along, suddenly the audience was onstage itself.'

The emergence of the Sisters Of Mercy, in late 1980, remains one of those pivotal events that is surrounded in mystery – and deliberately so. The spawn of an erstwhile Andrew Taylor, an Oxford-educated air force brat who renamed himself 'Eldritch' in calculated obeisance to its weird and spooky definitions, the band's roots lay in Leeds, where Eldritch had relocated when he discovered that, having already majored in French and German, his next choice of language was not offered at Oxford.

Only Leeds University catered for students of Mandarin Chinese, and he joined the course with wild enthusiasm. His interest faded, however, once he discovered that he'd have to spend a year in Beijing in order to complete his studies. According to the Sisters' legend, which may or may not be true, he simply wanted to learn Chinese, not live with them. So, he dropped out of school at the end of his junior year, and turned his intention instead towards the city nightlife.

The turbulence that had swirled through the streets for the past two years showed no sign of abating. Musical forces that, in the eyes of the London press, were little more than passing cults had themselves divided into sub-cults in Leeds – when the Damned played Leeds in 1980, there were more vampires in the audience than even Dave Vanian could have dreamed of, and more breeds thereof than that.

From the elite heights of the Warehouse to the down-to-earth grounding of the Faversham Arms, then scratching even lower than that, to the cluster of pubs around Headingley where any band could get up and play, so long as they looked like a band when they got there, Leeds itched with a self-contained musicality that permeated every facet of local youth culture. And youth consciousness.

The idea that Andrew Eldritch would contribute anything more than bodyweight to this ferment was, initially, one that even he never contemplated. 'I was banned from music classes,' he reflected years later, 'and told I would never, ever be able to understand anything. And I was quite prepared to accept that. I couldn't even play the recorder!'

But, when a friend stored his drum kit in Eldritch's basement, he could not resist having a crash around on it, eventually teaching himself sufficient rudiments that he was soon graduating through a series of local pub bands. He quickly discovered, too, that he had one attribute that no other drummer in town seemed to share. 'I was the only person who could play the drums in the whole of Leeds that could be relied upon never to hit the cymbals or do tom-tom rolls... mostly because I was completely incapable of it.' When one of his friends, guitarist Gary Marx, began scheming a band whose sound relied upon precisely that deficiency, Eldritch was the first person he contacted.

This unlikely duo did little more than tinker around for much of the year – according to an interview in the fanzine *Propaganda*, it was six months before they even realized they needed a singer. 'And, purely by default,' Eldritch related, 'it turned out to be me. Because I can't drum and sing at the same time, we bought a machine. Had we been able to buy a machine to do the singing, it might have turned out different.'

Christened Doktor Avalanche, the drum machine became the third and, for the time being, final member of the group – dubbed the Sisters Of Mercy out of allegiance to a favourite song on the first Leonard Cohen album. Scant weeks later, in November 1980, the group released their first single, a 1,000 strong pressing of 'Damage Done', on their own Merciful Release label. (The distinctive logo, designed by Eldritch, was adapted from a medical textbook, helpfully illustrating the autopsy cut-lines on a human head.)

High on ambition, low on virtually everything else, but certainly influenced by the Gang of Four's brand of mutant Punk-funk, 'Damage Done' was sufficiently intriguing to earn notice from the national press, but off-kilter enough to then be greeted with utmost caution. *Sounds'* Robbi Millar best caught the prevailing mood with the rumination, 'Sometimes I wonder what Ian Curtis was letting the world in for when he died... Certainly the Joy Division circus hasn't left us yet, and its impressions grow increasingly gloomy by the day.'

Eldritch himself would swiftly grow hostile to the record – a year later, with the Sisters of Mercy now joined by bassist Craig Adams, he mused, 'to all intents and purposes it was a different band, and is best forgotten.'

By the Sisters' still formative standards, Adams' recruitment was a major coup. In 1979, after all, he had stood on the stage of the Queen's Hall, regaling the first Futurama crowd as keyboard player with the Expelaires, a band whose renown had already stretched to a couple of singles on Liverpool's Zoo label and a John Peel session in June 1979. He quit, however, when the major labels came sniffing around and he discovered he was the only member of the band actually to welcome the attention.

He moved onto the synthi-duo, the Exchange, recording a demo with Jon Langford of the Mekons (whom the Expelaires had often supported), but that adventure was already paling when he met Eldritch at the F Club one night, falling into a conversation that apparently gelled around a shared appreciation of a distorted bass sound – ideal for Adams who, though he so hankered to play the instrument, had yet to master a single note.

With Adams and a passing Langford on board, the Sisters played their first ever live gig on 16th February 1981, opening for the then-formidable Thompson Twins at the University of York's Alcuin College. It was a rough and ready performance, of course, but sufficiently well-received to prompt the Sisters into playing a handful more shows around Leeds.

Few seem to have been at all memorable, not even the one at the F Club on 2nd July 1981 which drew Iggy Pop fleetingly into the Sisters' orbit. Earlier in the evening, Iggy headlined the somewhat roomier University, then headed down to the club to unwind. Sadly, nobody thought to record his reaction to the Sisters' increasingly stylised cover of his own '1969' – placed alongside Cohen's 'Teachers' and the Velvet Underground's 'Sister Ray' in a set that still screamed its influences out loud.

Yet the Sisters' reputation was growing. A definite audience had attached itself to them, a partisan bunch whose prodigious intake of amphetamines seemed peculiarly at odds with the often funereal beats that the band pumped out. As that crowd swelled, so did the number of promoters willing to book the band. And, in September, the most significant indication yet of the Sisters' progress was registered when they were added to the bill of Futurama 3, over the weekend of 5th/6th September 1981.

There they were joined by a band whose own emergence had paced the Sisters almost day-for-day, but whose renown had taken off from the moment the blue touchpaper was lit. Theatre Of Hate was the brainchild of vocalist/guitarist Kirk Brandon, whose last band, the Pack, released a brace of well-received singles and an EP during 1979-80. They earned a modicum of grassroots acclaim, but the Pack went nowhere and disbanded when Brandon quit to form a new group with former Strapps bassist Stan Stammers.

Drummer Luke Rendle and a classically trained saxophonist, Canadian squash champion John Lennard, followed and, in late 1980, Theatre Of Hate took their first tentative steps onto the London club circuit.

The noise the group made was swiftly matched by the noise made by its audience. Theatre Of Hate's strident manifesto of human politics, coupled with a roar that was two parts dying Punk, two parts embryonic Goth, and one part volcanic tribalism, was an instant magnet for madness – cast in a similar mould to UK Decay and Killing Joke for sure, but elevated immensely higher by the sheer dynamism of the Brandon persona.

Unfortunately, the group's two-year lifespan was to be severely troubled. The vaguely Communist overtones of the group's chosen logo, and song titles such as 'The Klan', 'Judgement Hymn', 'The Wake' and 'Freaks' marked Theatre Of Hate out as a band who danced on the thin edge of the revolutionary blade.

Their shows were chaotic, scarred by their fans' apparent and absolute inability to distinguish militancy from moronity. Nightly, it seemed, the group's audience was swollen by what we might euphemistically describe as 'troublemakers' – Rent-a-Fascist skinheads, Thugs 'R' Us bullies and disenchanted soccer hooligans, an alarmingly combustible mixture which was the utter opposite to the band's own creed of tolerance.

But there were happier times ahead as well, beginning in November 1980 when Theatre Of Hate released their first single, the soul-shaking 'Original Sin', and daubed Hatton Cross underground station with the memorably graffiti'd glower, 'Theatre Of Hate live on in your dreams and they will kill you.'

A tumultuous new single, 'Rebel Without A Brain', followed, alongside Theatre Of Hate's first album, *He Who Dares Wins – Live At The Warehouse*, recorded live in the band stronghold of Leeds. Bootleg tapes of Theatre Of Hate shows were already circulating widely and, over the years, a slew of similar "official bootlegs" would be released to try and calm what remained a very active underground market – with the sounds of an equally lively audience.

The group's third single 'Nero', was released in July 1981. Like its predecessors, it sold respectably and, as the band's live profile soared ever higher, Theatre Of Hate attracted the attention of Clash guitarist Mick Jones. The Clash were on hiatus for much of 1981, leaving Jonesy plenty of time to join Theatre Of Hate to record what would become one of the undisputable classic singles of the year, 'Do You Believe In The West World?'

A thunderous war-cry fed through a demented Burundi thunder that left Adam fans quaking in their anthills, 'West World' broke into the British Top 40 and, suddenly Theatre Of Hate were everywhere. Futurama was simply the next rung of the ladder.

Shifting from its Leeds home base, Futurama 3 took place in Stafford, with a magnificent – if somewhat splintered, in conceptual terms – line-up: Gang of Four, Bauhaus, the PiL spin-off Human Condition, Cure labelmates The Passions, Theatre Of Hate, OK Jive, Adrian Borland's The Sound, the Lines, Felt, Simple

Minds, Bow Wow Wow, Doll By Doll, the Virgin Prunes, Eyeless In Gaza, UK Decay, the emergent solo Richard Strange, A Flock Of Seagulls…

40 acts in two days illustrated the gulfs that were now yawning open within a scene that itself had been forged by a widening void. It was no shock at all, as the weekend progressed, to watch the audience literally revolving between auditorium and bar, depending on which band (or which style of band) was then on stage. Either you were a Happy Sod or you were a Gloomy Bastard. The latter, of course, worshipped the Sisters.

The same divide was visible just three weeks later when a similar circus returned to Leeds, in the guise of Daze Of Future Past. A handful of the same bands were on the billing: Gang of Four, Theatre Of Hate, B-Movie and Bauhaus all made an appearance, with the Cure, the Bunnymen and a pair of visiting Americans, the Cramps and Wall Of Voodoo, filling in some of the more notable gaps.

Again, however, it was the audience that most caught the attention, at least for Bauhaus – an audience that was suddenly, and very noticeably, coalescing into a solidly recognisable tribe.

Of course it had been gathering for a while – Bauhaus' earliest press had commented upon the near-uniform of fishnet, lace, frilly shirts and pointy shoes that patrolled the corridors of the crowd. More recent observers had professed amazement at the sheer dedication of its denizens. But Peter Murphy recalled, 'It took about a year for us to realize that we were actually drawing quite a large audience, post-Punks who were gelling into something which we called Wildebeests. We played [that] festival, and we toddled onstage to do our little bit… make way for the headliners… and suddenly there was this noise like a distant stampede coming towards us, and there they all were, flooding in. And we just thought, "My God! What have we done?"'

What they had done – they, and that clutch of other bands whose flirtations with aesthetics, theatre and darkness had suddenly and inextricably solidified into a definable stance – was give flesh to a term that had been kicking around the rock critic's thesaurus for a number of years, one that was simultaneously irresistibly implicit but frustratingly vague, as atmospheric as it was airless, as vivacious as it was vacuous. An adjective became a noun. Gothic became Goth. And, for the bands that had already been sucked into its maw, nothing would ever be the same again.

Part Two

Release

The Bats?

1982-1984

Pete Murphy, performing "Ziggy Stardust"

Chapter Seven
Releasing The Bats

In which we pause to take stock of what's gone before,
and how it will shape all that will emerge in the future.
Introduces a Cult rising in Bradford and two brothers
emerging from Wales. Bauhaus score a hit single, and
the Cure redefine pornography.

'I had nothing in common with the other white kids at my
school. I couldn't talk about soccer or music, they didn't know
who Bowie was, or Slade or T Rex, so there was nothing there.
But I had a lot in common with the [Native American] Indians
– there was more of a rapport with their beliefs, there were
more answers in the native stuff I was reading than in the stuff
I was reading at school and, as I grew older it became more
specific.' Ian Astbury

The word 'Gothic' crops up again and again in Joy Division's early reportage, both in the media and within the band's own circle. When Tony Wilson, head of the Factory label, joined Joy Division on BBC2's *Something Else* in September 1979, he described them as 'Gothic' in comparison with the rest of the pop mainstream. The following month, *Sounds*' Penny Kiley was complaining, '"Gothic" has become a somewhat overworked definition of the genre, but the effect of Joy Division is the same as... that of the Banshees.'

The band's supporters were undeterred. In an oft-excerpted interview with journalist Mary Hannon, conducted shortly after the release of *Unknown Pleasures*, producer Martin Hannett summed the band up as 'dancing music, with Gothic overtones.' In that same piece, Bernard Sumner added further fuel to the conceptual fire with his admission that his favourite film was *Nosferatu*, while Hannon herself insisted that the group were '20th Century Gothic.'

A year later, the term was still swirling around the rock lexicon. In November 1980, reviewing Bauhaus' *In The Flat Field*, the *New Musical Express* headlined with the delicious pun, 'Gothick as a brick' – with Bauhaus defined, as the review wandered along, as the latest product of 'a hard Punk/moderne monochrome crossover... on the verge of tapping a potentially massive market opened up by the earlier efforts of such as Siouxsie and the Banshees... [and] Joy Division.'

But it would be another twelve months after that before UK Decay's Abbo gave the interview with a European magazine that, as he recalled in conversation with *Sounds*' Steve Keaton in early 1982, confirmed him as the first musician to actually refer to a musical style called Gothic Rock.

UK Decay had just released their debut album, October 1981's *For Madmen Only* and Abbo was wrestling to explain how he would describe the band's music, having already acknowledged that it was neither Dance nor Alternative, New Pop nor Mod, but agreeing that 'suddenly there seemed a pool of bands – us, Killing Joke, Bauhaus – and that was when people started talking about a movement.' He told Keaton, 'I remember saying, "We're into the whole Gothic thing..." and we sat there laughing about how we should have gargoyle-shaped records and only play churches. Of course... it all [went] into the interview. For six months, everything went quiet, then... everyone was asking, "what's this Gothic thing you're into?" And it's a total joke!'

It just wasn't an especially funny one. Biographing Nico, the Velvet Underground chanteuse from beneath whose skirts the incipient movement drew so much of its iconography – but whose name could here be substituted for any of the so-called Gothic Rock acts – author Richard Witts quoted a promoter who booked some shows for her during the late 1970s.

'She was an icon to a whole generation of raincoated zombies. You felt you should have booked her into cemeteries rather than clubs. Her tours should have been sponsored by the Co-op Funeral Service. I used to tell promoters to stick a poster outside, "Free razorblade with the first 100 tickets." Do you know how miserable she was? She was more miserable than Joy Division and their singer hung himself. I used to have a hearse standing by at her gigs, just in case.'

'Ho ho ho,' responds Witts, but if you glance at any musical movement from a position of apathetic scorn, similar 'humour' is always close at hand – the safety-pinned scarecrows of Punk, the unnatural perversions of Glam, the unwashed acid-heads of the late 1960s. Even the Beatles were once longhaired layabouts who needed nothing so much as a few years in the army to straighten them out. 'That'll be "Yeah Yeah Yeah SIR," you miserable little specimen.'

The awkward thing about stereotypes is, there is generally some truth in them. A lot of hippies did forego bathing, a lot of Punks were a little less than kempt and, it is true, there are not that many shafts of light shining through the windows of Castle Goth. There are not that many windows, either – they were all bricked up years ago, around the time the master's first wife went mad.

Besides, even in the damaged middle age in which most of her acolytes finally saw her perform, Nico remains the most perfect vision of Gothic made flesh. And those artists whose own claims to laying Gothic Rock's foundation stones might be considered unimpeachable will always defer to the former Christa Päffgen when it comes to actually mapping out the site.

'Nico recorded the first truly Gothic album, *Marble Index* or *The End*,' confirms Peter Murphy. 'Nico was Gothic, but she was Mary Shelley to everyone else's Hammer Horror. They both did *Frankenstein*, but Nico's was real.'

'Nico was in there,' the Cult's Ian Astbury agrees. 'There's a direct lineage between the Velvets and Punk' – and an equally straightforward line from Punk to Gothic Rock. Nico, although her own career mapped out a considerably more convoluted path than such historical truths could ever encompass, nevertheless made the journey with unerring timeliness.

A former model and Fellini starlet, the oldest of the so-called classic Velvet Underground line-up, Cologne-born Nico was 28 when she was drafted into the group at co-manager Paul Morrissey's suggestion, to detract from the visually dour spectacle of Lou Reed monotoning the band's entire repertoire.

Both within the Velvets and without, tracing the solo career she first toyed with in London in 1965 under the aegis of Rolling Stone Brian Jones and his manager, Andrew Loog Oldham, Nico initially promised little of true musical note. A pleasant singer with an eye for sadder songs, only her statuesque beauty and Teutonic intonations separated her from any number of folkie singer-sometime songwriters plying the New York club circuit at that time.

Though they have since ascended to musical Valhalla, three Nico vocal performances on the first Velvet Underground album passed unnoticed by the world at large; it was her starring role in Andy Warhol's *Chelsea Girls* that prompted the Velvets' label, MGM, to give her a solo contract. But a 1968 album titled for the film was little more than a holding operation, a sideshow for the Velvet devotee, an opening line on Jackson Browne's resume.

It would be another year before Nico stepped out from that shadow, with the release of *The Marble Index*. Unheard and unsaleable at the time of release, the album's reputation now precedes it in every quarter.

Matt Johnson, future founder of The The, was so impressed that he named his first band for the album; *Rolling Stone* was so confused that it paired *The Marble*

Index with the latest waxing by Melanie, *Born To Be*; and the *New Musical Express* simply sighed, 'I can't make out a single real word.'

It is only with hindsight that we now comprehend. Ageless, sexless, hopeless, *The Marble Index*, as the opening stage in a triptych that would take five more years to complete, first ushered in, then set in stone, the Nico that the world now deifies, the Valkyrie ice maiden who pedalled her haunted harmonium and intoned medieval mysteries that still appear largely unfathomable.

Its highlights are as manifold as its prophecies: 'Frozen Warnings,' aptly emerging one of her iciest performances, is laden down with the imagery of the outsider that permeates the best of Nico's writing – and, of course, became something of a Gothic staple a decade later. The recurrent vision of the 'frozen borderline' is genuinely haunting, hoving into view in the *a cappella* opening verses, then growing closer as the instrumentation slides in, dense icicles (densicles?) of sound draping cathedral harmonium and sepulchral viola behind her stentorian Greta Gargoyle croon.

Desert Shore followed in 1971, delivering Nico's most perfect album and her most poignant song, the closing 'All That Is My Own.' Producer (and fellow ex-Velvet) John Cale's instrumentation is awe-inspiring, as a military fanfare propels the song with crashing percussion and skirling rhythms. But still Nico prevails, alternating her vocal between a harshly yearning melody, and childlike spoken passages, two songs in one which hinge around the plaintive request, 'meet me on the desert shore….' The effect is chilling, intense romance sandblasted by palpable loneliness.

Nico herself later described the song as a depiction of her own state of mind at this time. Living in self-imposed exile, apparently being hunted by the Black Panthers, certainly losing herself in a damaging heroin habit, she was about to embark upon a recorded silence that stretched for three years. 'All That Is My Own,' then, stands as a requiem of sorts, with that meeting on the desert shore her only hope of redemption. It would never happen.

A brief comeback in 1974 with *The End* was overwhelmed first by the howls of derision that greeted her twisted reinvention of the Doors' title track; then by the cries of outrage provoked by her (actually, rather lovely) rendering of her native country's wartime national anthem, 'Das Lied Der Deutschland' – better known, of course, as 'Deutschland Uber Alles.' When she followed that with a possibly misguided, and certainly misinterpreted remark about Jamaicans and cannibals, her fate was sealed. Her label, Island, dropped her; her audience, such as it was, abandoned her. Nico drifted into legend. But she would return.

All through Siouxsie and the Banshees' rise, Siouxsie herself cited Nico as an influence, one of the few that her own vocal style and lyrical predilections either admitted to or could be accused of having. 'Nico had an other-worldly character, which was enhanced by the choral quality of the organ she used,' Siouxsie reflected. "I was struck by the pictures on the records, how beautiful she was. It was the first time I'd heard such a deep voice and that made an impression on me. She was like a mature dark angel.'

Nico returned to the stage in 1978, performing a well-received show in Paris. Weeks later, she returned to the UK.

It should have been a triumph. Within the litanies of Punk, the Velvet

Underground were universally regarded amongst the most influential bands of all time, and both Lou Reed and John Cale had recently toured to unfettered adulation. But Nico's bookers, the Rough Trade agency, severely under-estimated the effect that the reality of the Nico experience would have on their earnest young acolytes.

At her first show, opening for Siouxsie and the Banshees at the London Music Machine on 19th April 1978, and again, ten days later, sandwiched between the Adverts and the Killjoys, alone on stage with her harmonium and voice, the original Femme Fatale was forced to beat an undignified retreat as her performance was punctured by flying cans and glasses.

Worse was to come. In September, the Banshees invited Nico to open on their next UK tour, their first since 'Hong Kong Garden' had catapulted them out of their earlier cult confines and into the provincial Punk mainstream. There, as Steve Severin put it, the headliners were faced with an audience 'who had never been to a Punk concert before. Nico was the last thing they expected to hear.'

Again barraged with abuse and bottles, Nico left the tour after just a handful of shows. At her final show, in Cardiff, however, she gave as good as she got. Staring down the baying audience as she prepared to walk off the stage, she drew herself up to her full height and swore, 'If I had a machine gun, I would shoot you all.' 'John Cale was born just up the road,' she mused a few years later. 'I expected more from those people.'

It was her meeting with a young Corsican reggae musician, Philippe Quilichini, which changed Nico's fortunes. She moved in to a London apartment with Quilichini, his girlfriend Nadett Duget, and a photographer friend, Antoine Giacomoni and, over the next couple of years, they began scheming her fifth LP. It would be titled, with determined irony, *Drama Of Exile*. And flavoured, with deliberate iconoclasm, by rock'n'roll.

'It was really boring, all that quiet stuff', Nico said of her past albums. 'And having been a member of the Velvet Underground, rock'n'roll is something I had to do at some point, even if only for one album'. Recorded at Gooseberry Studios in Tulse Hill, London, with a band comprising Quilichini, guitarist Mahammad Hadi, drummer Steve Cordona, Ian Dury's sax player Davey Payne and Andy Clarke, the keyboard player who so sparkled on David Bowie's *Scary Monsters* album, the first fruits of Nico's rebirth emerged on a single in early 1981, 'Saeta'.

The album followed weeks later, earning Nico some of the most favourable reviews of her entire career. This time, it seemed, the world was ready for her – and, more importantly, Nico was ready for the world.

Relocating to Manchester, where her impact on a scene that made no bones about its allegiance to the Velvets was akin to Jesus moving into the American Bible Belt, Nico began gigging anywhere and everywhere. Over the next nine years, until her death in 1988, it is estimated that Nico played well over 1,200 concerts, as far afield as New York and Berlin but, for the most part, on the same circuit of clubs and small theatres as the bands that had hitherto adored her from afar. On 28th October 1981, at Manchester's Fagins, she even got up onstage with Bauhaus to perform a ragged version of 'Waiting For The Man', the Velvet Underground staple that she herself had rerecorded for *Drama Of Exile*.

Not everybody was impressed, of course. Ian Astbury, present at the show, remembers 'Pete Murphy had to hold her up, she was so smacked out!' But he rated another Nico concert, at Dingwalls in January 1985, among the best live shows he ever witnessed and, in 2000, composed a song for her titled simply 'Nico', for the Cult's *Beyond Good And Evil* album.

For most observers, of course, the mere proximity of the legend was worth the price of admission and, besides, she gave a hell of a lot more good shows than bad, reaching as far back as the first Velvets album for material but unafraid, too, to try out new songs. No less than nine authorised live albums document these last years, while at least two readily available video recordings capture her in full, gloriously atmospheric flight.

Nico, then, epitomised the musical and iconographical bearing that Goth would wear – if not like sackcloth, at least an all-encompassing mantel. Marry that to any of the bands that was now perceived to be shifting into similar territory, be it Joy Division or Siouxsie and the Banshees, Bauhaus or even the nascent Sisters of Mercy and, inevitably, their offspring would have a heavy load to bear. Opening and closing the last two weeks of December 1981, the first of this unlikely union's children came scampering into view.

On 30th December 1981 at the ICA, Gene Loves Jezebel made their capital debut and were greeted with wild enthusiasm by *Melody Maker*'s Steve Sutherland. Sixteen days earlier, Southern Death Cult played their first ever London show, opening for Chelsea at the Marquee and prompting *Sounds*' Steve Keaton to compensate for misnaming them *Sudden* Death Cult by crowning them, too, among the most remarkable new bands of the entire year.

Although the intentions of the two groups could not have been further removed from one another, in imagery or sonic assemblage, it was an age when costume, not content, could brand a band for life. You could smell the sizzling flesh for miles around.

Steve Keaton's enthusiasm was certainly boundless. 'The singer is weird, really weird,' he wrote of his first sighting of Southern Death Cult. 'Eyeballs dilate and lug'oles dribble. His face (I presume he has a face) is hidden beneath an avalanche of red and black hair and rabbit skin pom-poms, and he wanders around the stage in authentic B-Movie western style. Dense, rhythmic and vaguely primitive... the music reflects the heavy Indian motifs. I later learn that [the singer] is named Ian.'

Indeed he was, but his stylistic credentials went somewhat deeper than a few afternoons spent watching reruns of old John Wayne films. Ian Astbury was born in the Merseyside town of Heswall, Cheshire, but spent most of his teenaged years in Canada, a land that made an immediate impression on him.

'It's been really well documented that I'm very influenced by North American Indian culture and religion. That came from Canada. I was exposed to native lifestyles, religious beliefs and ways.' Aged 12, he paid his first visit to an Indian reservation but, sensitive to the ways of journalism, he immediately added, 'I wasn't in a car that drove past a load of dying Indians when I was 6 and one of them jumped into my soul – there are a lot of parallels which are really a pain in the arse! But I went to the Mohawk reservation and what I saw really made an impression.

'At that time, the kids were all long haired, on horseback, I remember sitting next to this old guy, wearing a very typical big hat, eagle feather, smoking a pipe, and I was just blown away by how peaceful he was, and at one with everything around him. The kids were going wild, playing lacrosse, running round with their dogs, with no shoes on.

'We were there with this school trip and this really uptight teacher going on about how, "in 1763 the chief of the Mohawks made a compact with the British blah blah blah," but I was in this longhouse and it was just beautiful. I'd never seen an indigenous people in their native environment before, and it was quite overwhelming. The biggest experience in Britain is, you drive out into the country and you get to see a cow.

'So this extremely exotic, profound culture really had an effect on me because I had nothing in common with the other white kids at my school. I couldn't talk about soccer or music, they didn't know who Bowie was, or Slade or T Rex, so there was nothing there. But I had a lot in common with the Indians – there was more of a rapport with their beliefs, there were more answers in the native stuff I was reading than in the stuff I was reading at school and, as I grew older it became more specific. I was reading more. So this is something that's been omnipresent in my life from about the age of 12.'

Astbury left school, aged 16, in 1978 and enlisted in the Canadian army, lured by the glamour of the recruitment commercials ('girls, guns, travel'). He quit after 28 days. 'I had a lot of turmoil when I was growing up. I was forced to pretty much take over my father's role in the home because my mother was dying of cancer (she passed away on Astbury's 17th birthday), and my father was always away working. So, I had to look after my brother and sister. We were constantly moving. I went to twelve different schools. There was a lot going on, a thousand and one things, dysfunctional, horrible, get out your little violin sob stories.'

Finally, Astbury made his way back to Britain. 'I saw the Sex Pistols on Canadian television. This was after they'd broken up mind you, or around the same time, but the Punk thing looked so exciting, I wanted to see what it was all about for myself.'

Renaming himself Ian Lindsay (his mother's maiden name, an alias he would maintain until the pivotal month of January 1984), Astbury drifted first through his mother's hometown, Glasgow, before winding up in Liverpool, where he was involved in several bands, none of which ever got off the ground. Send No Flowers is the only band name he recalls.

Astbury's next move was to Belfast, Northern Ireland, where he fronted the similarly unknown Children of Lust but, by late 1981, he was back in England, sharing a house with some likeminded Punks in Bradford and attending every gig he could get to. Particularly the ones he could get into for free.

'One day, I went down to Sheffield to see Generation X at the Limit Club,' he remembers. 'I had my sleeping bag, I camped outside the club over night, and I was there the next afternoon when the band arrived.'

It was the last days of Generation X, the final three week tour that accompanied the *Kiss Me Deadly* album (still an Astbury favourite), and vocalist Billy Idol was already looking towards the stardom he was certain awaited him on the other side of the Atlantic. But he stopped and talked to the kid waiting outside and, when Astbury asked if he could get him into the show for nothing, Idol said yes, he could. Just so long as Astbury didn't mind working as guitarist James Stevenson's roadie for the evening. Astbury agreed.

Back in Bradford, Astbury continued his own dreams of musical success and, slowly, out of what he remembers as a chaotic aggregation of personalities and musical preferences, Southern Death Cult began to take shape around Astbury, drummer Haq 'Aky' Qureshi, guitarist David 'Buzz' Burrows and bassist Barry Jetson.

Adopting the American Indian imagery that was so precious to Astbury, but running it first through the wringer of English Punk, Southern Death Cult sprang out of Bradford in December 1981, the hottest young band of the age. Astbury still looks back on the period with absolute amazement.

'Things did happen very quickly, especially initially. The first concert I ever did was filmed by Yorkshire Television, for a show called *What Is Life*, a documentary about youth culture and life on the dole, and that was a really bizarre thing because the first time I ever walked on a stage, it was filmed. I don't know if they ever showed it, but they followed us around for three days, and filmed us and our lifestyle, the places we hung out, what we did, and we only had three songs! We'd been together about three weeks.'

Emboldened, Astbury began making regular trips to London to try and stir up more interest in the group. 'There was a lot of that, hitch-hiking down or getting on a bus with our ham-and-tomato sandwiches and a cup of tea with powdered milk in, and the bus driver singing away down the front. It was horrible!

'The first time, we went down there with a little demo tape we made at the local arts centre, a little four track cassette which cost us about eight quid to make. It was awful, atrocious, but it had the three songs on it that we had, and some photos we'd had taken by an art student. And naively, we had a bagful of about three copies of the demo tape and four photographs.

'I remember sitting outside RCA, CBS, EMI… we hit all the major labels, sitting in the lobby, waiting for hours. I remember sitting in the RCA lobby waiting for an A&R person. We thought the receptionist at the front desk was very important, and she made us wait there for three fucking hours. She was going to give us a call "when he was available," so we just sat there.

'Then, at CBS, Claire Grogan of Altered Images came down stairs, and we were going "wow! Claire Grogan of Altered Images!" So we ran over and asked her to give our demo tape to somebody, she said "sure," took our tape, ran upstairs and immediately came back down again and said there's nobody around – fucking Claire.

'Finally, we went to Cherry Red. We walked in the door and the guy was going "oh fucking hell, it's 5 o'clock, I've got to go," but he took the tape, played it right there in front of us and said, "Oh, it's not that bad – give us your phone number and, if we're interested, we'll give you a call. Give us the tape." And we're going, "We can't, we've only got one left!" But a little later, we got a phone call from him, arranging to meet us in a pub near Kings Cross train station.'

By that time, however, things had moved on a little, as Southern Death Cult finally made that crucial London debut, at the Marquee on 14th December 1981.

It was the band's fifth show ever, 'we'd been together four months, and we had six songs.' The gig was arranged by drummer Qureshi's brother, a promoter in Bradford. 'We'd get 30 quid for doing the gig, but we really earned it. We got stuck in Bradford in a snowstorm and we only just made it down to London. We got there, and Gene October was going crazy. The place was a complete shambles, there were about 30 people there, and it was the most exciting thing in my life. No, it wasn't – the most exciting thing was going to see Chelsea play in Leeds the week before, and hearing Gene announce onstage that we'd be supporting them at the London Marquee. We just looked at each other: "Wow, we've made it!"'

From the band's point of view, the show itself was a disaster. 'A friend of ours jumped onstage and pulled all the guitar plugs out. There were 30 people watching, and we had only six songs but we were supposed to play ten, so we played some twice. We were pretty raw, pretty poor, pretty amateurish.' Yet, the following week, the show was reviewed in *Sounds*, 'and it was brilliant. It said we were the Second Coming, sensational etc, and mass hysteria followed.'

Cherry Red's offer was simple. 'They said, "We'll offer you 500 pounds for your publishing," and we went, "Oh wow, each?" "No, for the whole group." It was a lot of money, but we wanted to think about it. Our drummer was very sharp, and he said 500 for the four of us was bullshit. We could get more than that. So we turned it down.'

The Marquee show also introduced the band to another facet of concert life they had never thought of before. 'This guy came up to us, introduced himself and said he was from an agency, a booking agency, and wanted to represent us. Now, I had no fucking idea what a booking agency did, I thought they did lights and PAs and shit. So he came up and introduced himself, "I really enjoyed your show" and "I'm from this agency," and I replied "well, we don't really need to book any lights or PAs, thank you very much," and we went back to Bradford.'

It was a month before Astbury realized his mistake. 'I called the guy up and the first thing he said was "thank God, you've phoned. We've been trying so hard to get in touch with you guys – we've pencilled you in to play five shows with Theatre of Hate next month." I just went, "Get out of here!" I was shocked, completely blown away! I dropped the phone, hung up on him immediately, phoned everyone else, and we were all just pissing our pants.' The headliners' 'Do You Believe In The West World' was still clattering through the firmament; their Clash connections remained strong as the two bands toured together; and Mick Jones had just completed producing Theatre Of Hate's *West World* album. Now Theatre of Hate were to be thrust deep into venues where they had once merely warmed up the audience, and Southern Death Cult were to make the journey with them.

Opening in front of 500 people at Keele University, Southern Death Cult's stint on the Theatre Of Hate tour was brief, but impressive – or so Billy Duffy, the headliners' increasingly dissatisfied lead guitarist, believed. An instant convert to Astbury's wild stage persona, Duffy recalled, 'He was absolutely unreal. And louder than the rest of the group put together!' By the time their five show allotment was up, Theatre Of Hate had already offered Southern Death Cult a further ten.

A Peel session in May 1982 accelerated Southern Death Cult's ascent, a four-song set that gave them another shop window for their wares. In July, Southern Death Cult were on the bill for high profile London showcases by both Theatre Of Hate and the Clash and, that autumn, they signed a one-off single deal with Situation 2, a subsidiary of Bauhaus and the Birthday Party's Beggar's Banquet home. Just as pertinently, however, Situation 2 was also the newly-acquired home of that other offspring of the previous December, Gene Loves Jezebel.

What would become Gene Loves Jezebel was formulated in twin brothers Michael and Jay Aston's Welsh hometown of Porthcawl in 1981. The band was originally called Slavaryan, a name, explained Michael, which was wholly influenced by Joy Division. 'We were playing around with the idea of the Slavs and the Aryans, the conflict of the races, we liked the idea of the duality of it. And it was dark, the Nazi nonsense, that was Joy Division's influence. We got rid of that name though, we thought it was too dark... Bauhaus, there's another one that was all Germanic, the great British obsession.'

With a line-up led by the Astons and guitarist Ian Hudson, Slavaryan played a mere handful of shows, including one semi-legendary spot with Crass, which ended when the Barry Town Hall audience spilled onto the stage for an all-out fistfight. The principle reason for Slavaryan's demise, however, was Michael's decision to relocate to London in mid-1981. By the time brother Jay joined him there with Hudson in tow, Michael had already recruited drummer James Chater (grandson, incidentally, of the owner of Led Zeppelin's Hedley Grange retreat) and bassist Steve Radwell.

Striking coiffed, dazzlingly flamboyant, the twins were already attracting attention even before their band took the stage. Indeed, the seeds of the new outfit's distinctive name were sewn by an aspiring film-maker, keen to include the pair in a movie he was shooting on the London club scene. Jay Aston: 'This filmmaker was introduced to me, and he thought I said my name was Jezebel – my Welsh accent, I don't know. It wasn't like I was going swanning around calling myself Jezebel!'

The name stuck, however, as did a nickname Michael had picked up after breaking a leg. 'He was limping around for a little bit, like Gene Vincent. And then one of my friends noticed that, even though Michael and I got into these huge arguments, in the end, we always came in on each other's side. "You guys just love each other, you always stick together," so I just went, "Oh... Michael loves Jay, Gene Loves Jezebel"'.

The name was confirmed in mid-December 1981, the day the Astons were asked how they wanted to be billed on the posters for their first ever gig, opening for the Higsons and the Electric Guitars at the ICA on 30th December. Jay concluded, 'We were aware of Bauhaus and Killing Joke wearing all black, so I thought we'll be totally colourful, we'll go the exact opposite way. And we won't have a one word name, we'll have a long name.'

Initially, the band was more of a performance art vehicle than a strictly musical show: 'when Gene Loves Jezebel began, the band was just a vehicle for Jay and my personalities,' Michael reflected. But other influences swiftly crept in. 'There's a very powerful history behind us being from southern Wales – the whole of Camelot, the singing, the mining. The people look to the past, its legends, its poetry, all that had an impact on us. Plus, our music was very, very moody, dark, and very lyrical. It was a marvellous time really – one, because we didn't know where we were going, and two, because we weren't really conscious of what we were doing. It was so pure.'

No less than Southern Death Cult's accelerated destiny, things moved astonishingly fast. *Melody Maker* journalist Steve Sutherland caught that first show and immediately began championing the group ('I have seen the future and I think we'll do lunch'). Situation 2 turned up at the band's second show; by the time of their third gig, Gene Loves Jezebel already had a record deal and an imminent single, a distinct echo of the now rolling Virgin Prunes' twin lead discordance, 'Shaving My Neck'. And, on 24th February 1982, less than two months after playing their first ever show, Gene Loves Jezebel were slotted in as support for labelmates Bauhaus, as that band prepared for life beneath the expectant banner of a defining hit single.

Or, at least, that's what everybody thought was about to happen.

Determined to break into the Top 30, Bauhaus abandoned their hitherto steadfast refusal to allow outsiders into their sessions, and recruited producer Hugh Jones to help them with a new single, the unapologetically spirited 'Spirit.'

It was an uncomfortable experience. Normally, Bauhaus worked quickly in the studio, knocking out albums in a matter of weeks. 'Spirit' took nine days to record, as band and producer argued furiously – and Jones came out on top every time. By the time the single was finished and trotting towards its ultimate placing of #42, Bauhaus weren't simply relieved that their dreams of chart domination had signally failed to come true, they were planning to rerecord the song from scratch, in the hope of consigning the 45 to the dustbins of eternal oblivion.

The group's chart ambitions by no means put an end to their earlier concepts of guerrilla art warfare, of course; indeed, if anything, the group's burgeoning popularity incited them to even greater radicalism.

Live, seeking any means of relieving the tedium that always creeps into the best-oiled machine, Bauhaus abandoned conventional set lists and relied instead on their already finely attuned powers of improvisation, a frustrating experience for audiences, but an educational one as well.

Every band offered its fans a chance to relive old records. Bauhaus were giving them a headstart on new ones as well, although Murphy admitted that the group's motives were not necessarily quite so altruistic. 'It came down to the fact that we were so miserable,' he swore. But it was also due to the band's own belief that the audience could never, ever, be allowed to get the upper hand. The partnership should always be an equal one.

'Once you release your music into the open, this is a communal exercise,' Murphy continued. 'The artist must never be so arrogant to own his music to the extent that he is the only authority on it. The audience are the authority, you become the servant in a sense. But, another danger is that you become subservient to the audience's wishes and that's most of what an artist must fight against – not denying his work, but denying the projection of it.' The media and, to an extent, the audience labelled Bauhaus. Bauhaus, as they toured through 1982, were doing their damnedest to cut those labels off.

One of the strangest activities that the band – or, at least, Murphy – indulged in was to become poster child for Maxell Tapes, starring in a memorable television commercial and, he agreed, revelling in the viewers' uncertainty. Apparently, the company had originally wanted to use Japan frontman David Sylvian, only turning to Murphy when the blonde boy proved unavailable. Murphy, on the other hand, didn't need to be asked twice.

'It was a wonderful art thing, it was a real subversive statement, and people were "who's that? It can't be!" I only got a couple of grand out of that, I did it out of pure vanity and the idea that it'd be amazing for real hardcore Bauhaus fans to switch on their TVs and see this fantastic looking model who was me! It'd twist their heads, "What the hell is he about then?" And then, people were recognising me on the street as the Maxell person, and that was the most brilliant way of opening the door. I'd say, "Oh yeah, and I'm also the singer with Bauhaus," so they'd come, see this Bauhaus show… it was a very great way of breaking down the doors.'

Other eyes were watching the band, too. Movie director Tony Scott caught Bauhaus performing 'Bela Lugosi's Dead' (alongside 'Kick In The Eye') on BBC2's arts program *Riverside* and promptly booked them to repeat the performance for his forthcoming new movie, the vampire flick *The Hunger*.

Utilising the same caged-singer idea that the band's own 'Telegram Sam' employed, Bauhaus' scene was shot at Heaven on 22nd March 1982 – the movie, starring David Bowie and Catherine Deneuve, would be released a little over a year later. The group's role in the finished flick would ultimately be harshly edited down to just a handful of flashes of Murphy himself. But the irony of a song about a film vampire appearing in a vampire film remained delightful. And, of course, it didn't hurt the Gothic image, either.

Back in the studio and still feeling the need for some outside guidance, Bauhaus assigned their latest album sessions to Derek Tompkins, the visionary hands-off presence who guided 'Bela Lugosi's Dead', installing him as the mediator between the band and their engineer, Ted Sharp. For a time, they even entertained the notion of returning to Tompkins' own Beck Studios, departing from that plan only when Tompkins himself convinced them that it simply didn't possess the kind of equipment they needed.

They turned instead to Rockfield, the same haunted halls as had inspired the Damned's most recent triumph. There, whatever presence may have guided that band to glory was awaiting them. The ensuing album, *The Sky's Gone Out*, would emerge as Bauhaus' best, a solid encapsulation of all that the band represented, and all that it was capable of, too. And yes, this time it did serve up a hit single.

Departing Rockfield for London, and killing some downtime in the studio one afternoon, Ash and Haskins thrashed out an impromptu rendering of David Bowie's 'Ziggy Stardust', a joking tribute to the artist with whom virtually every critic in the land had now compared them. The tapes were running throughout and J, when he played them back, was absolutely enthralled. The band had a John Peel session looming – what fun it would be to include the song in their broadcast.

Ash recalled, 'We'd been doing some recording at Trident Studios, which was where Bowie did a lot of his early albums, and when we got back to the office, we played "Ziggy" to the girl on the desk, a real Bowie freak. We told her we'd found it on an unmarked tape, that it was a rare Bowie out-take, and she was completely taken in. Which was the whole point.'

The Peel session was equally true-to-life – so much so that, when it came time to select a new single, the band had no hesitation in borrowing the performance back from the BBC. Bolstered by a version of Eno's 'Third Uncle', included in the same session and a recording of their live date with Nico, berating 'Waiting For The Man' in Manchester, 'Ziggy Stardust' was unveiled as the opening track on the *Covers* EP (oddly, the fourth track, 'Party Of The First Part', was an original) and immediately powered the group into the Top 20. *The Sky's Gone Out*, riding both the impetus of the single and the limited edition inclusion of a free live album, effortlessly followed it to #3.

From a musical point of view, *The Sky's Gone Out* was as unique as every other record in Bauhaus' canon; from a theatrical point of view, the band had materialised into territory that had no realistic reference point anywhere in rock. 'We were just clicking with energy,' reflects Peter Murphy. 'The energy that came off that band was quite amazing. It was very high-butane, very confrontational. You could touch the atmosphere in the air whenever Bauhaus were around.

'It was kind of heavy at times, but we made it so. There was an over-emphasis on the importance of what we were doing and what doors we were breaking down. But, really, there was no door there at all. We were just breaking. We were breaking down doors, but the doors were absent. We were just breaking, breaking, breaking.' What made that breakage all the more exciting, as the singer readily acknowledges, was the knowledge that Bauhaus were not alone. 'It was a real bastard period, bastard geniuses were springing up everywhere and they were sowing the seeds of something that's really amazing.'

The problem with bastard genius, however, is that it seldom survives long enough to actually reap the rewards of its endeavours.

* * *

No sooner had the *Faith* tour concluded and a new (non-album) single, 'Charlotte Sometimes', emerged to reinforce the Cure's cult literature credentials, than the band began preparing its fourth album, *Pornography*. If – as one reviewer shuddered – *Faith* had taken no prisoners, *Pornography* would not even recognize its allies. It was going to wipe out everyone.

'I'm hard-pressed to find any redeeming features,' *Melody Maker* complained upon the album's release in April 1982. That condemnation was echoed throughout a music press that had expected the new Cure album to be a lot of things, but had never even dreamed of such rancour or vitriol. *Pornography*, *Melody Maker* continued, 'plummets like a leaking submarine into depths unfathomable by man. Frankly, it's unhealthy. "100 Years" is the least depressing track; it's merely gloomy.'

Cure biographer Jo-Ann Greene would subsequently note that *Pornography* was, in fact, a considerably more positive-sounding record than its predecessor. But it was also 'a lot more violent' – a statement that Smith himself enlarged upon when he corrected, 'It wasn't really violent. It was the inability to be violent. It was a realization of shortcomings – the fact that the music couldn't be violent enough to break out of those confines.' Yet even he admits that there can be few more premonitory openings to an album than the first lines of *Pornography*, a plaintive wail of 'it doesn't matter if we all die.'

'The album was about things that have far-reaching effects,' Smith tried gallantly to explain. 'It was far more considered about some of the horrors that people go through just in everyday living, I suppose.' It was an indication of just how deeply felt those horrors were, therefore, that the Cure had no alternative but to allow them to impact on the band itself, as though they could not truly describe the nightmare until they had experienced it themselves.

Later, Smith acknowledged a distinct degree of calculation in the arc that the Cure's career had taken; admitted, too, that the fate that awaited it at the conclusion of that journey had been planned as far back as their first album. 'After *Three Imaginary Boys*, which I hated straightaway, to pull off a three-year project like *Seventeen Seconds* to *Pornography*, I realized we couldn't be seen to do it in a half-hearted way, so we threw ourselves into a whole lifestyle that was a vicious circle.' Unfortunately, 'by the time of *Pornography*, we weren't having any fun and it seemed pointless, because by then we were only doing it for other people and it all fell apart.'

Conducted early in 1982, the recording sessions for *Pornography*, he continued, were 'horrifying, chaotic... but not in a nice way. It was a very vicious, anarchic way. I seriously don't remember making a lot of it. But it turned out to be one of my favourite records.'

He is not alone. It is unlikely whether the Cure will ever escape from the three-headed hydra of *Seventeen Seconds*, *Faith* and *Pornography*, triplets of such unrelenting pressure and power that the very act of listening to them leaves one feeling both purged and punished. But it is even less likely that Smith, at least, would seriously want to escape.

Indeed, talking up 2000's *Bloodflowers* album, Smith admitted that he had returned specifically to the working practises that dictated the final state of *Pornography*: a dictatorship within which his bandmates were little more than additional instruments for him to tune and strum at will. Only one other Cure album had been made under similar circumstances, he claimed: 1989's *Disintegration*. It is no coincidence that, alongside *Pornography*, that album is generally counted among the band's greatest efforts.

Like its predecessors, *Pornography* was reasonably successful in UK chart terms; like its predecessors, it spawned what Smith now regards as hopelessly inappropriate (but, again, reasonably successful) singles. Unlike its predecessors, however, it was the sound of a band purposefully tearing itself into shreds, simply to see how far it could throw the fragments. As Smith himself has since remarked, when you are only selling 50,000 records worldwide, you have to do something to get yourself noticed. The Cure chose to destroy itself.

Of course, Smith argues, and with considerable conviction, there is a vast multitude of Cure fans out there for whom these albums have no more particular significance than any other record; that the so-called 'core' fans for whom they represent a musical Holy Grail are simply clutching a touchstone whose own magical properties were long since dissipated by time and tide.

'The difference between now and then – whenever 'then' was – is that it was all pure autobiography, taken exclusively from things that had worked me up to the point where I'd write a song. Now I can take situations that don't really upset my equilibrium I can hear something we could do musically and I'll write a song to compliment it, which in the old days I would never ever do. I had no interest in it, I just wanted to put my own point of view across and say this is how I feel about something, and the music was just a backdrop.

'But if you were to be totally dispassionate, if you listen to those albums on merit, they don't stand up to the later albums, not even emotionally and certainly not the songwriting. There's a completeness to the later albums that just isn't there.

'You're not really gonna expect someone who buys *Staring At The Sea* or *Galore* (compilations respectively documenting the first and second decades of the Cure) to then buy *Faith* and sit back and say, "Ah my life's changed." I don't think you're gonna buy the *Wish* album and then think, 'I'm gonna check out their back catalogue and pick up *Seventeen Seconds*. They're still good albums, but it's older fans who are gonna like the early stuff best because they were younger when we did it.' Perhaps wisely, in view of much of its lyrical content, he stops short of describing *Pornography* as the old lover you never quite got over, but the unspoken point is made regardless.

The counter to this argument, of course, can only ever be made from a personal viewpoint, simply because the songs themselves are never less than intense and intensely personal. But they are universal too and, besides, one can identify with the anguish of which Smith sings without ever having to twist one's own psyche into the same distorted misery that was the lot of Ian Curtis.

Pornography was a harrowing album. The accompanying *14 Explicit Moments* tour, which opened in Plymouth on 18th April 1982, has gone down in rock'n'roll folklore as one of the most disastrous, in personal terms, any band has ever undertaken. 'The tour was like a rerun of the worst movie you've ever seen,' Smith would flinchingly complain. 'We were cracking up, so all the people offstage began to fall apart as well. Twenty-three people reverting to primitive is not a pretty sight.'

On another occasion, he recalled, 'Everyone involved in that tour disintegrated somehow, their characters became distended. They seemed to revert back to something horrible inside them, and there was a lot of physical violence. We just took our lives up onto the stage. It was a distressing time and it made me go quite odd for about eighteen months. It all got too intense and depressing, everything was wrong, we were stagnating, me and Simon [Gallup, bassist] were fighting and we hadn't got anywhere.

'I was very proud of *Pornography*, but no-one else liked it'. So, when Gallup left the band at the conclusion of the tour in Belgium on 11th June 1982 (he would return to the Cure later in the band's career), Smith did not even bother replacing him. To all intents and purposes, the Cure was no more.

Of course, the split, in July 1982, was eventually proven to be nothing more than a simple parting of the ways. Smith and Tolhurst remained to keep the flag flying.

As it turned out, that was more than sufficient. But at the time, things looked very shaky indeed.

When *Flexipop* magazine requested an exclusive Cure track for a forthcoming freebie flexidisc, Smith handed over 'Lament', a song he'd recorded with Banshee Steve Severin alone, and which was less representative of the Cure than it was indicative of a looming Smith/Severin side project, the psychedelic Glove. When he returned to the stage, it was again alongside Severin, as he was drafted back into Siouxsie and the Banshees in November 1982 to replace his own replacement, John McGeoch.

'Talking about [the Cure] now is like going back to an old toy or game whose rules you've forgotten,' Smith mused. 'Do the Cure really exist anymore? I've been pondering that question myself.'

But, if he'd only cared to take a walk down Dean Street any Wednesday that summer, the answer would have been staring back at him from every kohl-eyed, shock-haired, graveyard-clad soul in sight.

Distinctively clad Batcave bouncers protect Specimen singer Ollie Wisdom from the hordes

Chapter Eight
Floorshow: Death
With Walls

An account of a visit to Specimen's Batcave, to meet sex gangs and sex fiends. Meanwhile, the curtain comes down on the Theatre of Hate, the Southern Death Cult soar, the Birthday Party sours and The Sisters redefine their sound for the masses.

'The people that we knew at the inception of the Batcave really were a diverse group... Other people, the media, just shut that out because they didn't want to hear it. They wanted Goth to be – Goth. But the Batcave exploded into a thousand, million, fragments.' Nick Wade

'Strange things happened at gigs. People had babies. This girl had a baby in the toilet. And, once, this guy came backstage and said, "You're my favourite band. I just got out of jail, I murdered my father and my whole family. And I love you so much, I'm going to murder you guys too!" We had a lot of people like that.' Andy Roberts, Sex Gang Children

**hen** Specimen opened the Batcave in London on Wednesday, 21st July 1982, a once-a-week intrusion into the life of a part-time West End strip joint called the Gargoyle Club, the black-slicked, white faced, be-fanged and Bela'd audience that would soon be forming funeral processions the entire length of Dean Street was the farthest thing from their minds.

Nick Wade, one of the club's first employees, explained, 'the Batcave really was an alternative to whatever else was happening at the time, an alternative independent. It was the perfect outlet for doing something that made no sense. I was always into Alice Cooper, but I was also into Salvador Dali so, for me, it was an opportunity to do something that was visually exciting, to an audience which was equally visually exciting.

'And it was marvellous. I wouldn't change a day about it. It was this mental idea of loads of people, photographers, clothes designers, musicians, artists, people from all different walks of life all thrown in together, everybody helps everybody through. The people that we knew at the inception of the Batcave really were a diverse group, which is something we [Wade and wife Christine] often commented upon. Other people, the media, just shut that out because they didn't want to hear it. They wanted Goth to be – Goth. But the Batcave exploded into a thousand, million, fragments.'

Specimen formed in Bristol in 1980, although vocalist Ollie Wisdom was no stranger to the streets of London. Three years earlier, at the height of Punk's first gleaming, he led the Unwanted, a band that formed in March 1977, and made both their live and recorded debuts simultaneously, onstage at the Roxy as the tapes rolled for the *Live At The Roxy* Punk sampler. Indeed, it was that precise prospect that dissuaded the band from going ahead with their original intentions, of naming themselves Smak.

A shambolic highlight of the ensuing album, the Unwanted wound up as one of the great also-rans of Punk – great because, at their best, in the seething dungeon of the Roxy, they left witnesses utterly boggled by how bad they were, a comedy turn that laughed at its own shortcomings, then laughed at the audience for being so shocked by them.

But critical disdain, commercial neglect, and increasingly miserable returns for their seldom-less-than wonderful live show took their toll. By the time the Unwanted split in late 1978, every instrument in the line-up had been played by at least two different musicians (including future Psychedelic Furs John Ashton and Vince Ely) and some by more than that.

Specimen were considerably more stable. The core line-up forged for their first ever concert, at a Royal Wedding street party in Bristol on 29th July 1981, would remain together for much of the band's career – Wisdom, guitarist Jon Klein and bassist Kevin Mills. They would be joined by drummer Johnathan Trevithick and, in late 1981, after one final Bristol show at Scamps nightclub, Specimen relocated to London in search of fresh excitement. They didn't find it, so they set about creating it themselves.

Klein later admitted that the band's very formation was an act of self-restoration.

Wisdom had spent the last six months travelling in Africa, while Klein himself had only recently left hospital, after suffering a broken back. 'Specimen was, in a way, our rehabilitation into civilisation,' he said, not even pausing to consider the irony of that statement.

Unrepentantly theatrical, unblinkingly glam, Specimen rehearsed a live show that blinded with its vivacity, a riot of costumes, cobwebs and kaleidoscopic colour that, even in the age of Adam Ant and Bauhaus, left the most open-minded onlooker reeling.

The comparison with the Antman, of course, was no coincidence. At their best, Specimen drew directly from the tribal chop of Adam's finest – witness the pounding 'Tell Tail' and 'Kiss Kiss Bang Bang.' But, whereas Adam's vivaciousness was based wholly on old panto traditions, Specimen drew their visual cue from the very underbelly of pop culture – old monster movies, new fetish notions and buckets of figurative blood.

It took Specimen just a couple of shows, support gigs at the Lyceum and Camden Town's Dingwalls, to discover that the conventional London circuit had little time for their savage entertainment and, by early 1982, the band was already booking its own shows, frequently taking over Bond Street's late night Embassy Club for what they modestly termed 'events.'

The audience they had been searching for swiftly sought them out – indeed, the very first 'event' landed the band a publishing deal with New Romantic figurehead-turned-entrepreneur Rusty Egan. The decision to begin organising such shows on a more regular basis, however, wasn't simply a natural progression for the band; it was also one that London itself needed. The conventional gig circuit was, if not dying, at least rotten – the handful of upstart newcomers that catered for the Punk movement had long since closed their doors. The traditional club venues, the Marquee, Dingwalls, the 100 Club, the Greyhound and so on, remained the same as they had been for a decade or more, with much the same booking policies as well.

Yet there was an entire new musical force brooding on the streets, one that didn't simply need somewhere to play, it also needed somewhere to call its own. The Batcave would fill that requirement. Klein continued, 'We built up a team of people to deal with many aspects of the club including finding cabaret, bands, decoration and the press. Initially the English music press responded well to our intentions and consequently people knew we were opening the club and a lot of people turned up. We had a 200 metre-long queue on our opening night, and this queue would become an integral part of the scene.'

The Batcave impressed from the moment you entered the premises. A tiny lift carried you four floors up, to pass through a coffin-shaped gateway into a tiny cinema-come-cabaret theatre-come-disco-come-live venue. Within a matter of months, Klein realised, 'It seemed we'd broken the circle at last.'

Still, refining the visuals-heavy stageshow that fell, as a cautious *New Musical Express* put it, somewhere between Bauhaus, the New York Dolls and vintage Marc Bolan, Specimen moved slowly but ambitiously. A fortnight before the opening of the Batcave, they made their recorded debut – not on vinyl or cassette but video, capturing the undeniable spirit of their live show on the video single 'Returning From

A Journey.' The *NME* called it 'lumpy rock of a transvestical bent,' but the band saw that as an honour, not a put-down. Good reviews in the *NME* were not, after all, something that their own intended audience would find overly encouraging.

The Batcave's brief was as far-reaching as its founders' influences. Although the leather, lace and monster movie décor would indeed play into the hands of all who would label it the quintessential Goth club, the Batcave was more a successor to the Cabaret Futura, a similarly themed weekly event helmed by former Doctors of Madness frontman Richard Strange during 1980-81.

A few yards down the road from the Marquee club, the Cabaret Futura shared its home with an Indian restaurant, and the strains (and smells) of one were frequently to be encountered within the other. But nobody really seemed to mind. For the club-goers, it was nice to know that an excellent curry was just a short flight of stairs away; for diners, it was reassuring to know that the Cabaret was not just another rock nightclub. Indeed, as Strange himself insisted, its very existence was 'challenging the rock biz by saying "it doesn't have to be like that." We're trying to get away from the established procedure of two bands a night, shunting people in and out, with no sense of occasion, no sense of spectacle, just a conveyor belt.'

Kissing The Pink, ex-Skids frontman-turned-acerbic poet Richard Jobson, Everest The Hard Way, Eddie & Sunshine and the infant Soft Cell all played there (so, though the night was scarcely memorable, did the newly formed Pogues), but their appearances were the exception. A night at the Cabaret was just as likely to feature mixed-media mime acts and performance art poets, film shows and plays – anything, in fact, but another lumpen rock band, clunking through its leaden paces.

The Batcave's repertoire, too, went far beyond mere live music. Drag acts, mud wrestling, fire-eaters and cult classic movies were also on the bill – anything, in fact, that offered some kind of escape from the increasingly anodyne and dreadfully clique-driven scene that had crushed the New Romantic scene pioneered by another of the Gargoyle's client clubs, Billy's. And that, too, paid tribute to the Cabaret Futura.

Strange had closed his own doors in 1982, tired of battling against the progressive distillation of a musical mood which had promised so much but had already been subverted into the New Romantic flash flood that valued haircuts higher than hair shirts. The Batcave was the sign for that battle to be renewed.

Specimen played the first Batcave night, but they were by no means representative of what the venue had to offer – what, after all, would have been the point of that? During its first few months of operation, the Batcave hosted eye-opening sets from Test Department, who played their first ever concert there on 4th August 1982; Brilliant, the new band formed by Killing Joke bassist Youth, who were there on 15th September (both bands would subsequently appear on the Batcave's own compilation album); and Zerra 1, who appeared on 6th October.

The venue even flirted with its own answer to Great Train Robber Ronnie Biggs, of Sex Pistols/Punk era infamy, when it welcomed Michael Fagin on stage with the band Red Lipstique. Weeks before the Batcave opened, on 7th July 1982, Fagin hit world headlines when he broke into Buckingham Palace, made his way into the Queen's bedroom, then sat at the end of her bed with a bottle of wine, waiting for her to wake up. Now, just a week after being released on remand, Fagin was taking the stage at the Batcave, a folk hero who had everything but longevity.

Another occasional highlight was provided by Marc Almond, one time nightclub entrepreneur, latter-day Top 40 confectioner, and now taking the stage with his Mambas side project. It was a deep, dark secret indeed that, behind the glossy hits and captivating synths, Almond's songwriting was scarcely your average teenybop fodder, while his very look – slimy black, bone-white jewellery and a lascivious smirk that was virtually etched into place – was certainly more De Sade than Duran.

But the pop kids loved him and, with that love, there came the freedom (not to mention the budget) to indulge his seamier side. The Marc and the Mambas side project's two double albums, *Untitled* and *Torment And Toreros*, offered, even by Almond's normal, and subsequent, standards, a bitter collision of commercial suicide and self-indulgent whimsy. Indeed, eight sides of vinyl alternate between psychic exorcism and physical relief, garage flamenco and jagged industrialism, the Banshees' Steve Severin and the brooding Jim Thirlwell, torrid torture and nihilistic nastiness. Of all the myriad happenings that the Batcave delivered during its lifetime, Marc and the Mambas' disavowal of even a hint of their makers' day-job appeal, ranks among the most honest of them all.

Almond notwithstanding and Specimen aside, the first of the so-called 'Batcave bands' to break into mainstream consciousness was the Sex Gang Children. Of course they baulked at the rest of the baggage that accompanied the term – echoing Nick Wade, frontman Andi Sex Gang summed up the objectives of both band and Batcave as 'just the epitome of human spirit. If you don't like control, you don't like mediocrity, if you don't like the way things are, and if you want to put freedom back into expression, you don't ask and you don't play the game to make it. You set out to destroy everything in your way.'

Sex Gang Children came together in early 1981 around a nucleus of vocalist Andi and bassist Dave Roberts, plus guitarist Terry MacLeay and drummer Rob Stroud. Roberts had previously been a member of Panic Button, an outfit that is otherwise best remembered for supplying two members to the first generation of Kirk Brandon's Spear Of Destiny but, as Roberts readily admits, 'when Andi and I put the band together, we had no idea. Basically we couldn't play. I was a guitarist, but he already had one, so I became a bassist instead.'

The actual band name, however, has a more intriguing genesis. A William Burroughs line that had been grafted into a song by Bow Wow Wow, 'Sex Gang Children' was promptly co-opted by one 'Boy' George O'Dowd, when he bowed out of the Wow Wows after just two live shows in February 1981. Co-vocalist there, he dreamed of becoming sole vocalist in his own band, a flamboyant pop dub outfit he was formulating with former Damned drummer Jon Moss and bassist Mikey Craig. Hopeful of a deal with EMI that spring, George conceded that Sex Gang Children was not a name that would take them far – as Moss remarked the first time they rehearsed together, 'it was good to have a sexy name' – but this one just wasn't 'commercial.' The group would become Culture Club. Sex Gang Children was consigned to the bin.

Or it would have been if Sex Gang and Roberts, rehearsing their own unnamed band down at the Elephant and Castle, hadn't heard the news. Immediately, Andi called O'Dowd to ask if he could take the name for his own band; the Boy, of course, graciously gave his blessings.

Queried by the media as to the name's origins, however, the band swiftly created a far less prosaic explanation. 'Go to a housing estate, a deprived area,' MacLeay told *Sounds*. 'You see that the kids there hang around in gangs and they're bounded by their desire to cause trouble. It's a sexual urge. That is what a Sex Gang should be.'

Working from a musical base loosely bordered by the snap of Bauhaus and the Sisters of Mercy, and the yowl of the Virgin Prunes and Gene Loves Jezebel, the Sex Gang Children rapidly became regulars at the Clarendon in Hammersmith, a venue that had, seemingly unwittingly but with remarkable conviction all the same, confirmed itself as home base for any number of bands who would eventually establish themselves at the Batcave or thereabouts. An early incarnation of Flesh For Lulu, Danse Society, the nascent Lords of the New Church, and the still rising Southern Death Cult all graced the halls. One of Sex Gang Children's earliest performances took place on 16th April 1982, when they opened for Astbury and co.

Other Sex Gang shows included appearances at the Royal College of Art, the Zig Zag Club (opening for Johnny Thunders) and the Embassy Club. But, when it came to preparing their first album, a cassette-only live album, it was the Clarendon's unique atmosphere that would be preserved on tape. *Naked* was released in May via Rough Trade, a snip at two quid and a thunderously percussive melange of Adam and the Ants and Theatre of Hate, with a hint of Johnny Rotten floating around the vocals, a smidgeon of Bauhaus about the bass, a bit of Banshees in the guitar.

So nothing too surprising, but it was an intriguing combination anyway, both musically and visually. 'Andi's eyes pierce the spotlights and his brilliant orange hair spouts cockatoo-style,' swooned *Sounds*' review of a June show at the Embassy Club. 'The guitarists claw at their instruments in their leathers, string vests and bowler hats. They look like Punks who have been to art school.'

Ian Astbury, too, has reflected on Sex Gang's audience, making a telling revelation: 'Andi Sex Gang used to dress like a Banshees fan. So, I used to call him the Gothic Goblin, because he was a little guy and he's dark. He used to like Edith Piaf and this macabre music, and he lived in a building in Brixton called Visigoth Towers. So he was the little Gothic Goblin, and his followers were Goths. And that's where Goth came from.'

True or false, those followers swiftly proved themselves to be as idiosyncratic as the band they worshipped. Roberts continued, 'for some strange reason, we had a very violent audience. I guess because the music was so fast and loud, and it wasn't smooth, strange things happened at gigs. People had babies. This girl had a baby in the toilet. And, once, this guy came backstage and said, "You're my favourite band. I just got out of jail, I murdered my father and my whole family. And I love you so much, I'm going to murder you guys too!" We had a lot of people like that.'

What would appear a simple case of cause and effect – weird music attracts weird listeners – was not, however, the band's intention, as Roberts explained. 'It really wasn't designed that way. The music wasn't deliberately discordant. It was just the way we played. I couldn't play bass, and I didn't know where to start, so I just started on the easiest strings – the high strings – and you're not meant to do that. Andi liked any rhythm that was odd, and he just stacked them together. Rob, our drummer, was like, "what do you want me to do?" Because he was a fairly straight player. So it was interesting how it came together.'

It was also interesting how it hung together. 'None of us liked each other very much,' Roberts concluded, recalling the Sex Gang Children's first John Peel session that November. 'We'd been bitching at one another for about an hour, when the engineer turned around and said, "The last band that was in here like that, was the Troggs." And we never did another radio session.'

Such chaotic discords notwithstanding, Sex Gang Children established themselves quickly. The Illuminated label moved in for them within weeks of the release of *Naked*; the band's first single, the four-song *Beasts* EP, was in the stores by August 1982. Days later, however, it was out of them again, after somebody realised they'd not procured the necessary permissions for the Diane Arbus photo on the picture sleeve. With a major lawsuit apparently imminent, the record was briefly withdrawn while the sleeves were removed, but still *Beasts* did all that could have been hoped for, reaching #8 on the Indy chart and hanging around the listings for much of the next twelve months.

The band was attracting attention from further afield, as well. Tony James, midway between playing bass with the now-sundered Generation X and masterminding the nascent Sigue Sigue Sputnik, was sufficiently impressed by Sex Gang Children to produce their next single, October 1982's 'Into The Abyss'.

He then added his own tongue-in-cheek interpretation of the band's reputation by insisting that the musicians played in full make-up and replacing the studio lighting with candles. It was, Rob Stroud, later complained, 'laughable,' but it was also effective. 'Into The Abyss' emerged as one of the year's most deliciously atmospheric singles, retaining the Ant attack that was the band's bedrock and further amplifying the aura of unbridled creativity that was now swirling around the Batcave.

The club's name was on everybody's lips that autumn. Maybe the BBC, filming a Halloween edition of *Riverside*, was distraught to discover the venue was not wall-to-wall celebrities, but still the Batcave guest list was as long as a winding cloth. Boy George, Ian Astbury, the Virgin Prunes, Gary Glitter, Ultravox, Jimmy Pursey, Siouxsie and the Banshees, Lydia Lunch, Marc Almond, Vince Clarke, Nick Cave, Wayne County and the future Sigue Sigue Sputnik were all regular visitors.

Not everybody had a good time, apparently. Unlike so many of his contemporaries, whose names and photographs constantly filled the *New Musical Express*' Ligger's Corner, Robert Smith was never a staunch fan of the Batcave. 'We used to go [there] because we got in free and it was a good atmosphere and the people were really nice. But the music was awful! That whole romanticism of death! Anybody who's ever experienced death firsthand could tell you there's nothing romantic about it.' The fact that *Pornography* remained a staple of the club's play list adds piquancy to his words.

Ian Astbury was more encouraging. 'The Batcave was really mixed. It wasn't just this dark death rock club. Specimen was the house band, and they were very dark, but they were as much Germanic as they were The Addams Family. They were like a Death Bowie.'

He could afford to be magnanimous. The same month that the Batcave opened, Southern Death Cult celebrated the first eight months of their meteoric rise by opening for the Clash at the Brixton Fair Deal and, though the headliners' mean-spirited audience would never admit it, blowing the headliners out of the room. Some groups are designed for success, some are simply lumbered with it. Southern Death Cult were one of the precious few who are actually born for it.

In September 1982, Southern Death Cult were among the star attractions at Futurama IV at the Deeside Leisure Centre, lining up alongside the Damned, Gene Loves Jezebel, Dead Or Alive, New Order, Danse Society and the March Violets, a Leeds band fronted by student Simon 'Detroit' Denbigh and still celebrating the release of their debut single, the *Religious As Hell* EP, on the Sisters Of Mercy's Merciful Release label.

The following month offered even further exposure, when Southern Death Cult were booked onto the bill for Bauhaus' latest tour, as that band, too, adapted to a new-found high life, riding the 'Ziggy Stardust' single up the chart. They were not, of course, the first of the putative Gothic bands to appear on *Top Of The Pops* – Siouxsie and the Banshees had long since beaten them to it. But they were the first to appear on the show after the movement was christened and, when they toured in the aftermath of that shell-shocking performance, it was the first Gothic gig that much of the audience had ever seen.

Southern Death Cult were perfectly poised to take advantage of the attendant furore. Astbury: 'Overnight, Southern Death Cult went from opening at the Marquee in front of 30 people to selling out Heaven, 3000 people, plus 600 rioting outside. [Disc jockey] Peter Powell fell down the stairs. Boy George was there. U2 were in our dressing room. It was hysteria.'

Released in December 1982, Southern Death Cult's long-awaited first single, 'Fatman' reached #43 on the national charts and topped the Indy listings for a couple of weeks in the new year.

It should have been a cause for wild celebration. Astbury, however, sensed a certain synchronicity in the timing. Exactly twelve months earlier, Theatre Of Hate had held that same position – and where were they now? Six months after "West World", just weeks after touring with Southern Death Cult themselves, Billy Duffy had departed the band. Six months after that, so did Brandon and Stammers, heading off to form the truly majestic (but utterly dissimilar) Spear of Destiny. Success had proven too much, too soon. Southern Death Cult were now suffering from precisely the same malaise.

Astbury kept his fears to himself for the time being. The Batcave was going from strength to strength – it seemed foolish, even foolhardy, to start rocking the boat so soon. New bands, after all, were appearing there regularly; new Goth bands were springing up all over the country; and, by late 1982, the sheer weight of numbers queuing for entry had forced the club itself to seek out an alternative home.

Early in the new year, the Batcave shifted to the top floor of the Subway Club in

Leicester Square, sharing the space, for whatever reason, with an American army jeep parked next to the bar. When that proved too cramped, operations shifted to the trendy nightclub Forberts; then onto the Cellar Bar, behind Heaven beneath Charing Cross Station.

At every location, Specimen were the most regular live entertainment, with Sex Gang Children close behind. The venue's first homegrown superstars, however, were Alien Sex Fiend, the band formed when Nick Wade finally gave up checking cloaks and stamping wrists, and became a reason for the cloaks to be checked and the wrists to be stamped in the first place.

Wade had already enjoyed a long, if not necessarily spectacular career, before he formed Alien Sex Fiend, playing around London in a string of little-known bands, whose strivings are best recalled as documents of Wade's love of classic Alice Cooper: the Earwigs, named for one of the Cooper band's own earliest aliases; Mr and Mrs Demeanour, for a track on the Coopers' *Easy Action* debut album.

Another Wade project, Demon Preacher (later the Demons and, occasionally, plain old Preacher) got as far as recording three 45s: 1978's 'Little Miss Perfect', inspired by the brief celebrity of one Joyce McKinney, who kidnapped a priest, then kept him chained up for sex; the *Royal Northern* EP in 1979 and 'Action By Example' in September 1980. They meant little, did even less, and have absolutely nothing in common with the sounds that Alien Sex Fiend would create. But future archaeologists may have fun trying to find them.

Wade was now going under the name of Nik Fiend, an identity that he perfected with cosmetics and clothing. Equally strikingly garbed, his wife Christine accompanied him to the club one evening – Wade remembered, 'I got as far as saying "this is my wife" and Ollie Wisdom just said, "ah yes, Mrs Fiend." And the name stuck.'

The Wades formed Alien Sex Fiend in late 1982, linking with guitarist David 'Yaxi High-rizer' James and drummer Johnny 'Haha' Freshwater and recording much of what would become their first album, the cassette-only *The Lewd, The Mad, The Ugly And Old Nick*, even before they made their live debut at the Batcave on 24th November 1982.

An instant hit with the club clientele, Alien Sex Fiend were back again the following week, completing the album with a handful of live recordings and placing it on sale at the Batcave before Christmas. When Sex Gang Children headlined the year's-end Christmas On Earth festival at the Lyceum, Alien Sex Fiend slid onto the bill as effortlessly as Ritual and the Sisters Of Mercy (also appearing, the Vibrators and Under Two Flags were less easily explained). It would be several years more before the Fiends' fascination with electronics and space rock saw them leave the gargoyle trappings of Goth behind. For now, Alien Sex Fiend were another garish gaslight glowing on the greatest show on the planet.

For the Sisters of Mercy, Christmas On Earth marked the end of a year that had seen the group finally slip the confines of unnoticed under-achievement and into a spotlight that they had scarcely dared dream of.

Still floundering in painful slow motion, the Sisters released their second single, 'Body Electric' in March 1982. Inspected with hindsight, 'Body Electric' – like its predecessor – has little of the visceral power that the band would ultimately achieve; rather, it is a virtual thrash, built around a harshly thumping drum program, a gratingly raw guitar and, buried in the mix, the merest glimmerings of Eldritch's most commanding vocal.

That said, there is an unproduced energy to the performance that raises it far above many other records of the age, a white heat focussed with pinprick accuracy and strengthened by some of Eldritch's most obsessive early lyrics – hardly surprisingly, the line 'this place is death with walls' became a particular favourite in British club land of the age.

Around the same time, the Sisters' line-up was further swollen by the arrival of second guitarist Ben 'Gunn' Matthews. It was a troubled period, though. The Sisters' own label, Merciful Release, was so strapped for cash that it couldn't actually afford to press the record; the eventual *Melody Maker* Single of the Week appeared instead on Mekon Langford's CNT (Confederacio Nacional de Trabajo).

Even with that accolade hanging in the air, however, gigs remained hard to find. Future Radio One DJ Andy Kershaw, Entertainment Secretary at Leeds University, was only one of a legion of promoters who steadfastly refused to book the band and, when bassist Craig Adams announced he was taking time away to work as a photographer's assistant on the Canary Islands, he missed only one show.

The media, meanwhile, seemed to be missing all of them. *Melody Maker* passed enthusiastic comment on the band's Vanburgh College, York, show on 5th February 1982, but the Sisters' appearances opening for Nico at the London Venue on 7th June and the Birthday Party at the Zig Zag Club on 10th July both passed unnoticed – except by the Birthday Party themselves. Asked for his opinion of the Sisters, Mick Harvey opined they were the worst band to have ever supported the Birthday Party. If, as so many subsequent observers have speculated, the Sisters Of Mercy deliberately set out to ride a black-clad bandwagon to calculated fame and fortune, they were certainly taking a long, and not especially scenic, route to the stars.

They were superstars in Leeds, however, and their confidence knew no bounds. At a time when so many bands were intent on breaking down the barriers between artist and audience – a hangover, of course, from the Punk era – Eldritch, in particular, maintained an aloofness that bordered upon absenteeism.

It was with their third single that the Sisters finally stepped out of the darkness. Eldritch met Psychedelic Furs guitarist John Ashton when the two bands played together in Leeds during the spring; in September 1982, Ashton joined the Sisters in the studio to cut 'Alice,' a song previewed to wild enthusiasm on their maiden John Peel session the previous month. Constructed around a darkly spiralling guitar line, racing to keep pace with Doktor Avalanche's most merciless metronome, 'Alice' remains one of the Sisters' most intriguing releases, its lyric a wealth of ambiguities, laced with knowing references to sex, drugs and Tarot – anything to make reality appear bearable.

Even better was the b-side, also cut with Ashton – indeed, the imprimatur of his own band is unmistakeable across the pulsatingly frenetic 'Floorshow' and, while a machine could never capture the visceral turbulence of the Furs' drummer, Vince Ely, Doktor Avalanche certainly gave it a go.

Eldritch's vocals, too, reached new heights of range and expression – proving to the doubters that he could do much more than the monochrome monotone that was his customary vocal performance. The heart of the song, however, is an old-fashioned dance rhythm ('slow, slow, quick, quick, slow,' commands Eldritch at one point), accompanying a helter-skelter lyric that is hypnotic in its manic metre. Set, as its title suggests, in a nightclub, 'Floorshow' captures all the hedonistic excitement of the evening but ends with a damning condemnation of the very culture it celebrates: 'it's populist, got mass appeal/the old religion redefined/for the facile, futile, totally blind.'

It was a fabulous release and deserved all the praise it received. 'Alice' climbed to #26 on the Indy chart, prompting *Sounds* to feature the band on its cover and earning them, at last, a concerted burst of gigs around the capital.

The first, an unlikely melange that still raises one's eyebrows, found the Sisters Of Mercy sandwiched between reggae band Aswad and the long-forgotten Maximum Joy at the Electric Ballroom on 28th November 1982. Five nights later, they were in the more hospitable surroundings of the Clarendon's Klub Foot, opening for UK Decay. But Christmas On Earth marked their true emergence, halfway up the billing of what was the biggest celebration of the so-called Gothic movement yet staged.

It would not, of course, be the last but it certainly gave its so-called forefathers pause for thought. The year ended with the *New Musical Express* inviting Nick Cave to write an article for their own Christmas issue, discussing the sudden influx of bands that the Birthday Party could be said to have inspired, the 'Superdeath tribe' as some enterprising sub-editor dubbed them.

Diplomatically, Cave refused. Only when the paper kept on at him did he finally relent and, in the process, drove a long sharp nail through the heart of every single one of his children. Any group, 'paper tigers', he called them, 'that reflects anything other than their own idiosyncratic vision is not worth a pinch.

'The Birthday Party are, in essence, a slug, nomadic… their trail of slime is their art and.. they are barely conscious of its issue, which bears little resemblance to anything bar ourselves – and we make no excuses for that.'

Thanks, Nick. And a Merry Christmas to you, too.

Andrew Eldritch

Bleddyn Butcher

Chapter Nine
Young Limbs,
Numb Hymns

Showing the cancerous spread of the sudden death cult, as the south goes north, Bauhaus bow out and the Cure stops working. The Party is over and the Banshees have flown. But the children are still playing, their Sisters are lovely, and even Lulu gets her pound of flesh.

"No more the wasted children of a bad Dave Vanian; no longer the idiot offspring of the Addams and the Munsters. Goth in 1983 was a wild celebration of imagination and magic, beauty and elegance, and few of the people who came in contact with it were ever left completely unmoved by the experience."

Record company interest in Southern Death Cult was approaching fever pitch. EMI came close to signing the band (several demos were recorded at the label's Manchester Square studios); they also worked with producer Mike Hedges, recording new versions of the two songs already issued by Situation 2, 'Fat Man' and 'Moya.' According to Astbury, another offer came from CBS. 'They offered us 100,000 pounds for our first year, but I walked away.'

His reluctance had nothing to do with the money. Quite simply, Astbury believed Southern Death Cult had reached the end of its tether. 'What happened was, I read this review in the NME, I think it was, of a gig at Manchester Poly and it said basically that we still had a long way to go before we'd even attain any accomplishment. It really struck a chord in me. I wanted to be a lot more serious about the music, because everything up to that point was so much more about the "success" – it had been so overwhelming, so fast, and I wanted to stay grounded.

'I wanted to get into my writing more. I was so fucking serious about the whole thing and everyone else was going, "Oh well, if we stay together for a few more months, we can do the Pistols thing and rip everyone off." I just said, "In six months time, we're gonna be nowhere." Several groups at that time had just signed big deals and were flopping miserably, simply because a lot of expectations were being heaped onto their shoulders, which is such a British phenomena anyway, the way young groups come up and get judged every week in the papers.

'There's so much pressure, the papers ripping them to shreds all the time, and there's no way to go. You can't grow under those circumstances. You can't go to America because you're not known; you can't tour Europe except on a very small scale. I didn't want that to happen to us. So I broke up the band.'

That Manchester show, on 26th February 1983, turned out to be the last gig Southern Death Cult would ever play. A month later, their demise was announced. Bassist Jetson immediately formed a new band, Getting The Fear, which eventually gave way to the remarkable Into A Circle; Aky, a decade later, would establish himself as a techno remixer, reworking, among other things, the Mission's 'Serpent's Kiss' for a 1993 hit single. And Astbury, of course, found himself having to deal with major success regardless. The final word on Southern Death Cult, however, was delivered three months after their demise, as Beggars Banquet released an eponymous album drawn from sources as disparate as the BBC Radio sessions, the Manchester Square and Mike Hedges demos, three tracks recorded live on a handheld cassette recorder in Manchester the previous December, and the single. Astbury looked on aghast. 'That album was really scraping the barrel!'

Locked into a series of increasingly dishevelled sessions at Rockfield, Bauhaus were feeling much the same way about their own efforts.

The Top 20 success of 'Ziggy Stardust' had changed much about the band, most notably their expectations. The members were genuinely dismayed when the follow-up, the whip-cracking 'Lagatija Nick', collapsed at a dismal #44, despite a second captivating Top Of The Pops performance. Tensions grew tighter as each member brought forth his own suggestions as to how they might regain their momentum, then soared even higher when Murphy found himself hospitalised with a bout of pneumonia. His bandmates simply went into the studio without him, and then proceeded to cut what amounted to an entire album – vocals (from Ash and J) included.

Returning to the fray, Murphy was furious and, with the remainder of the sessions simply sparkling with distemper, it was becoming obvious that Bauhaus, too, were on the verge of disintegration.

A sign of the wicked energies surrounding the sessions was delivered in February, when the band went into the BBC studios to cut a session for DJ David Jensen. Rather than preview material set for the new album, only one unheard song, the forthcoming single 'She's In Parties,' was aired. The remainder of the three-song session was given over to an only mildly revamped 'Terror Couple Kills Colonel,' and a throwaway cover of the old garage chestnut 'Night Time.' Any clue as to what the band was really up to was left deeply buried – because they, themselves, were no longer certain.

'She's In Parties' duly appeared in April 1983. It was, perhaps, Bauhaus' most commercial effort yet, a haunting melody powered by Haskins' pounding drums and J's pulsing bass, electrified by Ash's shimmering, shivering guitar and shadowed by chameleon vocals that shifted from evocative frailty to graveyard horror. It danced up to #26 – a fair return but not, apparently, fair enough.

Tours of Europe and the Far East, in the run-up to the release of Bauhaus' fourth album, the appropriately titled *Burning From The Inside*, kept the band members from one another's' throats, but they didn't still the discontent. A three-week swing through the UK in June only worsened affairs and, by the time Bauhaus returned to London in early July, rumours of a split were circulating freely.

The group confirmed them – at least to their own satisfaction – in a London hotel room on the eve of their two-night Hammersmith Palais tour closer. Amid dire recriminations, furious door slamming and bitter, betrayed tears, Bauhaus decided to call it quits. The final night at the Palais, 5th July 1983, would also be the final night of Bauhaus and, as David J walked offstage at the end of the dazzling six-song encore (culminating, of course, with 'Bela Lugosi's Dead'), he had just three words for the audience: 'Rest In Peace.'

Burning From The Inside was released one week later.

In a way, it was an inevitable collapse, as Murphy now acknowledges. 'Throughout Bauhaus' career, the performance was extremely tense. I would almost be the lamb to the slaughter in every show. I'd almost kill myself with the energy I put out, the pure passion, but I think we didn't know just how passionate it was. We were victims of the very energy that we were generating, and we weren't really protected with wisdom, we didn't know how to control this. We'd split the atom, but we had no idea of what to do with it. And, in the end, we became the fall-out.'

The Cure, Southern Death Cult and Bauhaus – in the course of just one year, the Gothic movement had lost three of its most potent forebears. The only consolation that any grieving onlookers could snatch was the knowledge that such things always come in threes. Except when they don't. In August 1983, just one month after Bauhaus' disintegration, the Birthday Party announced that they, too, were no more. The difference was those other break-ups came as near-bolts from the blue. The

137

Birthday Party, on the other hand, had been on the verge of collapse for over a year now. The end, when it came, was less dissolution and more a mercy killing.

Precisely twelve months earlier, in August 1982, the Birthday Party decided to relocate to Berlin. 'We abhorred everything about London,' shuddered Cave. 'We found it to be one of the greatest disappointments of our lives. After living in Australia and reading constantly about London, what an amazingly exciting place it was, we finally got there and found this horrible, very constipated society.'

Their resolve was strengthened by events earlier in the year. 1982 opened with the band returning briefly to Australia to record their next album and, hopefully, recharge their batteries. Instead, they watched aghast as Tracey Pew was sentenced to eight months' imprisonment for drunk driving; and in anger, as Phill Calvert's commitment to both the group and its future waivered. By the time Cave informed the drummer that the group intended relocating to Berlin, he had already determined that Calvert was not going to be invited – which was just as well, because Calvert himself had no intention of going. He would say goodbye to the band at the same time as they said goodbye to London, at the conclusion of their latest British tour.

With Magazine bassist Barry Adamson replacing Pew, the Birthday Party launched into another major tour in support of the newly released *Junkyard*, taking some satisfaction from the album's eventual performance – the most successful-ever Birthday Party release reached #73 on the UK national chart. It was a different story on the road, however, as tickets remained adamantly unsold and audiences utterly unmoved. Days after the tour wrapped up, at the London Venue on 5th August 1982, the band left for Germany.

Anyone who read Cave's interview with the *New Music Express* that same week, however, would have deduced that the Birthday Party was undergoing far more upheaval than a simple change of address and drummer. 'We consider what we have done to be so total and complete that there's no way it can be added to,' Cave announced. 'The Birthday Party has gone deeper than any of us thought possible. But, if we were to put out another record in the same style, we would only be watering down and lessening the effectiveness of what we've done before.'

He spoke of a radical new style of music, 'incredibly tense; slow, very slow, very moody and very soulful and extremely depressing' – the blueprint, of course, for his own early solo albums. The painfully protracted death of the Birthday Party over the next twelve months, was, in fact, merely the sound of Cave slowly resolving his own immediate future.

Severing their relationship with 4AD, the group's first new linkage was with Mute Records, who promptly despatched them into Berlin's Hansa-by-the-Wall studios to begin work on the new-style Birthday Party's maiden release, the *Mutiny* EP. There they were joined by Blixa Bargeld, leader of infamous industrialists Einsturzende Neubauten. The Australians had never made any secret of their love for that band – even before they met, Cave was moved to pronounce Bargeld 'a man on the threshold of greatness, a Napoleon victorious amongst his spoils, a conquering Caesar parading his troops, a Christ akimbo on Calvary.' Though Cave alone seems to have sensed it at the time, another element of his future career had clicked into place.

While Cave consummated one relationship, another continued to deteriorate. Somehow, the Birthday Party struggled through an American tour, but it could not even begin to paste over the cracks. On the eve of departure for their next Australian tour, Mick Harvey announced that he was quitting the band.

Stunned, if not necessarily surprised, the remaining Party pulled in a hasty replacement, the Marching Girls' Des Hefner, and the tour went ahead as scheduled. But the chaos was not at an end, as Rowland Howard began voicing his own overall displeasure with the way things were developing. Another tear rent the flimsy fabric holding what was left of the band together, as the guitarist revealed, 'I've come to realize that the Birthday Party has become in the last two years, more of a vehicle for Nick than anyone else.' He quit in July 1983, word of his departure simply rendering the inevitable official.

The Birthday Party was over and only once more would it be rekindled, at the London Town and Country Club on 1st September 1992. Cave's now-long-running Bad Seeds were performing one of their own shows when Cave announced, 'I'd like to give you a history lesson.' With Rowland Howard and Mick Harvey representing the Birthday Party and former Triffids bassist Martin Casey standing in for the now-deceased Tracy Pew, the ghost of a decade previous arose to stamp across 'Wild World', 'Dead Joe' and 'Nick The Stripper'. Then it was laid to rest once more, unlikely ever to walk again.

Why should it? Discussing his repertoire and reputation in 2001, asked how he responded to fans who recoiled from the ponderous intonations of his most recent solo albums (*The Boatman's Call* and *No More Shall We Part*) and mourned the death of his old piss and vinegar, Cave was unequivocal in his outrage.

'There's always the odd fan who sits and bemoans the glory days of the Birthday Party, who sits in the corner hugging his copy of *Junkyard* and wishing it could all be like that again. But I refuse to be bullied by what I see as their kind of conservative and basically reactionary attitude towards music. I just want to take it where it wants to go and I'm very grateful that a large part of our audience is happy to come along.'

He made, he insisted, grown-up music for grown-up listeners and was adamant that the Nick Cave of the 21st century, sonorously crooning to an audience spellbound by the sunken depths he revealed of his soul, is a far cry from the freakish, fiery, frenzied fuck-up that once stalked the streets of old London town, Nick the Stripper by name and nature, tearing down the walls of even the reactionary Punkers and rebuilding them with rubble gleaned from back street alleyways, bombsites and abattoirs. The question he refused to answer was: 'Which will ultimately make the most difference?' Or, perhaps, he didn't need to. Those odd fans hugging his furthest back catalogue have already answered it for him.

The near-simultaneous deaths of four of the genre's figureheads could have sounded the death knell for Gothic Rock. Nurtured by the Batcave, however, and in the safe hands of Specimen, Sex Gang, Sex Fiend and so many, many more, the movement scarcely even noticed. For many listeners, after all, the dearly departed represented little more than the musical extremes to which Goth was prone if left to ferment without supervision. Close in on the movement's heart, however, and the territory was considerably more landscaped – if no less disparate.

Spring 1983 saw Sex Gang Children's debut album, *Song And Legend*, top the Independent chart for a fortnight, before spinning off two hit singles, the title track and the tumescent, eerily fiddle-fired, 'Sebastiane'.

Gene Loves Jezebel, after a year of internal turbulence and constantly shifting line-ups, had finally succeeded in following the brilliance of 'Shaving My Neck', unveiling April 1983's yowling 'Screaming For Emmeline' (followed, in June, by 'Bruises'), then embarking on a UK tour with X-Mal Deutschland that confirmed the magnificence of their imminent debut album, *Promise*.

New Gothic-style bands were forming everywhere across the UK (and abroad, for that matter), some of them hopeless ingénues, attracted to the stage by Goth's stylism alone, others comparative veterans, fleeing other acts to pursue their own private visions.

From the churning nativity of Gene Loves Jezebel alone, guitarist Albio DeLuca linked with Abbo of the recently disbanded UK Decay in a hopeful new band, Furyo. Bassist Julianne Regan, a journalist for *Zig Zag* who joined the Jezebels after interviewing them, formed All About Eve; drummer Dick Hawkins joined the Bingley, Yorkshire, based Skeletal Family, their local presence simply reiterating Leeds' reputation as the Gothic capital of the north. There, they joined a scene ruled by the Sisters of Mercy but now bubbling with a host of other bands, too.

The March Violets, overlooked virtually everywhere else, were superstars in West Yorkshire. Since their primitive, drum-machine-fired sound was caught on their debut Merciful Release 45 in summer 1982, the March Violets had cut one further single for Eldritch's operation, November's 'Grooving In Green', before bad blood between vocalist Simon Denbigh and Eldritch himself prompted the band to depart for their own Rebirth set-up.

May 1983's 'Crow Baby', the final release by the original Violets' line-up of vocalists Denbigh and Rosie Garland, bassist Loz Elliott and guitarist Hugh, proved their biggest hit yet, soaring to #6 on the Independent chart and ensuring, at least for a few months, that the March Violets were being talked of as very serious contenders.

Great things, too, were predicted for another offspring of the Leeds axis, Red Lorry Yellow Lorry, a startling hybrid of post-Punk neuroses and grinding doominess formed in 1982 by vocalist Chris Read and drummer Mick Brown, and completed, by the time of their first single, by bassist Paul Southern and guitarist Dave Wolfenden, like Craig Adams, a former member of the Expelaires.

Three singles during 1982-83 and a pair of stunning Peel sessions constantly pushed Red Lorry Yellow Lorry forward, until the only surprise was not that they were so effortlessly peeling off so many classic singles, but that it actually took them until 1984 to release their greatest, the anthemic 'Hollow Hills'. Like the March Violets, Red Lorry Yellow Lorry would ultimately founder. But, again, in the music press of the day, the future seemed to be theirs for the taking.

The Sisters Of Mercy's momentum, meanwhile, was continuing to build. 1983 opened with a smattering of shows around northern England, where the band's grassroots support was it its strongest, then blossomed ever outwards following another BBC session for David Jensen in March, and a second Single of the Week honour, from *Sounds* for 'Anaconda.'

John Ashton resurfaced to finance the band's next release, a 12-inch EP for the American Braineater label, lighting the slow fuse on the Sisters' eventual American profile; in its wake, the band was finally able to piece together their first full British tour, criss-crossing the country throughout the spring, en route for their first major London headliner, at the Lyceum in London – a show that Eldritch quickly proclaimed the best the band had ever played.

Another new single, the *Reptile House* EP, brought the band their third successive Single Of The Week award, this time from the *New Musical Express*; hindsight, however, insists that the record deserved (and continues to deserve) even greater recognition. Hitherto, the media's growing insistence on a Gothic Rock movement had been hampered by its inability to settle on a specific Gothic sound. *The Reptile House* did the job for them, from the deliciously slow-building three-and-one-half minute instrumental passage that resolves itself into the grinding 'Kiss The Carpet' to the mephitic intensity of 'Lights', 'Fix', and 'Valentine', and onto 'Burn', a piece salvaged from total desolation only by the ethereal backing vocals.

All that Gothic Rock would ever become is captured on this one EP; all that a hundred, a thousand, bands have tried to recapture in their own variations was blueprinted across those five (six, if you count the reprise of 'Kiss The Carpet') songs. It is to the Sisters' enduring credit that they would not be counted among that number.

As the Sisters drove towards the future, Specimen continued subverting the present, subsuming some of London's most hallowed – literally – venues beneath a sea of rampant black. Joined now by synthesiser player Johnny 'Slut' Melton, a Batcave regular who rapidly transformed into what Klein affectionately dubbed 'the evil face of Specimen' (and layered the whisperingly foreboding 'Hex' with its synth-invocations of a seriously sinister Ultravox), the band played major shows at Heaven and, opening for rockabilly heroes The Meteors, the Lyceum, before taking over St Paul's Church in Hammersmith for what the handbills christened *Blasphemy, Lechery and Blood – Burning Martyrs Night*. Needless to say, the show lived up to that billing with fiery passion.

From there, the circus travelled to the USA for a two-night residency in the basement of New York's Danceteria, before spreading the madness further with gigs at CBGBs and Philadelphia's Eastside Club. Then, returning home, Specimen finally signed the major label deal they had been threatening for so long, linking with London and unveiling their debut single, the stirringly guitar-riffing 'The Beauty of Poisin' – cut, incredibly, with members of the London Philharmonic Orchestra.

Plans were also advanced for a full-length Batcave album, a collection to be headlined by Specimen and Alien Sex Fiend but also serving up a vivid snapshot of all the tastes that the Batcave catered for.

Sex Beat and Meat Of Youth (another brief flicker ignited by Abbo) joined the headliners in conforming to an approximation of the Gothic archetype. Other inclusions, however, purposefully shattered the mould.

Test Department was clattering atonality, a chanting shipyard of metallic clangs and brutal bangs; Patti Paladin offered up a weird Bowery approximation of early Lene Lovich; reformed Punker Jimmy Pursey spat poetry over a blistered drum track; Brilliant served up a scabrous funk fully informed by Public Image Ltd and old Killing Joke; and Marc Almond's Venomettes backing band wrapped things up with a keening chamber instrumental, all frightened violin and tentative tapping.

So, *Young Limbs And Numb Hymns* did not emerge the Batcave Be-all and End-all that the Gothic imagery led outsiders to expect, but of course it wasn't intended to. 'Look past the slow black rain of a chill night in Soho,' advised the liner notes. 'Ignore the lures of a thousand neon fireflies. Fall deaf to the sighs of the street corner sirens. Come walk with me between heaven and hell. Here there is a club lost in its own feverish limbo. For some, the Batcave has become an icon but, for those in the know, it is an iconoclast. It is the avenging spirit of nightlife's badlands, its shadow looms large over London's demi-monde. It is a challenge to the false idol. It will endure.'

Young Limbs was not the only long-playing celebration of the movement to be released that year, as Dave Roberts, guitarist with Sex Gang Children, set about organising his own collection of the weirdest sights and sounds, the album *The Whip*.

Featuring the Sex Gang's own 'Oh Funny Man' and, reconfirming the movement's mainstream possibilities, a duet between Andi and Soft Cell's Marc Almond on the caterwauling compulsion of 'Hungry Years', *The Whip* started life, insisted Roberts, as 'just some stupid idea I had in a club one night.'

But it touched a pulse regardless, drawing in contributions from as far afield as Play Dead and Brilliant (again), plus a pair of Damned spin-offs, the first and only solo performance by Dave Vanian, 'Tenterhooks', and the entire band's Naz Nomad & The Nightmares garage-psych alter-ego. A more conventional collection than *Young Limbs*, and certainly a lot less bewildering, *The Whip* went Top 3 on the Indy chart in May 1983 and even spun off a hit (the title track) for Carcrash International, a side project that Roberts, together with Crisis' Lester Jones had been nursing since 1981.

The Batcave was in the shops. Now it needed to get out on the road. In June 1983, Specimen and Alien Sex Fiend set off on tour with all the accoutrements of the Batcave affixed to their entourage. Night after night, clubs across the UK would be descended upon, darkened and decorated, and then unveiled as a taste of the grave that everyone was raving about, a sensational outing that, even the wearily seen-it-all organisers had to admit, brought some of the most dazzling Goths they'd ever seen out of the closet.

No more the wasted children of a bad Dave Vanian; no longer the idiot offspring of the Addams and the Munsters. Goth in 1983 was a wild celebration of imagination and magic, beauty and elegance, and few of the people who came in contact with it were ever left completely unmoved by the experience.

Sex Fiend remained on the tour for just a handful of dates, pulling out in preparation for the release of their debut single, 'Ignore The Machine'. They were replaced by Flesh For Lulu, a band sliced from influences that ranged from the Rolling Stones to the New York Dolls, then threw in the Stooges to ensure some variety.

The original Flesh For Lulu emerged in late 1981. A line-up, led by guitarist Nick Marsh and completed by bassist Philip Ames, former Tom Robinson Band keyboard player Mark Ambler and drummer James Mitchell, gigged around London throughout the next year and cut a tentative John Peel session in September 1982. But the group was not to make a true impression until Marsh shattered the line-up and linked with former Wasted Youth guitarist Rocco at the end of the year.

Rocco and Marsh met towards the end of Wasted Youth's lifespan. They began working together the moment it was over: Wasted Youth played their final show at the Venue on 6th December 1982; the new incarnation of Flesh For Lulu, featuring bassist Glen Bishop and drummer James Mitchell, was up-and-running by late January.

The band's insertion into the Gothic scene was not, according to Rocco, altogether calculated. 'We got roped into the scene just because of the way we looked. I think we kinda fell into a trap there. We found this image we liked, and we did it. I mean, Johnny Cash wears black all the time as well – and we did a country song on our first album.

'For me, the Gothic thing started with bands like Bauhaus, the Banshees, a general tribe of people walking around in black clothes and black spiky hair. For me, it was like listening to a Nico record, that atmosphere. We were always very unhappy with the idea of being labelled like that because we didn't want to limit ourselves to one particular audience. The Banshees, the Sisters, Bauhaus… compared to them, we were a straight-ahead rock'n'roll band.'

Indeed they were, but image was everything and theirs – towering quills of blackened, gelled hair, corpse-white make-up, dead black leather – was loaded with implications. Even Rocco's past could not detract from the force of their faces.

Not that the band went out of its way to dispel any lingering misapprehensions. The Batcave venture was followed by gigs with the Sisters Of Mercy – an association, of course, that tarred them with a very blackened brush. By late 1983, Flesh For Lulu had signed with Polydor, as that imprint joined the major label race for Gothic Rock.

Flesh for Lulu's debut EP, *Roman Candle*, was a powerful, confident debut and, for all the band's protestations, had no hesitation about leaping into Gothic waters. However, the masterful 'Subterraneans' single and an eponymous album in the new year did evidence the band's desire to broaden their horizons somewhat – even *Melody Maker* approvingly remarked that 'their days as a grim joke at the butt-end of Goth are behind them. In this mood, they could take on the world.'

And so it would eventually prove, although Polydor was unconvinced. Dropped after one final single, 'Restless', failed to twitch a limb, the Lulus lurched into a wilderness that yawned deep into the next year. By the time they resurfaced, with 1984's *Blue Sisters Swing* EP on the Hybrid Indy, the highlight of their recent career had been the departure of bassist Bishop, to be replaced by Kevin Mills, former bassist with the Lulus' own former mentors, Specimen, but long since convinced that the band was never going to get out of the traps.

A second Specimen single, a new version of the Video Single 'Returning From A Journey', had passed unnoticed. The inescapable conclusion was that London

Records simply didn't have a clue what to do with the group. Labelmates Bananarama and Blancmange were both scoring hits with effortless élan – Specimen, it seemed, simply required too much work to push them over the final hurdles to similar mass acclaim.

Further recordings lay unreleased, while hopes of igniting an American career petered out after just two releases on a seriously confused Sire label, the best-of-so-far *Batastrophe* EP and a single of 'Kiss Kiss Bang Bang' whose own sleeve notes allied the group with Hanoi Rocks and KISS. By the time Mills bade his farewells, both Sire and London had apparently forgotten that Specimen even existed. By the time Johnathon Trevithick departed, to be replaced by Chris Bell, the Batcave was simply the place where Batman lived. Though the fans who loved them continued to love them and Specimen remained a live draw both at home and abroad, they had no alternative but to lapse into recorded silence – ironically, at around precisely the same time as Sex Gang Children, too, discovered that record companies and contracts are not, necessarily, the answer to an artiste's prayers.

The band's contract with Illuminated expired in June 1983, at a time when, for all the media brickbats hurled at them, any number of major record labels were actively in pursuit. Buoyed by swaggering confidence, the band turned them all down, convinced that something better was just around the corner. Sadly, it wasn't.

Roberts explained, 'The major labels wanted us to take the word "Children" out of the name. We were like, "fuck that".' Unfortunately, though it might feel good having such high-flung principles in the face of courting corporate business, it doesn't often get you anywhere. Labels just want to sign new bands and, if one won't play ball, there's plenty more that will – particularly when the long line of suitors did, in fact, have very good reason for wanting to soften the Sex Gang Children's name.

For the past 18 months, the south coast of England had been terrorised by the so-called Brighton Rapist, a paedophiliac predator whose activities finally prompted *The Sun* to unveil a headline that, if one is utterly dispassionate about such things, was tailor-made for such sensationalism. It screamed SEX GANG CHILDREN. Even in the face of this adversity, however, the band would not be swayed. 'We were so hard-headed,' Roberts mourned.

Matters were made worse by relations with their former label. Illuminated had been desperate for Sex Gang Children to renew their contract, even if only on a disc-by-disc basis. They refused and, according to Roberts, the label avenged itself by not passing on the news that Island Records had made a massive and, apparently, unqualified offer for their signature. 'And that's how it began to fall apart.'

Rob Stroud was first to depart, simply not turning up to a show. (He later resurfaced in the Colne, Lancashire-based band Aemotii Crii.) The band initially replaced him with Steve Harle before turning to former Theatre Of Hate drummer Nigel Preston and, in September 1983, a one-off deal with the independent Clay label brought a new single, 'Mauritia Mayer'. Added to the stockpile of material cut since the first album – an impressive bundle that included fresh sessions with Tony James, the heart-thumping 'Ecstasy And Vendetta' and the yowlingly Antish 'Draconian Dream' – it boded well for a second Sex Gang album. Barely had this line-up settled down, however, than Preston received a call from Billy Duffy.

Since meeting Ian Astbury during the Theatre of Hate/Southern Death Cult tour, Duffy and the singer had become firm friends, all the more so following Southern Death Cult's demise. Astbury's musical dreams had turned towards a more rock-oriented direction than the tribal-based Southern Death Cult could ever have permitted, notions that he and Duffy thrashed out at the Brixton commune which had become an after-hours focal point for so many of the so-called Goth bands. According to legend, Astbury finally announced that he wanted to form a band with Billy on the same day as he arrived on the guitarist's doorstep with a bag of clothes.

The pair agreed immediately that the new band should at least try to capitalise on Southern Death Cult's high profile – they dubbed it Death Cult and set about recruiting a rhythm section.

Stan Stammers, Duffy's bass playing cohort in Theatre of Hate, was their first choice. When he declined the offer, Wasted Youth's Darren Murphy was approached. He, however, proved unsuitable and finally, Death Cult was completed by drummer Ray Taylor-Smith and guitarist-turned-bassist Jamie Stewart, both on the run from low-grade Goth rockers Ritual.

The press was onto the new band within weeks. Retaining Southern Death Cult's contract with Situation 2, upgraded to parent label Beggars Banquet, Death Cult had barely finalized its line-up before the group was featured on the cover of the *NME*. Beggars Banquet responded by rush–releasing the band's debut recordings as the four track *Death Cult* EP and, the following week, Death Cult made their live debut in Oslo, Norway.

A handful of shows around Europe, some low-key gigs in Scotland and a couple of continental festivals followed: Death Cult were not to make their official U.K. debut until autumn, when a short tour opened in Swansea and closed, a fortnight later on 18th September 1983, at the fifth and final Futurama Festival. They shared the billing, incidentally, with the Bay City Rollers.

On paper, Death Cult seemed set to pick up precisely where their predecessor left off, but the internal dynamic was still not right. Three days after Futurama, Taylor-Smith quit the group. Nigel Preston, with whom Duffy had worked so well in their own last band, was the natural choice for successor. With an odd and ultimately misplaced symmetry, Taylor then joined the Sex Gang Children – only to be forced out just months later when, returning to London from their first American tour, the band discovered that the Sierra Leone-born drummer was in the UK illegally. He was deported home, at which point Roberts, too, quit the band.

Andi and MacLeay kept the Sex Gang Children alive for a few months more, returning to Illuminated to release a new single, 'Draconian Dream', cut with producer Simon Boswell (ex-power pop hopefuls Advertising) and a new rhythm section of Cam Campbell and Kevin Matthews. Boswell also remixed 'Dieche', the b-side of the old 'Into The Abyss' single – this became the a-side and, in July 1984, Sex Gang Children scored their final independent hit. The band broke up weeks later.

Back in the autumn of 1983, unaware of the pending carnage, Death Cult marched on. October brought their second single, 'God's Zoo', together with their first and only BBC session, for David Jensen, and another British tour. A triumphant six months were rounded off in December when Death Cult were booked to make their national TV debut, on Channel 4's *The Tube*.

It was clearly an important event. Astbury and Duffy alone appreciated just how important. Over Christmas, both had travelled to the Americas – Astbury to visit his father in Canada, Duffy to holiday in New York. They returned home convinced that whatever happened in Britain, their own future lay in the United States – or, more specifically, in breaking big in the United States.

'And we were never going to do that with a name like Death Cult,' Astbury admitted. 'It was too Gothic, too gloomy. It wouldn't mean anything over there. Plus, it tied us in with too many bands that were on their way out, the whole Positive Punk thing. We wanted a name that was on its way in.'

Just two weeks into 1984, he made his intentions clear on nationwide television. The band was introduced as the Cult – nothing more, nothing less. The amplifiers were turned up full blast and Astbury, ever-mindful of the massive leap in musical credulity that he was now preparing to make, danced on stage with half his face painted, half his outfit flowing, and half his audience staring in disbelief. Goodbye, old, painted Ian – hello, new natural-born hard rocker.

The Sisters Of Mercy, meanwhile, had already paid their first visits to the United States, a few weeks apart in September (New York) and October (Los Angeles and San Francisco) 1983. They then returned home for the release of their next single and most adventurous record yet. Dispensing with the sound that culminated on *The Reptile House*, Eldritch completely reversed the Sisters' nose-dive into precocity with 'Temple Of Love', a driving number that was guaranteed to drive a serious wedge through the band's hitherto loyal support.

Crystal clear guitar, a twistingly haunting vocal and a triumphant, yelping chorus ensured 'Temple Of Love' emerged genuinely catchy and easily enjoyable, the sound of the group making a concerted leap out of the shadowy cultdom that had hitherto embraced them.

It was *too* concerted for Ben Gunn. Accusing his bandmates of 'taking things too seriously' and of 'selling out,' he quit the band for a return to school, enrolling at Liverpool University and only tentatively toying with any future musical projects, with a short-lived new band, Torch.

It was not difficult to respect his disdain but, a multitude of reservations notwithstanding, 'Temple Of Love' did everything Eldritch expected it to, a hurricane blast that blew straight into the upper echelons of underground success, with only the seeming eternity of New Order's 'Blue Monday' holding it back from the top of the Indy chart. In fact, had the Sisters been in a fit state to tour, it might even have accomplished the seemingly impossible and displaced the joyless division altogether. Instead, they were locked in the rehearsal rooms, frantically searching (but refusing to be rushed) for a new guitarist.

The Sisters of Mercy weren't the only band to be staging quite unexpected auditions that autumn. Although Robert Smith remained a member of Siouxsie and the Banshees throughout 1983 and into the following year, both he and Lol Tolhurst found it harder to let go of the Cure than they had ever imagined.

The first hint that things were going to be difficult arrived in October 1982, just four months after the band broke up, at a time when Smith himself was fervently denying that the Cure even existed any longer. That month, Fiction label head Chris Parry convened a band meeting to try and talk some sense into the pair. They arrived at his office unwilling and unco-operative; they departed having indeed agreed to revive the band name. Parry was forced to make one concession. Smith was determined that, whatever they did would destroy the myth of the Cure forever. To prove he was serious, the reluctant star delivered up the group's next single, 'Let's Go To Bed'.

A lightweight pop-tainted love song, it was indeed the absolute antithesis of everything the Cure had ever done before – so much so that, on the eve of release, Smith himself was having reservations about releasing it under the band's name. 'I never sit down and think, "I'll write a song",' he reflected years later, by way of explanation. 'I can't sit down in a calculating manner and say "I will write a song about..." I have done it, but the songs that come out are like "Let's Go To Bed", very flat. They're good on a certain level, but they don't resonate.'

But that was the point. Smith wanted to shatter the Cure's dreary image and the playful 'Let's Go To Bed', with its catchy chorus and doo-doo-doo backing vocals, could not have been further removed from that. Yet, in distancing itself from all that the band's audience once held Holier-than-Holy, it not only reinvented the Cure, it reinvigorated them, knocking them off the gloom-enshrouded pedestal upon which they had recently moped and allowing them a luxury which so few artists are ever granted – the chance to start again with a clean slate, and continue doing so forever more.

By proving so irreverently that there really was no such thing as a 'typical' Cure record (a point that was only reinforced by two follow-up singles, 'The Walk' and 'The Love Cats', and the groundbreaking videos associated with all three), Smith had given the band an option which only David Bowie, with his own continual self-reinvention, had ever successfully exercised in the past. Keep moving, keep changing and keep confusing people. As long as people cared enough to keep moving and changing with them, the group could get away with murder, stylistically if not literally.

Piecing together an *ad hoc* Cure line-up for promotional purposes, Smith and Tolhurst grasped the opportunity greedily. Summing up the three singles as a 'fantasy trilogy', they now promised a return to the abyss, with Smith warning, 'if *Pornography* took you to the edge of the cliff, the next one will plunge you over it.'

Of course it wouldn't; indeed, it couldn't. The Cure in 1983 was a completely different animal to the Cure of twelve months previous. It featured new members, Smith had new ideas and the band itself had a new commercial standing. While 'Let's Go To Bed' sputtered out at #44, 'The Walk' only narrowly missed the British Top 10, and 'Love Cats' soared to #7. *Japanese Whispers*, an eight-song mini-album that corralled all three singles and their b-sides, became one of the top stocking-stuffers of the forthcoming festive season. And it was all so wonderfully, wonderfully, wonderfully pretty.

Not all the abdicating warlords were so bent upon reinvention, however. Year's end also brought fruition to a project that had been germinating in the Batcave since the beginning of 1983. Relocated New Yorker Lydia Lunch was a seemingly permanent fixture on the Batcave scene, 'small, red-lipped and voluptuous in bosom-baring black lace,' as Marc Almond remembered her. 'The kind of woman who both fascinated and terrified me.'

Almond was introduced to Lunch at the Batcave. 'Little did I know it, but Lydia had plans for me. In fact she had the next nine months of my life planned out, whether I liked it or not.' She was planning a cabaret performance for New York's Danceteria on Halloween, around a line-up that made even a good night at the Batcave look like an episode of *Pop Idol*.

Fresh from the three-month old wreckage of the Birthday Party, Nick Cave would be making his first ever public appearance as a solo artist. Jim Thirlwell was the mastermind behind the cacophony of Foetus. Almond himself, taking time out from the looming disintegration of Soft Cell, was intent on demonstrating that recent collaborations with Psychic TV and Andi Sex Gang were as much a barometer of his tastes and abilities as the pop-tinged confections that his own band had brought to bear. Lunch herself was a spectacle that nobody could predict with any kind of certainty. Put the four together for three nights only, in New York and Washington DC, and the Immaculate Consumptives promised an event of extremities that even the participants were stretched to envisage.

The quartet were no strangers to one another. Lunch and Cave first met in New York on the Birthday Party's first American tour, forging a friendship that consummated on the joint Lunch/Party EP *Drunk On The Pope's Blood*. Foetus and Cave had been friends since their days in Australia, Almond and Foetus had been collaborating for a year or so, ever since they appeared on *The Tube* together, frightening the life out of teatime television with a version of Suicide's 'Ghostrider'. Foetus was also among the cast of madmen making mayhem with Marc & The Mambas.

Planning for the event lasted through the summer, Cave and Almond dutifully hauling themselves either to Lunch's flat in Baron's Court or Thirlwell's Brixton high-rise to plot the course of the event. Lunch's original plan to be orally raped by an oil-stained, crowbar wielding Cave had finally been passed over in favour of a more musical affair, but it would still be an unconventional event.

The show was divided into four inter-connected solo performances, held together by a backing tape recorded in a week by the musicians Cave and Almond had been working with recently: Blixa Bargeld, Barry Adamson and Mick Harvey from Cave's still formative Bad Seeds, Annie Hogan from Marc & the Mambas.

Almond continues, 'Each of us did duets with one other' – Almond and Lunch performed her 'Misery Loves Comfort' – before, as Almond recalled, 'Nick came on and stole the entire show.' Cave's set comprised just two songs, his brooding signature cover of Elvis Presley's 'In The Ghetto', and his own 'A Box For Black Paul', a lengthy piano dirge lamenting the demise of the Birthday Party.

At least, that was his intention. In fact, 'Black Paul' received only one full airing, on the final night of the Consumptives' existence. The first night at Danceteria, Foetus broke the piano, kicking the hapless instrument to death during his set, forcing Cave to abandon 'Black Paul' and play the Presley song only.

The second night, Foetus behaved and the piano survived, only for Cave himself to lose interest halfway through the song, suddenly informing the audience, 'then it goes on like that for another five minutes.' 'I was really pissed off about it,' Foetus remarked later. 'It really broke the atmosphere. But it was a lot of fun.'

The solo pieces at an end, the show wrapped up with all four musicians on stage, thrashing through a raw version of an Almond/Foetus original, 'Body Unknown'. The authors, respectively, sang and drummed, Cave screamed and Lunch strangled her guitar. It was a devastating performance, but would never be repeated. The Immaculate Consumptives parted company at the conclusion of the third show.

Cave: 'Lydia always had these grand ideas to do things, and she was always very much into roping other people in to do these things with her. I think the Immaculate Consumptives was one of her better ideas. But I don't know if I could be bothered getting something of that type together again, though. Lydia works in a kind of art-event area. To put a lot of effort into doing three shows that were never recorded, which is what this was about, I wouldn't be doing that.'

In fact, one of the shows was recorded – Almond himself has a bootleg video of it, although he's never watched it. 'I've always liked the memory. If I watched it, I'd probably think, "Oh God!"' It's an emotion Cave readily agreed with. 'It was better to be left in that mythological state, without anyone actually hearing what it was like.'

Indeed, the legend that has built up around the show, all four participants acknowledge, now far outweighs the event itself in terms of significance and historical resonance alike. Even at the time, though, for anybody who cared for such details, the Immaculate Consumptives proved that, beneath the rapid commercialisation of the 'Gothic' movement and its attendant slide into archetypal rock'n'role-playing, its fringes remained as creatively crazed as ever.

The Sisters of Mercy's Andrew Eldritch and Wayne Hussey

Chapter Ten
I'd Have Killed
Myself If It Wasn't
For The Alarm

Wherein homeland hatred translates to Trans-Atlantic joy, and an entire generation decamps for the Yankee dollar. Some of them get it, and never darken our doorstep again. Others just slink quietly home.

" [The Cult's] Love *itself sold over 200,000 copies in Britain, effortlessly spawning two further hit singles ('Rain', #17 in October 1985, and a remixed 'Revolution', #30 in December). It was its Stateside performance that mattered most, however. Love reached #87 in America, and neither the Cult nor their US label Sire Records were in any doubt that, with a more concentrated profile, the Cult could easily do even better next time. The band simply decided that 'next time' would be 'now.'"*

The newborn and freshly abbreviated Cult released their first single in May 1984. 'Spiritwalker' was not so great a departure from all that Astbury, at least, had accomplished in the past. Neither was the accompanying album, *Dreamtime*; it would be another year, and two more singles, before the Cult were truly ready to completely step into the promised land of hard riffs and bombast.

But still the Cult's intentions were laid bare. 'The word is out!' celebrated *Melody Maker*'s review of their late November 1984 Lyceum show. 'This time next year, the Cult should be enormous. The anthemic pace at which they take the slower numbers, the indiscriminate use of dry ice, the way Billy Duffy makes even tuning up sound important, all the ingredients are there. This time next year…'

Astbury read those words and agreed with every one of them. The only question in his mind was, would *Melody Maker* and the rest of the UK music press be a part of the equation? Britain, after all, is just a tiny island – there was a whole world beyond its shores and that, increasingly, was where his intentions lay. Just as one swallow does not make a summer, one good review does not make a career. Particularly when every other word written about the Cult seemed to be more damning than the last.

Billy Duffy once admitted that, if it wasn't for the Alarm, he'd have committed suicide: 'they were the only band getting worse press than us.' Astbury agreed. 'We got the most incredible slandering from the British press. I think it was because – a lot of things I said in interviews, the way I carried myself on stage and stuff, it was slightly loaded, so people took it as being a bit aloof and arrogant.

'They weren't able to accept the fact that, by the time I was 19 or 20 years old, I'd already lived the life of maybe a 60-year-old man. But when I was 19 or 20, I didn't want to talk about those things. The energy of my performance was a direct reaction against the way I'd been brought up. When I was that age, it was such recent history that it didn't appear to me to be traumatic or strange or anything, it was just the way my life was.

'Had I discussed all that stuff then, people might have lightened up on me because they'd have known that a lot of what I was saying and doing wasn't entirely contrived, it was really coming from a place of deep sincerity and a lot of experience. I guess the experiences that I was talking about outweighed the child's faith.'

The scorn, even hatred, with which many people regarded the Cult was palpable. Other bands could strut and show off and the critics would accept it as stagecraft. With Astbury, the feeling seemed to be that 'this is what he's really like – the prat'. And as the Cult's star rose higher, of course, that impression only grew stronger.

Astbury continued, 'We had our fair share of shit. By the time we were ready to start the *Love* album, I think I'd taken so much shit that it really began to weigh me down, and it really began to hurt a lot. I so desperately wanted to be accepted in Britain and was constantly ridiculed, criticized, put-down.'

Of course, the sheer weight of this negativity could only enhance the Cult's American resolutions and, as they commenced work on what would become their second album, *Love*, with its wide-screen guitars, pounding production and barked, barking choruses, they knew they held the key that would start to unlock the treasure chamber.

For the Sisters Of Mercy, on the other hand, America was simply another country in which to gain a foothold, an ambition they accomplished with the same sense of self-absorbed disinterest that they displayed in every other arena.

To this day, many Sisters' fans believe that Wayne Hussey was a strange choice for Gunn's replacement – brilliant, of course, but strange nonetheless. Eldritch himself may not have known precisely what it was that attracted the pair to one another, although ambition certainly came into it. Before Hussey's arrival, and the occasional flash of mass appeal notwithstanding, the Sisters existed entirely within a world of closeted cultdom, a band whose appeal was certainly far-reaching but was nevertheless firmly confined to Steve Severin's 'bracket of Goth.' Hussey, though his eye for what cynics might call 'the main chance' had still to fully focus itself, was nevertheless firmly entrenched in the notions of commercial appeal and, while Eldritch's contributions to the Sisters would not, for the most part, change too much, his willingness to permit Hussey full rein within the band's musical department certainly represented more than a casual lightening-up of the group's hitherto stygian visage.

Similarly, Hussey dragged the group into a spotlight where visual imagery was as crucial to the overall picture as its sonic counterpart. Never shying away from the black clothing that, of course, all good Gothic bands had in abundance, the earlier Sisters were a casually dressed bunch all the same. With Hussey evidently prompting as much attention to the wardrobe as to the music, an entire new look built around the band, a sepulchral spaghetti western feel that established a prototype from which neither Hussey nor Eldritch would ever truly escape.

That these visuals, whether in their purest, Sister-driven, form, or in the increasingly diluted state that they would be snatched up by other performers, were wholly superficial should not matter – the appearance of a successful band is, after all, as much a reflection of the times in which it thrives as any other aspect; no matter how loudly (or otherwise) a band decries the demands of the showbusiness machine, even the most naturalistic image is a product of marketing, subconscious or otherwise. The Sisters of Mercy, like the bands that preceded them in their little corner of the world, and those that followed, donned their distinctive garb not because it reflected their personalities, but because it reflected what they felt their audience should *perceive* as their personalities. And, again, while Eldritch, at least, already comprehended that truth, it took Hussey's arrival, and the subsequent remodelling of the entire group, to truly turn the theory into reality.

Born and bred in Bristol, where he was raised a devout Mormon, Hussey was 18 before he abandoned his parents' dreams of a future as a missionary, and relocated to Liverpool in 1976. There, he was to take his own place within the constantly evolving ferment of bands flowering there in the immediate post-Punk afterglow.

His first, Foxglove and the Ded Byrds, evolved into the Walkie Talkies in time for a solitary single, 1978's 'Rich and Nasty'. Hussey followed up with stints with Hambi And The Dance and David Knopov, and even tried a brief stab at solo recognition, when he contributed the foreboding promise of 'Trip To The Dentist' to the *And the Dance Goes On* compilation album.

Relocating briefly to Newcastle, he hooked up with former Penetration singer Pauline Murray's Invisible Girls, alongside former Buzzcocks drummer John Maher and Joy Division producer Martin Hannett. An eponymous album and the *Searching for Heaven* EP followed before Murray pulled the plug in 1981. Hussey returned to Liverpool to join Pete Burns' then-rising Dead Or Alive.

As a founder member of the now-mythic Mystery Girls with Pete Wylie and Julian Cope, Scouse androgyny Pete Burns was a familiar figure on the Liverpool Punk scene long before he happened upon a stolen keyboard 'and thought [I'd] better do something with it.' That 'something' was the proto-Gothic disco band Nightmares In Wax, a project unwrapped with the stated intention of becoming 'the worst group in history', but rapidly to develop into one of the most menacing.

Nightmares In Wax issued one just one record, the utterly tumultuous and grippingly subversive *Birth Of A Nation* EP. It led off with 'Black Leather', a hectic blend of Iggy Pop's 'Sister Midnight' and KC & The Sunshine Band's 'That's The Way (I Like It)', churningly revised into a homo-erotic paean to greasy motorcycle riders. Considerably toned down, 'Black Leather' would become the blueprint for much of what Burns would achieve over the next five years.

Retaining Marty Healey and Mitch from the ever-changing Nightmares' line-up, Burns formed Dead or Alive in April 1981, ten minutes before the band were due to appear on a radio program. The Ian Broudie-produced 'I'm Falling' and the swirling 'Number Eleven' singles followed for the local Inevitable label, before Burns formed his own Black Eyes concern for two further slabs of eminently danceable darkness, 'The Stranger' and the EP *It's Been Hours Now*.

With Hussey and bassist Mike Percy replacing Mitch and Sue James, the band's constant presence on the Independent chart saw Dead Or Alive begin attracting major label interest. They headlined the Futurama festival in late 1982, then signed with Epic in December.

With the hitherto dense sound gradually opening to embrace a dancier, club-friendly vibe, playing down the original Doors-ish keyboards in favour of party-pounding BPM percussion, the epic 'Misty Circles' – up there alongside 'Black Leather' as Burns' greatest ever achievement – opened 1983 to enthusiastic reviews. No matter that Burns had now been married (to Lynne) for three years, the media excitedly began linking his flamboyant image with the burgeoning gender-bender revolution forged by Boy George. Burns invariably responded with devastating wit, establishing himself as one of the most quotable men of the era and ensuring Dead or Alive would never be short of press.

Sales, too, were rising. Over the next year, Dead Or Alive released two further singles, 'What I Want' and 'I'd Do Anything', at the same time completing their debut album, *Sophisticated Boom Boom*. It was with untold self-assurance, then, that Hussey was able to walk away from the band on the eve of the album's release, immediately after shooting the video for their next single, a full-fledged revival of 'That's The Way (I Like It)' – and a full-fledged hit as well.

He had, he later admitted, finally tired of his bandmates' reluctance to take their show out on the road – during Hussey's two-year stint with Dead or Alive, they'd performed live no more than six times. He would never be so idle again.

Hussey spent a week fielding offers from other bands, including one from Holly Johnson as he formulated what would become Frankie Goes to Hollywood. Then came the call from Eldritch and, in September 1983, Hussey leaped.

Since that time, six months had elapsed without a squeak from the Sisters Of Mercy – six months that the fan base could not help but fill with increasingly speculative rumour and innuendo. They'd broken up, they'd changed direction and they'd all grown beards and renounced black clothing. By the time Eldritch finally broke silence to announce the new line-up's imminent unveiling, at Birmingham's Tin Can Club on 7th April 1984, the excitement in the air hung thicker than dry ice.

The fervour was well placed. True, Eldritch had grown a beard and a bushy beast it was! But a sheaf of new songs – 'Train', 'Walk Away', 'Body And Soul' and more – did more than complement the handful of oldies that were still in the set: they left them deathly-pale by comparison, as Hussey proudly reminded *Sounds* later in the year. The older songs, he said, 'were great, but never fully realised. I think my coming into the band has installed a high level of awareness of song arrangements and things like that. Embellishments and textures, rather than having one guitar line put through a fuzzbox.'

Whether this was precisely what Eldritch himself envisioned as the fate of the Sisters is, of course, a question that may never be answered. Certainly the vicious severance that ultimately closed this chapter of the band's development suggests that it wasn't, and more than one commentator has suggested that, in permitting this early flirtation with the commercial mainstream to reach the heights that it eventually reached, Eldritch was already working towards a preconceived masterplan – that is, drawing in the kiddies with a well-timed blast of well-tuned ditties, then turning around and hammering them with his real agenda. And woe betide anybody who tried to stand in his way.

The Birmingham gig was the Sisters' only UK show for the time being, before they headed to the US for a six-date mini-tour. Back in Britain in early May, however, they kicked into a full-blooded 16-show outing, climaxing at the London Lyceum around the same time as news broke of the next stage in the band's ascent, a major label deal with Elektra Records.

It was not the first label offer the band had received; it was, however, the first to allow them to retain the complete creative control that Eldritch deemed vital to the group's development. Music, merchandise, artwork, even label design (the Merciful Release logo, of course) were all his to decide, an arrangement that would, ultimately, lead to one of the most protracted stand-offs in record company history. It began happily enough, though, with the June 1984 release of the Sisters' latest single, 'Body And Soul'.

With major label sponsorship now behind them, the Sisters were no longer eligible for the Independent charts. They consoled themselves instead with breaching the nationals – 'Body And Soul' peaked at #46. 'Walk Away', a stop-gap issued after a bout of exhaustion kept Eldritch from completing the band's debut album in time for its scheduled autumn release, inched one notch higher in October.

The Sisters' *Black October* tour wound around Britain that same month, even incorporating a couple of shows in New York City (where Eldritch purchased his infamous black hat), before bleeding into a round of shows in Holland and Germany with Ian Astbury's Cult a crowd-pleasing choice for the opening act.

First And Last And Always, the Sisters' now long-overdue debut album, was finally released in March 1985, two days after the *Tune In, Turn On, Burn Out* tour kicked off at Glasgow University.

As the band's live shows had predicted, it was a powerful album, but one that was absolutely wrapped up within the verse-chorus-verse disciplines that, more than any other musical contribution, Hussey had firmly grafted onto the Sisters' sound. Indeed, there were moments when such adherances grew tiresome – the seemingl;y endless, and certainly mindless repetition bound up in such tracks as 'No Time To Cry' and 'Walk Away' really did not promise hours of entertaining repeat listens, while the constant reiteration of various sonic fingerprints (the oh-oh-oh backing vocals, for example), were similarly wearing. It was indeed telling that the album's most successful and, therefore, lasting numbers were those where Hussey's pop sensibilities were firmly eclipsed by Eldritch's interest in atmosphere – 'Marian' and 'Some Kind Of Stranger' aren't simply the best tracks on the album, they are also among the finest songs the Sisters of Mercy ever recorded.

Of course, such criticisms as the album deserved were of little import at the time – forgetting the sheer enthusiasm that the band's first long-player was inevitably to receive, there is no doubt that whatever Gothic Rock represented (or, more importantly, wanted to represent) in early 1985, it was both delivered and improved upon by *First And Last And Always* and, while neither album nor tour were especially well-received by the media, even the most spiteful responses were swiftly twisted to the Sisters' own wry advantage. When one critic dismissed the band as the drugged and drunken bastard sons of Led Zeppelin, the Sisters promptly added the behemoth's 'Kashmir' to their pre-show intro tape.

Of course, the press reaction was no reflection whatsoever of the audience response – every show was sold out, every one could have dragged them back for another set's-worth of encores. The band's delight at their reception, however, was tempered by the knowledge that Gary Marx would be departing immediately after the final UK date in Brighton, on 1st April. The ubiquitous 'personal differences' had claimed another casualty.

In the event, Marx made one further appearance with the Sisters of Mercy, a live appearance on BBC 2's *Old Grey Whistle Test* on 2nd April, performing 'Marian' and 'First And Last And Always' and choking the normally airless *Whistle Test* studio with the requisite dry ice.

Marx would eventually resurface at the helm of his own band, Ghost Dance. The Sisters, meanwhile, still had the scheduled European and American tour dates to fulfil. With only a week-long break, there was no time to seek out a replacement guitarist, and the band went out as a three-piece instead, pulling off the coup with such precision that several magazines accused them, erroneously, of using backing tapes.

There was a brutal beauty to the three-piece Sisters that past incarnations had only hinted at. Starkly lit and draped in fog, blatantly minimalist in an age when 'bigger' was generally regarded as 'better', there was little to look at but a great deal to watch: three figures choked in cloaking smoke, the now omnipresent hats and ponchos conjuring images that would not be out of place in a Peckinpah movie. And that was before the band kicked into either 'Phantom', with the ghosts of *The Good, The Bad And The Ugly* floating around its skeletal melody, or Dylan's 'Knocking On Heaven's Door', lifted straight from Peckinpah's own *Pat Garrett & Billy The Kid*. Other bands have toyed with the taut, tense expectation that was lay at the soul of the Sisters' experience. But none before had ever captured it with such chilling calculation.

Twenty-five dates were played throughout Europe during the three-and-a-half week *Trans-Europe Excess* tour; then, with just a ten-day break in between times, the Sisters were off to America for a tour that, opening in Long Beach, hit San Francisco, LA, Chicago and Detroit before wrapping up at the Ritz in New York City.

By now, however, fresh tensions were tearing at the band, as Eldritch on the one side, and Hussey and Adams on the other continued to fight the wars that Marx had already been sacrificed to. The conflict came down, of course, to the band's next move – the even broader assault on the hearts and minds of the mainstream that Hussey demanded, or the retrenchment into less populist but, building on the band's already established renown, hopefully equally popular, direction that Eldritch imagined.

Of course, the disparity of these two visions – compare, if you will, the two teams' own next releases – was such that there could never be equanimity; in the meantime, however, as they fought at least for compromise, the currents between the three would produce some of the group's most exceptional performances, as bootlegs of the trio's performances were to prove.

But the bitter clashes fed the rumour mill too. Nothing fought this viciously could maintain its equilibrium for long. When the Sisters christened their next scheduled concert, at the Royal Albert Hall on 18th June 1985, in ironic memory of the notorious Rolling Stones' festival of 16 years earlier, it was difficult not to regard it as a portent of some form. The gig was titled *Altamont – A Festival of Remembrance*.

In the event, the show turned out to be totally anti-climatic. Not only did it inexplicably fail to sell out, but the band didn't even seem to bother with an encore. The set ended, the lights came up, the equipment was turned off – even the cameras, filming the event under the auspices of director Mike Mansfield, had closed down. Most of the crowd was already spilling out onto the streets before the Sisters retook the stage, to finish off with a positively maniacal medley of 'Ghostrider' and 'Louie Louie.' And the rumours raged on.... What next?

The Sisters returned to America to shoot a video for 'Black Planet', an hysterical few minutes in which Eldritch delightedly pilots the Monkeemobile down the Ventura Freeway, while Hussey and Adams nap in the back. That accomplished, Adams returned to Leeds alone, while Eldritch and Hussey decamped for Hamburg to begin writing towards the next album. The fighting, meanwhile, never ceased.

The trio reunited in September 1984 to begin rehearsals for their next album, but the situation continued to deteriorate. Finally, Adams could stand no more and walked out. Hussey followed the next day.

Was it the end? No – just days later, on 21st September, Eldritch and Hussey reunited to join the Skeletal Family onstage in Hamburg. But the truce was temporary. A week after, a Merciful Release press statement made it official that the Sisters Of Mercy had split up. Amicably, of course.

As the Sisters collapsed, their erstwhile support band, the Cult, were effortlessly gathering speed. Reviewing one of the Cult's late-1984 live shows, *Melody* Maker confidently pinpointed 'the U2-ish "Hollow Man"' as a potential next single; thankfully, the Cult weren't listening. Instead, they delivered '(She Sells) Sanctuary', still the greatest record they have ever made because it is still the most potent distillation of everything that the Cult were – and could ever hope to become.

Built around descending guitars and one of Astbury's most breathlessly profound lyrics, plus a video that outdid the Sisters in the dry ice stakes, '(She Sells) Sanctuary' remains the Cult's most overt gesture yet to the basics of the Goth genre they were otherwise bent on mutating. Released in May 1985, it was the band's first placement in the UK Top 20 – and confirmed that there was a lot of record buyers who simply didn't give a damn what the music press told them.

It was a fraught time for the group, however. Nigel Preston was becoming increasingly unreliable, with drugs lying at the heart of many of his problems. Now, with new album sessions coming, Astbury, Duffy and Stewart had a difficult decision to make. 'We ended up sacking Nigel just before we went in,' Astbury related, silently acknowledging that, perhaps, a more pro-active response might have been better suited to the situation.

Preston's last recording with the Cult was a BBC session, taped on 16th June 1985 and broadcast on the Janice Long Show ten days later. Opening with 'Spiritwalker', the session then previewed three explosive new songs, 'Big Neon Glitter', 'Revolution' and 'All Souls Avenue', all confirming to even the most impartial listener that the impassioned stridency of 'She Sells Sanctuary' most certainly wasn't a one-off.

Preston was replaced for the *Love* album by Mark Brzezicki, late of Stuart Adamson's Big Country, but the dramatic change of style in this department was just one of many served up by the new recordings.

Astbury's costumes had long bordered on psychedelic vagrancy; now his writing was absorbing a similar sheen, as his preferred listening of the Doors and Hendrix boiled over into the Cult. A secret gig at Alice In Wonderland in London's Dean Street in May saw them execute a swirlingly ragged version of Hendrix's 'Hey Joe', alongside fellow '60s ravers 'I Can't Explain', 'Steppin' Stone' and 'Wild Thing'. From there, it was but a small step towards the blistered blues of Led Zeppelin and Free. As the Cult toured Japan in September 1985 and the US in December, with ex-Julian Lennon drummer Les Warner now filling in at the back, so these influences, too, began moving into focus.

Love itself sold over 200,000 copies in Britain, effortlessly spawning two further hit singles ('Rain', #17 in October 1985, and a remixed 'Revolution', #30 in December). It was its Stateside performance that mattered most, however. *Love* reached #87 in America. Neither the Cult nor their US label Sire Records were in any doubt that, with a more concentrated profile, the Cult could easily do even better next time. The band simply decided that 'next time' would be 'now.'

Gene Loves Jezebel were also eyeing America with wide-eyed enthusiasm, and for similar reasons to the Cult. After such a romantic start, their relations with the British media, too, had fallen into fractious decay, with the music papers' disinterest compounded by an even more damaging dispute with the BBC, sparked when the band attempted to cancel a Peel session in May 1984.

Bassist Steve Marshall had just departed the band but, when the Astons requested that the session be postponed while they regrouped, the BBC refused. It went ahead with Jay filling in on bass, but the performance, mourned Michael, 'was a complete mess. We told them that we weren't ready, that we couldn't do it. But they wouldn't allow us to reschedule, they accused us of being unprofessional. The whole thing was a disaster.' Even worse, it laid the groundwork for a feud that would dog Gene Loves Jezebel's UK standing for the remainder of their career. 'The BBC would never play us after that,' Michael believes, 'because we pissed them off over that session.'

The group's relations with their label, Beggar's Banquet, were at an all-time low. Two sets of high profile recording sessions, with John Cale and Steve Harley, had produced nothing that the label considered usable. Jay reflected, 'so far as they were concerned, we were spending all this money and nothing was happening. The Cale stuff hadn't come through, the Steve Harley stuff hadn't come through, some stuff we recorded with [producer] John Brand hadn't worked out. So finally, [Beggars] just said "to hell with you," and that was it. We were placed on hold.'

Over the next year, the band battled to win back its status. Pete Rizzo was recruited as the new bass player, former Klaxon 5 drummer Marcus Gilvear was installed on drums and, with a degree of stability finally in place, the Astons approached Beggar's Banquet label-head Martin Miller with an offer they hoped he couldn't refuse – a great album made on whatever budget he was willing to grant them.

The result, the John Leckie-produced album *Immigrant*, emerged in mid-1985; later in the year, it would become Gene Loves Jezebel's maiden American release, via Geffen. In early October, the group set off on its first ever US tour.

It was not their first taste of the country. The ill-fated John Cale sessions had taken place in New York, back in January 1984, and Jay recalled, 'We were all on the dole struggling, and then we were in New York. And it is just as fun as it gets for a couple of Welsh boys. We had a brilliant time, everyone loved us, and we were outrageous guys. It was an exciting period. I think it captured what was exciting about the band but, as I think about it, we must have just freaked people out the way we were.'

'That was one of the trippiest, scariest, most exhilarating experience of my life,' agreed his brother. 'I was the only one sober in New York, which tells you everything. It was our introduction to the netherworld.'

Now they were to renew the acquaintance, although, this being Gene Loves Jezebel, of course events could not go strictly according to plan. The tour had only just got underway when, according to Michael, 'Ian Hudson had a nervous breakdown. He cut his wrists, and tried to jump out of a 16th floor window.'

Hudson, the one musician who had remained with the group since the beginning, was packed off home, while the remaining band members tried to figure out what they were going to do next. Finally Michael suggested contacting James Stevenson, the mercurial former Chelsea and Generation X guitarist, now gigging with the Hot Club, a second division Punk survivors supergroup featuring Rich Kids Glen Matlock and Steve New and ex-Clash drummer Terry Chimes. He knew little about Gene Loves Jezebel – indeed, the first time he heard *Immigrant* was once he'd strapped himself into his seat for the flight to New York. 'I got on the plane and put on the tape,' he recalled, 'and the first thing I thought was "Oh my God, what IS this?"' It took three complete airings of the album before he finally decided not to jump out of the window and take his chances in America instead.

'He learned about three songs and went straight into a 60-date tour of America,' remembered Jay. To try and ease the transition, Michael continued, 'we would play the same songs and just exchange the lyrics. Then a few shows in, we got everything down.'

Immediately prior to departing for the US, Gene Loves Jezebel recorded their next single for release upon their return in November. 'Desire' was quite unlike anything the band had attempted before, a fist-punchingly catchy mantra built around a spiralling call-and-response routine, and an effectively economical Ian Hudson guitar assault. Destined for the Top 5 of the UK Indy chart, it also became an American college radio favourite, opening doors – both creative and commercial – that the band was swift to dive through.

Britain was simply too narrow-minded to accept Gene Loves Jezebel as anything more than a hold-over from the early 1980s art pack. Barely promoted and sparsely attended though it was (just 282 people turned out to see them play the 1,200 capacity First Avenue club in Minneapolis), the American tour convinced the band that a whole new audience was simply waiting to be introduced, an impression that Geffen Records, too, embraced enthusiastically. Nor would either party have to wait long for confirmation of their convictions.

America was also paying unqualified attention to another of the bands that the British media had long since painted into a very black strait-jacket, as the Cure finally put the chaos of the past two years behind them and resolved to lead a straightforward career once again. Or, at least as straightforward as any band fronted by Robert Smith can be.

Preceded by the band's most bizarre single yet, the totally whacked-out mock-turtled psychedelia of 'The Caterpillar,' the Cure's fifth album, *The Top*, appeared in May 1984 amid the band's longest British tour yet, one which saw them comfortably selling out the largest theatres in the land.

The album sat uncomfortably with this success. Smith himself admitted it was 'fucking deranged', a ragbag of styles and sounds far removed from the single-minded themes of its predecessors. Forgetting his earlier threat to out-porno *Pornography*, he acknowledged, 'I think subconsciously I made the decision to make *The Top* different [from our other albums]. It does resemble our first LP more than anything we've done, in as much as there is a variety of moods and styles. But

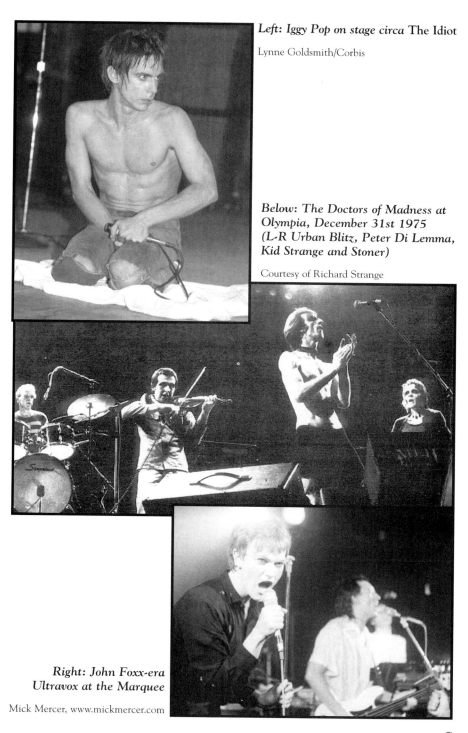

Left: Iggy Pop on stage circa The Idiot

Lynne Goldsmith/Corbis

Below: **The Doctors of Madness at Olympia, December 31st 1975 (L-R Urban Blitz, Peter Di Lemma, Kid Strange and Stoner)**

Courtesy of Richard Strange

Right: John Foxx-era Ultravox at the Marquee

Mick Mercer, www.mickmercer.com

Rikki Sylvan with the musicians for his KRL album Silent Hours *(L-R Stephen A Wilkin, Andy Prince, Rikki Sylvan, Mark Laff, Mike Taylor)*
Courtesy of Stephen A Wilkin

Left: Reluctant role model, The Damned's Dave Vanian

Rex Features

Below: UK Decay

Mick Mercer

Above: Bauhaus's Peter Murphy Live at the Rock Garden in 1982

Mick Mercer, www.mickmercer.com

Left: Bauhaus's Peter Murphy circa "Ziggy Stardust"

by Bleddyn Butcher

Left: Siouxsie

Bleddyn Butcher

Right: The Cure's Robert Smith

Bleddyn Butcher

Three Ages of Astbury

Southern Death Cult at the Zig Zag club: L-R, front, David Burrows, Ian Astbury, Haq Qureshi
Mick Mercer, www.mickmercer.com

Right: Death Cult: L-R, Ian Astbury, Billy Duffy, Jamie Stewart, Nigel Preston

Bleddyn Butcher

Left: The Cult: Astbury and Duffy

Bleddyn Butcher

The Birthday Party: Mick Harvey, Rowland S Howard, Nick Cave
Bleddyn Burcher

Alien Sex Fiend

courtesy of Cherry Red Records

Gene Loves Jezebel

Steve Jennings, Rex Features

Specimen singer Ollie Wisdom

Bleddyn Butcher

Right: The Mission (L-R Simon Hinkler, Mick Brown, Craig Adams, Wayne Hussey)

by Bleddyn Butcher

Below: Sisters of Mercy: Patricia Morrison and Andrew Eldritch

Photo by Brian Rasic, Rex Features

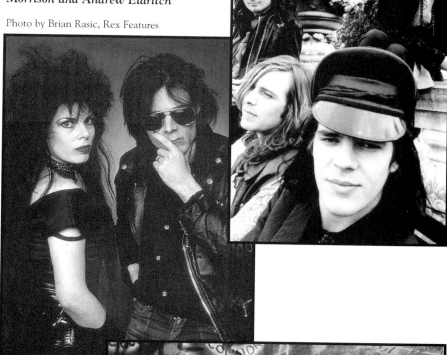

Right: All About Eve's Julianne Regan and Tim Bricheno, the latter would join a later incarnation of The Sisters of Mercy

Mick Mercer, www.mickmercer.com

Carl McCoy of The Nephilim

Mick Mercer, www.mickmercer.com

Below: Fields of The Nephilim

Bleddyn Butcher

although it's similar in its diversity, the content is very different.'

Stability was the secret; that, and the confidence to continue experimenting within the framework of the Cure. Smith had finally put his on-again/off-again relationship with the Banshees behind him, while other urges to work outside the Cure seemed to have been exhausted following a guest appearance on video director Tim Pope's debut single, the absurdly idiosyncratic 'I Want To Be A Tree.'

The Cure's own shifting membership had finally settled, with the band now lining up as Smith, Tolhurst, returning ex-members Porl Thompson and Simon Gallup, and former Thompson Twins drummer Boris Williams. *The Top* was still spinning when work began on a new album, *The Head On The Door*.

Named for a nightmare that plagued Smith during his childhood, *The Head On The Door* was very much a return to past (pre-split) glories in terms of musical intensity, if not subject matter. Boasting some of Smith's most deliberately contagious songs, the eternally effervescent 'In-between Days' and the Malice era 'On A Night Like This' among them, the album also had a naked spontaneity that harked back as far as *Seventeen Seconds*; indeed, Smith later confessed that eight of the performances were actually first takes, 'which is something we haven't done since that album.'

It would be another year before the Cure finally made any Stateside impression outside of the cult surroundings that they had already made their own. But for any historians attempting to date the dawn of the group's long-standing love affair with America-at-large, there is no better place to start than with the colourful videos and multi-hued songs that chased *The Head On The Door* up the college radio listings to become the band's biggest-selling album yet.

Not everybody who ventured across the Atlantic, however, was to find the milk and honey that the advertising slogans seemed to swear were there for the taking. Some didn't even want to look for it in the first place.

In early 1985, Specimen finally won their release from London Records, promptly linking with the newborn Trust label for what would be their final UK single, the thunderous (but distinctly dated-sounding) 'Sharp Teeth, Pretty Teeth'. It squeaked into the Independent Top 30 but it was clear that Britain had no time for Specimen.

The Batcave was still loyal, but what was that worth? More than a year had passed since the venue meant anything to anyone beyond a handful of curious tourists, a year during which the club itself had constricted so far that it was operating out of the Gargoyle again, from whence it had first taken flight.

The band's decline was remorseless. Headlining the Croydon Underground in April 1985, Specimen were completely blown offstage by the evening's support band, an untried glam revival combo called Sexagisma. 'They started out invigorating, swiftly fell into mundanity and, by the end of the set, I'd forgotten every last nice thing I'd ever wanted to say about them,' mused *Melody Maker's* review of the show. The only real surprise was that the paper had bothered despatching a critic to the gig in the first place.

Another blow fell when Chris Bell announced he was quitting, bound for Gene Loves Jezebel and the bright future that was now beckoning that band. Following

Bell's gaze westward to America, Ollie Wisdom knew that Specimen, too, needed to escape. When he announced that he was relocating the group to San Francisco, from whence he would re-establish the band around that city's own Gothic community, his bandmates were aghast. It wasn't a change of address that they required, it was a change of scenery.

Specimen scattered to the winds. Jonny Slut formed Playpen with former Soft Boy Matthew Seligman and future Stereo MCs' frontman The Head; Jon Klein, after spending close to two years out of sight, resurfaced in Siouxsie and the Banshees in 1987, as they embarked upon their *Peek-A-Boo* phase. He would remain on-board until the band itself split, seven years (but just three albums) later.

Only Specimen's newly-recruited drummer, Bone Orchard veteran Tim 'Rim Tim Cheese' Huthert, opted to follow his leader to America, there to discover that the even the Promised Land could renege on its pledges. They did cut another single – a barely recognisable 12-inch single that only came out, of all places, in Canada – but that was it. Just as the Batcave flickered to a barely-mourned, scarcely-noticed close in mid-1985, so Specimen were finally bottled just a few months later.

Part Three

The Sky's

Gone Out

(1986-2002)

Fields of The Nephilim

Bleddyn Butcher

Chapter Eleven
Left On Mission
And Revenge

An account of how two warring Sisters went their own dark ways, while the two parts of Bauhaus moved into the light. But we also discover that fame can be fed from a very distasteful chalice.

'If the Sisters of Mercy were ever booked for speeding, Fields Of Nephilism [sic] would be Exhibit A. The trip-hammer bass, crashing drums and sub-Smith guitar so beloved of the meek and unholy all [chase] each other around in breathless circles before disappearing offstage to a silence that was more shell-shocked than anything else. Last to the fade-out is a sissy.' Melody Maker

The success of the Sisters, so effortlessly scything across the generic lines now being drawn across the so-called Gothic field, was inevitable from the start. So, however, was their demise. 'It's well documented that Andrew [Eldritch] and I didn't get on,' Wayne Hussey explained. 'But it was a fruitful... relationship, and we did realize that what we had was very strong, both visually and musically.'

He didn't necessarily approve of the band's reputation, of course. 'If you looked at us, visually, we weren't a Goth band. People took one element of the way I dressed, the way Andrew dressed, or maybe they saw we had an armful of bangles, whatever. And they mixed it all up.' But he willingly acknowledged, 'we probably were guilty of taking ourselves too seriously, occasionally.' It was that seriousness, and the strength of that imagery, that allowed the Sisters' vision to persevere long after other acts within their circle of peers had moved on to other pastures.

By the mid-1980s, after all, the Gothic scene lay in tatters. The Batcave was gone and, with it, all the bands that once led the charge, mercilessly crushed beneath the combined weight of expectation and stereotype.

The Sisters were dead, but the composite elements had yet to stir further than their fax machines. The sundered remains of Bauhaus had produced little more than the tentative stabs of Daniel Ash's Tones On Tail and Peter Murphy's ill-begotten collaboration with Japan's Mick Karn, Dali's Car. New Order, the phoenix that arose from the ashes of Joy Division, were now plying their trade on the dance floor and in the remix studios of New York and London.

Nick Cave was still distributing his visions of doom, gloom and apocalyptic despondency, but he did so with an increasingly bright eye for an intellectual cult status that distanced him from even the most wishful fringe of schlock horror outrage. The Cult, the Cure and Gene Loves Jezebel were operating single-mindedly in the United States, where their baggage certainly didn't include the tags and tarring that the British media had saddled them with. It was, in short, a wipe-out.

But there *was* an audience, vast, unwieldy and untapped. If the masters were no longer interested in playing to it, then the pupils were going to take over the blackboard. The fact that one particular gaggle of musically incoherent, but stylistically well-hung acolytes were doing business under the soon-to-be notorious name of the Mission only adds piquancy to their story.

Natives of Stevenage, Hertfordshire, guitarist Paul Wright, his drumming brother Nod and bassist Tony Petit formed their Mission in 1983 after a earlier effort, the deliciously-named Perfect Disaster, fell apart. For all its future ramifications, of course, this particular Mission went nowhere and the name was abandoned. The core trio immediately regrouped, however, first recruiting a sax player rejoicing under the delightfully Beatrix Potter-esque title of Gary Whisker, but only really shifting into gear following the arrival of vocalist Carl McCoy, a figure whose own past allegedly included sundry local reggae bands.

It was McCoy who coined the group's new name, one that fit their intended *modus operandi* considerably more comfortably than their earlier soubriquet. The Fields of the Nephilim was derived in part from a race of Old Testament (Genesis 6:4) giants, cast upon the earth to cause havoc and destruction – a weighty tag –

but one that the group was determined to live up to. Interviewed on American radio in 1988, McCoy acknowledged, 'No one really knows that much about the Nephilim, it's a mysterious thing. We added "Fields" to suggest magnetic fields, pulling in toward the Nephilim, not green pastures.'

Basing their sonic assault on a twice-removed idealisation of the Sisters Of Mercy, all the way down to the hats, the Fields of the Nephilim gigged constantly around Hertfordshire, building enough of a local following to make it worth their while to self-release a single, the four-song *Burning The Fields* EP. That took off sufficiently for the Indy label Jungle to step in to handle distribution and, with Mr Whisker replaced by second guitarist Peter Yates, the Fields of the Nephilim landed a 1985 UK tour with Punk survivors Chelsea.

Other ventures, with Flag of Convenience and Balaam & The Angel, ensured the group continued zeroing in on its chosen audience, September 1985 found them at the 100 Club, opening for one of visiting American freak show Christian Death's sporadic London visits. Despite the growing sense that some kind of movement was gathering around the band, a passing *Melody Maker* was left stubbornly unmoved. 'If the Sisters of Mercy were ever booked for speeding, Fields Of Nephilism [sic] would be Exhibit A. The trip-hammer bass, crashing drums and sub-Smith guitar so beloved of the meek and unholy all [chase] each other around in breathless circles before disappearing offstage to a silence that was more shell-shocked than anything else. Last to the fade-out is a sissy.'

The hats continued to fascinate the band; ponchos and buckskin began to creep in as well – a Man With No Name stance that was rooted in the recent past. Forget the dry ice for tumbleweeds, the Fields of the Nephilim even had their own Ennio Morricone variation ("The Harmonica Man", from *Once Upon A Time In The West*) for an intro tape, echoing Eldritch and co's appropriation of *The Good, The Bad And The Ugly* for 'Phantom'. By the time the Fields of the Nephilim started headlining their own club gigs, the audience, the self-styled Bonanzas, was as black-clad as the Sisters could have wished.

So far, so Merciful. While criticism that the Fields of the Nephilim were little more than a second-hand Sisters could not be denied, it could be diverted by the role model's own absence. Not everyone wants to listen to the same old records over and again; not everyone wants to live in the past. The Fields of the Nephilim took the sound and ran with it. In mid-1986, Situation 2 stepped in for their signature, putting the group on the road with Beggars Banquet labelmates Gene Loves Jezebel.

'Power', the group's first single for the label, appeared towards the end of the year, rising to #24 on the Indy chart. But it was 'Preacher Man' in the new year, and a reissued *Burning The Fields* later in the summer, which truly pinpointed the Fields of the Nephilim's appeal. Both stormed to #2, leaving the country gagging for the band's first album.

While they waited, there was no shortage of equally enthralling diversions.

More than a year after quitting the Sisters of Mercy, Gary Marx finally got the long-anticipated Ghost Dance off the ground during 1985, uniting with vocalist Anne-Marie Hurst when she quit the Skeletal Family that spring, just as they signed with major label Chrysalis.

With the band completed by former Citron Girls bassist Paul Etchell and a drum machine named Pandora, Marx originally intended Ghost Dance as a vehicle for the songs he'd prepared for the Sisters Of Mercy. Early singles 'River Of No Return', 'Yesterday Again' and 'Grip Of Love' were all written during his time with that band. Ghost Dance also had as wry a taste in cover versions as the Sisters. Roxy Music's 'Both Ends Burning', Golden Earring's 'Radar Love' and the Yardbirds' 'Heartful Of Soul' all found a home in the band's repertoire, second cousins to the Sisters' legendary assault on Hot Chocolate's 'Emma', Dolly Parton's 'Jolene' and The Stones' 'Gimme Shelter'.

Swiftly, however, Ghost Dance outgrew that brief, going on to create some of the most dynamic, purposefully jarring music of the age. The recruitment of a human drummer, John Grant, in late 1986, and second guitarist Richard Steel (later of Spacehog) further loosened the most overt comparisons. But still, in the continued absence of the Sisters Of Mercy – at least in any form that actually resembled the Sisters Of Mercy – Ghost Dance, like the Fields of the Nephilim, were settling themselves very comfortably indeed into that band's vacant throne-room.

In fact, Andrew Eldritch was adamant that the Sisters themselves were long dead and buried, only for circumstance to completely redirect his thinking.

When the Sisters split, both parties agreed not to trade on the old group's name with whatever projects they might embark upon in the future. Hussey and Adams, however, reneged on that deal with the first show their new band played, at Alice In Wonderland on 20th January. They were billed as the Sisterhood, and seemed to be rubbing further salt into Eldritch's wounds first by recruiting a guitarist, Simon Hinkler, who'd actually applied for the vacant slot that eventually brought Hussey into the Sisters, then by bringing in a real live drummer, Mick Brown from Red Lorry Yellow Lorry.

That group was still celebrating the release of their debut album, *Talk About The Weather*, when Brown departed; he was replaced by former Girls At Our Best drummer Chris Oldroyd and the Lorries continued flirting very close to the breakthrough that both their audience and even their detractors were convinced was imminent.

Hussey/Adams' Sisterhood, on the other hand, appeared doomed from the outset, with their debut gig itself little short of a disaster. Despite readying a set that already contained such future standards as 'Wasteland', 'Severina' and 'Serpents Kiss', drawing from both newly-composed material and from Hussey's contributions to what would have been the second Sisters' album, the Sisterhood's 45-minute set was scarred by drunkenness and blighted by an audience that cared only for old Sisters songs.

'We don't play that stuff any more,' a huffy Hussey announced, but the barracking continued. Looking around the club, it was hard to miss Dave Vanian creased up laughing in the DJ booth or Eldritch himself, smiling smugly as the entire affair dribbled to its conclusion.

The battle was on. Eldritch immediately hit out with his own Sisterhood, debuting it with the single, 'Giving Ground (r.s.v.)', recorded with Lucas Fox, Motorhead's first drummer, and James Ray, a singer who legend insisted was simply an unknown Sisters' fan who had sent Eldritch a tape.

Less a song than a creeping malaise, 'Giving Ground' had only Doktor Avalanche in common with the Sisters themselves – Eldritch did not even take the lead vocal, handing the microphone instead to Ray. But, with the rumour mill insisting that a mere 200 copies of the single had been manufactured, 'Giving Ground' sold out wherever it was stocked, and in sufficient quantities that it went soaring to the top of the Indy chart.

The question was did Eldritch really intend reinventing himself under this new name? Or was it simply his first overt move in a battle over nomenclatural custody that was to engross the European media for much of the next two months, as Eldritch and Hussey barked out new insults and anger in a conflict which the papers, delighted to be the forum for this unseemly row, quickly dubbed the Corporate Wars?

The week after the Alice In Wonderland show, the Hussey/Adams Sisterhood recorded a four-song session for BBC Radio's *Janice Long Show*, featuring sharp takes on 'Severina', 'Sacrilege' and 'And The Dance Goes On', plus a rendering of Neil Young's 'Like A Hurricane' that suggested that there was more to the band than just a bold of funereal cloth, blowing in the dry wind. The session would ultimately be broadcast under the name of the Wayne Hussey and Craig Adams Band but, just days later, the team reclaimed the Sisterhood banner for their first tour, opening for the Cult on a twelve-day spin through Europe.

With only Hinkler a less than hoary old veteran of road work, the Sisterhood readily adapted to the rigours of the road, despite their absolute infancy. Venues holding between 2,000 and 5,000 people simply strengthened the group's resolve and boosted their confidence. Even better, though many of the audiences they faced were as smitten by the Sisters Of Mercy as the denizens of Alice In Wonderland had been, crowds also seemed willing to give the new boys a chance. By the time the Sisterhood returned to the UK, they were ready to take on anybody.

Anybody, that is, bar Eldritch. He had not been idle during their absence, although he had lost patience with the entire affair. Loudly proclaiming the existence of seven cast-iron complaints to throw at the rogue operation, Eldritch was threatening legal action. It was time, Hussey and Adams decided, to throw in the towel. But not before they made one final defiant gesture

At the end of February, the Sisterhood announced three UK shows – in London, Birmingham and Leeds – with only a carefully-worded rejoinder to inform their audience that this was not Eldritch's band. Eldritch promptly slammed an injunction onto the final show but, as it transpired, he needn't have bothered. On 27th February, at the end of a breathless set at the Electric Ballroom in Camden Town, Hussey quietened the crowd to announce, 'Thanks to Andrew Eldritch, we are no longer called the Sisterhood.' A curtain slipped down on the wall behind him and, once the roadies had finished untangling it, the stage lights lit up a backdrop proclaiming the band's new name – The Mission.

Eldritch had won. He wasn't above gloating. 'It is apparent,' read the latest press missive from Merciful Release, 'that Wayne and Craig have concluded that successful bands issue records not disclaimers, and appear in concert halls not courtrooms. Their logic is unassailable. We assume that their choice of name is entirely unconnected with the forthcoming Andrew Eldritch album which for some months has had the working title *Left on Mission and Revenge*.'

Hussey replied that the name had nothing to do with Eldritch's proposed album, claiming instead that it was inspired by a brand of guitar amps. Either way, Eldritch let the matter drop, and set about heeding his own advice. Successful bands issue records.

Retaining the Sisterhood name for the time being, and keeping Ray and Fox on board, he completed the new band's line-up with bassist Patricia Morrison – a friend since her last band, Gun Club, toured with the Sisters – and Suicide's Alan Vega, author, of the Sisters' showstopping 'Ghost Rider'. Thus constituted, they began work immediately on the Sisterhood's first (and only) album, *The Gift*.

Another skewed diversion from any paths that Eldritch had previously trod, with only the beautiful, claustrophobic 'Colours' sounding even remotely similar to the Sisters' pre-split vision, *Gift* opened with the seeds of another rumour, that the numbers 'two, five, zero, zero, zero' that Morrison reels off at the beginning of 'Jihad' represented the amount that the court ordered the Mission to pay Eldritch at the conclusion of another battle, this time over ownership of the unused songs for the second album. (It has also been explained as the advance Eldritch received for the album).

Hussey got at least a measure of revenge, however, when a conspiratorial *Sounds* invited him to review the album. Not too surprisingly, he was less than effusive, not only questioning Eldritch's mental health, but also remarking, 'There is absolutely no sign of... talent on this unwanted *Gift*...'

His vehemence was not wholly down to settling old scores. Although history now insists that *Gift* was a phenomenally underrated album, a light year leap in sound and substance, even non-partisan reviews were unanimously damning. While Eldritch appeared unabashed, announcing a new single, 'This Corrosion', for imminent release, clearly his plans were not set in stone.

With the exception of Morrison, the Sisterhood melted away. While Vega returned to New York and James Ray formed his own bands, Performance and, in 1989, Gang War (both bands' singles were issued by Merciful Release), Eldritch cancelled the single and returned to his familiar haunts in Hamburg.

From there, he would reclaim the old Sisters Of Mercy name, but it would be another year before either band or planned single finally appeared. In the meantime, the Mission ignited.

Reflecting upon the media coverage that had swirled around the Sisters Of Mercy, Wayne Hussey mused, 'Siouxsie, the Cramps and Bauhaus, even the Cure to an extent, were more archetypal [Goth] in the way they were than we [the Sisters] ever were.' The Mission, however, were to take that particular bull by the horns. 'The early Mission probably were Goth,' he mused. 'Songs like "Sacrilege" and "Serpent's Kiss" [based upon Aleister Crowley's *Moonchild*] were pretty incriminating, weren't they?'

Indeed they were. But, from the outset, the Mission designed their Goth with a genuine sense of humour, deliberately setting out the archetypes in song, but laying the ingredients on so thick that one needed, indeed, to be pretty thick not to get the joke.

Of course, that particular miscalculation proved easy for the music press of the mid-1980s, for whom the Mission were readily aligned alongside the Cult among the Aunt Sallies of the age, to be chastised and castigated with ever more invention as their career trundled along.

The band, cared not a whit. Fuelled by an unholy trinity of speed, coke and acid, driven by an audience whose own identity was as clearly defined as the band's, the Mission suddenly found that they could do no wrong, at home and across Europe.

It was Europe that, unwittingly, christened the most loyal of the band's fans with a title that is still whispered with awe in the presence of the Mission. As the group headed out on its first full continental tour, a small army of the most loyal supporters arranged to follow them to the furthest corners of the continent. It was on the German frontier that one particular fan was halted, questioned and finally released with one parting comment still ringing in his ears, a remark that was largely incomprehensible but sounded suspiciously like the word 'eskimo'. The name stuck.

The loyalty of the Eskimos ensured that even the lowest-key Mission gig turned into a celebration, although for some months it looked as though their support might never be rewarded with the one thing that all concerned most desperately wanted – a record deal. Hussey and Adams, as former members of the Sisters Of Mercy, remained contracted to WEA. Although the label clearly had no interest in what the new band had to offer, there seemed little chance of the conglomerate simply letting them go.

Indeed, early discussions with the company saw any number of increasingly bizarre suggestions and recommendations floated in the hope of transforming the group into something WEA deemed saleable – suggestions that ranged from a full-fledged Sisters Of Mercy reunion to the recruitment of a new lead vocalist. Peter Murphy, the Virgin Prunes' Gavin Friday, Andi Sex Gang and Modern Romance's Sal Solo were all put forward, but the Mission held firm. The band had been formed to perform Hussey's songs. It only followed that he should sing them as well and, if his voice wasn't up to WEA's standards, that was their look-out.

Desperate to force their gaolers' hand, the band arranged for the Birmingham independent label Chapter 22 to release a Mission single. A survivor from the sessions for a second Sisters' album, 'Serpent's Kiss' and the newly composed 'Wake (RSVP)' were both recorded as demos for WEA (the label also paid for them). The band snatched the tape regardless and, in May 1986, saw the record enter the Independent charts at #1, the first debut single ever to do so.

A churning rocker, an absolute explosion of undiluted joyousness, 'Serpent's Kiss' was a fabulous record, one of the Mission's finest ever singles. Flip it over, however, and 'Wake' was revealed as even more glorious, dark and atmospheric, as funereal as its title suggests. There were suggestions that the lyric was dedicated to Eldritch; suggestions, too, that the sepulchral edge to Hussey's vocal was designed specifically to further that impression. Hussey, however, remained silent on the subject. Diplomacy, after all, is just as damning as denial.

The Mission made their first video just three days before 'Serpent's Kiss" chart-topping status was made public, heading out to a local park to play soccer, while

Adams, dressed as a pantomime devil, chased them around. It was a rambunctious effort, gleefully amateurish, fetchingly childish, and it tickled another feather in the armpit of the band's so-called 'serious' side – all the more so after ITV's weekly *The Chart Show* took to broadcasting it at every available opportunity.

The Mission launched their first British tour, *Expedition I*, in the wake of the single, a solidly sold out 12-night outing that confirmed their ascendancy – but still failed to sway WEA. Neither, it seemed, would a second Chapter 22 single, as another Sisters survivor, 'Garden Of Delight', swung out in June to maintain the Mission's domination of the Independent chart.

Not only did it top that listing, it also breathed fresh life into 'Serpent's Kiss' and, for one memorable week, the band's first two singles lay side by side at #2 and #3. 'Garden Of Delight' also punctured the national Top 50 and, finally, WEA threw in their hand. They didn't want the band, like the band or even understand the band. Please go away.

The Mission signed with Mercury in July 1986, and immediately returned to the studio; by October, their major label debut single, 'Stay With Me,' was on its way to #30, while the band's first album, cut in five days in late summer, was in the stores by November and Top 20 by Christmas.

God's Own Medicine packed few surprises, but plenty of action – its contents, after all, had been hammered into shape across close to a year of gigging, breathing in and breeding with the enthusiasm of the audience. And so 'Wasteland,' the triumphal opener, emerged vast and symphonic, the raising of a gaudy curtain that, in lesser hands, would have proven better than the show itself. For the Mission, however, it was simply the first shot in a salvo that pulled every lyrical and musical trick out of the Gothic lexicon, then twisted them to the band's own ends.

Lyrically, the Mission were not impressive – a failing that Hussey would himself pronounce ever louder with his increasing reliance on soft pornography as the band moved further away from its original Gothic archetype. Where they stood head and shoulders over the rest of the pack, both chasing and distancing, was in an intuitive understanding of sound as a vehicle for atmosphere. The Mission appeared enormous because they sounded enormous, tsunamis of guitar crashing onto anthemic shores while Hussey's voice, yearning, imploring, demanding, echoed down from the mount with Biblical fervour. Even at their most preposterous – and the band's catalogue is littered with such moments – the Mission meant something, and you needed to be a very sour soul not to respond to it.

In every arena, the Mission excelled. They trampled all underfoot at the Reading festival in August, while *Expedition I* had proven one of the year's most talked-about tours. Even the Eskimos were riding high – as the band slammed into their version of 'Like A Hurricane', these doughty souls would form themselves into an eminently photographable human pyramid, swaying and trembling in front of the stage until weight of numbers, or the sheer force of the crowd, caused it to topple. Another self-contained band of fans, the Sausage Squad, lived up to their name by hurling sausages at the stage. Forget the band, watch the audience.

There was plenty of opportunity for that. On 28th October, a fan-club-only show at Nottingham's Rock City opened the Mission's first world tour – or *World Crusade* as they portentously dubbed it – a six month sprint that would take in 14 countries and over 100 shows, and confirm the band's reputation as rock's latest hell-raisers, rampaging across Britain and Europe, leaving a string of demolished hotels, deflowered maidens and delighted drug dealers in their wake.

While the Mission elevated frenzy to new levels of crazed Bacchanalia, a somewhat calmer rebirth attended the remains of another sundered legend, Bauhaus. Apparently stronger – and certainly happier – apart than they had ever been together, the musicians had followed in the footsteps of the Cult, Cure and Gene Loves Jezebel by turning their backs on Britain in favour of building an American momentum that their homeland could never have comprehended.

For Daniel Ash and Kevin Haskins, a few months pursuing the Tones On Tail spin-off they'd launched in 1982 with Bauhaus roadie Glen Campling had done little – a clutch of excellent singles and the sorely under-rated *Pop* album passed by unnoticed by all but the hardcore; a similar fate awaited David J's tentative dabbles, both solo and collaborative (with Jazz Butcher and original Bauhaus artist Rene Hackett) activities.

Peter Murphy, too, flexed his first solo muscles wracked by uncertainty. That intriguing, if not quite inspirational union with Japan's Mick Karn, as Dali's Car, left the world with nothing more palatable than an awkward album of misinterpreted art installations, one that ultimately gained more attention from the sleeve design (Maxwell Parish's *The Waking Hour*) that it inadvertently shared with the Moody Blues' last album than it did from the meeting of the musical minds.

An attempt to develop a career in mixed media, via a modern dance routine (to Bauhaus' 'Hollow Hills') on BBC TV's arts programme *Riverside*, was equally ill-starred. As he joined his erstwhile bandmates in silence, so the whispering began: Bauhaus were getting back together.

It was not to be, of course. Murphy found other fish to fry, linking with former Associates multi-instrumentalist Howard Hughes and beginning demo work for a new, assuredly solo album. But Haskins, Ash and J, rekindling the spirit of togetherness that made at least the first sessions for the final Bauhaus album a vague joy to recall, were not so readily discouraged.

Rehearsing through late 1984, the trio found themselves constantly returning to a darkly funk-infected version of the old Temptations chest-beater, 'Ball Of Confusion'. The song was originally J's suggestion – it was one of the first records he ever bought.

J: 'We were driving over to our rehearsal room, thinking "What shall we do? Shall we try to write a song?" We just wanted to get the thing going, to get the ball rolling – no pun intended – so we thought we'd do a cover version. And then we thought of that one. Lyrically, it was very pertinent to the time... the mid 80s. It's got a great riff. It's very solid. So that's what we did. We just concentrated on that for a week and nothing else, then went in straightaway and recorded it.'

The trio took the name Love And Rockets from the underground comic book created by Jaime and Gilbert Hernandez. They stayed with the pleasures of childhood when it came to furthering the new band's vision beyond what was already earmarked as their debut single, harking back to the golden era of glam, a decade or more earlier.

The three had just been entering their early teens at the time and, as Ash reflected, 'There's something about being that age, 13, 14, when you're first connecting with rock music, when it consumes everything, becomes a part of you.' He remembered the first time he saw Roxy Music: 'Eno was playing a tambourine, but it was triangular! I'd never seen a triangular tambourine. It was so weird!' And the first time he fell in love, standing at a bus stop and seeing a girl pass by, glammed out and befeathered. 'The Seventh Dream Of Teenaged Heaven', the title track to what would become Love and Rockets' first album, took its inspiration from that never-forgotten vision.

Though the years have deadened its impact somewhat, there is still a visceral thrill to be drawn from replaying *Seventh Dream*, a sense of the first step taken towards a brave new world, and a miasmic whirl of psychedelic intent that masks intents even darker than Bauhaus ever envisioned. Indeed, in so subtly aligning its makers with a destiny and fame that no-one could ever have predicted, *Seventh Dream* ranks among the most deceptive debut albums of the 1980s, its keys split between the churning guitar soup of 'The Dog End of a Day Gone By,' the sibilant glam sexuality of the title track, the chilling nursery-rhyme pendulum of 'The Game,' was choked by an opiate atmosphere as profound as any of the lauded trips of the original psychedelic era.

'Ball Of Confusion' in May 1985 and the self-composed 'If There's A Heaven Above' in September paved the way for the album, if the British press yawned and the public pecked delicately at its utter lack of Bauhaus-ness, Love and Rockets weren't paying attention. Without the band even having to leave the studio, 'Ball Of Confusion' was a Top 10 hit in Canada. In September, the group played their first ever live show, in Boston, Massachusetts.

Over the next twelve months, prior to the release of their sophomore *Express* album, the group would tour America three times, while playing just two shows in Britain: at the Marquee and the Astoria in London.

Gene Loves Jezebel, too, were eating up the miles on the road in America. The reception of their first two singles of 1986, 'The Sweetest Thing' in March and 'Heartache' in June, had already confirmed the promise that 'Desire' showed, while James Stevenson's decision on the eve of the band's latest US tour in April, to come on board permanently, gave an entire new dimension of flash and fire to the proceedings.

The singles were tasters for the band's forthcoming album, *Discover*, an album whose cohesion utterly belies the chaos of its creation. Jay Aston recalled, 'We were literally grabbing a few hours in the Roundhouse in London, a few hours in Rockfield, a few hours where ever we could find.' Even more disruptive was the loss of producer Gary Lyons when he suffered a heart attack early on in the proceedings. The album was ultimately completed with engineer Mark Dearnley and Jay marvelled, 'It's amazing the album sounds so cohesive because it really is so thrown together.'

The glue that bound it together was ambition, the perfect blend of all the parties, sounds and styles that had ever filed through the members' dreams. Stadium guitar, Bauhausian experimentation, pop and Goth all combined to forge a truly unforgettable brew, topped off by an even more unforgettable single, a rerecording of 'Desire', with Stevenson playing his heart out across a machine gun barrage of blazing licks, riffs, and leads.

'People hadn't noticed how good "Desire" was when I wrote it,' said Jay. 'We wanted to rerecord it, Geffen wanted us to rerecord it. So they put us together with producer Pete Walsh and he did a marvellous job.' Released in October 1986, 'Desire' did nothing whatsoever in the UK. In America, however, it soared to #7 on the Dance chart.

Having spent the summer back in Britain, Gene Loves Jezebel returned to the US to watch the single's rise. The difference it made was immediately apparent. Three months on the road sold out everywhere the band touched down: 600 people in Phoenix, 1,200 in Hollywood, close to 1,500 in Seattle. On 15th November 1986, Gene Loves Jezebel filled New York's Ritz to breaking point, but the greatest moment came at the very end of the outing as 4,400 fans crammed the Hollywood Palladium.

While Gene Loves Jezebel enjoyed their greatest hit, the Cure were preparing to introduce America to their greatest Hits, a compilation of past singles that Smith joked was a remarkable feat for a band whose actual chart successes would scarcely stuff an EP.

Standing On The Beach (the CD and an accompanying video were both titled *Staring At The Sea*) was a no-holds-barred survey of the Cure from the point of view of a singles fan. Every track had seen duty at 45rpm, regardless of whether or not it was actually suited for the medium, as Smith agrees today. But maybe that was the album's strength, the fact that it showed the Cure in every state of its being, from the speeding grime of 'Primary' to the idiot laughability of 'Love Cats', following them all the way from the naivety of 'Killing An Arab' to the in-built claustrophobia of 'Close To Me'.

'The whole point with *Standing On The Beach* was saying to people, "You wouldn't buy a Cure album, but this is what we've done and you might like it",' Smith explained. 'And it worked. For a lot of people, it was the first Cure album they bought and they thought, "I quite like this," and a lot of people who bought that, bought Cure albums after that, and found they liked them as well. It was like an old garage, you look around, "Ah, I recognize that, ah 'Love Cats,' I liked that, I'll get it to play in the car." They're not really buying a Cure album, they're buying songs they know.'

Both at home and abroad, the compilation became the band's biggest hit yet, even spawning a hit of its own, when Smith rerecorded the vocals to 'Boys Don't Cry', let it out as a single for the second time in its life, and was rewarded with the Top 20 status it ought to have grasped all those years before.

The group's powers of invention were further confirmed by their current live show, caught on camera in August 1986 for the *Cure In Orange* video. But, if *Standing On The Beach* set the scene for the Cure's imminent ascent to the top of their profession, it was up to their next studio album, *Kiss Me Kiss Me Kiss Me*, to confirm that they would have no problems once they got there.

TRALIA $1.25/NEW ZEALAND $1.50 (inc GST)/MALAYSIA $2.95/USA $1.95 (by air)/ SPAIN 230pb

MELODY·MAKER

THE RETURN OF THE SISTERS OF MERCY

ELDRITCH

HEAD · ANTHRAX
THE SUGARCUBES
CARMEL
HAMBURGER HILL
PET SHOP BOYS **ALBUM**

LIVE
NEW ORDER
ECHO & THE
BUNNYMEN

Melody Maker *announces The Return of Mister Sister*

Chapter Twelve
I'm Not Saying
Dylan's As Good As
Picasso...

Introduces Eve, and all about her. The Mission and the Cult discover the Bacchanalian vine, and the Fields are flourishing at home as well. Mister Sister returns to drop fall-out onto Middle America, and the Jezebels grapple with commercial demands and rip themselves apart.

'["This Corrosion"]'s directed at somebody and it doesn't take a genius to work out who, although it'll probably take the person concerned some considerable time. I find it embarrassing watching people humiliate themselves for their absurd idea of rock'n'roll.' Andrew Eldritch

reaking for Christmas 1986, the Mission prepared their next single, the heart-attack assault of 'Wasteland', then celebrated with a feat of endurance lesser souls would have baulked at. Booked to appear on Channel 4's *The Tube*, the group's first ever TV appearance, the Mission found their route to the show's Newcastle studios blocked by one of the heaviest snowstorms the country had endured in years.

The M1 was closed; entire swathes of the country were at a standstill. But the Mission made it regardless, together with an uninvited army of now aptly named Eskimos. The scheduled studio audience were trapped in their houses. The Eskimos were herded in to replace them and rewarded the show with one of the most exuberant audiences *The Tube* had ever hosted. The following week, 'Wasteland' was standing at #11 on the chart.

The Mission kicked off the next leg of their tour *World Crusade II* in Sheffield on 18th March 1987, just five days after *World Crusade I* closed. Their most ambitious outing yet, the venture would take them to the United States for the first time to add their voice to the growing British Invasion uproar. Before leaving, however, the band gifted the country with what remains their best remembered (if not, in commercial terms, most successful) single yet, the delicious 'Severina'.

A remarkable song to begin with, 'Severina' attracted attention, too, for the captivating co-vocal of All About Eve's Julianne Regan. While an absolutely spellbinding *Top Of The Pops* performance could not drive 'Severina' higher than #25, the session certainly drew the Mission and All About Eve together. Hussey would produce the group's forthcoming third single, 'Our Summer'; Mick Brown would play drums on the session.

While the music press continued to obsess on the dark side of Gothic Rock, All About Eve were the band that would come to exemplify its brighter aspects.

Regan had come a long way from her own formative days. The former *Zig Zag* journalist had found her way onto the other side of the typewriter by joining Gene Loves Jezebel as one of the revolving door bassists they'd employed in their earliest years.

Most dramatically audible on the band's first BBC radio session, for David Jensen in June 1983, Regan departed soon after for the short-lived Persian Flowers, and cut a solo track (under the pseudonym of the Nursemaids) for a sampler offered by *Artificial Life* fanzine.

By early 1984, Regan was rehearsing with former X-Mal Deutschland drummer Manuela Zwingman and bassist Richard Jackson, before recruiting guitarist Tim Bricheno via a *Melody Maker* classified. His own last band, Aemotii Crii, was best regarded for the presence of former Sex Gang Children drummer Rob Stroud, but the band seldom escaped its home base of Colne, Lancashire – when they did, hitting London for a well-received show at the Batcave in mid-1984, it was the last thing they ever did. Managerial problems split the band the following day.

Taking their name from an old Bette Davis movie and forming their own label, the appropriately named Eden, All About Eve were still finding their feet when, first Jackson, then Zwingman departed. Regan and Bricheno replaced the former with Andy Cousins, another veteran of Aemotii Crii, and the latter – as prevalent fashion apparently demanded – with a drum machine.

All About Eve debuted in March 1985 with the single 'D For Desire', a compulsively swirling effort clearly cut from a similar cloth to the Cocteau Twins, at that time firmly locked into their most obsessively musical phase.

They played their first live show soon after, opening for Chatshow at the Pindar of Wakefield pub in King's Cross, London. They also became regulars at the Underground in Croydon, while a year's-end tour with Play Dead brought them further visibility.

Things continued moving at a snail's pace. Close to a year elapsed before All About Eve released their second single, 'In The Clouds', in spring 1986; another passed before they hooked up with Hussey for 'Our Summer'. And that was the end of the band's so-slow gestation. The two groups toured together; Mission manager Tony Perrin took over All About Eve's affairs and promptly – with the group's fourth single, 'Flowers In Our Hair', topping the Independent chart – landed them a deal with the Mission's own label, Mercury. Everything else that the Mission touched, after all, was turning to gold. How could All About Eve do anything but?

The Mission themselves, meanwhile, headed for the USA, on the brink of a greatness even U2 could only wish for, a status that U2 themselves readily agreed with. Bono, scarcely a man prone to unconsidered hyperbole, personally informed Hussey that the Mission were going to be massive. Hussey, of course, knew exactly what he meant.

Unfortunately, even the most exhilarating roller-coaster has to come to a screeching halt at some point: on 15th May 1987, the Mission's year-long joy-ride flew off the rails, almost exactly halfway through a 41-date American tour that the group, with a self-belief that flew in the face of all received wisdom (and all human endurance), insisted on completing in exactly 41 days. On the road in Britain, you can drive from one end of the country to the other in a matter of hours. Get into the American mid-west and you can motor for days without seeing a single town. Even by private jet, hopping from venue to venue in straight succession is a remarkable feat. To do it by bus is practically super-human. After a year of running full-tilt without a break, the Mission were a lot frailer than they realised.

Adams, in particular, had been growing increasingly fragile as the outing progressed. He finally cracked in Los Angeles, racing onto Hollywood's Sunset Strip in the early hours of the morning, there to be run down by one of the police cars that was despatched to investigate reports of a crazed, barefoot Englishman jumping up and down in the middle of the road.

Miraculously unharmed and somehow escaping without being charged, Adams spent the remainder of the day sinking drink after drink. Then, just an hour before that evening's concert, he took his passport and fled. Within three hours, he was on a flight back to Blighty, leaving his bandmates in utter disarray. Of course they cancelled that evening's show – the question was, what about the other 20 that still loomed ahead of them?

The show would go on. Sound engineer Pete Turner agreed to stand in for a few nights, an American friend named Surf completed the outing. But, if the immediate future – which now included a batch of shows opening for the Psychedelic Furs – was in safe hands, the group's long-term prognosis was not good.

The Mission were not the only British band haring their way across America that summer of 1987. The Cult, too, were on the road, with Ian Astbury, in particular, doing his level best to live up to an honour that Wayne Hussey had bestowed upon him with the b-side of the Mission's 'Stay With Me' single. The pair were, the song insisted, 'Blood Brother[s]', which meant they thought alike, dreamed alike and, when it came to raucous on-the-road activities, behaved alike.

Britain scarcely figured in the group's calculations any longer. The Cult played just three British concerts during 1986, a one-off London show at the Brixton Academy and festival dates in Glasgow and Milton Keynes (opening for Simple Minds). Their only other performance was a return to the Janice Long Show, previewing four new songs on a session broadcast on 3rd March: 'Love Removal Machine', 'Conquistador', 'Electric Ocean' and 'King Contrary Man'.

The album that those songs would eventually dignify, however, could scarcely have suffered a more painful gestation. Still trying to cushion himself from the continued savagery of his homeland media, Astbury had turned to alcohol for solace, with the inevitable consequences. 'I'm *still* too sensitive to criticism,' Astbury explained in his defence. 'It really hurt me, it just crushed me over a period of time, and I began to drink a lot more heavily than I ever had.'

According to the Cult's own mythology, the sessions for what became the *Electric* album passed by with Astbury in an perpetual stupor; he himself admits that 'when we did *Electric*, I was drunk every day of the sessions. That record is like my evil twin, the Mr Hyde to *Love*'s Dr Jekyll, a really dark album. I mean, all we did was drink. I was completely fucking wasted all the time, I don't remember being sober during that period at all.'

The initial *Electric* sessions, at Richard Branson's lavish Manor Studios outside Kidlington, Oxfordshire, were undertaken with *Love* producer Steve Brown again at the helm. Within weeks of completing the record, however, Astbury and Duffy acknowledged that the album left much to be desired. Brown, Duffy condemned, had resorted to as 'much the same approach as before. Whereas we'd changed.'

In November 1986, he and Astbury flew to New York where Def Jam supremo Rick Rubin was waiting to remix the album's key tracks. Remixing became rerecording, which in turn led to the Cult scrapping the entire album and starting again under Rubin's supervision. In February, 1987, four months after *Electric* was originally to be released, the first fruit of the sessions, the single 'Love Removal Machine', was released. 'Lil' Devil' followed, alongside the album itself, and the Cult hit the road.

A short UK tour debuted a newly revised line-up. While Jamie Stewart shifted to rhythm guitar, Kid Chaos, formerly of Zodiac Mindwarp, came in on bass. Less than three years after they supported Big Country at Wembley Arena, the Cult were back at that cavernous pit, as headliners in their own, much-deserved right.

More important developments, however, were afoot in America. *Electric* broke the band into the Top 40 for the first time, while spinning off a sequence of videos that remain staples of MTV-style programming today. Even more significantly,

Electric's tumultuous barrage, the rabble-rousing choruses, the glam guitars set to stun and a lyrical bent that seemed obsessed with cheap thrills and the rawk'n'rawl lifestyle set the stage for the glam-metal outburst that would utterly reshape the second half of the United States' hitherto-stagnant 1980s music scene.

'It wasn't our intention,' Astbury is adamant. 'But it was rewarding. The whole scene was changing, and we became part of it. I think it was inevitable because of the way Punk fell into the Eighties. Suddenly Phil Collins was omnipresent... Phil Collins was Buddha, Mick and Keith, Bruce Springsteen, Sting, Eric Clapton... the Live Aid crowd just permeated the Eighties, and the younger groups couldn't come through because there was no way through that hierarchy. I mean, how do you get past Phil Collins?

'Then in the late Eighties, groups like Metallica burst through, Guns N'Roses burst through, we burst through, the rap scene burst through. Suddenly, there was something happening again, and whatever it turned out to be, it was a changing of the guard. Goodbye Mr. Spandex Seventies Rocker, hello Mr. New Hair Eighties Rocker. Only the new guard became the old guard very quickly, to the point where Guns n'Roses are now the establishment themselves, and we rubbed shoulders with that a little, we got dangerously, incredibly, close to that.

'But it was kind of fun in a way, driving on the edge. It was really quite exciting to go there when we absolutely had no business being there, being in their world, competing with them and doing quite well. Actually, it was incredible.'

This latest Cult line-up toured the US incessantly through 1987. Throughout the spring and summer, they hauled around the nation's sports arenas with Billy Idol, playing to four- and five-figure crowds nightly for close to four months. That outing over, they were immediately despatched on their own headlining tour, supported by the infant Guns n'Roses on a tour that was swiftly to enter into the annals of Rock Legend as the drunken episodes mounted up as quickly as the wrecked hotel bills. By the time the band finally came off the road, in March 1988, the Cult – like the Mission before them – was reeling in shellshock.

Chaos of a very different nature had also gripped Gene Loves Jezebel. The success of 'Desire' placed immense strains on the group – or, more specifically, upon the twins. For the first time in their lives, they were forced to face an issue they had barely imagined even existed, a conflict over just how far they were prepared to go in search of success.

Michael Aston: 'It was difficult for me, because I was trying to aim the visuals between [Pete] Rizzo and [Chris] Bell, who were essentially very middle class, bourgeois boys, in my opinion, so they couldn't see where Michael Aston was coming from. Neither could Jay, because Jay's pretty puritan about it all too. Things have to be harmonies, a bridge has to go there, a chorus has to go there. But I come from a more Patti Smith position, where the emotions, the delivery, what you convey, is far more important than the sum of the parts.

'Onstage, I'm the shaman. Jay's always saying, "Why can't you stand still?" But I don't care if I look like Isadora Duncan on LSD, I have to express my emotions. I came from a performance standpoint, working at the ICA, seeing artists – it's very powerful to me seeing artists, seeing an individual dance to music, and express themself.'

The presence of James Stevenson, too, confounded Michael Aston's intentions. Jay enthused, 'James is very much on the same wavelength as me, musically. I can just strum him something, and he can transpose it into something else. We both like interstellar guitars, the kind that blow you away, that wake you up, hopefully make you cry. It's very much a celebration of our lives.' Michael, however, simply could not understand the guitarist.

'I remember sitting down with James once,' Michael mused, 'and being shocked that he didn't like Bob Dylan. I don't care what anyone says, he's an incredible lyricist. Not to understand that is like saying, "Picasso doesn't matter." I'm not saying Dylan's as good as Picasso, there's a lot better poets, but the fusion of the music and the delivery and whatever else, you have to appreciate it. But James loves the Velvet Underground, which I never could understand. Philosophically, we differed. Retrospectively, bringing James into the band was probably the worst decision we ever made, certainly from Jay's and my position as a working partnership.'

'Musical differences' is an industry euphemism for a variety of sins, from personality clashes to chemical dependence but, in this instance, it meant precisely what it says, and it was tearing the group apart. By the time Gene Loves Jezebel returned to the studio to record their next album, the record that Geffen said would break them wide open in the United States, Michael Aston was 'desperately unhappy. So I walked out of the band. I love James as a person, but I think he really narrowed our vision, he lent himself to the more poppy side of Jay, which is only one side of him, really. In my opinion, it took away the art of Gene Loves Jezebel, completely marginalized me from purely an artistic, performance standpoint.'

His brother agreed – with reservations. 'Mike was right, James did pull us slightly in a poppier sense. He doesn't come from the same angles as Mike and I. Some people would argue the genius of Gene Loves Jezebel was the stuff I did with James, other people would argue the dark spaces. "Stephen" [from *Immigrant*] is the most classic song I've ever written, it's very dark and there's great beauty in that, a vulnerability. But there's vulnerability in the poppier stuff too. My point is, you try to create where your head is at in that space. You can look to the real dark quality, or you can try to breathe, stop yourself hanging yourself, and hang onto something that glows, a spark.

'If people don't love things James and I did together, it's because we have this love of melody. We'd always bounce on each other what I thought was the genius of something, that a lot of people didn't get. They want to hear a story of how someone was raped that night, and to them that is important. To me there's another side to it too, which is the genius of the pop single.'

And pop singles were what Geffen wanted this latest album, *House Of Dolls*, to be filled with. Jay Aston: '[People] forget the pressure the record company was putting on us for that record. They spent a lot of money, and product's money to them. It's just a business. It was all a nightmare.'

As the album sessions loomed, Geffen began searching around for the appropriate producer to draw out the band's magic. They settled on Jimmy Iovine, renowned for a string of mega-million sellers ranging from Dire Straits to Stevie Nicks, Simple Minds to Joan Jett. The adventure perished after just one single.

Having completed 'Motion Of Love' to what they thought was everybody's satisfaction, Gene Loves Jezebel were mortified to discover that Geffen had commissioned an entirely new mix from Iovine, to be carried out while the band wasn't even in the country. Jay Aston shuddered, 'By the time "Motion Of Love" came back from LA, it had turned into this horrible little song. If I played you the original, you wouldn't recognize it, it's Joy Division. And now it comes back a poppy nothing.'

Refusing ever to work with Iovine again, the band put forth their suggestions for a suitable producer – Michael Aston, in particular, was keen to try Dave Allen, producer of the Cure's most recent albums, or else return to John Leckie. Geffen ignored him completely. Instead, they suggested a return engagement with 'Desire' producer Peter Walsh and the rest of the band, anxious simply to get on, agreed. It was a decision that they would quickly come to regret.

'The thing about *House Of Dolls*, none of us in the band actually like it,' condemned Jay. 'We love the songs; the way we do it live, whatever version of the band we've had. But we don't think the album captures the songs. We didn't like the production on it, it's too slick, we didn't feel good about it at the time.

'We were fucked with a lot, and don't forget the era we were in, the producers ruled literally. Listen to "Gorgeous" – they cut things about. The song doesn't become clear anymore. These things are frustrating. Suddenly we were both forced to sing things that we didn't want to sing, almost.'

The frustrations mounted quickly – and were resolved with shattering suddenness. Two songs into the session, Michael Aston quit the band – dropping his bombshell just days before Jay planned unleashing one of his own. 'I was going to leave the group. That was the original plan. Only Mike picked up the wrong signals and thought *we* didn't want *him* in the band. And suddenly, I was stuck with this band that were totally on my side, or just picked me because they thought I was the better horse at the time.'

Geffen were unimpressed by the turmoil and, so far as they were concerned, such tantrums made no difference anyway. *House Of Dolls* emerged an astounding album, at least by the sonic standards of the time. A watertight rhythm section, glittering guitars, yowling vocals that oozed lascivious excitement: it was a devil of a long way from *Promise* or *Immigrant* or even *Discover*. But it was a mainline to America's heart all the same. 'Motion Of Love'. 'Suspicion' and '20 Killer Hurts' all peeled off as club and MTV staples – '20 Killer Hurts' even squeezed into an episode of TV's *Miami Vice*. That, so far as the record company suits were concerned, was all that mattered.

Though he played very little part in the album sessions, Michael Aston remained a vital component within the band itself – the more so once the promoters and booking agencies had set to work and presented Gene Loves Jezebel with a six month world tour. It opened with two months around the American stadium circuit, sharing the bill with Echo and the Bunnymen and New Order, followed by assaults on South America, Japan and Europe, and a return to the US in January 1988 for three more months of clubs and theatres. Agreeing to put the recent past behind them, the brothers decided to reunite. Except the past would not stay buried.

Out on the road, the tension between the twins just kept mounting. Half the time they were fighting, the other half they weren't speaking. By the time the band finally limped home in early 1988, the only certainty was that Michael Aston's resolve was set in stone. He moved to Los Angeles to plan a career of his own; Jay remained in London to maintain the band. While they would reconvene in late 1988, with six months' cooling-off time behind them, it was apparent that nothing had changed. A handful of desultory sessions with producer Steve Brown collapsed in nerve-shredding disarray and Michael Aston quit for good that autumn.

Some good did come out of that final American tour, however – and Flesh For Lulu, the support band, grasped it with both hands.

The Lulus were late arrivals on the American rock scene, just as they were – or so glumly disapproving critics continued to snipe – late arrivals on the British Goth scene.

Not quite confirming, but certainly not negating the brilliance of their debut, the Lulus' second album, *Big Fun City*, was cautiously received by a media that thought the band might have finally gone away, suspicions that appeared to be confirmed when the band lapsed into further silence for much of the next year. They resurfaced in late 1986, however, with the release of a positively angelic new single, 'Idol'. 'Siamese Twist' followed in the new year, before their third album, confidently titled *Long Live The New Flesh*, dynamited even the most cynical doubter's forebodings.

Signed now to Beggars Banquet and reinvented as an utterly skewed pop band, still capable of dipping into blacker waters when it suited them (the death-country opus 'Dream On Cowboy') but just as happy evoking '60s hit memories with some simply soaring melodies, Flesh For Lulu had already spent over a year promoting the album when they were added to labelmates Gene Loves Jezebel's US tour.

With Flesh For Lulu not quite taking advantage of the turmoil that was shattering the headliners, but certainly turning in performances that were a lot easier to digest than some of Gene Loves Jezebel's petulant displays, *Long Live The New Flesh* began edging into the US Top 70 at a time when its British sales, like the band's British profile, could be reckoned up on one hand. 'And, as time went by, we just forgot about England,' said Rocco. 'The English press just wouldn't give us a chance.' America, on the other hand, couldn't get enough.

The Fields Of The Nephilim, too, greeted the last years of the 1980s from a position of astonishing strength. 1987 opened with the band preparing for the release of their debut album, *Dawnrazor*, unveiled that May and a guaranteed chart-topper, both at home and, gradually, across Europe.

Occasionally miasmic, oft-times myopic, and furiously derivative if you cared to think in such terms, *Dawnrazor* was everything that the band's live show had promised, harnessed to the disciplines of the studio but still loose and lurid enough to recapture the thrill of the stage show. The vocals that seldom descended below a loud growl, the guitars that wailed out sepulchral hymns, it was very easy to write the whole thing off as just another pantomime-horseman of the apocalypse. But there was a churning conviction to the vinyl as well, the knowledge that if one just shut down the critical faculties and dived headlong into the Fields' glorious din, one would be converted on the spot.

And so, in many cases, it proved. Lifted from the album and transplanted into the soundtrack of the Italian horror film *Demons 2*, 'Power' topped that country's national Indy chart. The reissued *Burning The Fields* followed it to similar heights. Germany, too, succumbed to the Fields of the Nephilim's charms. At home, in August 1987, they were among the heroes of what was otherwise the dullest Reading festival since the last one, while anybody capable of digging a little deeper than whatever music television was currently being drip-fed into their own homes swiftly discovered the Fields of the Nephilim to be knocking out some of the most remarkable videos of the age.

Directed by *Hardware* visionary Richard Stanley, the zombies, mutants, cowboys and cemeteries-laden 'Preacher Man', and the *MacBeth*-ian 'Blue Water', in particular, were triumphs of the genre. But, as *Helter Skelter* magazine pointed out, you had to go to a lot of effort to see them. Television certainly wasn't going to show them.

"Yes, well, it's not the acceptable sort of video thing really, is it?" Petit responded. "Most videos these days are performance videos with everyone looking really nice, smiling and having a good time, cars and women, et cetera. If you do something a little bit different, no-one wants to know.

'It seems to be the primary objective at the moment to make videos that...you don't have to think about the music, like Stock, Aitken and Waterman and all that old bollocks. You know what I mean, just a beat with lots of people running around smiling. Yes, I did think some of these people such as Channel Four did have a bit more brains to try something different." But no, they were no more willing to take a chance than *Top Of The Pops*.

1987 also took the Fields of the Nephilim to the US for the first time, although unlike the ever-broadening profile that other bands sought, this was simply a low-key outing designed, as Petit put it, 'to test the water and see how we would go down over there.' Keen to sample the nation's wares and return home in one piece, the Fields of the Nephilim laid their conditions out long before the tour began. There was to be none of what Petit called 'big advertising or hype,' an important consideration because, as he continued, 'RCA, who we're with over there, could have gone well overboard. They could've tried to really push us down people's throats and we're not that sort of a band. [But] the reaction was good...' The Fields of the Nephilim returned home to continue their slow-burning ascent.

Watching with a similar detachment, Andrew Eldritch was also preparing to stir once more, reclaiming the Sisters Of Mercy's hallowed name and restaking his claim on feverish grandiosity. By now, all but Patricia Morrison and the ever faithful Doktor Avalanche had departed from his side, but producer Jim Steinman was on hand to compensate for any paucity of band members and, from Eldritch's home in Hamburg, plans were laid for the most purposefully ostentatious project yet in the Sisters' convoluted history.

For anybody waiting for Eldritch to follow through on his oft-quoted opinion that Motorhead was one of the most important bands of the recent age, Steinman appeared a peculiar choice – but was he really? Motorhead's importance, after all, lies not in their ability to drive heedlessly through the pain threshhold, but in the sheer bombast and overture of their sound, the construction of vast, unyielding symphonies in power trio drag. Steinman adhered to precisely the same agenda – he just wrung it through a mangle of considerably greater sonic complexity. From his earliest public emergence alongside Todd Rundgren at the helm of Meatloaf's stupendously over-the-top *Bat Out Of Hell*, through to the selective succession of similarly grandiose gestures he had delivered since then, be it Bonnie Tyler's 'Total Eclipse Of The Heart,' or his own dramatically mad solo releases, Steinman's fist was clenched firmly around exactly the same adrenalin pump as Lemmy's. And it was a grip that Andrew Eldritch instinctively knew the Sisters needed to feel.

'This Corrosion', summed up by Eldritch as 'power in the face of misery,' was released in September 1987, sailing in on the waves of a vast operatic backdrop (provided by the 40-piece New York Chorale Society) and defying even the sourest listener not to feel a slight fission of excitement and awe. It was, at its heart, another jab at the Mission, although Eldritch was suitably coy when he told *Melody Maker*, '[it's] directed at somebody and it doesn't take a genius to work out who, although it'll probably take the person concerned some considerable time. I find it embarrassing watching people humiliate themselves for their absurd idea of rock'n'roll.'

'Wake (RSVP)' had been answered in the most fitting way possible, but there was so much more to 'This Corrosion' than simply another bout of handbags. There was its 'glorious stupidity,' as Eldritch smirked. Its 'bombast' – such effective bombast – that added up to one of the most impressive sounding records of the age. Supported by a Stuart Orme video that slammed Eldritch and Morrison into wet leather and wasteland (actually London's Docklands), one of the most memorable visual experiences too. Indeed, it could have been even more dramatic – Eldritch's initial vision for the video included shots of caged Americans being taunted by rioting Middle Easterners. With an eye for both MTV and political sensitivities, however, the record company insisted that the scenes be cut.

Eldritch's partnership with Jim Steinman unfortunately stretched to just one more song on the forthcoming Sisters album, the similarly vast 'Dominion/Mother Russia', a towering behemoth constructed around crashing drums, operatic chorales, stentorian vocals and a rhythm that could run a marathon.

On album (an edited version was issued as a UK single), it is an astonishingly powerful piece, a soaring opus that disguised an anti-American diatribe flavoured by the Chernobyl nuclear disaster. For the accompanying video, Eldritch and Morrison travelled to the ancient city of Petra to film a semi-intelligible adventure epic amid the ruins. But, in an interview with *Melody Maker*, Eldritch painted the portrait that he truly intended, Americans 'huddled in their mobile homes while Mother Russia rained down on them. They deserve it.'

The *Floodland* album was released in November 1987, a unanimously praised masterpiece that, in spiralling so far from the home base that the Sisters had made their own, confirmed all that Eldritch had sworn he would accomplish, once he had cut away what he called the 'deadwood' – an expression that clearly translated to the need to sustain the appearance of a functioning 'band.' The Sisters Of Mercy was his vision alone.

Despite the success of the album and the singles that flew off it – 'Dominion' and 'Lucretia, My Reflection' (described by Eldritch as his 'welcome aboard, Patricia' song) both followed 'This Corrosion' into the UK Top 20 – Eldritch adamantly refused to tour the album. Rather, he sat back and let the videos do the hard work, with the Bombay cotton factory shoot of 'Lucretia, My Reflection' offering a visual blueprint for every industrial record of the next five years. Coupling this unimagined stance with the vitriol evinced by the unseen 'This Corrosion' footage and 'Mother Russia''s wishful thinking, clearly this was one horse from the stable that was not going to America to graze the tempting green of the Yankee dollar.

The Cult's Ian Astbury and Billy Duffy

Chapter Thirteen
50 Machines, One Black Heart

A description of how the best-selling singles of the American year came to include the Cure, the Cult and three quarters of Bauhaus. The Sisters and the Jezebels, too, find a new lease of life, but it's not only pride that comes before a fall. So do hit records.

'So that left Billy and I having to deal with each other, which is when we discovered all the debts and the legal messes which were left over from before. We were falling out with our new manager, and the whole thing had become incredibly cynical. It was horrible. It was like something out of one of those old b-movies where they have about 50 medical machines hooked up to one tiny little black heart.' Ian Astbury

If the Sisters were purposefully drawing back from the musical demands of the rock'n'roll lifestyle, the Mission were finally distancing themselves from its physical attributes.

Coming off the road in early August 1987, with only a headline appearance at the Reading festival's 25th anniversary at the end of the month to punctuate the calm, the surviving threesome set about repairing the bridges that separated them from Adams, luring him (not altogether unwillingly) back into the camp to begin work on their second album.

The sessions, at the Cult's old stomping ground, the Manor studios, would consume the remainder of the year as the band painstakingly constructed an album that would not only consolidate all that their debut had promised, but would also shed its own, beguiling light on one of the harshest criticisms of the band's musical career so far – that they (like the Sisters Of Mercy before them) were little more than a reconstructed Led Zeppelin, as prone to musical hyperbole and symbolic meaningless as that most hairy of hallowed pre-Punk dinosaurs. Zeppelin's own bass player, John Paul Jones, would be producing the sessions.

It was a cautious courtship. The Mission had approached Jones the moment they heard he was considering widening his own horizons to begin working with 'new' bands; Jones, however, was not at all keen, first experiencing the band through their press coverage and then, having recanted slightly after hearing *God's Own Medicine*, being utterly underwhelmed by their live show, witnessed at Leeds United's Elland Road stadium in June, when the Mission opened for U2.

Meeting the band, however, he rapidly changed his mind again; meeting Jones, the Mission in turn reversed their entire perspective on studio work. Tim Palmer, producer of their debut, had been content to let the band work as fast and frenzied as they wished. Jones, on the other hand, had a meticulous touch that could spent days trying to perfect the most minute element of a song.

The Mission acceded to his every command – only Jones' reservations about the band's continued indulgence in amphetamines, scarcely a drug suited to such an agonising approach, rattled the composure of the sessions. When *Children* was finally released in March 1988 (on the heels of the hymnal 'Tower Of Strength' single), it was clear that the new approach had worked. Still recognisably the Mission, still a florid flourish of smirking Gothic cliché and unashamed 70s rock excess, *Children* emerged the best album Led Zeppelin never made – in the best sense of the phrase.

It was also a deeply personal record. Hussey's first child, daughter Hannah, had recently been born but the singer and the mother were no longer on terms. 'You can see the sense of guilt there about being an absent father,' Hussey mourned.

The depth of his emotions, however, was more than equalled by the sheer vastness of the record, a symphonic rock experience that surely reached its peak with the latest in the band's always well-chosen catalogue of covers. As if the rest of the message was not hard-hitting enough, the closing number, American hard rock giants Aerosmith's 'Dream On', addressed the Mission's ambitions with neon clarity.

Riding a riff that could have been cut from the Cult, shotgun-wedded to the galloping rhythm of Zeppelin's own 'Immigrant Song', opening the verse with a stadium-shaking yelp, then throwing in a primary school choir for added anthemic piquancy, 'Hymn (For America)' was so blatant as to be blinding. But only time, and the band's next US tour, would tell whether the country could really be so easily swayed.

If their last world tour had been enormous, the Mission's next outing was immense, a year-long escapade that would take them to 26 countries, opening in the UK in February 1988 (the latest incarnation of Mick Brown's old band, Red Lorry Yellow Lorry, were support) and then vanishing into the wider world with only periodic news flashes reaching home to record another triumphant concert, another slice of off-stage ribaldry, another audience swayed and sucked into the Mission's web.

A string of American shows opening for John Paul Jones' Zeppelin bandmate Robert Plant started badly, as audiences reacted with uncertainty to the Mission's appropriation of the 'Dream On' anthem and shifted restlessly throughout the remainder of the show. But Plant himself adored the group, going so far as to tell them that, of all the Zep disciples he'd ever seen, the Mission came closest to the original's ideal.

They played their first major American headline shows, too, going out with Balaam & The Angel as a most suitable support and forging, for the first time, the same kind of links with Stateside audiences as they'd already accomplished in Britain and Europe. Out of what Brown disparagingly called the Enormodomes, into the clubs where the audience could smell the band's sweat, the Mission played some of the most triumphant dates of their career so far – certainly since those first, Eskimo-enhanced club dates – and were rewarded with accolades from every angle of the industry.

'Hymn (For America)' may not have done the trick single-handedly – short of being released as a monster, career-defining hit 45, no individual song could ever do that. But the spirit with which the Mission romanced the heartland left nobody in any doubt that next time out, they'd be scraping the sky.

Peter Murphy was also reaping the rewards of exquisitely careful planning.

Like Love and Rockets, Murphy's true post-Bauhaus career got underway with a radical reinvention, a positively simmering cover version, Pere Ubu's 'Final Solution.' That and, the following year, a dynamic revision of Magazine's Glitterstomp 'The Light Pours Out Of Me' indicated that whatever his past might have portended, the solo singer was going to move far, far away from the narrow confines of reputation and renown.

Should The World Fail To Fall Apart, Murphy's solo debut, was released in mid-1986 to warm reviews but low sales: a flickering appearance at #82 on the UK chart set few pulses racing. In fairness, the album was more memorable for its intent than its contents – and that despite a brief reunion between Murphy and Ash in the most surprising place of all.

'Movement Of Fear', a track from the Tones On Tail album, was widely proclaimed (and perceived) as a vicious dig at Murphy; turning the song's lyrics back on their writer, Ash himself, Murphy retaliated with 'The Answer Is Clear', then invited his victim in to play on the song. The guitarist, as Murphy delightedly chuckled later, 'blitzed all over the thing.'

The apparent failure of *Should The World Fail To Fall Apart* notwithstanding, evidence that Murphy was made of at least as stout material as Love And Rockets was swiftly forthcoming.

Although he'd been unable to arrange a US release for the album, Murphy nevertheless insisted on touring the country, kicking off his first American adventure in February 1987. 19 shows opened in Boston and proved a wild success – far more than their UK counterparts, where a sea of empty seats bespoke only the speed with which Bauhaus' once loyal audience had found other thrills. Murphy ensured, therefore, that American concert-goers were amply awarded for their loyalty.

In a live set built around the largely unheard *Should The World Fail To Fall Apart*, Murphy still found time for a clutch of old favourites – 'The Passion Of Lovers', 'Spirit', 'Kick In The Eye' and 'She's In Parties' were all in the set. Nor was Murphy averse to throwing a taste of 'Bela Lugosi's Dead' into the mix either: just enough to get the crowd up on its feet, before he snatched it away and moved elsewhere instead. It was a brilliant tease, making for stunning theatre.

But it also sowed seeds of expectation that Murphy had no intention of cultivating. Back home, writing with former B-Movie keyboard player Paul Statham, Murphy began formulating his second album, *Love Hysteria*, around the passion for so-called 'world music' that he had recently begun to incubate.

It was not exactly a bolt out of the blue. Dead Can Dance, a band he had admired since their inception, frequently dipped into those waters, while Murphy's wife-to-be, Turkish dancer Beyhan Foulkes, not only opened his ears to the music of her homeland, she also ensured that he remained aware of the pitfalls of diving into another culture, without first understanding the sub-cultures that it comprised.

'There's enough of that done in Turkey,' Murphy reflected. 'They call it Arabesque, and what they mean by that is a bastardization of sources, and it's not respected. I took a lesson from that in a way. It seems a bit tired now, done to death, and not always very well, although there are people who do it brilliantly, like Dead Can Dance. But, since I can't pull it off properly, it seemed better to steer away, and take a realistic view of it."

Solidly backed by his own new band, the 100 Men, Murphy unveiled the compulsively haunting 'All Night Long' in February 1988, a fabulous 45 that rode around upon an eastern motif and an all-but perfect hookline, dramatic and anthemic in equal proportions.

Backed on the 12-inch single by Murphy's own tribute to the album that started so much, a cover of Iggy Pop's *The Idiot* showstopper 'Funtime', 'All Night Long' failed to chart. But, if his first American tour had shaped an American cult, regular airings for 'All Night Long' on MTV's *120 Minutes* alternative rock showcase ensured an undercurrent of imminent excitement that was already equalling Love And Rockets'. For the first time, he said at the time, he felt as though he was being treated as an individual. Bauhaus was still there, of course: interviewed on MTV, the first question was 'Peter Murphy, how do you feel about being a legend in your own time?' Even so, the band was no longer the sole source of his fame.

That much was apparent from the *Love Hysteria* tour, as the black-clad, distinctly Bauhausian hordes who attended the first tour suddenly began to appear the minority, overtaken by the college kids who'd seen the video, heard the album and made up their own minds what Murphy represented.

Love and Rockets were experiencing a similar rejuvenation. Another year of American touring had concluded with 1987's *Earth-Sun-Moon* album, a vivid reversal of all that the preceding *Express* had indicated, but a stunning contrast as well. Where *Express* had maintained its predecessor's psychedelic angle, tightening the noose around such acid-washed rockers as 'Kundalini Express' and 'It Could be Sunshine,' then drawing back to the stoned folk of 'An American Dream" and 'Life In Laralay,' great swathes of *Earth-Sun-Moon* could have fallen out of an early 70s Traffic rehearsal, as remixed by the Ozric Tentacles. 'That,' Ash explained, 'came down to where we'd record. We did an electric album on *Express*. So then we said, "Let's do a strumming-guitars-in-the-country album," which was *Earth-Sun-Moon*. So we recorded in the country. *Express* was recorded in London. We'd always go somewhere that was completely different from where we recorded the previous album to keep it fresh."

Now the band was reinventing its sound again. Work on Love and Rockets' fourth album consumed much of 1988, a public silence broken only by the pseudonymous appearance of the bumble-bee bodied Bubblemen, wacky post-Residents alter-egos whose cartoon visages were scribbled across the last album's inner sleeve and who would emerge with their own 'The Bubblemen Are Coming' single.

Love And Rockets themselves returned in January 1989 with the four song *Motorcycle* EP. After all the soporifics of *Earth-Sun-Moon*, things could not have been more different. Again. Cacophonous and electronic, guitar-driven and synth-laden, cracked by Ash's scaling saxophone, the songs on *Motorcycle* were an intense combination of house, trance and the industrial nation, a bridge between styles, a catalyst to metamorphosis. It was also positively earth-shaking.

J explained the transition. 'In London in 1988, that's when acid house was coming in. We'd listen to these pirate stations on the radio. "This is really interesting." The influence of that can be heard on "Bike Dance"' – and its impact can be felt on 'So Alive', one of *the* monster defining singles of late 1980s America, one of the biggest hits of 1989 and one of the heaviest nails ever to be banged into a band's coffin.

'So Alive' was released in America in spring 1989, and hurled itself straight to the top of the US charts, peaking at an absolutely unbelievable #3. The band's fourth album, the sensibly-titled *Love And Rockets*, peaked one place lower in September. It was a glorious coup, all the more so since it was so unexpected.

At a time when 'alternative music' was still a media hype waiting to happen and the mainstream muddied everything that crept close to success, bands like Love And Rockets – and, indeed, the Cult, the Mission, Gene Loves Jezebel, Flesh For Lulu, all the odd little acts that had come creeping out of Britain's post-Punk underbelly with the words 'Gothic Rock' prominent in their letters of referral – were still regarded as a self-sustaining anomaly, acts whose audience cherished them as the world's best-kept secret; whose detractors viewed every new hit a fluke; whose own record company essentially despaired of them.

Robert Smith once remarked, without a shred of false modesty, 'our record company only like us when we're selling records,' and that was more than likely true. Right now, though, Love And Rockets – and the Cure – were selling records. Lots of them. Their record companies must have liked them very much indeed.

A double album released exactly one year after the *Standing On The* Beach hits collection, the Cure's next effort, May 1987's *Kiss Me Kiss Me Kiss Me*, undoubtedly disillusioned many of the group's long-time followers with its sheer bulk and diversity. Their cries of dismay were barely audible, lost beneath the keen and trample of an entire-new Cure audience, drawn from around the globe.

In the space of a year, eighteen months at the outside, Britain, Japan, Europe and, finally, the United States had succumbed to the band. While *Standing On The Beach* breached the US Top 50, *Kiss Me* stormed the Top 40. MTV bled the string of enchanting videos which paired the band with director Tim Pope across some of the most memorable images of the decade; radio stumbled across the Cure's latest single, 'Just Like Heaven' (originally written as the theme to a French TV show); and the American public dispatched it into the Top 40 too.

When the Cure convened in mid-1988 to begin working on the songs which would, less than a year later, emerge as the band's eighth studio album, it was in the knowledge that the group's commercial standing was at an all-time high.

From the outset of the new album, however, those feelings were clouding with concern. The Cure's greatest hits so far had been the ones which, in the hands of any other band, might be called 'novelty' records: 'The Love Cats', with its bouncy swing and singalong jingles; the demented dance-pop of 'Why Can't I Be You', a lasciviously lurid love song made all the more cataclysmic by its accompanying video; and 'Hot Hot Hot', unadulterated jazz pop fed through the same kind of musical time machine that Sparks, darling doyens of 70s' eccentricity, had developed around the time of 'Looks Looks Looks'. The Cure's reputation painted them as unabashed doom-mongers. But their greatest hits were the opposite entirely.

These latest sessions didn't even glance towards the lighter, brighter pastures into which the Cure had strayed of late. When Smith spoke of it, even during its embryonic phase, he peppered his conversation with comparisons to *Faith* and *Pornography*, an incarnation of the Cure that many of the band's most recent fans had no idea even existed. Older fans, too, would have cause for concern: the period in question was, of course, also that which climaxed with the Cure's total collapse. When Smith, too, appeared to be thinking along those lines, most patently with his choice of title for the new record – it was, of course, *Disintegration* – the alarm bells were set ringing everywhere.

But Smith had a lot to write about. His 30th birthday was swiftly approaching – on 21st April 1989 – and he admitted that the event was weighing heavy on his mind. Many of the songs that would be included on *Disintegration* started life as possible inclusions on Smith's own, long-mooted, solo album, itself a reaction to the looming chronological milestone. He'd been thinking about the project for years and, following his marriage to long-time girlfriend Mary in August, he retired to the couple's new home on the south coast and started writing for it.

'I took [the songs] to the rest of the group, knowing that if they were resistant to the ideas of going back to the Cure of eight years ago, I would use them myself. I would have been quite happy to make those songs on my own. This record has the same kind of continuity and theme of our earlier material. I didn't want any songs that didn't conform to that mood. It will be compared to those records, but I think it's better.'

The difference between past and present, however, was immense. Smith admitted that 'the things that bother me seem to crystallize, rather than go away. The same things still disturb me, but I scream in private now, rather than in public. The group is there for me to scream.'

One of the key moments in the gestation of *Disintegration* came when Smith sat down one evening and listened to *Faith*. It was the first time he had absorbed himself in that album in some years and, he confessed, 'It disturbed me. I realized I hadn't resolved anything. I reached the point a long time ago where I don't have any kind of spiritual faith and so I have to find something else, some form of release otherwise everything would become unbearable.'

The theme of most of the *Disintegration*-bound material, he continued, 'is age – what happens with age, and your inability to feel as keenly, and that sense of loss all the time. Which either depresses you or it doesn't. I've always felt the perfect age was 17, and I don't wander about crying about it all the time, but those things do bother me.' This latest crop of songs, in particular, was written 'at a time when I was feeling completely awful. I was very aware that I was reaching my 30th birthday, I realised that I didn't want to go on juggling my different personalities. I didn't want to keep on worrying about the difference between the public me and the private me.'

It was, of course, a theme that also haunted *Seventeen Seconds*, written when Smith was just 20 and already realizing 'we're not young any longer.' To return to past pastures was not unusual for Smith; to return to them with such a self-flagellating vengeance was. Smith, then, was adamant that he had to get it right this time. *Disintegration*, he insisted, marked 'the last time I'll write about internal disintegration, because there's nothing left to say about it now. I was writing about the things that troubled me for the last time. They're all gone now.'

Producer Dave Allen continued, 'For *Disintegration*, we were trying to knit it into one long entity so it's obsessively non-diverse.' *Disintegration* was meant to test those fans who had maybe picked up on the Cure as a result of their recent pop successes with the singles from *Head On The Door* and *Kiss Me Kiss Me Kiss Me*.

'I want people to like the Cure for the right reasons,' Smith explained, 'because it's different to everything else, and not really accessible. It's a bit of a crass generalization, but people whose favourite Cure albums are *Pornography* and *Disintegration* are generally more alert, and have thought about things.' As for the band's long-cherished reputation for performing miserable, or at least moody songs: 'I don't think it's in the human nature to write inspiring material about happiness. It's just meant to be enjoyed. You can really wallow in sadness.'

The sessions were hard work. The band would play through the night, something they hadn't done since the making of *Pornography*. Smith: 'Things got very intense. We put songs like 'Disintegration' into a key I can't sing, so it hurt me. It sounds really good from a physical point of view.'

While Smith was deliberately inviting musical history to repeat itself, he was also encouraging other demons from the group's past to re-emerge. Shortly after the album was complete, Lol Tolhurst – Smith's fellow co-founder and the only other constant member in the band's twelve-year history – was sacked, loudly and angrily.

'It was about halfway through *Disintegration* that things weren't working out too great,' Tolhurst later remarked. 'I wasn't feeling that well in myself, and I guess the Cure psychosis struck again. Big time! I thought the whole ethos of the Cure had become slightly warped as far as I was concerned. It became very undemocratic and a lot of people around the band, like the record company, found it better that way because they only had to deal with one person, and that was a bit upsetting, as over the years I'd put a lot of my life into it.'

His departure stunned observers, all the more so since Tolhurst would go on to form his own band, Presence, whose debut album *Inside*, many observers felt, actually sounded more like the Cure than the Cure sometimes did – and deserved a lot more attention that it ultimately received. The fact that his departure appeared not to affect the Cure one iota, meanwhile, simply added further weight to his reasons for departing. When you listened to the Cure, you were now only really hearing one person.

With Perry Bamonte replacing Tolhurst, the new-look Cure finally emerged from its public isolation at the end of April 1989, just days after Smith's birthday, when they appeared on *Top Of The Pops*, to promote the album's first single, the haunting 'Lullaby'.

It was a controversial appearance. The band's make-up, based upon that worn in the accompanying video of arachnophobic night-sweats, was deemed 'too frightening' for the show's younger viewers, prompting a tense stand-off between the show's director and the band. For a time, it seemed that the Cure would simply walk out of the studio. Ultimately, however, they agreed to remove the make-up.

The pain of the appearance was, of course, worthwhile. 'Lullaby' became the Cure's biggest UK hit yet, a Top 5 smash. The following month, as the Cure set out on the Prayer tour, *Disintegration* itself rocketed to #3, another all-time best; later, as if to confirm both the musical and commercial supremacy of this period of the band's career, the live *Entreat*, recorded during the tour, and essentially reprising *Disintegration* in its entirety, made #10.

In Europe, the Cure were undisputed festival headliners – even the Mission, having vowed to maintain a reasonably low profile throughout the year, were no more than special guests at three such events in May, alongside such cult powerhouses as the Pixies and the Sugarcubes. At home, meanwhile, the Cure filled the vastest arenas with ease.

It was in the United States, however, that the true measure of the Cure's popularity could be taken. Even before the tour reached American shores, *Disintegration* had smashed into the album chart at #12, provoking an outbreak of Cure-mania that saw Smith's bird's-nest hair and bloodied-nose lipstick adorning every even vaguely music-oriented magazine throughout the summer.

Even more spectacularly, the single of 'Love Song', which peaked at a meagre

#18 in Britain in September, effortlessly duplicated the efforts of its parent. Chasing Love and Rockets' 'So Alive' up the chart, 'Love Song' went one better, coming to rest at #2. Suddenly there could be no doubt of the Cure's stature. Nor that behind them, the floodgates were straining.

As many have found before, however, a lofty roost is not necessarily an enviable position. Major success brings major responsibilities – not least the battalion of accountants, promoters and PR professionals that would now flock to the banner, professing undying love and life-long commitment. 'I've loved you guys since the beginning,' they'd say, and with such wide-eyed sincerity that you could almost believe that this time, they really meant it. Some bands found themselves capable of dealing with such sycophancy. For others, however, the strain was too great.

On 22nd June, a month after 'So Alive' commenced its rise up the US chart, Love And Rockets unwrapped their latest American tour at the prosaically named and quaintly intimate Tupperware Auditorium in Kissimmee, Florida. A month later, they closed it at the vast Irving Meadows auditorium in California. A month after that, they were on the road again with another round of shows that would take them through to the end of September.

It was a gruelling operation. For a band that had never previously stretched their legs beyond a two-week tour, the 45 shows that yawned through the summer left Love and Rockets' nerves shredded and their tempers frayed. 'By the time we went into the final stretch,' Haskins recalled, 'we were scarcely even talking to one another.'

Love and Rockets got real big, real fast. RCA couldn't believe their luck. One more push, boys, and you'll be top of the world. The number-crunchers were already lining up the band's next tour, a winter-long avalanche that would elevate them to the stadiums and sports arenas that are the hallmark of genuine superstardom.

But Love And Rockets weren't playing ball. 'There was pressure from the label and from the promoter as well,' recalls David J. 'And it was very tempting in a way, being offered huge amounts of money as well. But it just didn't feel right.' On the final night of the September tour, with 10,000 young Americans baying them on, the band encored with a hastily improvised Clash cover – 'Should I Stay Or Should I Go.' The answer was obvious.

They didn't want to play football stadiums, they didn't want to go super-nova, they didn't want to trade cult for the Cult. While their label wrung its hands and their advisors glared darkly from beneath storm cloud brows, Love And Rockets announced their decision. They were taking a year off to concentrate on solo projects – a year that would stretch into three before the trio were ready to re-animate the monster they had made.

Flesh for Lulu, too, were suddenly staggering as they came to terms with the momentum that had built around them so abruptly. Sliced from the soundtrack to John Hughes' latest teen-spolitation flick, *Some Kind Of Wonderful*, the hyper-infectious 'I Go Crazy' opened the group up to an audience they had never imagined, a post-*Pretty In Pink* 'alternative' rock crowd whose spending power, already evinced by the success of Love And Rockets and the Cure, was now being targeted by every label in the land.

Remaining with Beggars Banquet in the UK but eschewing that label's traditional American partnership with RCA, Flesh For Lulu signed instead with Capitol and promptly found themselves shipped to Australia to record their next album at INXS' studio. It had worked for that band, after all.

Unfortunately, it wasn't about to work for them. 'That's when the band started to split up,' Rocco mourned. 'James and Kev in one camp, me and Nick in the other. We got back and Nick said, "I'm leaving," and I said "I'm leaving, too." But then we got asked to do an American tour with Public Image at the end of 1989, so we auditioned new members [bassist Mike Steed and drummer Hans Persson] and went along with it.

'But the tour was just wrong. And that was the beginning of our demise in the public eye. We just didn't want to play, didn't know what we wanted to do.' *Plastic Fantastic*, the album that Capitol was convinced would break the band, broke them up instead. 'It was too clinical,' Rocco slammed. 'It lost all the rough edges, it was too over-produced. It was awful!'

Flesh For Lulu shattered less than a year later, although Marsh and Rocco would remain together, relaunching as the Infidels in 1995. Augmented by bassist Dave Blair and drummer Al Fletcher, the band changed its name to Gigantic after discovering a Candian band with the same name.

Having first been courted by the Disney subsidiary Hollywood, Gigantic signed with Columbia, recording an album, Disenchanted, with Mission producer Tim Palmer. Although it was well-received in Europe, the album was completely lost in Britain and the US and, following tours with Bush and the Goo Goo Dolls, Gigantic broke up in 1998. Barker resurfaced briefly with the techno band Space Police but, by 2000 had reunited with Rocco in a reborn – but, as yet, unrecorded – Flesh For Lulu.

For other bands, self-destruction was a way of life, with self-reinvention less a necessary response than an automatic one. After some seven years of spontaneous self-immolation, the Cult had grown accustomed to combusting on a regular basis. It was the painful reconstruction. The knowledge that they were doomed to repeat the exercise was most wearing.

The most immediate casualties of the latest ructions to sweep through the Cult camp were the band's management team, as well as Kid Chaos and Les Warner, all of whom were let go in early 1989. Chaos, or Haggis as he was now calling himself, immediately formed his own new band, the Four Horsemen; Warner retaliated by fighting his dismissal through the law courts, claiming that he'd been taken on as a full-time band member (Astbury and Duffy argued he was simply employed for the duration) and was thus titled to more substantial compensation than the 2,000 pounds and a new drum kit that the Cult allegedly offered him.

Astbury, Duffy and the ever-loyal Stewart, meanwhile, were now operating out of Los Angeles, casting around not only for a new rhythm section and management, but for a new producer as well, one whose vision might lift their own strivings to the next level of competitiveness. They eventually settled on Bob Rock, best known for his engineering work with Aerosmith. With Jamie Stewart reverting to bass, session drummer Mick Curry was recruited and the team headed to Canada to begin work.

Let loose in April 1989, *Sonic Temple* remains the most contentious inclusion within the Cult's entire album catalogue, a record that finally won them the respect and acceptance of the Heavy Metal crowd with whom they'd been flirting for so long, but stripped away every last shred of 'alternative' credibility the band had ever mustered. Indeed, Beggars Banquet's UK marketing campaign made no bones whatsoever about courting the Metal marketplace, even including a free sew-on patch, the emblem of Britain's metallic hordes, with early copies of the album. Their efforts paid off, too. *Sonic Temple* reached #3 in the UK, #10 in America.

Similarly, the singles 'Fire Woman' and the heart-wrenching power ballad 'Edie (Ciao Baby)', a tribute to the late Warhol superstar Edie Sedgwick, catapulted the Cult into the chart on both sides of the Atlantic.

It was time to go for the throat. With Matt Sorum moving into the drum seat, the Cult set out on their latest world tour on 29th April 1989 as special guests on Metallica's *Damaged Justice* jaunt across the US. The Cult's own *Prayer Tour* would follow immediately afterwards.

'*Damaged Justice* was madness,' Astbury attested, 'the height of Bacchanalian fucking living off the vine, white line fever, trashing hotel rooms, groupies… you name it, it was going on. I was right in the heart of this thing and it's going on every fucking night. It was like a bordello every night, travelling in a mobile whore house. Everywhere we were, it was happening.' And everywhere, he was leaving another little piece of himself behind in the wreckage.

On 6th September 1989, the Cult appeared at the MTV Video Music Awards, before returning to Europe to tour with the recently – and surprisingly – rejuvenated Aerosmith. Again, it was a destructive mess, personally if not musically – Astbury himself remembers running into Jason Bonham, the scheduled support act on the Cult's next US tour, and being told that the young drummer had been advised not to go near him, 'because I was a dangerous influence. On John Bonham's son.'

The sick thing was, he probably would have been. 'There were times when I got out of order. I've been put in jail several times, I've got a dislocated shoulder to show for some of my obnoxious behaviour, I've got a few scars. And that's the point. If I was out of order, I certainly got put back in my place pretty quickly.'

Proof of this came in Copenhagen, when Astbury allegedly beat up a fan who was innocently chatting to his long-time girlfriend Renee Beach (the star, incidentally, of the band's *Edie* video). It was one abuse too many. Beach walked out on him, never to return. 'It was a mad time,' Duffy later recalled. 'Ian was totally out of his mind. He'd split up with his girlfriend and had been drunk for 14 days straight.'

The Cult were back in Britain in November 1989, returning to Wembley Arena, but first discovering that controversy was already waiting for them. Plugging their latest single, 'Sun King', on TV's *Jonathan Ross Show*, Astbury appeared completely out of control and horribly out of shape. The last the cameras saw of him, he was on his knees on the floor, smashing his microphone into the stage, while the band howled out the dying chords of 'Born To Be Wild', the ultimate biker anthem suddenly, and sickeningly, transformed into the macho anthem of a man who'd spent too long believing his own hard-drinking, hard-rocking reputation.

Yet it was not Astbury who earned the following morning's headlines, but Billy Duffy, who appeared on screen wearing a T-shirt emblazoned with a reversed swastika. The ensuing outcry barely even registered the fact that Duffy himself is half-Jewish.

The Cult opened another US tour in Tempe, Arizona, in the New Year – it was the end of March before they finally came off the road once more. As they packed up their last hotel room and waited for the last flight home, each of them had just one conviction rooted in their soul. The Cult was over.

'Basically, the band had split up,' Astbury explained. 'We were done, we were burned out. Gone. Relationships were in tatters, I was basically hanging on by a thread, I was a complete burned-out wreck.' At the beginning of the month, Astbury's father died. Two weeks later, so did Andrew Wood, vocalist with the Seattle band Mother Lovebone and one of Astbury's closest friends. Devastated, the singer mourned, 'I just couldn't do anything any more. My relationship with Billy [Duffy] was incredibly tarnished. Matt Sorum was offered x amount to join Guns N'Roses so he just kind of went "this is a much more secure seat" and left. Jamie Stewart's wife basically pulled him out of our black world and he went off to be a domestic house-husband and he's much more happy being a producer.

'So that left Billy and I having to deal with each other, which is when we discovered all the debts and the legal messes which were left over from before. We were falling out with our new manager, and the whole thing had become incredibly cynical. It was horrible. It was like something out of one of those old b-movies where they have about 50 medical machines hooked up to one tiny little black heart.' And it was time, he believed, to start pulling every plug out of its socket.

The Mission's *Wayne Hussey*

Chapter Fourteen
Everything Falls Apart

From which it will appear that the early 1990s took an awful toll on the biggest and the best while the air grew thick with the stench of Teen Spirit.

'Some of the people who came through at the same time as us had all moved up a notch to different planes...' – Depeche Mode, REM, the Replacements, U2 of course. 'But everyone else was just there to be scattered, and that included us. We were still there as an alternative act, but it had altered, it all became "rock" again, people were allowed to have long hair and punch the air again, buy pretzels and shout "way to go." It had changed, and there wasn't really a place for what we did any more. Our stuff was far too musicianly and middle-aged.' Robyn Hitchcock

Contemplating life beyond the Cult, Ian Astbury also found himself considering life *around* the band, the nature of the business in which he had spent the last ten years of his life, the way in which increasingly focussed marketing had bound each group into its own little box from which there could never be an escape. Picking up a British music paper, the Cult were still dismissed as Gothic Rockers – or, at best, Gothic *Cock* Rockers – years after they'd abandoned even the most generous trappings of that genre. And, of course, they were not alone.

It wasn't only Gothic Rock that was pigeonholed, however. For every band there was a genre, for every genre there was a stereotype. Gone were the days when a band could just get up and play rock'n'roll. Now they had to announce what kind of rock'n'roll it was, before anybody would even give them a listen. Neither was it the media alone which insisted on playing these silly games. Bands, too, were dividing themselves down party lines, a box for everyone and everyone in their box.

'For some reason, I made the observation that there was a complete lack of harmony between young musicians. The communal spirit that had come through Punk Rock didn't exist any more.

'I was really intrigued by N.W.A. when they came out, they reminded me of Punk, they were so radical. I liked Ice T, and I'd been to see Soundgarden play a couple of times and I really liked them and I thought, there's all these groups around, these counter-culture groups, and no-one's hearing them outside of their own camps. They're all in their little boxes, they don't recognize each other's presence, there's no linkage between rap and rock, between rock and alternative, and certainly not folk or traditional. It was very formatted, nothing was crossing over, and I just felt depressed about that…

'I was talking to my agent about how it would be amazing if we could bring together all these different groups for a concert to show people as a whole what's going on with our generation, so we wouldn't have to deal with Phil Collins and Bruce Springsteen any longer. It would be a concert showcasing all the different options, showing the linkage, and he thought it was a brilliant idea.'

Over the next six months, the dream would expand to encompass two massive counter/cross-cultural festivals that Astbury titled the Gathering Of The Tribes. Staged at the Shoreline Amphitheatre in Mountain View, California (6th October 1990) and the Pacific Amphitheatre in Costa Mesa (7th October 1990), the Gathering featured the very cream of 'what's going on with our generation' – the Cramps, the Charlatans, Soundgarden, Queen Latifah, Steve Jones, the American Indian Dance Theater, the Indigo Girls and Michelle Shocked all appeared. There was also room to restate the one musical bond that neither time nor turmoil had prevented Astbury from enjoying: the appearance of the Mission.

At the conclusion of the Mission's first ever live show, the night they shed the banner of the Sisterhood, Astbury and Billy Duffy had ambled onstage to proclaim the newcomers 'the future of rock'n'roll.' Six months after the release of their third album, *Carved In Sand*, the Mission seemed to have borne out that prediction.

Wayne Hussey made no bones of the fact that it was the stellar success, three years earlier, of U2's *The Joshua Tree*, which fired the overwhelming ambitions of

Carved In Sand. He, too, believed that rock'n'roll had been standing still for too long, and should be broadened not simply to embrace other moods and forms, but to do so in a way that allowed one single album to embrace every conceivable emotion.

The Joshua Tree, revoltingly overblown and ridiculously melodramatic though it was, had achieved that, thrusting U2 to a position of utter unassailability through its admixture of benign belligerence, pointed polemic, unbridled joy and some rattling good tunes. *Carved In Sand,* recorded with *God's Own Medicine* producer Tim Palmer back at the helm, set out to echo that achievement. Considering the 18 songs that were completed during the year-long sessions, there was no doubt that the Mission had touched a similar plateau... touched it and then, somewhere along the line, they lost their grip.

The best of the *Carved In Sand* material is, indeed, as good as it gets: the embittered 'Amelia', written in a fit of fury after Hussey read a letter from a young fan whose father had been sexually abusing her; the heartbroken 'Butterfly On A Wheel', dedicated to Simon Hinkler's recently sundered romance with All About Eve's Julianne Regan; the deliciously vicious 'Mercenaries', penned after the Mission's road crew upped and left to join Andrew Eldritch for the (again revitalised) Sisters Of Mercy's first tour in five years.

'Into The Blue' and 'Deliverance' even recast the old Gothic sensibilities, hurtling out of Hussey's love affair with Marion Bradley's *Mists Of Avalon* retelling of the Arthurian legends. 'It's a great book,' he enthused, 'very inspiring, and that's where a lot of the lyrics came from. Too many, perhaps. But it is one of the few books that actually makes you reappraise your whole way of thinking.'

As the band deliberated on how much of this vast arsenal of material they could fit onto a single disc, Hussey could not resist proudly boasting, 'if the next album is half as good as we think it is, it's gonna blow worldwide.'

And it could have, it really could. But something was not quite right, the songs didn't sit as well as they should have, the mood was too easily broken. Finally, Hussey acknowledged what the reviews had already suggested and insiders were readily murmuring. *Carved In Sand* was only half of the album it could have been. The other half was lying on the cutting room floor. They'd picked the wrong bloody songs.

Hastening to make amends, the band released a second album in October 1990, on the eve of their Gathering of the Tribes performance. *Grains Of Sand* swept up the remainder of the sessions and, sure enough, the missing magic was there for all to see. But it was too late. *Carved In Sand* had swept to #7 in the UK album charts. But singles 'Butterfly On A Wheel', 'Deliverance' and 'Into The Blue' barely nuzzled the heights the Mission should have been smooching, while *Grains Of Sand* barely made the Top 30. The moment had passed and, with it, the momentum.

Live, the Mission could still cut the mustard with ease. The recently sundered Red Lorry Yellow Lorry's Dave Wolfenden had been added as rhythm guitarist, bringing untold additional attack to the band's symphonic wall, and the *Deliverance* UK tour that kicked off in Leeds on 1st March 1990 drew some of the most breathless reviews of their career, and some of the most exhausted audiences.

The Eskimos and the Sausage Squad had long since been snowballed beneath the sheer enormity of the Mission's audience. Their protests could still be heard in the uproar. When the *New Musical Express*, for so long the one voice that could be relied upon to smash the Mission into the mud, turned around and proclaimed their Wembley show a masterpiece, it spoke for masses beyond the mound of unkempt die-hards who'd supported the band all along.

Behind such triumphs, however, old demons were surfacing once more. Alcohol and cocaine were rife on the tour and, with them, arguments and insecurities that had not been heard – or allowed to be heard – since the earliest days of the band. Back in 1986, at the conclusion of the Sisterhood's European tour with the Cult, Simon Hinkler had been sacked, his bandmates convinced that he would never see eye-to-eye with the rest of them. Of course he was reinstated after a matter of days and, since then, all had been calm.

Now, however, it was Hinkler who regarded the rest of the band as the odd men out. On 21st April 1990, the morning after the Mission's latest North American tour opened with a fractious show in Montreal, the guitarist simply upped and quit. The first the band knew of his disappearance was when one of the crew picked up a message at the hotel desk. It said, simply – and somewhat suavely – 'Mr Hinkler sends his apologies, but he will not be doing the rest of the tour.'

Dave Wolfenden was promptly promoted to lead guitar for the remainder of the American dates, his own spot being filled by Malcolm Treece of the supporting Wonder Stuff. The following month, back in Europe for a string of festivals, Treece stepped aside for Tim Bricheno of All About Eve – after three years of regular, if seldom more than minor, hits, Bricheno had left the band to continue pursuing its increasingly wayward folky 60s bent. Regan promptly delved deeper into those pastures – in 1992, she even appeared as a special guest of arch-traditionalists Fairport Convention, at their annual Cropredy Festival. Bricheno, on the other hand, found himself playing louder and faster than he'd been able to in years.

For the Mission, however, the turbulence was still not at an end. By the time the band reached the United States in October 1990 for the final lap of the *Deliverance* tour, Bricheno had already departed and the Mission were sporting their fourth rhythm guitarist in six months as Paul Etchell was lured away from Ghost Dance.

Having dominated the Independent singles chart through 1986-87, Ghost Dance looked like making the same transition to the mainstream after they were picked up by Chrysalis and immediately went to #66 with the single 'Down To The Wire'. A summer 1989 album – the band's first – went nowhere, however, and the band were touring Europe when they learned they'd been dropped. The departure of Etchell was the final straw. Ghost Dance broke up.

With profound circularity, meanwhile, Tim Bricheno was now to be found with the Sisters Of Mercy.

It was late 1989 when word began circulating that Andrew Eldritch, Patricia Morrison and former Only Ones guitarist John Perry were working together towards a new Sisters of Mercy album – pretty much the same time, in fact, as Morrison herself quit the combo, beneath a glowering cloud of both artistic and financial dissatisfaction. Claiming she'd been paid just 300 pounds a month for her tenure in the band, she described Wayne Hussey, Craig Adams and Gary Marx as 'the only three people on the planet who will ever understand what has happened to me.'

Eldritch shrugged her complaints away, as he had those of her predecessors, and continued scheming the new album. Alone with Perry, Hamburg-based guitarist Andreas Bruhn and, of course, the good Doktor Avalanche, Eldritch relocated the sessions to Denmark with producer Jim Steinman again at the helm.

Then, in February 1990, he broke cover to announce, with barely disguised glee, the constitution of the next incarnation of the Sisters of Mercy, to be built around the hitherto unknown Bruhn and the excessively famous Tony James – ex-Chelsea, ex-Generation X and, damningly to all but the handful of fans who sensed just how visionary the whole scam was, ex-Sigue Sigue Sputnik. Tim Bricheno and former Mike Oldfield Group vocalist Maggie Riley would complete the troupe.

Eldritch explained, 'I've known [James] a long time and he was playing exactly the same kind of bass lines in Generation X as he is now. And I thought, "Well, that'll annoy a few people," which is a helpful bonus. [So], we'll see if he cuts it. I think he will. You can only do the Sigue Sigue Sputnik thing once, and that's not going to let him die with any self-respect.' Indeed, James had offered Eldritch himself the role of frontman in Sputnik back in 1982. Eldritch turned him down.

Five years to the day since the last Sisters' gig, the *Festival Of Remembrance* at the Royal Albert Hall, Eldritch and his new conspirators appeared onstage at the Lorelei Festival in Germany to announce the band's forthcoming plans: a new album in the autumn, with a tour to follow. That, however, was all they did and it was one of the bizarre highlights of the entire event when Eldritch, James and Bruhn took the Lorelei stage to read out the tour dates.

It would be another four months before the 'More' single unveiled the sound of this latest melange, unsurprisingly retaining all the epic quality of the *Floodland* singles but adding a full-frontal hard guitar assault that slammed the band full into a towering Monsters of Rock role even before the accompanying video was uncaged, 'a Fellini parody of a heavy metal video,' as Eldritch put it.

Neither the sound nor the vision was an aberration, as the LP readily proved. *Vision Thing* – oddly recorded before Bricheno or James was on the scene, but hingeing anyway around the 'eight-to-the-bar bass riffs' that Eldritch credited James with creating – followed in late October and made even *Floodland* sound strangely under-produced.

With Bruhn's 'Panzer attack riffs' fully to the fore, conjuring an aggression and rage that threatened to melt the speakers, the album was viciously contemporary. 1990 saw the United States prepare to lead a coalition of nations into action in the Persian Gulf to remove the invading Iraqis from neighbouring Kuwait – 'Vision Thing' itself dove into the sound-byte heart of the then-President George Bush, the father of the current incumbent, teasing his speeches ('vision thing' itself was a Bush quote) and mocking the apparently heriditary belief that the only solution to any problem was to send another army in to kill it.

The result blazed with an industrial fury that would not be truly resolved for another year or more, until a new wave of American noise-mongers arose behind Ministry, a band that so thoroughly absorbed all that *Vision Thing* portended that they even paid tribute to the video with their own, equally Bush-bashing 'New World Order'.

The album also provided, if such was needed, final food for thought for anybody still pondering the true reasoning behind Eldritch and Hussey's break-up four years earlier. While the Sisters of Mercy were conceiving an all-out assault of sound and imagery, and executing it with a power whose echoes would still be reverberating around the industrial-gothic scene a decade or more later, the Mission were up to their eyeballs in heartache, hobbits and grand acoustic anthems. Any hopes of reunion, grounded as such an event would have been in so disparate a battleground, were kicked out of the park from the opening squall of 'Vision Thing' itself.

With ex-Big Audio Dynamite keyboard player Dan Donovan fleshing out the sound, the Sisters Of Mercy embarked upon a sequence of gigs that opened in Ireland, warmed up in Brazil and Yugoslavia and then made their official kick-off in Hamburg on 16th November. With a set pulled from throughout the band's career, peppered with such tried and trusted covers as 'Gimme Shelter' and 'Jolene', it was a violent exorcism of the past five years of reticence, a festival of noise that verged on, and sometimes descended into, the realms of unapologetic thrash.

It was a short series of dates, wrapping up with two nights at London's Wembley Arena just ten days later, in front of an audience that included Wayne Hussey and bandmate Mick Brown. The pair wandered backstage after the show, there to finally put to rest the Corporate Wars that had waged, sometimes violently, sometimes merely unspoken, for half a decade. Eldritch celebrated the truce the following month, when the next Sisters' single, the album's twitchily riffing 'Doctor Jeep', arrived with a 1985-era live b-side, Dylan's 'Knockin' On Heaven's Door'.

But even this full-blooded rock assault served an agenda that was far from the dreams of other bands, as Eldritch proved when an MTV video jock asked him whether he had any hopes of an American hit with the song. If that had been the intention, Eldritch responded, it would've been an instrumental.

If the Sisters continued holding America at arm's length, their peers embraced it wholeheartedly.

Whether by design or coincidence, Peter Murphy was silent through Love and Rockets' year of greatest acclaim, but returned in 1990 with a second soaring classic, 'Cuts You Up', and a similarly classy album, *Deep*. This time, he was rewarded with a pair of at least minor American hits, sales of 250,000 and a #55 placing for the single, #44 for the album.

Gene Loves Jezebel, too, were confidently assaulting the lower reaches of the chart, even though the gestation of their latest album, 1990's *Kiss Of Life*, had proved just as fraught as any of its predecessors.

With Michael Aston's departure and out of deference to all that the earlier band had achieved, the remaining members floated the possibility of changing the band's name, only for Geffen to slap the suggestion down without a second thought. Bowing to higher wisdom and abandoning the tentative sessions they'd commenced with the errant twin the previous autumn, the reconfigured Gene Loves Jezebel returned to the studio in spring 1989 with producer Paul Fox.

Since widely acclaimed for his work with XTC, Phish and Sky Cries Mary, Fox was not at all to Gene Loves Jezebel's tastes. Jay Aston slammed, 'We go to San Francisco, and we work with a guy called Paul Fox who sucks. And it cost us a fortune, because we ended up having to rescue the album back in London with [Mission producer] Tim Palmer, rerecording some bits, retracking other bits. It ended up being so much pain to record – we'd just come through the war with Mike, with *House Of Dolls*, and then we had another war doing that album. And then there was the San Francisco earthquake in the middle of the damn thing; we should've taken that as a sign.'

What sustained the band was the knowledge that *Kiss Of Life* was to pack some of their best songs yet. 'When we recorded the demos, we thought we'd made our best album. You'd just die, it's fucking awesome, to use a cliché, but it is. It's a beautiful album.'

What then turned around and destroyed them was the brief that Geffen handed to Fox. A clean record, an upbeat record, a *pop* record. The demos, with their mood and shade and intensity, were thrown out of the window. Verses were cut from songs, tempos shifted, rhythms mutated. 'Evening Star' live was an awesome sight to behold. On record, it scarcely whimpered. Elsewhere, 'Jealous', the first single from the album in June 1990, lost a set of lyrics that Aston still insists were essential to the song's meaning.

Of course, such behind-the-scenes machinations did not prevent 'Jealous' from hustling into MTV rotation and crowning the Modern Rock chart for weeks on end. When 'Tangled Up In You' joined it at the top, it was obvious that with just one more push... and inevitable that the band wouldn't take it.

'What is it about these whiney Brits?' a top American record executive demanded a year or two later. 'They come over here, work their balls off, work everyone else's balls off, and then the moment they're in sight of what everybody wants, they turn tail and run back to their miserable island, complaining that America was eating them alive. And people wonder why American record labels don't want to even bother promoting them any longer?'

In this case, of course, the blame lay far from Gene Loves Jezebel's own door. America was entering a recession, one that seemed to be biting the record industry even harder than it normally would. When a projected two-month summertime tour pairing Gene Loves Jezebel with the similarly rising Concrete Blonde fell apart, the best the band could replace it with was less than a dozen dates with Billy Idol, as he limped along on a tour which, itself, was scarcely pulling in the punters – a far cry indeed from the triumphant foray he had undertaken just three years before with the rising Cult were his opening act. Less than 3,000 fans rattled around the 18,000 capacity Sandstone Arena in Kansas, barely 8,000 in the 40,000 seater Alpine Valley Music Theatre, and so on.

Back in Britain, Gene Loves Jezebel did land the opening slot at David Bowie's Milton Keynes shows, performing a riotous set to the biggest homeland audience they had ever had. But their America dream was unravelling fast. A tour in November, supported by the newly-emergent Posies, literally returned Gene Loves Jezebel to the same size venues they'd been playing the first time they went over, while another outing in April/May 1991 was even more desultory, as those same clubs stubbornly refused to even pretend to sell out. The only consolation was the knowledge that they were not alone among their peers in suffering the slings and bows of outrageous concert promotion.

* * *

To mark the tenth anniversary of the Sisters of Mercy's first ever live show, in February 1991, two special 'fan club' shows were scheduled in Leeds, with the first, at Leeds University (the same venue that, so long ago, had refused outright to book the burgeoning band), taking place ten years to the day of that debut gig in York. The group then returned to their rehearsal studio in Sussex to prepare for a tour of southern Europe which kicked off on 26th February in Lisbon, Portugal, meandered through Spain and Italy, before ending up in Yugoslavia on 11th March.

An 18-date North American tour followed, including one delirious day out at the Irvine Amphitheatre, the Sisters joined by Gene Loves Jezebel, Danielle Dax and Lush – at the time still firmly under the miasmic spell of the Cocteau Twins' Robin Guthrie. From the States, the Sisters returned to Europe, then it was back to the US again, with their eyes suddenly filled with the promise of a breakthrough – on their own terms entirely. Remixed for radio play, a DJ-only single of 'Detonation Boulevard' was picking up speed, while MTV clearly adored the accompanying, purposefully uncontroversial video that accompanied it.

Unfortunately, this latest tour was to undo all of that. Ambitiously echoing the tenets of both Ian Astbury's Gathering of the Tribes and, earlier in the year, Perry Farrell's similarly-styled Lollapalooza outing, the Sisters were booked onto a circuit of arenas in the company of Gang of Four and rappers Public Enemy.

But the sluggish ticket sales that had benighted every other major package of the last two years had not improved; they had, if anything, slowed even further. Gig after gig was cancelled until, finally, the entire outing was postponed. The Sisters returned to Britain and lapsed into absolute silence.

The cultural slack that was released by the Sisters' recorded silence through 1991 should have been taken up by the Fields of the Nephilim. Instead they, too, commenced their disintegration.

Confirming the success of *Dawnrazor*, the Fields of the Nephilim's second album, *The Nephilim*, had opened doors across the stratosphere, as the band nailed their imagery into place. No longer the bastard offspring of some impatient Sisters' copyist that their harshest critics described them as, the band had found a voice and, more importantly, a vision that was wholly their own.

Of course the old media criticisms still rode roughshod across the band's visage; of course the group still looked and sounded far too serious for their own good. But *The Nephilim* was nothing if not the sound of precocious growth, a prediction not of the direction the most obvious role models would have progressed had they only wished, but of the concerns and fascinations that had enfolded great swathes of the Fields of the Nephilim's own audience.

'Moonchild,' the first single from the album (in May 1988), 'Shiva' and the tremulous finale 'Last Exit for the Lost' were all the sound of the band in general, and Carl McCoy in particular, broadening their outlook beyond, one imagines, even their own dreams. The popular image of the band's make-up, one *bona fide* mad genius and four average blokes from the burbs, might never truly be shrugged off, but the best of *The Nephilim* proved that whatever personal conflicts might lay down the road, right now the members' conjoined imagination over-rode all. Besides, the early Pink Floyd was built around much the same combination, and *The Piper At The Gates Of Dawn* didn't turn out so bad, did it?

Revelling in the arcane, deliriously draping themselves in an imagery and mysticism that might have been drip-fed from some all-powerful Gothic lexicon, the Fields of the Nephilim drew their sources from across the cultural spectrum. They plundered movies for samples – *Texas Chainsaw Massacre*, *The Evil Dead* and *Nightmare On Elm Street* were all effectively employed across *Dawnrazor*; *The Name Of The Rose* was referenced in *The Nephilim*; and that most fabled of Black Art bibelots, the Necronomicon, would be quoted in 'Psychonaut', the 1989 single that raised the Fields of the Nephilim's standing to untold heights, a prelude to the album that would become their schemic masterpiece.

In every arena, the Fields of the Nephilim were constructing a world within a world, a private mythology which, though accessible to (or even comprehended by) only an apparent handful of the most devoted fan/scholars, nevertheless communicated itself far beyond the realms of the group's still cultish following. From the music to their artwork, from their concerts to their merchandising, every aspect of the band's being was inextricably bound to a single point of identity.

But there was nothing so garish as the floating islands of Yes infamy, nor anything as obvious as the conceptual troughs from which Jethro Tull fans were fed. Therefore, when the band announced that their next album, 1990's intensely ambitious *Elizium*, was to be a philosophical concept set based upon the band's own private beliefs and mythos, even their detractors barely batted an eyelid. What else could it be?

A considerably gentler album than either of its predecessors, at least in terms of its sonic impact, *Elizium* drew at least grudging comparisons with the darker efforts of the Cocteau Twins and Dead Can Dance, not via any dallying with purposeful precocity or, heaven forbid, world music disciplines, but through its so-effective reliance on moody soundscapes and textures to evoke emotions that would hitherto have been cloaked in bombast and battery. Certainly the Gothic scene of early-mid 1990s America, drenched as it was in ethereal whispering and understated drones offered up a deeply reverential opinion on the minimalism that gave *Elizium* so much of its punch, and locked into this private world, the Fields of the Nephilim could have churned on forever. Their gigs were no longer simple concerts – they were virtual festivals, the very air crackling with a reverence that is as audible on the *Elizium*-era live album *Earth Inferno* as it is visible on the accompanying video *Visionary Heads*.

Yet, of course, immortality was not an option. The energy of performance and the reverence of their audience placed the band in a no-win situation, a high-intensity, zero-gravity battlefield in which it was impossible for the band members to maintain any kind of equilibrium. Musical differences, the bug-bear of so many acts, gave way to the more specialised skirmishes of philosophical concern. The entire existence of the band, once forged around a vision of singular purity, was unravelling. Something had to give and, in 1991, it did. Barely audible beneath the cries of anguish from the Bonanzas, the Fields of the Nephilim announced their final gigs – the Fire Festivals at London's Town and Country Club.

The shows were triumphant, the fall-out was tragic. Although Petit, Yates, and the Wrights remained together, recruiting vocalist Andy Delaney for their own Rubicon project, bereft of McCoy's vision, they had little to offer that even began to approach the pinnacles of their earlier work.

But McCoy, too, seemed to have stalled. Though he immediately announced a new Neph, this time employing the alternative Hebraic spelling of the Nefilim, he, too, ground to a standstill. By 1992, a year in which so many other institutions were fatally falling to pieces, it was as though the Fields of the Nephilim had never existed. It was only with a hindsight borne of the events of the first months after the break-up that one could muse, maybe they did the right thing after all.

The trick, a wise man once said, is 'to keep one's head when everybody else is losing theirs'. After September 1991, that trick became even more difficult to pull off, because the axe was swinging so indiscriminately. It was being wielded, of course, by Nirvana.

Nirvana were a Seattle three-piece that had hitherto barely registered outside the narrow confines of the *Melody Maker* reviews page and a few ragged inkies in the Pacific Northwest. Nobody, least of all the band and its record label, Geffen, expected much from their new album: American sales of 250,000 would leave everyone slapping each others' backs; any more than that, and they'd be reaching for the sedatives.

But that was before 'Smells Like Teen Spirit' rocketed out of radio and MTV; that was before the world heard *Nevermind*. It sounds absurdly melodramatic to say so but, from that moment on, the established music scene would never be the same again.

Nirvana's impact was as immediate as it was profound and the casualty list was as long as the decade that stretched behind it. Robyn Hitchcock's latest album, *Perspex Island*, was top of the American alternative chart when *Nevermind* was issued; indeed, it was the Seattle band that knocked it off the #1 spot and, Hitchcock mused later, 'Some of the people who came through at the same time as us had all moved up a notch to different planes…' – Depeche Mode, REM, the Replacements, U2 of course.

'But everyone else was just there to be scattered, and that included us. We were still there as an alternative act, but it had altered, it all became "rock" again, people were allowed to have long hair and punch the air again, buy pretzels and shout "way to go." It had changed, and there wasn't really a place for what we did any more. Our stuff was far too musicianly and middle-aged.'

Though it ultimately amounted to little more than a short icy snap, for many acts the change in temperature was shattering, as destructive in its own way as the Punk killing fields of 14 years before had felt to those bands whose own lives were to be irreparably scarred. Others, however, welcomed the emergence of 'Grunge' as the breath of fresh air they themselves had spent so long working towards.

Ian Astbury was especially excited, all the more so since two of the acts riding closest to Nirvana, fellow Seattle-ites Pearl Jam and Soundgarden, were already old friends: the former had grown from the wreckage of Mother Love Bone, the group destroyed when Astbury's friend Andrew Wood passed away in 1990; the latter were among the most triumphant inclusions at Gathering of the Tribes.

The shattered shards of the Cult had begun piecing themselves together on the very eve of the Gathering of the Tribes. Rejuvenated by the experience of organising the event, excited once more about making music, Astbury and Billy Duffy reconvened in September 1990 and began preparing for a new album, one that would stand as their own signpost for the musical future.

Of course it was never going to turn out like that, no matter how desperately Astbury wanted it to. Augmented by session musicians Charley Drayton (bass) and *Sonic Temple* drummer Mick Curry, Astbury recalled, 'we went in, and the songs really weren't too bad. But we spent a ridiculous amount of money making it, and the way we recorded it was really bad.'

In retrospect, the portents were dodgy from the outset. The sessions united the band with producer Richie Zito, but Astbury confessed that 'the only reason we used him was because he was the first person to walk into the room and stay there. Rick Rubin took one look at us and said, "Not right now," Bob Rock was with Metallica, so we just went, "okay, Richie, you're a maker of fine confectionery, you've got the job." He'd sold like five million records with Heart and all that kind of bullshit, and we thought maybe he could do the same with us. And it was a fucking shambles.'

Poll the band's most loyal acolytes and all will admit that every Cult album has its flaws. None, however, are as inherently flawed as the bloated travesty that emerged as *Ceremony*, an album that might have traced its title, like its makers' lineage, back to Joy Division, but which remains a severed horse's head in the bed of even Astbury and Duffy's own increasingly discredited Gothic boudoir. Neither were its makers in any doubt as to its overall worth. Astbury himself sought immediate solace outside of the studio – although, this time, it was neither drink nor drugs to which he turned. 'I met my future wife, Heather, at the time, so I just went off with her all the time. I just started hanging out with Heather, having the greatest time, and I started rediscovering myself, not drinking as much, and eventually I started to get a bit wider as a person.

'It seemed that I was suddenly connecting with so many people in similar circumstances to me, who'd been through similar experiences, and who were carrying a lot of the same grief and burdens. We'd all seen our role models and heroes and friends fade or die; we'd all been around for a little while, and were noticing the way the musicians we came out with had dissipated and crumbled, and a lot of our heroes had turned into flabby, cynical... turned out to be John Lydon or whatever. Actually, I really like John Lydon a lot, but – Joe Strummer to an extent. I realized this, and I didn't want to turn into them myself.'

It was too late to halt the rot that was already consuming the new album: opting to bide his time, Astbury simply allowed the sessions to meander to their stodge-rocking conclusion; vowed, too, to get through the accompanying ('fucking inevitable!') world tour, a six-month marathon that he regarded with the dread most people reserve for blood tests and dental work. All of it, he told himself, was a time of healing.

As the *Ceremony* tour neared its end, Astbury personally invited Pearl Jam to join the Cult for the finale, the mammoth Cult In The Park festival in Finsbury Park in June 1992. It was an absolute triumph, both musically – for all the ramifications of the new movement's emergence, Pearl Jam had a lot more in common with the Cult than they did with the rest of the Grunge scene – and personally. 'I'd started hanging out more with Billy and we became friends again, and we'd decided that once the tour was over, it was time to get our shit back together.

'We had a lot of soul-searching to do, because we'd been together for ten years, and a lot of stuff came out, a lot of stuff about how we wanted to work with each other and shit started coming out. But we kept going. We got a new manager who worked very closely with us and was a real Cult fanatic, we built a lot of things around the band, and sorted out a lot of financial bullshit which was going around.'

Shrugging off a battery of difficulties, legal and personal, the Cult's re-emergence was signalled by their gift to the cult hit movie of 1992, *Cool World*, the grinding electro-thrash of 'The Witch'.

Recorded with Rick Rubin, 'The Witch' remained recognizably the Cult. But it was looser and dirtier than anything they had released in a long time, a brutal shock of unrepentant industrial noise that could, as Astbury reflected later, have utterly reinvented the band. 'The thing about "The Witch" was, it was a song I'd written back in December 1989, way ahead of the pack. It was an impressive song, an influential song, a song which really could have changed the Cult's direction. Throughout the *Ceremony* period, that's where I thought we should have gone. Shaved our heads and done songs like "The Witch."

'But the commercial pressures surrounding the band wouldn't allow that, and the emotional things as well. I didn't want the hassle of having to go out there and fight and be a martyr for this music. So I kinda let Billy take over, instead. Throughout that whole period, we were going sideways. "The Witch" was just a little step forward at the end of it.' Overlooked on the soundtrack, ignored on the dance floors, 'The Witch' disappeared virtually without a trace and the Cult seemed doomed to follow it. In the new musical climate, it wasn't enough simply to have a new sound. Audiences wanted new names as well. Because who wants to groove on the same bands as their father did?

Gene Loves Jezebel, too, were reeling. Chris Bell quit the group in early 1991, to be replaced by Robert Adam, ex-Promise and one of Fleetwood Mac founder Peter Green's past outfits – coincidentally, Jay had recently recorded a track for a Green tribute album. Unfortunately, the new man couldn't have arrived at a worse time.

Having quit Geffen in the aftermath of *Kiss Of Life*, Gene Loves Jezebel were lured over to Savage, a thrusting new label whose stated intentions promised the world, but whose reality was to be considerably more sobering.

Gene Loves Jezebel weren't alone in falling for the spiel, either – David Bowie, too, pledged his troth to Savage, only to be left reeling when it all went belly-up. 'We could have gone to Atlantic,' Jay Aston recalled, 'but we decided to go to Savage. We needed the money. We were broke, and they were offering a lot of money. And they loved us to death. Then they sign David Bowie, go broke, and we get cut off in the middle of the tour.'

Even before then, however, the group was swiftly aware that they'd made a dire mistake, delivering up what they assumed was a completed new album, spring 1992's *Heavenly Bodies*, then watching while the salesmen tore it to shreds, then wrapped it in a sleeve so garish, as Jay Aston put it, that it 'totally misrepresented what was ultimately a very sensitive album. But that was the fate of it.'

Savage's precipitous downfall, of course, spelled the end for *Heavenly Bodies*. The album disappeared from the stores, barely weeks after it reached them. Reeling in total disbelief at this latest twist of vicious fate, Gene Loves Jezebel disappeared alongside them.

1992 saw the Mission, too, finally run out of brick walls to crash through, their apparent demise finally completing a process that began with Simon Hinkler's departure two years earlier. That September, with the failure of their latest album, *Masque*, already tolling the last rites, a terse Wayne Hussey press release announced, simply, that Adams had been sacked from the band. He had lost interest in the band, lost faith in their ability to pull themselves out of the hole. Observers watching events from a distance simply wondered how he'd lasted as long as he had.

Closing out the *Carved In Sand* era with one final show at London's Brixton Academy on 12th December 1990, making no secret of the bitter rows that now gripped the band whenever they met, the members had only one thought in common: what was the point of continuing?

The last rites were suitably atypical, a reunion with Hinkler for a glam-flavoured tribute to the early 1970s, under the Bolanic totem of the Metal Gurus. Christmas 1990 saw this unlikely-garbed gathering cut a delightfully reverent version of Slade's 'Merry Xmas Everybody' for the holiday market, but the venture lost its appeal even before the final turkey leg was eaten.

The Gurus, too, went their separate ways and, by early 1991, Wayne Hussey was seriously considering joining All About Eve, as a full-time replacement for the errant Tim Bricheno. Marty Wilson-Piper of the Australian band The Church was filling in for the time being and, had he not decided to make his sojourn permanent, Hussey might have acted on his instinct. Instead, he kept his Mission options open but, even if his sympathies were turning back towards the band, still there seemed any number of stumbling blocks.

Personal problems aside, the Mission were now warring furiously with Mercury. The UK branch of the label's commitment to the group had certainly waned in recent years, even as their overseas counterparts grew ever more enthusiastic. Even before the band members themselves knew whether or not there'd be another Mission album, manager Tony Perrin was in discussion with other labels – both within the Phonogram conglomerate that ran Mercury and elsewhere – in search of a suitable new home.

He finally settled with Vertigo, one of Mercury's sister companies and, two decades before, the distinctively clad home of the best in British prog and heavy metal. Even more impressively, he received a guarantee that whatever the Mission decided to do was fine by the label. There would be no interference, no argument, no attempts to redefine the band's direction. Whatever and whenever they chose to record, the label would be behind them.

Using Hussey and wife Kelly's newly acquired Barn home studio as their base, Adams, Brown and Hussey reconvened in late 1991, alongside producer Mark Saunders – he had remixed 'Into The Blue' for a single and also had a hand in the Cure's recently-released and so revolutionary *Mixed Up* collection of rerecorded classics, a stop-gap released while they strove to complete their follow-up to *Disintegration.*

Saunders proved a wise choice, as Hussey and Adams were both eyeing the then-prevalent dance scene with increasing interest, moving themselves further away from the standards that had once defined the Mission. In the event, little about the resulting album, June 1992's *Masque*, addressed such topics in any overt fashion, but the inspiration, at least, was there.

Rather, *Masque* reaffirmed the Mission's Zeppelin-esque rock credentials, at the same time as thoroughly demolishing the more airy-fairy lyrical notions that had begun to tire even the most faithful observers. One song, 'She Conjures Me Wings', could even be described as Hussey's own farewell to his former preoccupations: the dragons have departed, the fairies have fled and the apples of Avalon have withered and died. Even in the grip of a barrelhouse romp *à la* the Small Faces or the Kinks, a better summary of the Mission's current mindset could scarcely be imagined.

Much of the album's strength, Hussey affirmed, came from the surroundings in which it was conceived. The Barn (which was, literally, a barn) was located some 50 miles away from the nearest major highway, in the absolute heart of middle-England nowhere.

'I originally went there to lick my wounds,' Hussey revealed. 'A lot of shit went down in 1990; by the end of that year, I had no self-esteem, no self-belief at all, I was very low – lower than I'd ever been before.' Only as the Barn filled with rented recording equipment did his confidence return and, with it, a way of dealing with the negativity. 'The songs on *Masque* were written way after the event. It was a case of putting myself back into a particular situation and feeling all the anger, the betrayal or whatever, but being more objective about it. If I'd written those tunes while all that shit was going down, the album would have been a lot darker.'

Nothing about the Mission's reinvention was going to be easy, however. Having previewed much of the new material at their own show in Finsbury Park on 1st June 1991, the group then announced that, for the first time, they would not be touring in support of the album. It was a stunning decision from a band that had built its reputation, not to mention its record sales, on live work. It backfired spectacularly.

The group hoped that their absence might create an aura of mystery. Instead, their first single in 18 months, April 1992's 'Never Again', belly flopped at #34. *Masque* itself limped no higher than #23, assailed further by some of the most hostile reviews in the band's entire career.

Just when it seemed things could get no worse, the entire debacle was kicked firmly in the face when Andrew Eldritch, having already dipped into his archive for an album-length retrospective of the Sisters' early years, *Some Girls Wander By Mistake*, unleashed an audacious remake of 'Temple Of Love', featuring Israeli vocalist Ofra Haza.

While the Mission foundered at the foot of the chart, 'Temple Of Love' raced to the top, coming to rest at #3; *Some Girls Wander By Mistake*, buoyed by both the single's success and, a boon for collectors, the inclusion of material dating back to 'Damage Done', climaxed at #5. The following year, the rest of the Sisters' story was told by a second compilation, *A Slight Case Of Over-Bombing* and, again, an audacious new single, 'Under The Gun'.

A duet with Terri Nunn of Berlin infamy, 'Under The Gun', at least through its first three minutes, was little more than a chest-beating power ballad, a love duet that hinged around Nunn's demand to know, 'are you living for love', and Eldritch's apparent reluctance to even bother answering. Compared to the sonic slaughterhouse of past Sisters' epics, truly there was more Meatloaf than meathook to 'Under The Gun'.

But that was simply the first three minutes. Persevere a little longer and matters take on a very different complexion as Eldritch drifts into a lengthy deconstruction of all that Nunn was yowling about, a bitter rant that makes even greater sense if you can lay your hands on one of the television appearances the band made to promote the single. Even at the outset of the song, the distance between the singers was disconcerting; by the time Eldritch hits his monologue, he might as well be absolutely alone. Which, as his musical peers his continued to fall apart all around, he was.

Robert Smith

Chapter Fifteen
Friday I'm In...
What???

How the Cure were able to carry on, while everyone else lost their heads – and how a handful of people found them again.

'I'm not going to worry about the Cure slipping down into the second division, it doesn't bother me, because I never expected to be in the first division anyway.' Robert Smith

nly the Cure seemed immune to the convulsions that were shattering the order of things. Buoyed by the grotesque hall of mirrors that was the *Mixed Up* remix collection, the band spent much of 1991 at work on the true follow-up to *Disintegration*, as heedless of what was taking place in the outside world as ever.

Looking back on *Disintegration*, Smith remarked, 'Hitting 30 was a real benchmark. I wanted to change everything about the way I was doing things, and that was the album. After that, it changed, it became a much easier-going group. Whether you think the albums suffered or not is irrelevant. The way it worked within the context of the group was immeasurably better than the albums leading up to being 30.'

As the first full-scale example of this new egalitarian regime, 1992's *Wish* remains perhaps the most contentious, and certainly misunderstood, album in the Cure's repertoire. Its success simply cannot be argued with – it blustered its way to #2 in the US, dragging the 'Friday, I'm In Love' single into the Top 20 in its wake, and sending the band out on a world tour that seemed to last forever.

Was it a good Cure album, though? In places, yes – 'From The Edge Of The Deep Green Sea' certainly merited all the applause it won, while 'High' also ranks amongst Smith's better later compositions. And 'This Twilight Garden', a session out-take that was held over for a b-side, was so great that even Smith later mourned, 'I cannot believe I left it off the album.'

Overall, *Wish* was patchy, with 'Friday I'm In Love' representing a nadir from which even Smith's 'tongue-in-cheek' defence could not salvage it. But in terms of consolidating the monster, proving that the dreaded Grunge had not changed absolutely everything, it did its job with room to spare.

Wish was followed by two new live albums, *Show*, which Smith describes as the 'official' set, and *Paris*, which he compiled purely for the old time fans who were demanding an airing for the sometimes stunning versions of older, 'more obscure' songs that the band was occasionally capable of unleashing during the 1992-93 tour.

Smith enthuses, '*Show* is a fantastic album, it's the Cure live at their best, there's no better collection of songs ever in our history, than that tour. Everyone was playing so well, I just wanted to capture that. I just thought "I want this, this is my testament, this is what we were like when we were doing this stuff."

'*Paris*, on the other hand, came out because there was actually fan demand. I didn't want to put stuff like 'Drowning Man' and that on a live album that I thought was a showpiece album, but a lot of people wanted our interpretations – in a good setting, recorded well – of some of the older stuff, the more hardcore fan stuff, so that's what *Paris* was. It honestly had nothing to do with me in a funny sort of way, I really didn't mind if it was out or not. We didn't promote it, it had no advertising, it was just sort of there, and it sold a handful of copies. It was unusual to bring two live albums out at once,' he conceded, 'but they were such totally different records.'

Simon Gallup continued, 'with the *Wish* tour, we knew Porl [Thompson] was going to leave... we didn't at the time know Boris [Williams] was also going, but it seemed like a good way to end that chapter. And, to be quite honest with you, we didn't know if we were going to do another record. We're not that clever that we

think "Oh, in two years time we're gonna do another record." We tend to get together and get excited if someone's got a tune, which is what we did with *Wish*.'
Both discs, then, could have been the Cure's farewell. But, of course, they weren't. They simply prefaced a delay that, at times, appeared interminable.

The Cult, meanwhile, had had their time off and greeted 1993 by stirring for their biggest push in three years. Still moribund in the wake of the failure of 'The Witch', the band was both startled and gratified when the 1993 studio/live compilation *Pure Cult For Rockers, Ravers, Lovers And Sinners* not only returned the band to the charts, it also suggested that media and public alike were prepared to rehabilitate the group.

The recruitment, in May, of Dag Nasty drummer Scott Garrett and former Mission bassist Craig Adams offered Astbury and Duffy a stability that they'd not experienced in years, with Adams an especially welcome addition. Astbury and Duffy had never made any secret of their admiration for his playing and, within six months of his dismissal from the Mission, they were in touch. Neither could Astbury conceal his delight in interviews of the time. 'Craig had just about had it with the Mission after they'd attempted another Glam Rock Christmas record or one of those novelty things. The Mission, and this year they're Father Christmas, and next year they're Slade.

'He'd got bored with all that, he and Wayne [Hussey] were pretty much finished, so we got together with him and it was great. He'd grown up the same as we had, he was the same age, has the same cultural references. All we had to say was "Billy Bremner," and that was that.'

This new Cult line-up played a handful of UK dates that summer, including an appearance at Guns n'Roses' Milton Keynes Bowl festival, followed by a 40-date European tour with Metallica. 'Seven times they asked us and I said no, but finally, they told us Alice In Chains would also be on the bill, and that sounded a bit more liberal than just us and Metallica, so we said okay.'

In the event, the Seattle grunge-meisters pulled out, to be replaced by Suicidal Tendencies, 'with us sandwiched between them,' shuddered Astbury. 'And we were thinking, there was no way we could do it, because at the time we were wearing baggy Levis and old Punk T-shirts and boots, and we'd all cut our hair off. We looked like a shower of Punk art students from the Seventies.

'But we went out and did the shows and, at first, we were really pissed off, thinking "We should not be here, this is not the place for us." But after a while, it was "Fuck this, let's just have a good time," and it was brilliant, a complete riot. Then we did our own shows and suddenly we found we had this audience that had never gone away. We were even selling out places we'd already played with Metallica, it was just overwhelming. People were so fanatical about us, and it was like starting over again. To me, it was a brand new band and, when we went into record the new album, it was a product of that energy.'

Having assured himself that the Cult in 1993 was a far cry from the dishevelled beast that had contacted him prior to recording *Ceremony*, Rick Rubin was originally scheduled to produce this latest album but, according to Astbury, 'it was not to be. We expected him to come down to rehearsals, but he was working with

Tom Petty. We expected him to come down to rehearsals, but he was working with Mick Jagger. He was hanging out with Donovan, he'd just signed Joe Cocker, he was working with Johnny Cash… in the end we went "Fuck this shit," and forgot it. And then Bob Rock called me up and said, "I really want to work with you guys again."

'Now, I really wasn't too keen on *Sonic Temple* in some respects, although it was a commercial success, but I went up to meet with him and he just blew me away. He said he really understood my criticisms of that album but, as far as he was concerned, he never got a fair crack of the whip. So we went to Vancouver and recorded in this little warehouse, and it was brilliant.

Titled with a simplicity that echoed its conception, *The Cult*, said Astbury, 'was really humble pie. We didn't have any frills, we weren't going out to nightclubs or anything, we were just turning up at the studio every day around two, knocking off at one in the morning, every day for three and a half months. We had no illusions of grandeur, we didn't think we were going to make a record that was going to set the world on fire, we just went in wanting to do something that was turning us on every day, and that's what happened. We were trying out all our ideas.

'We knew we wanted to make a dry record. We didn't want any more grandiose, over the top records, we wanted to make a very sincere, honest, truthful record, and that was the challenge, to be honest. It's very strange, but I felt that this was an album I should have made when I was 17 or 18 years old, but I wouldn't have been able to. I don't think I'd have been able to face the issues.' Shortly before *The Cult's* September 1994, release, he admitted, 'It's bloody killing me waiting for it to come out, like being an expectant father again!'

The Cult's return to the stage opened with a low-key show at Vancouver's Commodore Ballroom in October 1994. The line-up had shifted slightly again, with the addition of rhythm guitarist James Stevenson, moonlighting from the still-hibernating Gene Loves Jezebel but, 15 years before, guitarist with Generation X that night in Sheffield, when a 19-year-old Punk named Ian Astbury carried his gear in return for a free concert ticket. 'He used to be my roadie,' Stevenson laughed. 'Now he's my boss.'

British, European and Australian dates followed, before the Cult made it back to the US in February 1995. South American shows carried them further into the year. With a set divided squarely between new material and old favourites, with Astbury positively demonic both onstage and, given his new-found penchant for fearless stage-diving, off, the Cult played to packed houses everywhere, and every night sent audiences away in amazement. 'When people thought of the Cult, they thought of a tired old rock band,' Astbury declared. 'Then they come to see us, and we're anything but.'

A matter of weeks later, he would break up the band.

As 1994 turned to 1995, Love And Rockets, meanwhile, were wondering why they hadn't done the same thing.

Their solo hiatus had completely rejuvenated the musicians. No matter that neither Ash nor J's solo albums really confirmed anything more than the already entrenched belief that Love and Rockets together were an awful lot stronger than

Love and Rockets in pieces, still they served a purpose. J explained, 'It was healthy because there are certain things – more so with my stuff – that don't fit into the Love And Rockets idiom. We can get those off our chest. And it's also healthy to be your own boss, having that final and only say on what you do, and not having to compromise it. Then it makes it that much easier to compromise when you go back to work with a band.'

J released his third solo album, *Songs From Another Season* in June 1990, completing a triptych that commenced in 1983 with *The Etiquette Of Violence* and paused in 1985, following *Crocodile Tears And The Velvet Cosh*; Ash unleashed the menacing, mood-splintering *Coming Down*. By mid-1992, 'We had our solo things out of our systems, and it was time to begin work again.'

Sessions began for what would become Love And Rockets' epic foray into the world of electronica, the consummation of musical instincts they had toyed with on *Love And Rockets*. Working with an enthusiasm they had all but forgotten existed, the sessions represented an absolute and violent rebirth, rebuilding the band from the ground up and dispensing with even Ash's trademark guitar riffs in favour of electronic loops and samples. Tight songs were eschewed for broiling moods. Anybody searching for even the ghost of 'So Alive' was left staring into a vacuum. RCA, naturally, hated every minute of it.

The label wanted another 'So Alive'; the band didn't care if they never heard the song again – it was the main reason why they'd taken a break in the first place. Love And Rockets had always been pushing for creation, not stagnation; to back-pedal now would ruin everything. Although the label tried to make them see reason, so far as the trio was concerned there were no terms to discuss. 'RCA couldn't see the single,' shrugged J. 'They couldn't hear the guitars, they didn't know what we were doing. So they let us go.'

It would be another eight months before Love And Rockets found a new home – with Rick Rubin's American label – a period that sent Ash and J scurrying back to solo pastures while the looming Love and Rockets masterpiece was given time to gestate and, maybe, reconsider its position.

'It was very textured, moody, ambient,' Ash mused. 'It was only when we went back to it a year later, that I thought it maybe needed some more conventional elements' – a few guitars, a handful of solos, a few more vocals, a few more melodies.

Scheduled for release in September 1994, side by side with the Cult's comeback, *Hot Trip To Heaven* should have been Love And Rockets' biggest album yet. Instead, it sank like a stone. 'The plan was to put out *Hot Trip To Heaven* and really make it very low-key,' J recalled. 'In fact, Rick Rubin at one time just wanted to put it out without any name on the sleeve, with just a white sleeve and a white label. That low key. And the idea was, people would talk about it and then would find out it was Love And Rockets.'

Unfortunately, 'it was a plan that really backfired on us,' and even the early release of two great singles, 'This Heaven' in Britain and 'Body And Soul' in America, didn't stop the slide. The majority of mainstream reviews simply couldn't comprehend how *their* Love And Rockets had recorded something so *un*-Love And Rockets-ish; mainstream radio simply ignored it altogether. By the time *Hot Trip To*

Heaven's projected release date rolled around, Beggars Banquet had decided not to even bother releasing the album in Britain. American did give it a US issue, but its fate was sealed. 'It was a commercial catastrophe,' reflected Ash. 'We all thought it would be like *Dark Side Of The Moon* or nothing. It turned out to be nothing. We completely lost faith. And things kept getting worse.'

Shaken, the band immediately began work on a new album – 'I think subconsciously we were like "Okay, that didn't work, so let's get back to guitars again",' Ash mused, but even that decision caused problems. 'We were having a complete identity crisis. It was "Where are we going with this?"'

They were still trying to figure that out when a catastrophic fire destroyed the studio where they were recording, reducing their demos and gear to ashes. J: 'We lost all our instruments that we'd had since Bauhaus. It's indescribable, really. Because when you've had an instrument since you were fifteen, it becomes a very soulful thing. But then again, there was something beautiful about it, purging.'

The band resolved to start again, only for a second disaster to strike as American, unmoved by their musical efforts so far, froze their recording budget. The band finished recording in what Ash described as a friend's garage, then sat back while the world completely ignored Love And Rockets' most fragmented effort yet, the perhaps aptly-titled *Sweet FA*. That, after all, was how much promotion it received, that was how much buzz surrounded its release.

On the road, even long-term fans were astonished to see the band in town without any advance warning or, apparently, any new product to push. For many people, the first they knew of the new album was when they heard the songs in concert. American had dropped the ball. Then they dropped the band.

As Love And Rockets faded from view, the Cure – the band alongside whom they had topped the world just five years earlier – finally began moving into sight again.

Work on their next album had commenced in late 1993. 'We started doing demos but, because we didn't have a drummer, it's a bit weird rehearsing with a drum machine, so there was a lot of things going on,' Gallup recalled. 'Then, after about two years, Jason [Cooper] came in and we knew he was going to be permanent, so things started moving on.'

The sessions eventually wound up in a west country mansion rented from actress Jane Seymour. It was there that *Wild Mood Swings* slowly began taking shape. Very slowly: the album would not appear until early 1996.

The first release from the sessions was a single, the bizarre '13th'. Unanimously, the press leaped to praise it as a considerable departure for the Cure – much, of course, as they had done with 'Love Cats' and 'Hot Hot Hot', as Gallup pointed out.

'Doing things as a departure makes it sound like it's contrived. If I looked at "13th" and wasn't involved in it, I could say, "oh look, it's got a Latin beat in it, it's got all this stuff," but because we've all been involved, we all think it's a good song. And I'll be thoroughly honest, we're not trying to break new ground with it because its actually quite a sleazy song in a way. But if we were to go out tonight and we heard that song, we'd dance to it.'

'I think we lost our belligerence years ago,' Smith continued. 'I think people have become used to the fact we'll do what we do, we're not trying to upset or shock or amuse anyone, we just want people to think it's fun.'

By past mighty standards, however, *Wild Mood Swings* was not regarded by many people as fun. Uniformly criticized by the press, it entered the charts at #1, then plunged straight down from there. Recent reports have sales bottoming out at around half of whatever *Wish* did. Smith, however, was not downhearted. 'It kind of reflected a trend, I suppose. I was told "oh, it was the lack of hits and blah blah blah," but I think really, we took too long making it and, even though I wouldn't go back and make it in any other way, because it was really good fun, I did accept the criticisms.

'But I've never yet evaluated a Cure album by what it's done globally. *17 Seconds* did something like 25,000 worldwide, but it couldn't take away from what it meant to me. So I'm not going to worry about the Cure slipping down into the second division, it doesn't bother me, because I never expected to be in the first division anyway.'

The attendant tour was not without its problems either, including the technical hiccups that resulted in the entire British leg of the jaunt being postponed for six full months. The *Five Swings Live* live EP which was drawn from the shows, however, sold out its limited edition run of 5,000 within days. Only available through the band's website, it did, in fact, show off the recent material in far stronger surroundings than the actual album.

Smith could not completely ignore *Wild Mood Swings*' relative failure, however. 'It did prompt me to re-valuate why I'm doing it, and the reasons why I started. And I decided I should just go back to pleasing myself.' 2000's *Blood Flowers* album, an oasis of modernity released sandwiched between the retrospectives *Galore* and *The Cure's Greatest Hits*, was the first evidence of this resolution, its miasmic recreation of the *Pornography/Disintegration*-style sound that Smith regards as the very soul of the Cure flying furiously in the face of everything the band had accomplished in the previous decade. A lot of listeners thought it was also the best thing they'd done in as long.

Back in Los Angeles, Ian Astbury, too, was contemplating dropping a spanner into the machinery that had erected itself around him. Reflecting on the tempestuous end of the 1994-95 version of the Cult, Astbury explained, 'I walked out in March 1995. We had a big impassioned brawl on the Copacabana Beach. I was at the end of my tether, exhausted, and I basically lost my mind. We'd been together since 1983, pretty much non-stop, tour-album-tour-album and the one time I tried taking a vacation for ten days, I couldn't handle it. So, come 1995, it was just a case of getting away from it.'

He didn't go far. Four weeks after the Brazilian showdown, Astbury and drummer Scott Garrett had a new band, the Holy Barbarians, up-and-running. 'There you go. I had a month away and couldn't wait to get back in again. I'd left the Cult, but I still had a pile of songs and I wanted to record them. But I wanted to do things differently. The Cult had become all about accountants and record labels and doing everything on a grand scale. The Holy Barbarians rehearsed in my garage.

'It was making music for authentic reasons, for the sake of making music. It wasn't intended to be a big commercial thing, we just did it. It was great, we toured in a van, we didn't do anything we didn't want to. If we wanted to be a degenerate mess, we could. It was like being in my first band again and it reaffirmed my love of music.'

The Holy Barbarians' *Cream* album, however, was barely even noticed when it emerged during 1996 and silence now reigned where Astbury had once blustered so beautifully. It would be another four years before the singer resurfaced. In the meantime, his most recent cohorts scattered – and unerringly headed for home.

James Stevenson was the first to resurface, his experiences with the Cult not only breathing fresh life into his own outlook, but encouraging him to push the Aston brothers into giving Gene Loves Jezebel another crack of the whip.

Of the two, Michael had been the most active of late. While his brother relocated to New York, contemplating a solo career that peaked with the acoustic album *Unpopular Songs* but ultimately fizzled out through lack of impetus, Michael formed a new band, Edith Grove, signed with the LA Indy Triple X, and set to work on a new album.

Edith Grove would emerge a dramatically esoteric record, its contents raging from the dulcimer-driven 'Venus In Rags' and the rustic madrigal 'Kings Horsemen', to the 'All The Young Dudes'-esque 'Wheel' and on to a tribute to Marc Bolan. It was an incredibly forward-looking record and, followed as it was by the similarly superb solo album *Why Me Why Now Why This*, Aston should have been poised to take full advantage.

Instead, he turned towards reunion. Both Stevenson and Jay Aston guested on *Edith Grove* and, having toured the album during spring 1996, Michael linked up again with Jay in June, to record three songs: 'When We Were Young', 'The Goodbye Girl' and 'Who Wants to Go To Heaven', a beautiful ballad based, at least partly, on the Birthday Party's 'Sonny's Burning' and originally intended for the soundtrack to the movie version of *Interview With A Vampire*.

They were backed, for the occasion, by Edith Grove: Tommy Andrews, Dick Hawkins, and Morad. However, when Avalanche, the US label that issued the Edith Grove album, suggested that the pair reconvene Gene Loves Jezebel to cut a couple of new songs for a forthcoming Best Of collection (1995's *From The Mouths Of Babes*), Edith Grove were cut loose and Stevenson returned to the unit.

The trio cut two songs, 'Body And Soul' and 'No Sweat', neither of which exactly rekindled the fondest memories of the original pairing; neither of which was accomplished without a fight. But Jay looked back and reflected, 'it wasn't uncomfortable, we had a nice time doing it. It wasn't a big deal.' Barely were the sessions complete than the Astons were looking for further projects to combine on.

Some new material was demoed but went it nowhere; finally, Michael recalled, 'I called Jay in England, and said "Let's do a little tour together." Why not? It'd been 15 years since Gene Loves Jezebel began.' Dubbed the Pre-Raphaelite tour, it was not strictly a reunion – indeed, the initial plan was to go out without any reference to the Gene Loves Jezebel name whatsoever.

Jay Aston continued, 'The idea was I was going to do five or six of my songs and he'd do five or six of his songs, and we'd do some older Jezebel stuff together. Then Mike found that, obviously, the promoters were offering 20 times the money for

Gene Loves Jezebel, and that opened a whole new can of worms. But I felt the same as Mike: "yeah, let's do it"'

Aware that no gathering of past members of the band could please them both, the twins decided to piece together an entirely new band line-up: guitarist Michael Ciravolo, on loan from Human Drama, drummer Pete Parada and the singularly named Yugoslavian bassist Slobo.

Still, Jay insisted, the intention was to feature the older material at the very end of the show. 'But, once we started rehearsing, the agent sold a lot of the gigs as some kind of '80s flashback thing.' The die was cast.

With the band touring the US through summer 1997, the outing was seized upon as an opportunity for fans to witness something they believed they might never see again, as both brothers set out in pursuit of what had been the guiding principle behind the Gene Loves Jezebel in the first place. 'The most important thing for me was for Gene Loves Jezebel to be different from anything else on this planet,' Michael explained. 'When Jay was involved, what we had was so unique, so rare, so painfully, primitively honest, that it would knock people's heads off. As to what extent it could still do that, I didn't know but I knew it was really powerful. That was the vision of it. It was a remarkable thing on every level. It was incredible.

'But Jay and also I needed to work a lot of stuff out. I knew it would be a painful process. We both have such different perspectives on what occurred but, in there, there's the truth. We needed to do this, because we dearly love each other, and we both needed to learn something from this.'

Stage as therapy couch is an unusual concept, but Gene Loves Jezebel were always an unusual band. 'What we're both finding out on this tour is that the battle continues, and it always will,' Jay admitted, as the outing approached its midway point. 'It's amazing we even got out of LA. We're on the highway out, and we're screaming at each other.

'But, ultimately, our power is enormous and, as much as we can hate each other sometimes, generally we're on each other's side. I guess the lesson is, when Mike and I work together, things always go right, when we're not together they go wrong.'

His brother agreed. 'What Gene Loves Jezebel should be perceived as is, the ongoing relationship of the bad twins. And that's why it's interesting, cathartic, whatever else. It's worth the pain.'

Unfortunately, this new-found truce was but a passing phase. Though plans for further touring and recording seemed far advanced, no sooner were the pair back home again than the disagreements began once more and, this time, dragged further and deeper than they ever had before. Few familial disputes, after all, can become as rancorous as those which divide twins and the Astons, for all the deep love that undoubtedly conjoins them at heart, split with all the vicious rage and betrayal that such a sundering could muster. Both looked towards the courts to put the other's claims to rest, both ignited fresh confusion amid their fan base as they strove to assume supremacy, establishing their own rival versions of the band.

Jay's unadorned Gene Loves Jezebel were first to get off the mark with the *VII* album, reconstituting the classic Stevenson/Rizzo/Bell line-up; his twin's Gene Loves Jezebel Featuring Michael Aston, meanwhile, contented themselves with a darkly effective 'All The Young Dudes,' cut for a Gothic-themed David Bowie tribute album, before cutting their own *Love Lies Bleeding* in 1999. In the two teams' eyes, both bands represent a new beginning. For fans, it is, perhaps, a different story.

Chapter Sixteen
Give The People
What They Want

In which, as the reunion roadshow rattles into life, the past is always lurking around the corner. It's not the happiest ending you'll ever read, but who said the story was over, anyway?

'Wayne and I have an understanding. But I still wish he wouldn't stick his tongue down your ear when he's playing at the affectionate.' Andrew Eldritch

As Gene Loves Jezebel splintered into two, the two halves of Bauhaus were planning to do quite the opposite. They, too, were marking a 15th anniversary – of their original demise, of course – but the event seemed worth noting regardless, all the more so since recent events had seen them both depart from Beggars Banquet and wind up, instead, on the independent Red Ant.

The rollercoaster horrors of Love And Rockets' last few years had brought the band to the brink of a very public collapse. Peter Murphy, on the other hand, had slipped quite contentedly from view. He waited two years to follow up 1990's *Deep*, completing a triptych of remarkable singles with the suitably claustrophobic 'You're So Close' but, with the accompanying *Holy Smoke* album, the moment of magic that he had come so close to touching had clearly dissipated. The album sold no more than 100,000 copies nationwide, crushed – as so much else was crushed – by the American predilection for all things Grunge and Seattle-shaped (ironically, Seattle has always been a strong market for Murphy).

Equally pertinent, however, was the gathering gloom of America's own burgeoning Gothic Rock revival, a peculiar hybrid that owed little to the artistic stretches that characterised the movement's UK heyday and an awful lot to remaining within the tightest confines of miasmic melancholy it could devise.

Regardless of its own tenets, however, this reborn genre was snatching back as many of its icons as it could lay its hands on. A reborn Sex Gang Children, the band's releases and reissues flooding out alongside a simultaneous Andi Sex Gang solo catalogue, were readily adopted. Both Gene Loves Jezebel and the Cult had noticed the increasing number of black-clad reverents clustered around the stage when they played and the Cure, of course, had never seen them leave.

The reissue racks groaned beneath belated releases for albums previously available on import alone – Beggars Banquet, as befit the largest repository of relevant releases, gave American debuts to Dali's Car, early Peter Murphy, the pre-Cult convolutions, and the Fields of the Nephilim. From LA, the Cleopatra label sought out sometimes stunning compilations of Specimen, Red Lorry Yellow Lorry, Alien Sex Fiend and Theatre of Hate, then reinforced the catalogue with glimpses into America's own early 80s Goth scene, Christian Death, 45 Grave and the Superheroines.

New bands, too, were filtering through, on both sides of the Atlantic, as Children On Stun, London After Midnight, Rosetta Stone and many more piled into view. The dichotomy of their existence, in an age that had wrought so many changes upon the Dark Rock scene, was shocking enough to their traditional audience – what next, a Dick Emery comedy revival? Imagine how it must have seemed to someone with no expectation or even advance warning of such happenstance. But, with so much active interest, Peter Murphy, whose own moody ruminations had never sought to evade the basic tenets of *a* (if not *the*) Gothic sensibility, was a sitting duck.

Nevertheless, he was shocked, upon returning to the country to tour *Holy Smoke* in 1992, by the turnaround; shocked, too, to discover that the 'Godfather of Goth' tag that *Deep* had so successfully buried, was alive and well once again. A handful of interviews, both on this tour and again three years later when he returned to promote his fifth album, *Cascade*, turned decidedly prickly as he struggled to distance himself from the reborn preoccupation, unaware as he was that it was not his own distant past that was returning to haunt him but a segment of the American scene's own present.

The gulf that divided Murphy from what other artists might have conceded was their core audience was not simply obstinacy. Based now in Ankara, his wife's home city, Murphy acknowledged that his own awareness of western market forces was hopelessly out-dated – and he preferred it that way.

'I don't know what the latest sequencer is, I don't know the proper BPM speed for the latest records. But the upside of that is, I can be terribly uninformed and that sometimes helps make music which comes completely out of nowhere, that doesn't go along with the obsessive following of the masses.

'I'm a very dislocated personality anyway. It's not that I'm introverted, but I have an aesthetic, a sense of myself in the music business, as being completely dislocated and not linked with the general musical community. That allows me to live my own psycho-dramatic alter ego. It's a very subconscious thing, but I sort of retain a purity in that. I tend to store up a lot of energy and let it out in one main burst, and it's that energy which constitutes the power you hear on the records. I'm kind of like this floating mist, which I bring out of the cupboard to play with.

'When I come to rationalize it, I definitely like living in the desert and visiting the city occasionally, to speak metaphorically. Because when I go to the city, it informs my work with an originality which hasn't been tainted by familiarity, or what's happening at that time.'

1995's *Cascade* album, Murphy's last major label American release (Beggars Banquet dropped him at the same time as they bade farewell to Love And Rockets), was his last album even to toy with commercial respectability and the first to map out the directions that would haunt his next two releases, the *Recall* EP in 1999, and the *Dust* album in 2002. Those subsequent releases would see him moving at light speed away from the mainstream, into areas that not only confirmed, but also justified, his own standing as a serious artist.

It was a lesson that others of his generation would have been well advised to absorb. Murphy himself only absorbed it after he bowed to the pressure that had been building for much of the last decade-and-a-half: The Bauhaus reunion.

There had been several false starts earlier in the decade, rumours arising and then collapsing again as one or other of the band members – usually Murphy and/or Ash – backed out at more-or-less the last minute. 1998, however, found all four members agreeable, despite both parties having their own new releases waiting at the gate, Murphy's *Recall* EP and Love And Rockets' valedictory *Lift* album. Maybe the hope was that the publicity surrounding the Bauhaus tour would give both projects extra buoyancy of their own. Maybe such matters never entered their heads. Either way, the Bauhaus tour was on, a four-month gallop that, opening in mid-August 1998, would draw packed houses across the US, Europe and, finally, the UK.

Past and present collided loudly, of course, but the harshest jolt for many onlookers was the reality that was sandwiched in between: Bauhaus' own reality, as opposed to the idealized Gothic legend that history had constructed around them.

The fable, perpetuated across a slew of steadily more refined compilations, is of a band whose sole sound was that of unparalleled savagery: the guitar crunch of 'Double Dare', the immolation lope of 'Terror Couple Kills Colonel', the ragged dub of 'She's In Parties' and, of course, the Better Than Bowie of their 'Ziggy Stardust' cover.

The truth, however, was always less comfortable, a blend of untutored experimentalism and idealistic spontaneity careening into the savage murder of convention: 'Party Of The First Part' epitomised that; so did 'King Volcano'. so did a chilling cover of John Cale's 'Rosegarden, Funeral Of Sores' and so, though it had long been dulled by familiarity, did the still chillingly dislocated 'Bela Lugosi's Dead', the ten-minute epic that spawned Goth in the first place and, as the American *Goldmine* magazine pointed out, 'landed Bauhaus in their present pickle. Without it, they'd be ranked with Pere Ubu and the Pop Group, sociopathic pioneers with a penchant for the piquant. With it, they were on a hiding to nothing.'

The first night of the tour, in Seattle, was plagued by gremlins. Reclaiming a visual trick that had characterised their first incarnation, the band intended opening the show with 'Double Dare', with Murphy's place on stage filled by a closed-circuit television set. As the band began playing, the screen flickered into life and Murphy, deep within the bowels of the venue, appeared to sing the opening lines of the song. The TV didn't work, however, so the band took another tack entirely, and opened the show with 'Bela Lugosi's Dead'. Neither band nor audience recovered from the jolt.

Afterwards, Murphy grinned, 'I like it when we have to work harder,' but a stony and so-Gothed-out crowd, having already heard what they'd waited so long to experience, barely moved a muscle all night, simply watching in intensifying disbelief as their idols romped through a shattered rendition of 'Wild Thing', a seemingly endless cover of Dead Can Dance's 'Severance', then closed up with a 'Passion Of Lovers' that was neither passionate nor loving... but did capture the dichotomy which the original Bauhaus espoused with blinding fury.

They were never a slick band, nor a crowd-pleasing circus turn. Later in the reunion tour, Daniel Ash insisted, 'we want to give people what they want' – in contrast, presumably, to the original band's insistence on supplying what they need. But the fact remains, Bauhaus thrived on dissent and adversity, and the more they fought to win back that first night crowd, the more like 'old times' the show became.

The following night, by contrast, ran like clockwork, the opening 'Double Dare' restored to the show and everything falling into place from there. Songs that landed flat the first night were now acknowledged with astonishment, and the band responded in kind. Maybe they did lose a little of the previous night's edge; maybe they did turn the cruise control on for a few rehearsed routines and riffs. But even as Bauhaus strove for perfection, they never lost sight of the tightrope they walked, nor lost the knowledge that collapse was always around the corner.

It never came. For more than 70 minutes, that night and every other night on the tour, Bauhaus played a show that could (and, the following year, would) grace the most demanding live album, slammed 'Telegram Sam' into the inevitable 'Ziggy Stardust', then wound up with a breakneck 'Bela' that was not so much dead as simply breathless. 'The tour went amazingly, it was just like one long show,' Murphy reflected once it was all over. 'It was incredible.'

The rejuvenation continued as Bauhaus returned to the studio for the first time in 15 years. They cut just two songs, but even they proved that the old magic was still intact. A slow-burning version of the in-concert cover 'Severance', intended for inclusion on the live album *Gotham*, was described by Murphy as 'one of those songs which just immediately felt right. Thematically, it fit Bauhaus. It has that very yearning, dark, long quality to it, but it has a spiritual element to it as well, which is nice. And of course we went in and experimented with it, and it became quite a powerful, challenging thing which was happening every night.'

The second recording, 'The Dog's A Vapour', meanwhile, was one of several new songs the band originally hoped to record. It was destined for the *Heavy Metal 2* movie soundtrack. Murphy continued, 'We started to play around with some original material which was coming along really well but, since we only had one day in the studio, we couldn't really do anything. It was very confident, a very strong session.' It was also, unfortunately, the only session they played. When the tour was over, so was the reunion.

The moment they returned to America from the European leg of the Bauhaus bash, Daniel Ash, David J and Kevin Haskins began gearing up for their own band's next outing, promoting *Lift* with a string of one-off shows that, according to Ash, were united in just one purpose... to prove that Love And Rockets didn't just escape from Jurassic Park.

'There's a feeling in the industry now that anyone who was around in the 1980s, and is still around today, has to be some kind of nostalgia thing. But if we've already got one 80s band, why would we need another?'

To his mind, Love and Rockets remained a real, functioning, forward moving band, and *Lift*, a frenzy of electro-squawk rock shot through with some of the band's most savage riffs and head-thumping comedowns, developed from impromptu onstage jams through tracks from *Hot Trip To Heaven*. It should have completely rehabilitated the band. Instead, it was the final nail in their coffin. By the time the tour was over, the album had already sunk; by the time the last live reviews were in, the band was at an end, and David J was preparing to sell all his souvenirs off on e-bay and the internet. An era wasn't simply over, it had been expunged from the record.

Reunions were in the air throughout the late 1990s, although – again – often with unforeseen consequences. In quick succession, the Mission, the Fields of the Nephilim, the Sisters of Mercy and, perhaps inevitably, the Cult all followed Bauhaus and Gene Loves Jezebel back into circulation, each confounding the nay-sayers with some excellent performances and, in two instances at least, some intriguing new music as well.

Little of the Mission's post-*Masque* (or, perhaps, post-Craig Adams) career had gone according to plan. In early 1993, just months after his long-time partner's departure, Wayne Hussey unveiled an ambitious new Mission line-up, featuring former Spear Of Destiny guitarist Mark Thwaite, keyboard player Ric Carter and, following All About Eve's final collapse, bassist Andy Cousins. (Regan would reform the band during 2001.)

Immediately, however, even the most fanatical fans' eyes were directed away from the main event and onto what was surely little more than rampant wishful thinking. In August 1993, Andrew Eldritch made his first live appearance in two years, appearing alongside techno mavens Utah Saints at the Off The Streets benefit in Leeds. Where things got interesting was in the presence on the bill, also, of the rekindled Red Lorry Yellow Lorry and, sharing a venue with Eldritch for the first time in eight years, Wayne Hussey and the Mission.

The rumours of a reunion were rife from the moment the billing was announced. Hussey, after all, was finally debuting the new, post-Craig Adams line-up of his band. The way the music press (led by an extraordinarily conspiratorial *Melody Maker*) saw it, a few extra song rehearsals would be no problem whatsoever.

Neither Hussey nor Eldritch was playing ball, however. Although the two remained on good terms, Hussey joked he'd only rejoin his old partner onstage if 'he pays me loads of money.' Eldritch, on the other hand, simply left the room when the question was put to him. Later, he did agree to talk, but he was no more pliable than Hussey. 'Wayne and I have an understanding. But I still wish he wouldn't stick his tongue down your ear when he's playing at the affectionate.'

The event, then, was a non-event, an outcome that, sadly, set the scene for much of the remainder of this latest Mission's career. A pair of EPs and two final albums, 1995's *Neverland* and the 1996 compilation *Blue*, offered little more than tentative recastings of all that the band had once pioneered. It was telling that the biggest hit single the band enjoyed during these years was a Youth remix of 'Tower Of Strength'; the biggest hit album was the *Sum And Substance* hits collection.

Hussey continued making plans but few came to fruition. Finally, Hussey rung down the curtain on the Mission, staged an elaborate farewell concert, then moved his family to Los Angeles, wife Kelly's home town.

'As far as I'm concerned, The Mission as a democratic and working band ceased to exist the day Simon checked out of the hotel in Toronto back in 1990,' he confessed. 'With each subsequent album and tour, The Mission became less and less a band, and more and more a vehicle for the things that I wanted to do. And, even though people such as Mark Thwaite and Rick Carter came into the line-up and did a fantastic job, it was never to really function as a band again.

'There were times that I encouraged people to take more of an active involvement, both in the creative process, promotion and at the business end of things, but no one ever really took the initiative and the onus of responsibility came to rest more and more with me.'

Now it was exclusively his. Working alone, but still utilising the Mission name, Hussey contributed a pair of songs to the *Shadow Of Doubt* movie soundtrack in 1997; the following May, he flashed again into the media eye when the newly resurgent Gary Numan passed through LA on his much-praised Exile tour: Hussey leapt onstage to layer some brittle guitar into 'Metal' and 'Dead Heaven'. The pair had talked about working together back in 1995, going so far as to plan a new band together, but it never happened. This one night in Los Angeles at least gave a taste of what might have been.

Hussey also remixed a couple of tracks for the South African Goth band No

Friends Of Harry, an engagement that led to a longer flirtation with remix culture in general.

Recent years had seen a massive explosion in the popularity of classic rock remixes, updating (or sometimes, simply mutilating) past hits to create, supporters claimed, a fresh experience for modern listeners. The fashion had now crept further, into 80s rock and even beyond. Hussey commenced reworking material for a series of albums created by the Cleopatra label. Operating under the United States' preferred 'Mission UK' banner, Hussey handled versions of Gene Loves Jezebel's 'Desire', Bow Wow Wow's 'WORK' and Christian Death's 'Spiritual Cramp'.

Such endeavour was not necessarily a sideline he recommended to his former audience: 'It's not a new Mission track or even a cover version but a Wayne Hussey interpretation of someone else's song. The tracks I do only ever use the original vocal. Everything else is done by me. Guitars, backing vocals, production and programming etc. [But] I would suggest trying to hear the track before buying...'

He also recorded a version of the old Sisters Of Mercy live favourite, the Stooges' '1969', for inclusion on a Gothic box set produced by the same label, and a surprisingly fresh cover of David Bowie's 'After All' to accompany Michael Aston's 'All The Young Dudes' on the *Goth Oddity* tribute album. Further tributes to U2, A Flock Of Seagulls, Madonna and the Doors similarly featured 'new' Mission recordings, a process that finally culminated with the 1999 creation of an entire new Mission album, comprised almost wholly of rerecordings of the band's greatest past moments.

It was a controversial move, of course, but Hussey at least had a stab at justifying it. 'Whilst I think the songs are good, some of the original recordings were not, and really don't stand the test of time very well. Also, things like "Like A Child Again" were always better than the recorded version and I've always wanted the opportunity and excuse to re-record some of these songs.' Nevertheless, the sense that the adventure was finally over had never seemed stronger. Or sadder.

Out of such rampant revivalism, however, there sprang fresh hope – a reunion with Craig Adams, unemployed since the demise of the Cult, and a massive American tour winding through October/November 1999. Joined on the bill by Jay Aston's version of Gene Loves Jezebel, and with the Mission's own line-up bolstered by former Cult/Holy Barbarians drummer Scott Garrett and *Neverland*-era guitarist Mark Thwaite, the outing was an unlikely success, not only presenting a fresh take on the two bands' old material, but offering hope for the future as well.

Gene Loves Jezebel, sadly, would not follow through on that promise – since then, their only new releases have been archived live recordings. The Mission, however, dove straight into their first world tour in a decade, Mission Recon2000 and released a comeback album, *Aura*, in November 2001. *Q*'s review, describing it as the band's 'most satisfying album to date' might have overdosed on the excitement of the return. But their best since the masterpiece that *Carved In/ Grains Of Sand* could have been? Certainly. After all, as America's *Alternative* Press put it, 'you can't keep a good Goth down – hell, even a good Goth can't keep a good Goth down.' No matter what convolutions Wayne Hussey had led his merry mob of morbid minstrels through over the last decade, at his heart he remained the same

235

swords'n'sorcery goblin we've always loved so heartily. *Aura* arrived armed with everything that the band always used to be and none of the baggage that sent you packing away from them.

The opening 'Angeline' set the scene, riding the same stirring anthemic guitar lines that underpinned all the band's classic oldies with vocals piping like the spawn of 'Severina' and a title that rhymed with 'whiplash queen'. True, a total of 13 tracks, including two behemoth epics at the end of the disc, may have been a bit more Mish than nostalgia needs, but they were atmospheric kickers regardless. The boys, to wring out an assuredly unwelcome hard-rockin' cliché, were back in town.

Would the band remain intact to enjoy their newborn success? On 19th April 2002, the Mission opened a South American tour with four shows in Brazil; five days later, the night before flying on to Argentina, Craig Adams announced that he was quitting for personal reasons.

Boldly, Hussey completed the tour as a solo act; back home, he insisted that all was not lost: while 'Craig's departure will be felt deeply... the European tour is going ahead with a temporary replacement. We will also play all other scheduled European festival shows over the summer.' However, he also confessed, 'one of the promises I made to myself when we reformed The Mission in 1999 was that this time it would be fun.

'Well, since the release of *Aura*, there has been a lot of business to take care of that has had nothing to do with making music, and quite frankly, working as The Mission over the last few months has not been fun.' In July 2002, still refusing to bury the band, but certainly not skimping on the funeral expenses, Hussey launched another solo acoustic tour of Europe and the UK.

The return of the Fields of the Nephilim was also marked by a certain amount of chaos and disarray, with the band's tentative re-emergence in 2000 merely one more uncertain step of a journey that began a full three years before when the original quartet – Carl McCoy, Tony Petit and Paul and Nod Wright – reconvened for the first time in five years to begin working through new material.

The past half-decade had been one of brutal under-achievement. Both Rubicon and the Nefilim had eventually stirred themselves to record, although a pair of Rubicon albums, *What Starts, Ends* and *Room 101*, captured no more than the ghosts of past glories. There was more intense interest in rumours, emanating from the German media, that McCoy was undergoing psychiatric treatment than there was in *Zoon*, the Nefilim's 1996 album.

A projected Nefilim tour was cancelled but McCoy was quick to scotch tales of his mental collapse, revealing instead that there were far more prosaic reasons for the non-event. He told the *Zillo* fanzine, 'I have heard a lot of rumours, most of them are quite funny because there is not much truth in it. The reason why [the] tour was cancelled is that there was a dispute between the record company, Beggar's Banquet, and me. The tour wasn't gonna go ahead because I planned it, so we didn't do it. We had to do it the way we need it, the right shows, the way we want it to do at the right time. That was the main reason why it was cancelled, because of this big disagreement.'

That disagreement, it was quickly surmised, was the reason for the old band's return. Again, McCoy was swift to deny it – the members had remained in contact throughout the hiatus, with Petit going so far as to say both the break and the comeback were all part of a secret seven-year plan formulated around the time of *Elizium*.

Whatever the reasoning... it didn't happen. A projected new album, targeted for late 1998, failed to materialise. When the Fields of the Nephilim did finally resurface in 2000, McCoy and Petit alone represented the old guard.

McCoy: 'Some of the old members of the band are a bit out of touch with what we were doing, and also the material we were writing didn't seem totally suitable for the future so, you know, we felt that the band had to be kind of scrimped, so by choice we kind of scrimped the band the way we felt suitable, just to put across what we do as best we can. Me and Tony were the original founders and builders of the Nephilim.'

Reflecting on the 1997 sessions, he continued, 'We did do some work... it was okay for doing some of the older material but, looking toward the future, it's definitely not radical enough for getting the profile back out there nowadays, really. So we found us some extra strength.'

While the Wright brothers flew off to their own new band, Last Rites, the reconstituted Fields of the Nephilim got to work on reintroducing themselves to their early roots, rerecording two of their earliest songs. Both 'Trees Come Down' and 'Dark Cell' originally appeared on the *Burning The Fields* EP at the dawn of the band's career. The band also returned to the live arena, crowning weeks of speculation by joining the bill for the Woodstage Open Air Festival in Glachau in March 2000, then following through at the high summer M'era Luna festival in Hildesheim.

With the band running through a set that mixed original Fields of the Nephilim material with selections from McCoy's own *Zoon*, it was difficult to perceive the show as anything more than a straightforward retread. McCoy and Petit's promise that new material was in the wings would remain unfulfilled until autumn 2002 finally delivered *Fallen*, an assuredly Nephish collection of (largely) new material that not only updated all that they'd achieved in the past, but drove a few stakes through the hearts of sundry latterday pretenders as well.

For most observers, however, simply the sight and sound of the band back onstage after so long away was sufficient – all the more so when, as at Hildesheim, other idols of the era were proving themselves as vital as they had ever been.

Also among the M'era Luna headliners were the Sisters of Mercy, undertaking one more in the seemingly endless series of sporadic live performances which had been the devoted fan's only opportunity of hearing the group for eight long years... and counting.

Locked into a seemingly endless dispute with Warner Brothers, overlords of his recording contract, Eldritch had essentially downed tools and gone on strike following the release of *A Slight Case Of Overbombing*. Since that time, he had stirred only occasionally, for annual or thereabouts tours and festival shows.

Accompanied by an entire new coterie of musicians, the Roadkill tour in 1996, and a short UK/European outing in summer 1997 confirmed that Eldritch remained a vital performer – indeed, watching him perform or experiencing the performance via the wealth of bootleg videos and CDs that chronicled every move he made, it was difficult not to curse each and every one of the circumstances that had ground his momentum to a halt.

From the convoluted amateurisms of the earliest Sisters recordings, to the unforgiving Passchendale of *Vision Thing*, Andrew Eldritch entered the 1990s as the living epitome of Dark Rock in all of its guises and at each of its extremes, from the loopiest ruminations of the ethereal pack, to the mutant noiseniks of the Black Metal scene. Even more importantly, however, he was confirmed as the one figure on the scene to whom everybody looked for guidance, whether they admitted it or not.

Like David Bowie through the 1970s, Eldritch led by example and his own apparent disinterest in the obeisance of his followers only increased his impact. Had he only been permitted (or, perhaps, amenable) to maintain any kind of recording career, his dominance would not simply haver dictated the direction in which the decade moved, it might well have derailed many of the pretenders who did rise up to take advantage of his absence – Trent Reznor and Marilyn Manson among them. Instead, with the studio stalemate showing no sign of breaking, Eldritch's recording plans remained as pointlessly uncompromising as ever.

The label was demanding a new album, Eldritch was demanding freedom. Finally, however, he appeared to have crumbled. In mid-1997, he informed the company that a new album had been recorded and that, under the terms of his original deal, granting him complete control over every aspect of his career, he was now free to depart. The label took one listen to the proffered disc and refused to accept a moment of it.

Not that Eldritch ever believed they would, as he confirmed in a late 1997 press release. 'Bearing no resemblance whatsoever to the Sisters Of Mercy, this album will be released – if at all – under a completely different name, which is just as well... [because] the rather bad sub-techno music [within] was under-average and boring even before the drums were mysteriously removed.'

In fact, he intended the album to be released under the acronym SSV-NSMABAAOTWMODAACOTIATW – 'Screw Shareholder Value – Not So Much A Band As Another Opportunity To Waste Money On Drugs And Ammunition Courtesy Of The Idiots At Time Warner.' Time Warner, on the other hand, had no intention of releasing it whatsoever and the legal minds continued wrestling with the impasse.

Finally, in 1998, Eldritch informed the world that the dispute was finally over, as his contract had expired; the news was accompanied by the announcement of a new Sisters of Mercy single, co-written with latter-day band member Adam Pearson. 'Summer,' Eldritch promised, was 'very pretty, and probably very cruel. It goes like a freight train painted in the shiniest yellows and blues.'

Unfortunately, no sooner was the news released than it was withdrawn again: 'Sorry,' said Eldritch's website, 'but what with one thing and another, [it] was not to be. We *are* working on an album, *inter alia*, but the matter of single releases is currently on hold.'

Four years later, the album was still gestating; in the meantime, the Sisters continued their odd touring schedule, celebrating their 20th anniversary in 2001, as they had for the 10th, with a Leeds University show on 17th February – the previous evening, the official opening night of a near-two month European outing, saw them return to York University where it had all begun.

If the Sisters' workload was characterised by the group's continued refusal to release the new material that was increasingly dominating their live repertoire, , and other bands on the 'comeback' trail seemed content merely to take whatever rewards were thrown to them, one group was considerably less bashful.

Work on the first new Cult album since 1994 commenced in 2000. Since the demise of the Holy Barbarians, Astbury had finally cut the solo album he'd often dreamed of, and which the Cult's own 'The Witch', back in 1992, had apparently been hinting at all along. The startling electro-techno hybrid *Spirit/Light/Speed* did, in fact, reprise that song, dirtier and angrier than the original ever was but, when Astbury took to the road in July 1999 to begin setting the stage for the record's release, he did so under a very unexpected name. The Cult were back.

Recalling Billy Duffy from his recent stint with ex-Alarm frontman Mike Peters, Astbury explained, 'Billy and I got together again and said, "if we're going to do this, we have to do it properly, get the best band line-up we've ever had, and just hit it. No hiding behind the big rock sound, no worrying about whether the record will sell ten million or twenty, just make the music we both want to make, in the way we want to make it." So we got Martyn Lenoble [ex-Porno For Pyros] in, and Matt Sorum came back, and it was exciting again.

Beyond Good And Evil was, of course, archetypal Cult. You knew from the opening guitar who it was and, while subsequent developments might surprise you – the churning riffs, the hammering rhythms, the snatches of solo which slice through the swamp – at it's heart it was still the Cult. And for that, as more than one critic admonished his readers, one should be grateful. Too many reunions collapse when the members remember why they split in the first place, too many emerge insipid renovations. The Cult, however, simply picked up where they'd left off on whichever occasion it was that they really did leave off. Louder than ever before, heavy in the best sense of its modern meaning, and so thunderous that even the occasional moments of reflection were simply oases of calm in the turbulence around them.

Which, as Astbury continued excitedly, 'is exactly what the Cult should be.'

Epilogue

𝕴n the end, Goth went down like a sinking ship in reverse. The captain and the crew were off first, the passengers and rats reluctantly followed. By the time the floatation devices kicked in, only a handful of stowaways were left on board, and they didn't even know where the ship was headed. So they pointed it away from the sun and let the tides do the rest.

Americans – for that, for the most part, was who they were – have always had a hard time with British rock. They take it all so seriously, for a start. We gave them the fun loving mop tops, they gave us Bob Dylan. We gave them the Animals, they gave us an electric Bob Dylan. We gave them Glam, they gave us KISS, we gave them Punk, they gave us Black Flag.

In every instance, the correlation was correct. It was the interpretation, the underlying sense of mischief, irony and fun fun fun – itself, how ironic, such an all-American concept – that was lost, or discarded, or eased out in the translation, to bounce back a distorted excess, a bloated parody, an evil twin. We gave them Def Leppard, they gave us Metallica, we gave them the Cult, they gave us the Cult. And we gave them Goth.

The roots of American Gothic lay in the Death Metal movement that spread around the Los Angeles underground in the direct aftermath of Punk, fashioned by such bands as 45 Grave, the Superheroines, the Castration Squad, the Speed Queens and, most pointedly of all, Christian Death. Fronted by the spectacular outrage of teenaged transvestite Rozz Williams, an unrepentant Bowie freak who saw nothing at all wrong with clashing Ziggy with the zeitgeist of his hardcore punk-fired bandmates, the original Christian Death broke up in 1982, although Williams promptly hooked up with another LA band, Pompeii 99, to fulfill his own band's scheduled European tour. Among the first bands he encountered when he reached that continent were the Sisters of Mercy.

The Superheroines' Eva O (later to become Williams' wife) remembers the point where 'there definitely seemed to be something happening, how it went from Post-Punk to Death Rock at the same time as the Gothic thing was happening in England. It was when English Gothic and American Death Rock collided that it started getting really interesting.'

In later years, Williams furiously dismissed the impact that the Sisters had on his band and on his contemporaries. 'I'd rather listen to a 30-minute guitar solo by Jimmy Page than anything by the Sisters of Mercy!'

At the time, however, the cross-fertilization of his own roots and theirs was regarded as a major step forward on the LA scene, igniting not only a seriously devoted sub-culture of 'true' Goths, but also opening the door for the first stirrings of the Industrial music scene that would come to fruition in the early 1990s.

'Suddenly,' recalled Eva O, 'it was a drum machine, somebody playing a two-stringed guitar and, if it's a boy singing, it's the Sisters' sound and, if it's a girl, it's the Banshees'. It was these two disparate consequences that were to dictate the music's course over the remainder of the decade – on the one hand, an increasingly ethereal sound that verged, at times, on airless ambience; on the other, an ever-more aggressive, violent and nasty noise that churned even the vestiges of melody out of its system.

The merging of Gothic Rock, in its purest sense, to Industrial Rock, in its most media-friendly designation, was accomplished by Trent Reznor, a Cleveland-based musician who had already tried his hand at several other musical hybrids before finally settling upon a dark, existentialist brew forged in equal parts from moody (read 'self-pitying') lyricism and intense (read 'clattering') sonics. It was, if you want to be cynical about such things, an obvious next step although nobody could have predicted the ease with which his debut album, 1989's *Pretty Hate Machine*, slid into a marketable gap somewhere between the pure rage of Ministry and the burgeoning victim culture of 'alternative' rock.

That ease initially had very little to do with musical style *per se*. Rather, it was a philosophical wedding, embellished by the existence of both musical forms on the edge of convention. Yet it became so deeply rooted that, by the mid-1990s, the American public at large was no more able to distinguish between the Gothic and Industrial species than between different species of caribou.

For some bands, the cross-fertilization of imagery (if not always purity) offered a welcome adjunct to already flourishing reference points. 'There's also a lot to be said,' acknowledged Electric Hellfire Club's Thomas Thorn, 'for a rock group all dandied-up in psycho-goth-adelia, who are bigger and meaner than any of the shaved-head, stompy-boot aggro industrial boys around.'

From their peaks of already lofty ambivalence, self-confessedly serious Goths – those raised on the singularity of the genre's influences and schooled in the increasingly narrow tunnel that time had forced those influences into – treated such extremes with absolute disdain, regarding Nine Inch Nails' Trent Reznor as little more than a pretentious modernist who wallowed in ugliness, the living antithesis to Goth's own (albeit equally stereotyped) ideal of 19th-century Romanticism and beauty.

Yet Rozz Williams readily pointed out just how ugly and pretentious their own vision was. 'It's kind of baffling. How do these people maintain it? *Wake up, put in my fangs, do my hair... Got to make it down to the graveyard before it's closed.* It really gets bad when people get stuck just in that, where they can't go outside of that. Where it's so strict with so many rules.'

At the same time, many people who had never hitherto contemplated investigating the Gothic lifestyle were drawn into its periphery, first by Reznor and, in his footsteps, self-styled Antichrist Superstar showman Marilyn Manson.

Still, it was inconceivable to even the most morbidly pessimistic observer that it would be this same apparently superficial coterie who would, with the Internet a willing partner in their own fantasies, present Gothic Rock with its first taste of widespread media condemnation.

'The beauty of the Internet' Rozz Williams continued, 'is that it gives everybody a voice. You don't have to shout to be heard. The problem is that it tends only to be the extreme cases who want to be heard in the first place, so you log onto what looks like a Gothic site, and you're as likely going to read about mutilation, fetishism, mass murder and Hitler, as you are about vampire novels and the best place to buy little gargoyles. I can imagine a lot of people getting some very strange ideas about it all.'

These 'strange ideas' were already surfacing. In December 1996, a 26-year-old self-styled vampire named Jon C Bush was charged in the nation's capital with raping and sexually molesting 13 girls, all aged between 13 and 16, under the guise of initiating them into his own 'vampire club.' Less than a month later, 17-year-old Alex Barayni a member of a Gothic role-playing club called the Dark Ballad Gaming Society, butchered a family of four in the Seattle suburb of Bellevue. A little over a year later, in March 1998, four teenage vampires were charged with desecrating and then burning a Dallas church. The following April, two heavily armed and deeply disaffected teens walked into the cafeteria of their Littleton, Colorado, high school, Columbine High, to fire the first shots in a massacre which would leave 12 students, one teacher and both gunmen dead.

Across the media, reporters rushed to compile hard-hitting 'investigations' into the evil 'new' Gothic cult which was so poisoning America's children, a damning blend of vampiric ritual, apocalyptic prophecy and sex crime ceremony, all dancing to the distorted beat of metal machines gone mental. Their information, of course, was drawn from the internet, repository of sufficient digital DNA to condemn an entire generation.

German industrial (and decidedly un-Gothic) band KMFDM, whose song lyrics were found all over the gunmen's apocalyptic website, found themselves issuing a public apology for events which they never imagined possible. Marilyn Manson, whose scheduled concert in neighbouring Denver the following week was cancelled within hours of the shootings, postponed his entire American tour rather than face the nation with notions that were now so maligned. And the handful of courageous voices raised in defense were shouted down beneath the hysterical baying.

Across America, where rapprochement should have followed the grieving, ignorance, prejudice and hypocrisy flourished instead. Gothic – that is, black – clothing was banned from school campuses across the country. Vigilante bands of 'concerned' 'decent' citizens took to targeting, abusing and even attacking any passers-by they deemed too Gothic. While the hatred would eventually die down, still the scars of those few madness-wracked weeks remained, in the distinctly poor performances of new albums by Ministry and Nine Inch Nails later that year, and by Manson two years later. It's no coincidence that, as the popular spotlight swung away from those artists who beautified ugliness as a source of musical madness, it returned to those who had initiated at least one strand of the hybrid in the first place. When Peter Murphy toured America in spring 2002 and the Mission followed him around a few months later, audiences looked younger than those either artist had performed to in the best part of a decade – younger, but no less committed to the ideals that the artists stood for.

It is said that no musical genre is capable of developing any further after two or three years in the spotlight. Historically, this is true. Rock history divides even the most potent movement into comfortable bite-sized spans – 1967-69 (Psychedelia), 1971-73 (Glam), 1976-78 (Punk), 1991-93 (Grunge) – yet the harshest dismissal of Goth as a living, breathing force is forced to expand its growth over three or four years, and even that ignores crucial developments before and after. Between the emergence of the Banshees and the flourishing of Fields of Nephilim, a colossal eight years passed. If one then allows the Americans their due, from the birth of Nine Inch Nails to the denouement of Columbine High, another decade of at least some form of development is opened up for inspection.

Neither have the 'classic' artists totally abandoned the precepts for which they first came to attention, whether they are returning to their own roots for a 'comeback' album (the Mission's surprisingly stimulating *Aura* set and the Fields of the Nephilim's charring *Fallen*) or pursuing the future as doggedly as ever (the Cult's *Beyond Good and Evil*, Peter Murphy's *Dust*). Indeed, with only the handful of exceptions that one could have predicted 20 years ago, the bands that mattered at the dawn of the age still rank among those which matter today; have, in fact, not only retained, but also maintained, exactly the same musical values that they started out with.

If Dark Rock, Gothic Rock, call-it-what-you-will rock, can be summed up in any single phrase, the music, its makers and its story have never heard it. In twenty years of development, and two decades beforehand of antecedents, the only common thread is surely the individualism that any artist, in any field, must strive towards.

No matter that the success that many came so close to acquiring was ultimately snatched away; no matter, either, that few beyond the faithful even care what most of the musicians involved in Goth's golden era do today. Still, as Ian Astbury says of the Cult, and as his peers could say of their own continuing endeavours, 'the music we're making is dark, sexy... brave. This isn't a nostalgia thing. We want to make music that's going to be influential on the future. We don't care about the past.'

Neither were his words simply hollow boasting. They had a pedigree, and a portentousness, that reached back a full quarter century to when Iggy Pop was preparing to leave his own battered, shattered reputation behind to move into the brave new world of *The Idiot*. He, too, denied that he was living off former glories; he, too, declared that history was dead. And he, too, was correct.

The Idiot is still making sense.

The Dark Diary

A chronology of significant events, sessions and record releases.

1976

March
DOCTORS OF MADNESS: Release LP *Late Night Movies, All Night Brainstorms.*
DOCTORS OF MADNESS: UK tour.

March 30
DOCTORS OF MADNESS: Marquee, London.

September
DOCTORS OF MADNESS: Release LP *Sons Of Survival.*

September 20
SIOUXSIE & THE BANSHEES: live debut at the 100 Club Punk Festival, London.

November 25
DOCTORS OF MADNESS: Record first John Peel session: 'Out'/'Brothers'/'Suicide City.'

December 7
DOCTORS OF MADNESS: First John Peel session broadcast. (Radio One).

December 21
SIOUXSIE & THE BANSHEES: Roxy, London – supporting Generation X.

1977

March 1
IGGY POP: Opens first UK tour at Aylesbury Friars.

March 7
IGGY POP: London Rainbow.

April
THE CURE/EASY CURE: enter and win Ariola/Hansa talent contest.

April 2
THE UNWANTED: live debut at the Roxy, London, recording *Live At The Roxy* compilation.

April 9
IGGY POP: LP *The Idiot* enters UK Chart (peak #30).

May 18
THE CURE/EASY CURE: Sign with Ariola/Hansa.

May 29
JOY DIVISION: Adopt name Warsaw.

June 3
THE CURE/EASY CURE: Queen's Square, Crawley (footage on *Staring At The Sea* video compilation)

June 29
RIKKI & THE LAST DAYS OF EARTH: Roxy, London (audition night).

June 30
JOY DIVISION: Warsaw-open for Johnny Thunders at Rafters, Manchester with new drummer Steve Brotherhood.

July 18
JOY DIVISION: Warsaw record first demos.

July 21
SIOUXSIE & THE BANSHEES: Roxy, London with THE UNWANTED.

August
DOCTORS OF MADNESS: Release single 'Bulletin.'
DOCTORS OF MADNESS: UK tour.

August 4
RIKKI & THE LAST DAYS OF EARTH: Roxy, London.

August 19
BOYS NEXT DOOR: Swinburne Tech, Melbourne. First major show.

August 24
JOY DIVISION: Steve Brotherhood quits. Replaced by Stephen Morris.

October
THE CURE/EASY CURE: Record first demos for Ariola/Hansa.

October 2
JOY DIVISION/WARSAW: Manchester Electric Circus (final night)

November 18
BOYS NEXT DOOR: Rowland Howard, then a journalist, reviews gig at Bananas, Melbourne.

November 21
SIOUXSIE & THE BANSHEES: London Vortex

November 29
SIOUXSIE & THE BANSHEES: record first John Peel session: 'Love In A Void'/'Mirage'/ 'Metal Postcard'/'Suburban relapse'

December 3
Sounds publishes its New Musick issue.
SIOUXSIE & THE BANSHEES pictured on cover.

December 4
THE CURE/EASY CURE: Rocket, Crawley (one track on *Curiosities* compilation LP)

December 5
SIOUXSIE & THE BANSHEES: First John Peel session broadcast (Radio One).

December 11
SIOUXSIE & THE BANSHEES: London Roundhouse.

December 31
THE CURE/EASY CURE: Orpington Hospital.

1978

DEMON PREACHER: Release single 'Royal Northern (N7)'.

January 25
JOY DIVISION: Adopt new name.

January 27
SIOUXSIE & THE BANSHEES: London College of Fashion.

February 6
SIOUXSIE & THE BANSHEES: Record second John Peel session: 'Hong Kong Garden'/ 'Overground'/'Carcass'/'Helter Skelter'.

February 9
DEMON PREACHER: Roxy, London.

February 19
DOCTORS OF MADNESS: London Roundhouse

February 23
SIOUXSIE & THE BANSHEES: Second John Peel session broadcast (Radio One).

March
DOCTORS OF MADNESS: Unreleased single 'Sons Of Survival'.
THE CURE/EASY CURE: Depart Ariola/Hansa.

April
DOCTORS OF MADNESS: LP *Sons Of Survival*.

April 4
THE CRAMPS: Release single 'Surfin' Bird'.

April 14
JOY DIVISION: Stiff/Chiswick Challenge, Rafters, Manchester.

April 19
SIOUXSIE & THE BANSHEES, NICO: Music Machine, London.

April 29
NICO: Music Machine, London, with the Adverts.

May
DOCTORS OF MADNESS: US LP *Doctors Of Madness*.

May 3
THE CURE: Shorten name.

May 27
THE CURE: Record new demos, from which the Fiction label deal will result.

June
DOCTORS OF MADNESS: Dave Vanian (DAMNED) replaces Urban Blitz.
JOY DIVISION: Release EP *An Ideal For Living*.

June 4
JOY DIVISION: Release single 'An Ideal For Living'.

June 9
SIOUXSIE & THE BANSHEES: Sign to Polydor.

June 16
JOY DIVISION: Featured on *Short Circuit* live album (compilation)

June 28
DOCTORS OF MADNESS: London Lyceum.

July 31
DEMON PREACHER: Release single 'Little Miss Perfect'.

August 18
SIOUXSIE & THE BANSHEES: Release single 'Hong Kong Garden'.

August 26
SIOUXSIE & THE BANSHEES: Single 'Hong Kong Garden' enters UK Chart (peak #7).

September 9
JOY DIVISION: Liverpool Eric's, supporting Tanz Der Youth.

September 13
THE CURE: Sign with Fiction.

October
SIOUXSIE & THE BANSHEES: UK tour.

October 10
JOY DIVISION: Rerelease 'An Ideal For Living'.

October 26
DOCTORS OF MADNESS: Music Machine, London – farewell concert.

November
BAUHAUS: Daniel Ash, Peter Murphy, Kevin Haskins, Chris Barber form band SR.

November 14
SIOUXSIE & THE BANSHEES: Release LP *The Scream*.

November 20
THE CURE: Support UK Subs at the Moonlight Club, West Hampstead.

November 24
THE CURE: Open UK tour supporting Generation X.

December
BAUHAUS: SR debut at the Racehorse Pavilion, Northampton. David J is also on bill.

December 2
SIOUXSIE & THE BANSHEES: LP *The Scream* enters UK Chart (peak #12)

December 4
THE CRAMPS: Release single 'Human Fly'.
THE CURE: Record first John Peel session: 'Killing An Arab'/'10.15 Saturday Night'/ 'Fire In Cairo'/'Boys Don't Cry'.

December 5
THE CURE: Dismissed from Generation X tour.

December 11
THE CURE: First John Peel session broadcast (Radio One).

December 16
THE CURE: First major press interview in *New Musical Express*.

December 22
THE CURE: Release single 'Killing An Arab' on Small Wonder label.

December 25
JOY DIVISION: Included on *A Factory Sample* compilation EP.

December 27
JOY DIVISION: Hope & Anchor, London.

December 31
BAUHAUS: David J replaces Chris Barber in SR and changes band name to Bauhaus 19.

1979
UK DECAY: Release split single.

January 26
BAUHAUS: Bauhaus 19 record first demo, including 'Bela Lugosi's Dead'.

247

January 31
JOY DIVISION: record first John Peel session:
'Exercise One'/'Insight'/'She's Lost
Control'/'Transmission'.

February 9
THE CURE: Rerelease single 'Killing An Arab'
on Fiction.

February 14
JOY DIVISION: First John Peel session
broadcast (Radio One).

February
THE CURE: Open UK tour in Newport.

March 23
SIOUXSIE & THE BANSHEES: Release single
'Staircase (Mystery)'.

March 31
SIOUXSIE & THE BANSHEES: Single 'The
Staircase (Mystery)' enters UK Chart (peak
#24).

April 3
THE CURE: Open four week residency at the
Marquee, London.

April 7
SIOUXSIE & THE BANSHEES: London Rainbow
(MENCAP benefit).

April 9
SIOUXSIE & THE BANSHEES: Record third
John Peel session: 'Placebo Effect'/ 'Playground
Twist'/'Regal Zone'/'Poppy Day'.

April 16
SIOUXSIE & THE BANSHEES: Third John Peel
session broadcast (Radio One).

April 25
THE CURE: Final night of Marquee residency.
JOY DIVISION support.

May
BOYS NEXT DOOR: Release Australian LP *Door
Door*.
THE CURE: New single 'Grinding Halt'
withdrawn after one poor review in *NME*.

May 5
THE CURE: Release LP *Three Imaginary Boys*.

May 9
THE CURE: Record second John Peel session:
'Desperate Journalist In On-going Meaningful
Review Situation'/'Grinding Halt'/ 'Subway
Song'/'Plastic Passion'/'Accuracy'.

May 16
THE CURE: Second John Peel session
broadcast (Radio One).

May 17
JOY DIVISION: Acklam Hall, London with ACR,
OMD, John Dowie.
THE CURE: Open UK tour at Memorial Hall, Northwich.

May 26
BAUHAUS: Bauhaus 19 support Throbbing
Gristle and shorten name.

June
BAUHAUS: Sign one-off single deal with Small
Wonder.
SIOUXSIE & THE BANSHEES: Release single

'Mittageisen' in Germany.
THE CRAMPS: UK tour with the Police.

June 2
THE CURE: LP *Three Imaginary Boys* enters
UK Chart (peak #44).

June 14
JOY DIVISION: release LP *Unknown Pleasures*.

June 15
JOY DIVISION: Royalty Theatre, London,
supporting John Cooper Clarke.

June 17
THE CURE: London Lyceum.

June 20
THE CRAMPS: Release LP *Gravest Hits*.

June 26
THE CURE: Release single 'Boys Don't Cry'.

June 30
SIOUXSIE & THE BANSHEES: Release single
'Playground Twist'.

July 1
THE CURE: London Lyceum.

July 5
BAUHAUS: London debut. Billed as
'Bauhouse', open for Patrick Fitzgerald/Wall/
Teardrop Explodes at Music Machine, London.

July 6
THE CURE: Manchester Factory.

July 7
SIOUXSIE & THE BANSHEES: Single
'Playground Twist' enters UK Chart (peak #28).

July 13
BAUHAUS: London Nashville.

July 29
THE CURE: First European date at a festival in
Holland.

August 13
JOY DIVISION: London Nashville.
THE CURE: First David Jensen session recorded:
'Boys Don't Cry'/'Do The Hansa'/ 'Three
Imaginary Boys'.

August 24
THE CURE: Reading Festival.

August 27
JOY DIVISION: Leigh Festival

August 28
NIGHTMARES IN WAX, THE DAMNED: Eric's,
Liverpool.

August 29
THE CURE: Second David Jensen session
broadcast (Radio One).
THE CURE: UK tour opening for SIOUXSIE &
THE BANSHEES.

August 31
JOY DIVISION: London Electric Ballroom
SIOUXSIE & THE BANSHEES: Release LP *Join
Hands*.

September
BAUHAUS: Release single 'Bela Lugosi's
Dead'.

September 6
SIOUXSIE & THE BANSHEES: Kenny Morris and John McKay quit band during UK tour.

September 7
BAUHAUS: London Marquee.

September 8-9
FUTURAMA 1

September 9-10
JOY DIVISION: London Rainbow, opening for the Buzzcocks.

September 10
THE CURE: Headline Rotterdam New Pop Festival.

September 18
SIOUXSIE & THE BANSHEES: Relaunch UK tour with Robert Smith (THE CURE) and Budgie (ex-Slits) replacing Morris and McKay.

September 22
SIOUXSIE & THE BANSHEES: LP *Join Hands* enters UK Chart (peak #13).

September 28
JOY DIVISION: Manchester Factory with Teardrop Explodes.

September 29
SIOUXSIE & THE BANSHEES: Import single 'Mittageisen' enters UK Chart (peak #47).

October
JOY DIVISION: Open UK tour supporting the Buzzcocks.

October 15
SIOUXSIE & THE BANSHEES/THE CURE: Hammersmith Odeon.

November
THE CURE/THE CULT HEROES: Release single 'I'm A Cult Hero'.
THE CURE: Michael Dempsey quits band, to be replaced by Simon Gallup and Matthieu Hartley.

November 2
THE CURE: Release single 'Jumping Someone Else's Train'.

November 16
THE CURE: UK tour opens at Liverpool Eric's – first show with new line-up.

November 17
JOY DIVISION: Release single 'Transmission'.

November 26
JOY DIVISION: Record second John Peel session: 'Love Will Tear Us Apart'/'24 Hours'/'Colony'/'Sound Of Music'.

December
THE CURE: European tour.

December 4
BAUHAUS: record first John Peel session: 'A God In An Alcove'/'The Spy In The Cab'/'Double Dare'/'Telegram Sam'.

December 7
BAUHAUS: 11 Club, Axis Records launch party.

December 8
JOY DIVISION: Eric's, Liverpool.

December 10
BAUHAUS: Rock Garden, London. Approached by Axis records (later 4AD)

JOY DIVISION: Second John Peel session broadcast (Radio One).

1980
DEMONS (ex-DEMON PREACHER): Single 'Action By Example'.

January 3
BAUHAUS: First John Peel session broadcast (Radio One).

January 10
BAUHAUS: Rock Garden, London.

January 19
JOY DIVISION: LP *Unknown Pleasures* enters Independent Chart (peak #1).
JOY DIVISION: Single 'Transmission' enters Independent Chart (peak #4).

January 26
BAUHAUS: Single 'Bela Lugosi's Dead' enters Independent Chart (peak #8).

January 28
UK DECAY: Moonlight Club, London.

January 29
BAUHAUS: Open residency at Billys, London.

February
BIRTHDAY PARTY: Relocate to London.

February 8
JOY DIVISION: University of London.

February 16
BAUHAUS: First major press interview in *Sounds*. Single 'Dark Entries' enters Independent Chart (peak #17).
BIRTHDAY PARTY: Release single 'Riddle House'.
RICHARD STRANGE: Single 'International Language' enters Independent Chart (peak #48).
UK DECAY: EP *The Black 45* enters Independent Chart (peak #42).

February 29
JOY DIVISION: London Lyceum (with Killing Joke, ACR, Section 25)

March 3
THE CURE: Record third John Peel session: 'A Forest'/'17 Seconds'/'Play For Today'/'M'.

March 6
SIOUXSIE & THE BANSHEES: Release single 'Happy House'.

March 6-8
THE CURE: Marquee, London.

March 10
THE CURE: Third John Peel session broadcast (Radio One).

March 15
RICHARD STRANGE: Nashville, London.
SIOUXSIE & THE BANSHEES: Single 'Happy House' enters UK Chart (peak #17).
UK DECAY: Acklam Hall, London.

March 18
JOY DIVISION: Release single 'Sordide Sentimentale'.

March 22
THE CRAMPS: LP *Songs The Lord Taught Us* enters Independent Chart (peak #1).

March 23
THE CURE/THE CULT HEROES: Marquee, London, supporting the Passions.

March 27
BAUHAUS: Open first European tour in Moers, Germany.

March 27-28
SIOUXSIE & THE BANSHEES: Music Machine, London.

March 29
NIGHTMARES IN WAX: Release EP *Birth Of A Nation*.

April
BAUHAUS: UK tour with Magazine.
THE CURE: Release LP *Seventeen Seconds*.

April 3
THE CURE: Robert Smith guests with the Stranglers at the Rainbow, London.

April 4
JOY DIVISION: Ian Curtis suffers epileptic fit onstage supporting Stranglers at the Rainbow, and again at the Moonlight Club later in the evening.

April 5
THE CURE: Release single 'A Forest'.

April 10
BAUHAUS: Support Gary Glitter at the Lyceum, London.
THE CURE: Open first North American tour in Cherry Hill, NJ.

April 12
THE CURE: Single 'A Forest' enters UK Chart (peak #31).

April 15
THE CURE: Hurrah's, NYC.

April 18
JOY DIVISION: Release single 'Komakino'.

April 22
UK DECAY: Record first John Peel session: 'Rising From The Dead'/'Unwind Tonight'/ 'Sexual'/ 'For My Country'.

April 24
THE CURE: UK TV *Top Of The Pops*: 'A Forest'.

April 25
THE CURE: Open UK tour at West Runton Pavilion, Cromer, supported by the Passions.

April 26
JOY DIVISION: Rock Garden, London.

April 29
UK DECAY: First John Peel session broadcast (Radio One).

May
THE CURE: European tour.

May 1
BAUHAUS: London Lyceum, supporting Magazine.

May 2
JOY DIVISION: Birmingham University.

May 3
THE CURE: LP *Seventeen Seconds* enters UK Chart (peak #20).

May 9
NIGHTMARES IN WAX: The Factory, Manchester.

May 15
BAUHAUS: Play Grand Re-opening of the Moonlight Club, West Hampstead.

May 18
JOY DIVISION: Death of Ian Curtis.

May 29
BIRTHDAY PARTY: Release LP *Birthday Party*.

May 30
SIOUXSIE & THE BANSHEES: Release single 'Christine'.

June 7
SIOUXSIE & THE BANSHEES: Single 'Christine' enters UK Chart (peak #22).

June 28
JOY DIVISION: Single 'Love Will Tear Us Apart' enters Independent Chart (peak #1).
JOY DIVISION: Single 'Love Will Tear Us Apart' enters UK Chart (peak #13).

July
THE CURE: Dutch festival tour.

July 26
JOY DIVISION: LP *Closer* enters Independent Chart (peak #1).
JOY DIVISION: LP *Closer* enters UK Chart (peak #6).

July 29
THE CURE: Auckland, New Zealand.

August
THE CURE: Australian tour.

August 1
SIOUXSIE & THE BANSHEES: Release LP *Kaleidoscope*.

August 1-2
VIRGIN PRUNES: Dublin Project Arts Centre.

August 2
BIRTHDAY PARTY: Single 'Mr Clarinet' enters Independent Chart (peak #43).

August 9
BAUHAUS: Single 'Terror Couple Kill Colonel' enters Independent Chart (peak #5).

August 11
BAUHAUS: Open first UK headlining tour at Scamps, Oxford.

August 16
SIOUXSIE & THE BANSHEES: LP *Kaleidoscope* enters UK Chart (peak #5).

August 19
UK DECAY: #1 Club, London, supporting Wasted Youth.

August 30
JOY DIVISION: LP *Unknown Pleasures* enters UK Chart (peal #71).

September 5
BAUHAUS: US debut at Tier 3, NYC.

September 6
UK DECAY: Release single 'For My Country' enters Independent Chart (peak #13).

September 13
THE CRAMPS: Single 'Drug Train' enters Independent Chart (peak #5).

September 13-14
FUTURAMA 2

September 15
UK DECAY: Music Machine, London.

September 18
BAUHAUS: Music Machine, London, supported by Dead Or Alive.
BIRTHDAY PARTY: Hope & Anchor, London, celebrating 4AD deal.

September 23
UK DECAY: Dingwalls, London

September 25
BIRTHDAY PARTY: First John Peel session broadcast (Radio One).

September 29
DEMONS/DEMON PREACHER: Release single 'Action By Example'.

October
SIOUXSIE & THE BANSHEES: UK tour, supported by Altered Images.
THE CURE: European tour.

October 4
JOY DIVISION: Single 'Atmosphere' enters Independent Chart (peak #1).

October 8
BIRTHDAY PARTY: Moonlight Club, London, supporting DAF.
UK DECAY: Music Machine, London, supporting Dead Kennedys.

October 15
BAUHAUS: Open second UK tour at Granary, Bristol.

October 16
DEMONS: #1 Club, London, supporting the Dark.

October 23
BIRTHDAY PARTY: Music Machine, London.

October 24
THEATRE OF HATE: Clarendon, London, supporting Killing Joke.

October 28
DEMONS: Music Machine, London, supporting Discharge.

October 29
JOY DIVISION: Single 'Love Will Tear Us Apart' re-enters UK Chart (peak #19).

November
THE CURE: UK tour.

November 1
BIRTHDAY PARTY: Single 'The Friend Catcher' enters Independent Chart (peak #21).

November 3
THE DAMNED: release The Black Album.

November 5
SISTERS OF MERCY: Release single 'Damage Done'.

November 15
BAUHAUS: LP In The Flat Field enters Independent Chart (peak #1).

November 15
BAUHAUS: LP In The Flat Field enters UK Chart (peak #72).
VIRGIN PRUNES: McMordie Hall, Belfast.

November 17
THEATRE OF HATE: Music Machine, London.

November 19
BAUHAUS: Open European tour at Klacik, Brussels.

November 22
BAUHAUS: Single 'Telegram Sam' enters Independent Chart (peak #3).
BIRTHDAY PARTY: Crystal Ballroom, St Kilda – first Australian show in 10 months.

November 28
SIOUXSIE & THE BANSHEES: Release single 'Israel'.

November 29
THE DAMNED: LP Black Album enters UK Chart (peak #29).

December 1
THEATRE OF HATE: Record first John Peel session: 'Rebel Without A Brain'/'The Wake'/'63'/'It's My Own Invention'.

December 4
THE CRAMPS: Single 'Fever' enters Independent Chart (peak #12).

December 6
SIOUXSIE & THE BANSHEES: Single 'Israel' enters UK Chart (peak #41).

December 8
THEATRE OF HATE: Rock Garden, London.

December 9
THEATRE OF HATE: First John Peel session broadcast (Radio One).

December 13
THEATRE OF HATE: Single 'Original Sin' enters Independent Chart (peak #5).

December 18
THE CURE/SIOUXSIE & THE BANSHEES: Notre Dame Hall, London.
THEATRE OF HATE: Music Machine, London.

December 20
DEAD OR ALIVE: Single 'I'm Falling' enters Independent Chart (peak #22).

December 30
SIOUXSIE & THE BANSHEES: Hammersmith Palais, London.

1981
DANSE SOCIETY: Release single 'The Clock'.

January 7
THE CURE: Record fourth John Peel session: 'Holy Hour'/'Forever'/'Primary'/'All Cats Are Grey'.

January 9
UK DECAY: Acklam Hall, London.

January 15
THE CURE: Fourth John Peel session broadcast (Radio One).

January 25
RICHARD STRANGE., THEATRE OF HATE: London Lyceum.

January 28
RICHARD STRANGE: US release of live LP *The Live Rise Of Richard Strange.*

February 4
DEAD OR ALIVE: Record first John Peel session: 'Nowhere To Nowhere'/'Running Wild'/'Flowers'/ 'Number 11'.

February 7
VIRGIN PRUNES: Single 'Twenty Tens' enters Independent Chart (peak #5).

February 10
SIOUXSIE & THE BANSHEES: Record fourth John Peel session: 'Halloween'/'Voodoo Dolly'/ 'But Not Them'/'Into The Light'.

February 12
VIRGIN PRUNES: Ladbroke Grove Tabernacle, London.

February 13
VIRGIN PRUNES: North London Poly, supporting Pere Ubu.

February 16
SISTERS OF MERCY: Live debut at Alcuin College, York, supporting Thompson Twins.

February 16-17
SIOUXSIE & THE BANSHEES: Hammersmith Palais, London.

February 17
DEAD OR ALIVE: First John Peel session broadcast. (Radio One).

February 18
SIOUXSIE & THE BANSHEES: Fourth John Peel session broadcast (Radio One).

February 19
THEATRE OF HATE: Marquee, London.

February 24
BAUHAUS: Open second North American tour at Blitz, NYC.

February 26
THE CURE: Record first Richard Skinner session: 'Funeral party'/'Drowning man'/'Faith'.

February 27
UK DECAY: Clarendon Hotel, London.

March
BIRTHDAY PARTY: Return to London.
THEATRE OF HATE: UK tour.

March 2
THE CURE: First Richard Skinner session broadcast (Radio One).

March 7
UK DECAY: Single 'Unexpected Guest' enters Independent Chart (peak #4).
UK DECAY: EP *The Black Cat* enters Independent Chart (peak #21).

March 11
BIRTHDAY PARTY: Moonlight Club, London.

March 12
BAUHAUS: US TV debut, *New York Dancestand*: 'Kick In The Eye'/'Stigmata Martyr'.

March 18
BIRTHDAY PARTY: Rock Garden, London.

March 19
BIRTHDAY PARTY: Venue, London.

March 27
THE CURE: Release single 'Primary'.

March 28
THEATRE OF HATE: Live LP *He Who Dares, Wins* enters Independent Chart (peak #1).

April
RICHARD STRANGE: Single 'International Language' (new version).
SISTERS OF MERCY: Circulate first demo tape: 'Teachers'/'Floorshow'/'Lights'/'Adrenochrome'.

April 4
THE CURE: Single 'Primary' enters UK Chart (peak #43).

April 11
THE CURE: Release LP *Faith.*

April 12
THEATRE OF HATE: Hyde Park, London, with Classix Nouveaux, Specials, etc.

April 13
BAUHAUS: Release single 'Kick In The Eye'.

April 18
THEATRE OF HATE: Single 'Rebel Without A Brain' enters Independent Chart (peak #3).
BIRTHDAY PARTY: LP *Prayers On Fire* enters Independent Chart (peak #4).
THE CURE: UK tour opens at Aylesbury Friars. The movie *Carnage Visors* opens the show.
BAUHAUS: Single 'Kick In The Eye' enters UK Chart (peak #59).

April 21
BIRTHDAY PARTY: Record second John Peel session: 'Release The Bats'/'Roland Around In That Stuff'/'Pleasure Heads Must Burn'/'Loose'.

April 25
THE CURE: LP *Faith* enters UK Chart (peak #14).

April 29
BIRTHDAY PARTY: Second John Peel session broadcast (Radio One).

May
THEATRE OF HATE: UK tour.
UK DECAY: UK tour.
RICHARD STRANGE: LP *The Phenomenal Rise Of Richard Strange.*

May 1
THEATRE OF HATE, BIRTHDAY PARTY: University of London.

May 3
UK DECAY: London Lyceum supporting 9.

May 11
PLAY DEAD: Release single 'Poison Takes Hold'.

May 15
SIOUXSIE & THE BANSHEES: Release single 'Spellbound'.

May 19
UK DECAY/PLAY DEAD: Venue, London.

May 30
SIOUXSIE & THE BANSHEES: Single 'Spellbound' enters UK Chart (peak #22).

June
THE CURE: European tour.
RICHARD STRANGE: Single 'The Phenomenal Rose Of Richard Strange'.

June 4
SIOUXSIE & THE BANSHEES: Record first Richard Skinner session: 'Arabian Nights'/'Red Over White'/'Headcut'/'Supernatural Thing'.

June 7
SIOUXSIE & THE BANSHEES: LP *Juju* enters UK Chart (peak #7).

June 14
THEATRE OF HATE: Lyceum, London.

June 16
SIOUXSIE & THE BANSHEES: First Richard Skinner session broadcast (Radio One).

June 17
BAUHAUS, BIRTHDAY PARTY: Open UK tour at University of Newcastle.

June 19
SIOUXSIE & THE BANSHEES: Release LP *Juju*.

June 25
BAUHAUS, BIRTHDAY PARTY: Lyceum, London.

June 27
DEAD OR ALIVE: Single 'Number Eleven' enters Independent Chart (peak #15).

June 29
BAUHAUS: Release single 'The Passion Of Lovers'.

July
SIOUXSIE & THE BANSHEES: UK tour.
DOCTORS OF MADNESS: Compilation LP *Revisionism 15-78*.

July 2
SISTERS OF MERCY: F Club, Leeds.

July 4
BAUHAUS: Single 'The Passion Of Lovers' enters UK Chart (peak #56).

July 20
ARTERY: Record first John Peel session: 'The Clown'/'Into The Garden'/'[Potential Silence]'/'Afterwards'
DANSE SOCIETY: Release single 'Clock'.

July 23
THE CURE: North American tour opens at the Ritz, New York City.

July 24
SIOUXSIE & THE BANSHEES: Release single 'Arabian Nights'.

July 27
UK DECAY: Record second John Peel session: 'Last In The House Of Flames'/'Stagestruck'/'Glass Ice'/'Duel'.

July 28
ARTERY: First John Peel session broadcast (Radio One).

July 29
SPECIMEN: Play final gig for a year, at a Royal Wedding party in Bristol.

August
THE CURE: Australian/New Zealand tour.
DANSE SOCIETY: Release single 'There Is No Shame In Death'.

August 1
SIOUXSIE & THE BANSHEES: Single 'Arabian Nights' enters UK Chart (peak #32).

August 5
UK DECAY: Second John Peel session broadcast (Radio One).

August 8
VIRGIN PRUNES: Single 'In The Grey Light' enters Independent Chart (peak #50).

August 15
THEATRE OF HATE: Record second John Peel session: 'Love Is A Ghost'/'Conquistador'/'Propaganda'/'Westworld'.
THEATRE OF HATE: Single 'Nero' enters Independent Chart (peak #2).
NICO: LP *Drama Of Exile* enters Independent Chart (peak #14).

August 24
THEATRE OF HATE: Second John Peel session broadcast (Radio One).

August 29
BIRTHDAY PARTY: Single 'Release The Bats' enters Independent Chart (peak #3).

September 5-6
FUTURAMA THREE.

September 10
BIRTHDAY PARTY: Venue, London.

September 23
BIRTHDAY PARTY: Launch first North American tour at the Underground, NYC.

September 25
SIOUXSIE & THE BANSHEES: CREATURES side project release *Wild Thing* EP.

September 26
DAYS OF FUTURE PAST, LEEDS.

September 30
THE CURE: French tour.

October
BAUHAUS: David J/Rene Halkett release single 'Nothing'.
BAUHAUS: Release LP *Mask*.
THEATRE OF HATE: UK tour, some dates with the Clash.
VIRGIN PRUNES: UK tour with the Fall.

October 2
THE CREATURES: Record first David Jensen session: 'Mad Eyed Screamer'/'So Unreal'/'But Not Them'/'Wild Thing'.

October 3
THE CREATURES: Single 'Mad Eyed Screamer' enters UK Chart (peak #24).

October 6
NICO: Imperial Cinema, Birmingham, with the Fall.

October 8
SIOUXSIE & THE BANSHEES: North American tour opens in Vancouver, Canada.

October 13
THE CREATURES: First David Jensen session broadcast. (Radio One).

October 17
JOY DIVISION: Compilation LP *Still* enters UK Chart (peak #5).
NICO: Single 'Saeta' enters Independent Chart (peak #13).
THE CURE: Single 'Charlotte Sometimes' enters UK Chart (peak #44).

October 19
VIRGIN PRUNES: North London Poly, supporting The Fall.

October 22
BAUHAUS: Open UK tour at Reading University.

October 24
UK DECAY: Single 'Sexual' enters Independent Chart (peak #10).
BAUHAUS: LP *Mask* enters UK Chart (peak #30).
JOY DIVISION: LP *Still* enters Independent Chart (peak #1).
RICHARD STRANGE: Chelsea College.

October 28
BAUHAUS: Fagin's, Manchester. NICO joins band onstage to record joint live version of 'Waiting For The Man'.

November
VIRGIN PRUNES: Release EP *A New Form Of Beauty Part Two*.

November 3
BIRTHDAY PARTY: Launch first European tour in Berlin.

November 8
THEATRE OF HATE: London Lyceum.

November 13
SOUTHERN DEATH CULT: Queen's Hall, Bradford.

November 14
VIRGIN PRUNES: EP *A New Form Of Beauty Part One* enters Independent Chart (peak #44).\

November 17
BAUHAUS: Open European tour in Brussels, Belgium.

November 21
DANSE SOCIETY: Record first John Peel session: 'Sanity Career'/'We're So Happy'/ 'Woman's Own'/'Love As Positive Narcotic'.

November 22
RICHARD STRANGE: Maestro's, Glasgow.

November 25
PLAY DEAD: Release single 'TV Eye'.
THE CURE: UK tour opens at the Lyceum, Sheffield, with And Also The Trees.

November 26
BIRTHDAY PARTY: Venue, London with Lydia Lunch.

November 30
DANSE SOCIETY: First John Peel session broadcast (Radio One).
FLESH FOR LULU: Rock Garden, London.

December
VIRGIN PRUNES: Release EP *A New Form Of Beauty Part Three*.

X MAL DEUTSCHLAND: Release single 'Schwarze Welt'.

December 2
BIRTHDAY PARTY: Record third John Peel session: 'Big Jesus Trash Can'/'She's Hit'/'Bully Bones'/'Six Inch Gold Blade'.
DANSE SOCIETY: Release single 'There Is No Shame In'.

December 4
SIOUXSIE & THE BANSHEES: Release LP *Once Upon A Time* (compilation).
THEATRE OF HATE, UK DECAY: Central Poly, London.

December 5
UK DECAY: LP *For Madmen Only* enters Independent Chart (peak #8).

December 7
RITUAL: Record first John Peel session: 'Playtime'/ 'Mind Disease'/'Human Sacrifice'/'Brides'.
PLAY DEAD: Golf Club, London.

December 10
BIRTHDAY PARTY: Third John Peel session broadcast (Radio One).

December 11
BIRTHDAY PARTY: Central London Poly; last show before returning to Australia to record.

December 12
SIOUXSIE & THE BANSHEES: Compilation LP *Once Upon A Time* enters UK Chart (peak #21).

December 14
SOUTHERN DEATH CULT: Marquee, London with Chelsea.

December 17
X-MAL DEUTSCHLAND: Release single '12 Schwarze Welt'.

December 21
THE CURE: Record fifth John Peel session: 'Figurehead'/'100 Years'/'Siamese Twins'/'The Hanging Garden' (not broadcast)

December 28
LORDS OF THE NEW CHURCH: Venue, London, with the Members.

December 30
GENE LOVES JEZEBEL: Live debut at ICA London, supporting the Higsons, Electric Guitars.

1982

January
NICO: UK tour.

January 4
THE CURE: Fifth John Peel session broadcast (Radio One).

January 8
LORDS OF THE NEW CHURCH: Dingwalls, London, with Lightning Raiders.

January 13
PLAY DEAD: Record first John Peel session: 'Effigy'/'Metallic Smile'/'Pray To Mecca'/ 'Propaganda'.

January 14
VIRGIN PRUNES: Venue, London.

January 16
BIRTHDAY PARTY: as THE CAVEMEN, Tiger
Lounge, Richmond, Australia.
LORDS OF THE NEW CHURCH: Hope &
Anchor, London.

January 17
BIRTHDAY PARTY: Tracey Pew arrested for
drink-driving. He will be sentenced to 8 months
imprisonment.

January 21
GENE LOVES JEZEBEL: Venue, London with
the Sound, King Trigger.

January 23
THEATRE OF HATE: Single 'Westworld' enters
Independent Chart (peak #1).
THEATRE OF HATE: Single 'Westworld' enters
UK Chart (peak #40).

January 25
LORDS OF THE NEW CHURCH: Bridegouse,
London.

January 26
SISTERS OF MERCY: Release single 'Body
Electric'.
NICO: New Albany Empire, London.

January 28
PLAY DEAD: First John Peel session broadcast
(Radio One).

January 29
FLESH FOR LULU: Clarendon Hotel, London.

January 30
ARTERY: Record second John Peel session:
'The Ghost Of A Small Tour Boat Captain'/'Louise'/
'The Slide'/'The Sailor Situation'.

February
BAUHAUS: Release EP *Searching For Satori*.
BAUHAUS: UK TV debut, *Riverside*: 'Kick In
The Eye'/'Bela Lugosi's Dead'.
DEATH IN JUNE: Release single 'Heaven Street'.
THEATRE OF HATE: UK tour.

February 4
VAMPIRE BATS FROM LEWISHAM: Record first
David Jensen sesison: 'Ordinary Scheme'/'Real
Lovers'/'Petrol'/'Milk With Knives'.

February 5
SISTERS OF MERCY: Vanbrugh College, York.

February 8
THEATRE OF HATE: Record third John Peel
session: 'Dreams Of The Poppy'/'Incinerator'/
'The Hop'/'The Klan'.

February 14
FLESH FOR LULU: Starlight Club, London.

February 15
ARTERY: Second John Peel session broadcast
(Radio One).

February 16
LORDS OF THE NEW CHURCH: Marquee, London.

February 18
THEATRE OF HATE: Release LP *Westworld*.
THEATRE OF HATE: Third John Peel session
broadcast (Radio One).
GENE LOVES JEZEBEL: Rock Garden, London.

February 19
VAMPIRE BATS FROM LEWISHAM: First David
Jensen session broadcast (Radio One).

February 20
FLESH FOR LULU: Clarendon, London.
UK DECAY: Ladbroke Grove Tabernacle,
London.

February 23
VIRGIN PRUNES: Release compilation LP *A
New Form Of Beauty*.
DANSE SOCIETY: Venue, London, with
Zeitgeist, Airstrip One.
UK DECAY: Hammersmith Palais, London with
Killing Joke.

February 24
BAUHAUS, GENE LOVES JEZEBEL: New
Victoria Theatre, London show recorded/filmed
for release.

March
BIRTHDAY PARTY: UK tour with Cocteau Twins.
DANSE SOCIETY: release single 'Woman's Own'.
MARC & THE MAMBAS: Release single 'Fun City'.
THEATRE OF HATE: UK tour.
VIRGIN PRUNES: UK tour.

March 1
DEAD OR ALIVE: Record second John Peel
session: 'Misty Circles'/'Number 12'/'Untitled'.

March 5
BIRTHDAY PARTY: Venue, London: Barry
Adamson fills in for Pew.

March 6
VIRGIN PRUNES: Single 'A New Form Of
Beauty' enters Independent Chart (peak #47).
BAUHAUS: EP *A Kick In The Eye* enters UK
Chart (peak #45).

March 13
BAUHAUS: record second John Peel session:
'The Party Of The First Part'/'3 Shadows:
Departure'.
BIRTHDAY PARTY: EP *Drunk On The Pope's
Blood* enters Independent Chart (peak #2).
THEATRE OF HATE: LP *Westworld* enters UK
Chart (peak #17).

March 18
DEAD OR ALIVE: Second John Peel session
broadcast. (Radio One).

March 22
BAUHAUS: Film 'Bela Lugosi's Dead' for movie
The Hunger.

March 26
UK DECAY: City Poly, London.

March 27
DEAD OR ALIVE: EP *It's Been Hours Now*
enters Independent Chart (peak #13).
SEX GANG CHILDREN: Clarendon Hotel,
London.

April
BAUHAUS: Open Italian tour.
THE CURE: Release LP *Pornography*.

April 1
FLESH FOR LULU: Le Kilt, London

April 8
DANSE SOCIETY: release EP *Continent*.

April 12
BAUHAUS: Second John Peel session broadcast (Radio One).

April 15
SOUTHERN DEATH CULT: Rock Garden, London.

April 16
SOUTHERN DEATH CULT, SEX GANG CHILDREN: Clarendon, London.

April 17
SOUTHERN DEATH CULT, UK DECAY, DANSE SOCIETY, 13 AT MIDNIGHT: ZigZag Club, London.

April 18
THE CURE: UK tour opens at Skating Bowl, Plymouth, with Richard Jobson, Zerra 1.

May
GENE LOVES JEZEBEL: Release EP *Shaving My Neck*.

May 1
LORDS OF THE NEW CHURCH: Single 'New Church' enters Independent Chart (peak #34).
THE CURE: Hammersmith Odeon, London.
DANSE SOCIETY: Clarendon Hotel, London

May 2
THE CURE: Open European tour.
SOUTHERN DEATH CULT: Moonlight Club, London.

May 4
THEATRE OF HATE: Release single 'The Hop'.

May 8
TONES ON TAIL: EP *Tones On Tail* enters Independent Chart (peak #15).
BIRTHDAY PARTY: Zig Zag Club, London.

May 9
LORDS OF THE NEW CHURCH: Marquee, London.

May 13
SIOUXSIE & THE BANSHEES: Record first David Jensen session: 'Coal Mind'/'Greenfingers'/ 'Painted Bird'/'Cascade'.
SEX GANG CHILDREN: Zig Zag Club, London, with Johnny Thunders, Dirty Strangers.

May 15
THE CURE: LP *Pornography* enters UK Chart (peak #8).

May 16
THEATRE OF HATE: Release live LP *He Who Dares, Wins (Live In Berlin)* enters Independent Chart (peak #3).

May 18
GENE LOVES JEZEBEL: Venue, London, with Modern English.

May 21
SIOUXSIE & THE BANSHEES: Release single 'Fireworks'.
SOUTHERN DEATH CULT: Record first John Peel session: 'Fat Man'/'Today'/'False Faces'/'Or Glory'.

May 23
SEX GANG CHILDREN: Release live cassette *Naked*.

May 24
SIOUXSIE & THE BANSHEES: First David Jensen session broadcast (Radio One).

May 26-27
BIRTHDAY PARTY: Clarendon Ballroom, London, with the Go-Betweens.

May 27
THE CURE: A post-show fight between Robert Smith and Simon Gallup precipitates the end of the band.

May 29
SIOUXSIE & THE BANSHEES: Single 'Fireworks' enters UK Chart (peak #22).
THEATRE OF HATE: Single 'The Hop' enters UK Chart (peak #70).

May 31
GENE LOVES JEZEBEL: Release single 'Shaving My Neck'.

June
BAUHAUS: Release 'Spirit' single.

June 3
BIRTHDAY PARTY: With Pew released after 3 months, Birthday Party launch European tour in Eindhoven, Holland.

June 4
BIRTHDAY PARTY: Band meets Blixa Bargeld at Paradiso, Amsterdam.

June 5
VIRGIN PRUNES: Single 'Pagan Lovesong' enters Independent Chart (peak #13).
DANSE SOCIETY: Clarendon, London.

June 7
NICO, SISTERS OF MERCY: Venue, London.
SEX GANG CHILDREN: Embassy Club, London.

June 10
SOUTHERN DEATH CULT: First John Peel session broadcast (Radio One).

June 11
BAUHAUS: Rioting at Adelphi Theatre, London show leads to cancellation of second night.
THE CURE: Ancien Belgique, Brussels. Final show.

June 17
BAUHAUS: Open North American tour (three shows).
THEATRE OF HATE: Record first David Jensen session: 'Legion'/'The Solution'/'The Americans'/ 'Anniversary'.

June 18
SOUTHERN DEATH CULT: Moonlight Club, London.

June 19
BAUHAUS: Single 'Spirit' enters UK Chart (peak #42).

June 24
THEATRE OF HATE: First David Jensen session broadcast (Radio One).

June 25
BIRTHDAY PARTY: Begin the 'Oops, I've got Blood on the End of my Boot' tour of Germany.

June 26
SOUTHERN DEATH CULT: Central Iberico, London.

June 27
LORDS OF THE NEW CHURCH: ICA, London.

June 29
SPECIMEN: Release video single 'Returning From A Journey'.

July
BIRTHDAY PARTY: UK tour.
LORDS OF THE NEW CHURCH: UK tour.
THE CURE: Release single 'Hanging Garden'.
THEATRE OF HATE: Release flexidisc single 'Ghost Of Love' with *Masterbag* magazine.

July 1
BAUHAUS: record first David Jensen session: 'Third Uncle'/'Silent Hedges'/'Swing The Heartache'/'Ziggy Stardust'.

July 3
THEATRE OF HATE: Billy Duffy quits band.

July 4
THEATRE OF HATE, SOUTHERN DEATH CULT: Hammersmith Odeon, London.

July 10
BIRTHDAY PARTY, SISTERS OF MERCY: Zig Zag Club, London.
MARCH VIOLETS: Record first John Peel session: 'Radiant Boys'/'Steam'/'1-2 I Love You'/ 'Grooving In Green'.
X-MAL DEUTSCHLAND: Release EP *Incubus Succubus*.

July 11
DANSE SOCIETY, 13 AT MIDNIGHT: Zig Zag Club, London with Nightingales

July 15
UK DECAY, SEX GANG CHILDREN: Zig Zag Club, London

July 21
SPECIMEN open the Batcave.

July 22
BAUHAUS: First David Jensen session broadcast (Radio One).
DANSE SOCIETY: Klub Foot, London with Wasted Youth, New Model Army.

July 24
BIRTHDAY PARTY: LP *Junkyard* enters Independent Chart (peak #1).
BIRTHDAY PARTY: LP *Junkyard* enters UK Chart (peak #73).
LORDS OF THE NEW CHURCH: LP *Lords Of The New Church* enters Independent Chart (peak #3).
THE CURE: Single 'Hanging Garden' enters UK Chart (peak #34).

July 29
SEX GANG CHILDREN: White Lion, Putney.
SOUTHERN DEATH CULT: Clarendon, London.

July 30
SOUTHERN DEATH CULT: Brixton Fair Deal, London, with the Clash.

July 31
LORDS OF THE NEW CHURCH: Gateshead Stadium with the Police, U2, Beat, Gang of Four.
LORDS OF THE NEW CHURCH: Single 'Open

Your Eyes' enters Independent Chart (peak #7).
MARCH VIOLETS: Release EP *Religious As Hell*.

August
THE CURE: Release flexidisc single through *Flexipop* magazine.

August 2
MARCH VIOLETS: First John Peel session broadcast (Radio One).

August 3
LORDS OF THE NEW CHURCH: Venue, London.

August 5
BIRTHDAY PARTY: Venue, London – final gig with Phill Calvert. Final gig before move to Berlin.

August 9
SEX GANG CHILDREN, RITUAL: Marquee, London.

August 12
GENE LOVES JEZEBEL: Le Beat Route, London.

August 21
UK DECAY: EP *Rising From The Dead* enters Independent Chart (peak #9).
FLESH FOR LULU: Record first John Peel session: 'Dancer'/'Walk Tired'/'Missionary'/'Spy In Your Mind'.

August 25
SISTERS OF MERCY: record first John Peel session: '19'/'Alice'/'Good Things'/'Floor Show'.

August 26
RED LORRY YELLOW LORRY: Release single 'Beating My Head'.

August 28
DANSE SOCIETY: Record second John Peel session: 'Clock'/'Ambition'/'Godsend'/'The Seduction'.

September 4
SEX GANG CHILDREN: Single 'Beasts' enters Independent Chart (peak #8).

September 6
FLESH FOR LULU: First John Peel session broadcast (Radio One).

September 6-8
NICO: Band On The Wall, Manchester.

September 7
SISTERS OF MERCY: First John Peel session broadcast (Radio One).

September 9
UK DECAY, SEX GANG CHILDREN, RITUAL: Klub Foot, London.

September 11-12
FUTURAMA 4, DEESIDE LESIURE CENTRE

September 13
DANSE SOCIETY: Second John Peel session broadcast (Radio One).

September 17
BIRTHDAY PARTY: First gig as a four piece, at a festival in Athens.

September 18
MARCH VIOLETS: EP *Religious As Hell* enters Independent Chart (peak #32).
DEAD OR ALIVE: Single 'The Stranger' enters

Independent Chart (peak #7).

September 19
SEX GANG CHILDREN, MARCH VIOLETS:
Lyceum, London, with Wasted Youth &c.

September 22
UNDEAD: Release single 'This Place Is Burning'.

September 23
GENE LOVES JEZEBEL: Rock Garden, London.

September 24
THEATRE OF HATE: Break-up.
TONES ON TAIL: Release single 'There's Only One'.

September 29
DANSE SOCIETY: Marquee, London.

October
SEX GANG CHILDREN: UK tour.
THE CURE: Release single 'Let's Go To Bed'.

October 1
SIOUXSIE & THE BANSHEES: Release single
'Slowdive'.

October 2
BAUHAUS: Release 'God In An Alcove' flexidisc.
NICO: Single 'Procession' enters Independent
Chart (peak #33).

October 4
BAUHAUS: Release single 'Ziggy Stardust'.

October 6
DANSE SOCIETY: release EP *Seduction*.
RITUAL: Release first single 'Mind Disease'.

October 7
BAUHAUS: UK TV *Top Of The Pops*: 'Ziggy
Stardust'.
SOUTHERN DEATH CULT: Brixton Ace, London.

October 8
BAUHAUS: UK TV *Old Grey Whistle Test*: 'Spy
In The Cab'/'Ziggy Stardust'

October 9
BAUHAUS, SOUTHERN DEATH CULT: Open
UK tour at Brighton Dome.
BAUHAUS: Single 'Ziggy Stardust' enters UK
Chart (peak #15).
DANSE SOCIETY: LP *Seduction* enters
Independent Chart (peak #3).
SIOUXSIE & THE BANSHEES: Single
'Slowdive' enters UK Chart (peak #41).

October 14
BAUHAUS: Release LPs *The Sky's Gone Out*
and *Press The Eject & Give Me The Tape*.
SISTERS OF MERCY, MARCH VIOLETS,
RITUAL: Klub Foot, London.

October 16
MARC & THE MAMBAS: LP *Untitled* enters UK
Chart (peak #42).

October 21
BAUHAUS, SOUTHERN DEATH CULT: Lyceum,
London.

October 24
THE CURE: Record second David Jensen session:
'Lets Go To Bed'/'Just One Kiss'/'1 Years'/'Ariel'.

October 27
SEX GANG CHILDREN: Record first John Peel

session: 'Kill Machine'/'German Nun'/'State Of
Mind'/'Sebastiane'.

October 30
BAUHAUS: LP *The Sky's Gone Out* enters UK
Chart (peak #4).
VIRGIN PRUNES: Single 'Baby Turns Blue'
enters Independent Chart (peak #15).

October 31
VIRGIN PRUNES, Heaven, London.

November
BIRTHDAY PARTY: UK tour.
DEATH IN JUNE: Release single 'State Laughter'.
MARC & THE MAMBAS: release single 'Big Louise'.
SIOUXSIE & THE BANSHEES: Robert Smith
(THE CURE) replaces John McGeoch for UK tour.

November 1
THE CURE: Second David Jensen session
broadcast (Radio One).

November 5
SIOUXSIE & THE BANSHEES: Release LP *A
Kiss In The Dreamhouse*.
THE TUBE debuts on Channel 4.

November 6
SEX GANG CHILDREN: Single 'Into The Abyss'
enters Independent Chart (peak #7).
THEATRE OF HATE: Single 'Eastworld' enters
Independent Chart (peak #3).

November 11
LORDS OF THE NEW CHURCH: Release single
'Russian Roulette'.

November 13
SIOUXSIE & THE BANSHEES: LP *A Kiss In
The Dreamhouse* enters UK Chart (peak #11).

November 15
BIRTHDAY PARTY: Record fourth John Peel
session: 'Pleasure Avalanche'/'Deep In The
Woods'/'Sonny's Burning'/'Marry Me'.

November 19
BAUHAUS: UK TV *Oxford Road Show*: 'Passion
Of Lovers'/'Lagartija Nick'/'Antonin Artaud'.

November 22
BAUHAUS: Open North American tour at Reds,
Levittown, NY.
BIRTHDAY PARTY: Fourth John Peel session
broadcast (Radio One).

November 23
NICO: Venue, London.

November 25
BIRTHDAY PARTY, VIRGIN PRUNES: Brixton
Ace, London.
MARCH VIOLETS, RITUAL, BRIGANDAGE:
Klub Foot, London.
X-MAL DEUTSCHLAND: Record first John Peel
session: 'Incubus Succubus'/'Geheimnis'.
Qual'/'Zinker'.

November 26
SIOUXSIE & THE BANSHEES: Release single 'Melt!'

November 27
VIRGIN PRUNES: LP *If I Die I Diei* enters
Independent Chart (peak #8).

November 28

SISTERS OF MERCY: Lyceum, London with Aswad &c.

December 1
ALIEN SEX FIEND: Live debut at the Batcave, London.

December 4
LORDS OF THE NEW CHURCH: Single 'Russian Roulette' enters Independent Chart (peak #12).
SIOUXSIE & THE BANSHEES: Single 'Melt' enters UK Chart (peak #49).

December 5
MARC & THE MAMBAS: Drury Lane Theatre, London.

December 11
SISTERS OF MERCY: Single 'Alice' enters Independent Chart (peak #8).

December 12
RED LORRY YELLOW LORRY: Record first John Peel session: 'Sometimes'/'Happy'/'Silence'/'Conscious Decision'.

December 13
SPECIMEN, ALIEN SEX FIEND: Heaven, London.

December 17
X-MAL DEUTSCHLAND: First John Peel session broadcast (Radio One).

December 22
LORDS OF THE NEW CHURCH: London Marquee.

December 23
UK DECAY, SISTERS OF MERCY, BLOOD & ROSES: Klub Foot, London.

December 25
SOUTHERN DEATH CULT: Single 'Moya' enters Independent Chart (peak #1).

December 26
SEX GANG CHILDREN, SISTERS OF MERCY, ALIEN SEX FIEND, RITUAL: Christmas On Earth Festival, London Lyceum

December 28-29
SIOUXSIE & THE BANSHEES, MARC & THE MAMBAS: Hammersmith Odeon, London.

December 30
DAMNED, DANSE SOCIETY, UK DECAY, RITUAL: Brixton Ace, London.

1983
SPECIMEN: Release the Batcave compilation LP *Young Hymns And Numb Limbs*.
SPECIMEN: Release debut single 'The Beauty Of Poison'.
SPECIMEN: Release second single 'Returning'.
SPECIMEN: Release US EP *Batastrophe*.

January
SIOUXSIE & THE BANSHEES: Far Eastern tour.

January 8
THE CURE: Single 'Let's Go To Bed' enters UK Chart (peak #44).

January 13
RED LORRY YELLOW LORRY: First John Peel session broadcast (Radio One).

January 15
BAUHAUS: Release single 'Lagartija Nick'.

MARCH VIOLETS: Single 'Grooving In Green' enters Independent Chart (peak #14).

January 20
SOUTHERN DEATH CULT: Record first David Jensen session: 'Apache'/'The Patriot'/'Flower In The Desert'/'False Faces'.

January 22
BAUHAUS: Single 'Lagartija Nick' enters UK Chart (peak #44).

January 24
SOUTHERN DEATH CULT: First David Jensen session broadcast (Radio One).

January 27
BAUHAUS: UK TV *Top Of The Pops*.

February
BIRTHDAY PARTY: Short UK tour.

February 1
MARC & THE MAMBAS: Record first John Peel session: 'Empty Eyes'/'The Bulls'/'Once Was'/'Your Aura'.

February 17
BAUHAUS: Record second David Jensen session: 'She's In Parties,' 'In The Night-time,' 'Terror Couple Kill Colonel'.

February 19
BIRTHDAY PARTY: EP *The Bad Seed* enters Independent Chart (peak #3).

February 24
MARC & THE MAMBAS: First John Peel session broadcast (Radio One).

February 26
SOUTHERN DEATH CULT: Manchester Polytechnic – final gig.

March
THE CURE: Former members Simon Gallup and Matthieu Hartley form new band, CRY.
THE CURE: UK TV Riverside: Robert Smith, Lol Tolhurst and Steve Severin perform 'Siamese Twins'.

March 5
DANSE SOCIETY: Single 'Somewhere' enters Independent Chart (peak #2).
SEX GANG CHILDREN: LP *Song And Legend* enters Independent Chart (peak #1)

March 6
SISTERS OF MERCY: Record first David Jensen session: 'Heartland'/'Jolene'/'Valentine'/'Burn'.

March 10
SISTERS OF MERCY: First David Jensen session broadcast (Radio One).

March 19
MARCH VIOLETS: Record second John Peel session: 'Strange Head'/'Slow Drip Lizard'/'The Undertow'/'Crow Baby'.

March 23
BAUHAUS: Second David Jensen session broadcast (Radio One).

March 24
MARCH VIOLETS: Second John Peel session broadcast (Radio One).
BIRTHDAY PARTY: Launch final North American tour in Boston, MA.

March 26
BLOOD AND ROSES: Single 'Love Under Will' enters Independent Chart (peak #4).
SISTERS OF MERCY: Single 'Anaconda' enters Independent Chart (peak #3).

March 29
AUTO DA FÈ: Record first Janice Long session: 'Girl Boy Difference'/'Blood Into Life'/'Sensitive Eyes'.

April
BAUHAUS: Release single 'She's In Parties'.
THE CURE: UK TV *Oxford Road Show:* 'Figurehead'/'1 Years'.
BIRTHDAY PARTY: Mick Harvey quits following show at the Electric Ballroom, London.

April 3
DANSE SOCIETY: record first David Jensen session: 'Wake Up'/'The Sway'/'So Lonely In Your Crowd'/'We Know The Place'.

April 6
VIRGIN PRUNES: Brixton Ace, London.

April 9
BAUHAUS: Single 'She's In Parties' enters UK Chart (peak #26).
RITUAL: EP *Kangaroo Court* enters Independent Chart (peak #28).

April 12
DANSE SOCIETY: First David Jensen session broadcast (Radio One).

April 14
BAUHAUS: UK TV *Top Of The Pops*: 'She's In Parties'.

April 16
SEX GANG CHILDREN: Single 'Song And Legend' enters Independent Chart (peak #6).
SKELETAL FAMILY: Single 'Just A Friend' enters Independent Chart (peak #50).

April 20
BLOOD AND ROSES: Record first John Peel session: 'Theme From *Assault On Precinct 13*'/'Possession'/'Spit Upon Your Grave'/'Curse On You'.

April 23
ARTERY: LP *One Afternoon In A Hot Air Balloon* enters Independent Chart (peak #15).
THE CREATURES: Single 'Miss The Girl' enters UK Chart (peak #21).
X MAL DEUTSCHLAND: LP *Fetisch* enters Independent Chart (peak #3).

April 26
BLOOD AND ROSES: First John Peel session broadcast (Radio One).

April 30
AUTO DA FÈ: First Janice Long session broadcast (Radio One).

May 3
BIRTHDAY PARTY: Launch Australian tour at Mainstreet Cabaret, Auckland.

May 7
THE CRAMPS: Reissued EP *Gravest Hits* enters Independent Chart (peak #41).
MARCH VIOLETS: Single 'Crow Baby' enters Independent Chart (peak #6).

May 11
SKELETAL FAMILY: Record first John Peel session: 'Black Ju Ju'/'The Wind Blows'/'Someone New'/'And I'.

May 12
BAUHAUS: Open world tour in Paris.

May 14
BRIGANDAGE: Record first John Peel session: 'Let It Rot'/'Heresy'/'Hope'/'Fragile'.
Compilation LP *The Whip* enters Independent Chart (peak #3).

May 17
NICO: Ace, Brixton.

May 18
BRIGANDAGE: First John Peel session broadcast (Radio One).

May 19
SKELETAL FAMILY: First John Peel session broadcast (Radio One).

May 21
PLAY DEAD: LP *The First Flower* enters Independent Chart (peak #10).

May 26
DEAD OR ALIVE: Record first David Jensen session: 'Far Too Hard'/'Give It To Me'/'What I Want'.

May 28
TONES ON TAIL: Single 'Burning Skies' enters Independent Chart (peak #11).
GENE LOVES JEZEBEL: Single 'Screaming' enters Independent Chart (peak #18).
THE CREATURES: LP *Feast* enters UK Chart (peak #17).

June 1
DEAD OR ALIVE: First David Jensen session broadcast.

June 2
MARC & THE MAMBAS: Single 'Black Heart' enters UK Chart (peak #49).

June 4
UK DECAY: LP *A Night For Celebration* enters Independent Chart (peak #9).

June 9
BIRTHDAY PARTY: Seaview Ballroom, Melbourne. Final concert.

June 11
BAUHAUS: Open UK tour at Aylesbury Friars.
X MAL DEUTSCHLAND: Single 'Qual' enters Independent Chart (peak #9).

June 15
PLAY DEAD: Record second John Peel session: 'The Tenant'/'Total Decline'/'Gaze'.

June 16
BONE ORCHARD: Record first John Peel session: 'The Mission'/'Shall I Carry The Budgie Woman'/'Fat's Terminal'.
GENE LOVES JEZEBEL: Record first David Jensen session: 'Sticks And Stones'/'Bruises'/'Upstairs'/'Scheming'.

June 18
SOUTHERN DEATH CULT: LP *Southern Death Cult* enters UK Chart (peak #43).

June 22
X-MAL DEUTSCHLAND: Record second John Peel session: 'In Motion'/'Vito'/'Reigen'/'Sehnsucht'.

June 23
PLAY DEAD: Second John Peel session broadcast (Radio One).

June 25
THE CRAMPS: LP *Off The Bone* enters UK Chart (peak #44).

June 27
X-MAL DEUTSCHLAND: Second John Peel session broadcast (Radio One).

June 30
GENE LOVES JEZEBEL: First David Jensen session broadcast (Radio One).

July
THE CURE: Release single 'The Walk'. Appear twice on *Top Of The Pops*.
THE CURE: Robert Smith and Steve Severin debut side project THE GLOVE on UK TV *Riverside*: 'Punish Me With Kisses'.

July 2
DEATH IN JUNE: LP *The Guilty Have No Pride* enters Independent Chart (peak #13).
THE CRAMPS: LP *Off The Bone* enters Independent Chart (peak #1).

July 5
BAUHAUS: Final live show at Hammersmith Palais.
RED LORRY YELLOW LORRY: Single 'Take It All' enters Independent Chart (peak #23).

July 7
SPECIMEN: Record first David Jensen session: 'Lovers'/'Syria'/'Wolverines'/'Stand Up Stand Out'.

July 9
BIRTHDAY PARTY: EP *Birthday Party* enters Independent Chart (peak #8).
SEX GANG CHILDREN: Single 'Sebastiane' enters Independent Chart (peak #19).
SISTERS OF MERCY: EP *Reptile House* enters Independent Chart (peak #4).
THE CURE: Single 'The Walk' enters UK Chart (peak #12).

July 14
SPECIMEN: First David Jensen session broadcast (Radio One).

July 15
BAUHAUS: Release LP *Burning From The Inside*.

July 16
DANSE SOCIETY: Single 'Clock' enters Independent Chart (peak #11).
THE CREATURES: Single 'Right Now' enters UK Chart (peak #14).

July 23
DANSE SOCIETY: Single 'We're So Happy' enters Independent Chart (peak #22).
BAUHAUS: LP *Burning From The Inside* enters UK Chart (peak #13).

July 28
BONE ORCHARD: First John Peel session broadcast. (Radio One).

July 30
DANSE SOCIETY: Single 'There Is No Shame In Death' enters Independent Chart (peak #26).
DEATH CULT: EP *Brothers Grimm* enters Independent Chart (peak #2).

August
THE CURE: Elephant Fayre, St Germains, Cornwall.
BIRTHDAY PARTY: Break up.
THE CURE: North American tour.

August 4
BAUHAUS: Official split announcement.
PETER MURPHY: Solo UK TV debut, *Riverside*: 'Hollow Hills' (dance routine)
LORDS OF THE NEW CHURCH: Clarendon, London.

August 13
THE CURE: Compilation LP *The Walk* enters US Chart (peak #179).

August 20
MARC & THE MAMBAS: LP *Torment & Torreros* enters UK Chart (peak #28).

August 26
THE CURE: Record third David Jensen session: 'Speak My Language'. 'Mr Pink Eyes'/'Lovecats'

August 27
ALIEN SEX FIEND: Single 'Ignore The Machine' enters Independent Chart (peak #16).
DANSE SOCIETY: Single 'Wake Up' enters UK Chart (peak #61).
SKELETAL FAMILY: Single 'The Night' enters Independent Chart (peak #41).

September
BAUHAUS: Release EP *4AD* (compilation).
SISTERS OF MERCY: USA tour.

September 3
THE CURE: Compilation LP *Boys Don't Cry* enters UK Chart (peak #71).

September 10
GENE LOVES JEZEBEL: Single 'Bruises' enters Independent Chart (peak #7).
X MAL DEUTSCHLAND: Single 'Incubus Succubus' enters Independent Chart (peak #5).

September 15
UNDER TWO FLAGS: Record first David Jensen session: 'Land Of The Rising Guns'/'Masks'/ 'Can't Take Love'/'The Feeling Of Resistance'.

September 17
GENE LOVES JEZEBEL: Record first John Peel session: 'Pop Tarantula'/'Brittle Punches'/ 'Upstairs'/'Screaming For Emmalene'.
THE GLOVE: LP *Blue Sunshine* enters UK Chart (peak #35).

September 18
FUTURAMA 5

September 21
THE CURE: Third David Jensen session broadcast (Radio One).

September 24
SALVATION: Single 'Girl Soul' enters Independent Chart (peak #24).

September 26
GENE LOVES JEZEBEL: First John Peel session broadcast (Radio One).

September 29
UNDER TWO FLAGS: First David Jensen session broadcast (Radio One).

September 30
SIOUXSIE & THE BANSHEES: first of two nights at Royal Albert Hall, London – gig taped for *Nocturne* live album.

October 1
BAUHAUS: EP *The Singles* (compilation) enters Independent Chart (peak #5).
PLAY DEAD: Single 'Shine' enters Independent Chart (peak #14).
SIOUXSIE & THE BANSHEES: Single 'Dear Prudence' enters UK Chart (peak #3).

October 15
SISTERS OF MERCY: Single 'Temple Of Love' enters Independent Chart (peak #1).
UNDER TWO FLAGS: Single 'Lest We Forget' enters Independent Chart (peak #32).

October 16
DEATH CULT: Record first David Jensen session: 'Too Young'/'Butterflies'/'With Love'/ 'Flower In The Desert'.

October 17
BIRTHDAY PARTY: Reissued single 'Mr Clarinet' enters Independent Chart (peak #18).

October 20
DANSE SOCIETY: Record first Janice Long session: 'Lizard Mad'/'Red Light'/'Where Are You Now'/'The Night'.

October 27
DEATH CULT: First David Jensen session broadcast.

October 29
BAUHAUS: Compilation EP *The Singles 19-* enters UK Chart (peak #52).
DANSE SOCIETY: First Janice Long session broadcast (Radio One).
GENE LOVES JEZEBEL: LP *Promise* enters Independent Chart (peak #8).
SEX GANG CHILDREN: Single 'Maurita Mayer' enters Independent Chart (peak #7).
THE CURE: Single 'Love Cats' enters UK Chart (peak #7).

October 31
LORDS OF THE NEW CHURCH: Lyceum, London.

November
AND ALSO THE TREES: Release single 'Shantell'.
BONE ORCHARD: Release EP *Stuffed To The Gills*.
FLESH FOR LULU: Release single 'Roman Candle'.
MARC & THE MAMBAS: Release single 'Torment'.
THE CURE: UK TV *Top Of The Pops*: 'Love Cats'.

November 4
DAVID J: Release LP *The Etiquette Of Violence*.

November 5
DANSE SOCIETY: Single 'Heaven Is Waiting' enters UK Chart (peak #60).
RED LORRY YELLOW LORRY: Record second John Peel session: 'See The Fire'/'Strange Dream'/'Monkeys On Juice'.

November 12
DEATH CULT: Single 'God's Zoo' enters Independent Chart (peak #4).

November 16
RED LORRY YELLOW LORRY: Second John Peel session broadcast (Radio One).

November 19
ALIEN SEX FIEND: Single 'Lips Can't Go' enters Independent Chart (peak #12)
RED LORRY YELLOW LORRY: Single 'He's Read' enters Independent Chart (peak #20).

November 26
THE CRAMPS: LP *Smell Of Female* enters Independent Chart (peak #1).
THE CRAMPS: LP *Smell Of Female* enters UK Chart (peak #74).

December
BAUHAUS: Release single 'Sanity Assassin' (fan club only).
SEX GANG CHILDREN: Release compilation LP *Beasts*.
THE CURE: Release LP *Japanese Whispers* (compilation).

December 1
FLESH FOR LULU: Record first David Jensen session: 'Restless'/'Dog Dog Dog'/'Lame Train'/ 'Hyena'.

December 3
BIRTHDAY PARTY: EP *Mutiny* enters Independent Chart (peak #8).
SIOUXSIE & THE BANSHEES: Live LP *Nocturne* enters UK Chart (peak #29).

December 10
ALIEN SEX FIEND: LP *Who's Been Sleeping In My Brain* enters Independent Chart (peak #10).

December 15
FLESH FOR LULU: First David Jensen session broadcast (Radio One).

December 17
CARCRASH INTERNATIONAL: Single 'The Whip' enters Independent Chart (peak #34).

December 24
THE CURE: Compilation LP *Japanese Whispers* enters UK Chart (peak #26).

December 25
THE CURE: UK TV *Top Of The Pops* – Robert Smith appears twice, performing 'Love Cats' and, with SIOUXSIE & THE BANSHEES, 'Dear Prudence'.

1984

January
BAUHAUS: Release video *Shadow Of Light*.

January 11
PLAY DEAD: Record third John Peel session: 'Break'/'Return To The East'/'No Motive'.

January 18
PLAY DEAD: Third John Peel session broadcast (Radio One).

February 2
THE CURE: Record fourth David Jensen session: 'Bananafishbone'/'Piggy In The Mirror'/ 'Give Me It'/'The Empty World'.

February 11
DANSE SOCIETY: LP *Heaven Is Waiting* enters UK Chart (peak #39).

February 12
MARCH VIOLETS: Record first David Jensen session: 'Walk Into The Sun'/'Deep'/'Kill The Delight'/'Big Soul Kiss'.

February 18
MARCH VIOLETS: Single 'Snakedance' enters Independent Chart (peak #2).
SKELETAL FAMILY: Single 'Alone She Cries' enters Independent Chart (peak #8).

February 22
THE CURE: Fourth David Jensen session broadcast (Radio One).

February 25
THE CURE: Compilation LP *Japanese Whispers* enters US Chart (peak #1).

February 28
MARCH VIOLETS: First David Jensen session broadcast (Radio One).

March
AND ALSO THE TREES: Release LP *And Also The Trees*.
DANSE SOCIETY: Release single '2,000 Light Years From Home'.
SIOUXSIE & THE BANSHEES: release single 'Dear Prudence' and launch UK tour.

March 2
TONES ON TAIL: Release single 'Performance'.

March 10
RED LORRY YELLOW LORRY: EP *This Today* enters Independent Chart (peak #18).
SEX GANG CHILDREN: LP *Live* enters Independent Chart (peak #15).

March 17
ALIEN SEX FIEND: Single 'RIP' enters Independent Chart (peak #4).
THE CRAMPS: Single 'Faster Pussycat' enters Independent Chart (peak #7).

March 24
DEAD OR ALIVE: Single 'That's The Way I Like It' enters UK chart (peak #22).
SIOUXSIE & THE BANSHEES: Single 'Swimming Horses' enters UK Chart (peak #28).

March 28
NICK CAVE & THE BAD SEEDS: Record first John Peel session: 'Saint Huck'/'I Put A Spell On You'/'From Her To Eternity'.

March 30
THE CURE: Release single 'Caterpillar'.

April
AND ALSO THE TREES: release single 'The Secret Sea'.
BONE ORCHARD: Release EP *Swallowing Havoc*.
FURYO: Release LP *Furyo*.
TONES ON TAIL: Release LP *Pop*.

April 7
AND ALSO THE TREES: Record first John Peel session: 'There Was A Man Of Double Deed'/'Wallpaper Dying'/'Impulse Of Man'/'The Secret Sea'.

THE CRAMPS: Single 'Gorehound' enters Independent Chart (peak #2).
SISTERS OF MERCY: Tin Can Club, Birmingham – first gig with Wayne Hussey.
THE CURE: Single 'The Caterpillar' enters UK Chart (peak #14).

April 8
SKELETAL FAMILY: Record first David Jensen session: 'Don't Be Denied'/'11.15'/'Burning Oil'/'Promised Land'.

April 9
NICK CAVE & THE BAD SEEDS: First John Peel session broadcast. (Radio One).

April 11
SISTERS OF MERCY: Launch North American tour in Boston MA.
X-MAL DEUTSCHLAND: Record third John Peel session: 'Nachtschatten'/'Tag Fuer Tag'/'Mondlicht'/'Augen-blick'.

April 25
X-MAL DEUTSCHLAND: Third John Peel session broadcast (Radio One).

April 26
AND ALSO THE TREES: First John Peel session broadcast (Radio One).
THE CURE: UK tour opens at Edinburgh Playhouse.

April 28
DEAD OR ALIVE: LP *Sophisticated Boom Boom* enters UK chart (peak #29).
DEATH IN JUNE: LP *Burial* enters Independent Chart (peak #9).
GENE LOVES JEZEBEL: Single 'Influenza' enters Independent Chart (peak #11).
MARCH VIOLETS: Single 'Respectable' enters Independent Chart (peak #48).
PLAY DEAD: Single 'Break' enters Independent Chart (peak #9).

April 30
SKELETAL FAMILY: First David Jensen session broadcast (Radio One).

May
FLESH FOR LULU: Release single 'Subterraneans'.

May 2
ALIEN SEX FIEND: Record first John Peel session: 'Attack'/'Dead And Buried'/'Hee Haw'/'Ignore The Machine'.

May 5
THE CURE: Apollo, Oxford. Four songs recorded for *Concert* live album.
CARCRASH INTERNATIONAL: Single 'All Passion Spent' enters Independent Chart (peak #47).
SEX GANG CHILDREN: Live cassette *Ecstacy & Vendetta* enters Independent Chart (peak #20)

May 8-10
THE CURE: Hammersmith Odeon. Remainder of *Concert* recorded.

May 11
TONES ON TAIL: Release single 'Lions'.

May 12
GENE LOVES JEZEBEL: Record second John Peel session: 'Waves'/'Shame'/'Five Below'.
THE CURE: LP *The Top* enters UK Chart (peak #10).

UNDER TWO FLAGS: Single 'Masks' enters Independent Chart (peak #20).

May 13
THE CURE: Open European tour.

May 15
ALIEN SEX FIEND: First John Peel session broadcast (Radio One).

May 20
THE CULT: London Lyceum show taped for *Dreamtime Live* LP.

May 24
GENE LOVES JEZEBEL: Second John Peel session broadcast (Radio One).

May 25
THE CULT: First Richard Skinner session broadcast. (Radio One).

May 26
PLAY DEAD: LP *From The Promised Land* enters Independent Chart (peak #5).
SIOUXSIE & THE BANSHEES: Robert Smith quits. Replaced by John Carruthers.
SKELETAL FAMILY: Single 'Recollects' enters Independent Chart (peak #7).
THE CULT: Single 'Spiritwalker' enters Independent Chart (peak #1).

June
SIOUXSIE & THE BANSHEES: Release LP *Hyaena*.

June 2
SIOUXSIE & THE BANSHEES: Single 'Dazzle' enters UK Chart (peak #33).

June 12
MARCH VIOLETS: Record third John Peel session: 'Lights Go Out'/'Love Hit'/'Electric Shades'/ 'Don't Take It Lightly'.

June 16
GENE LOVES JEZEBEL: Single 'Shame' enters Independent Chart (peak #14).
SIOUXSIE & THE BANSHEES: LP *Hyaena* enters UK Chart (peak #15).
SISTERS OF MERCY: Single 'Body And Soul' enters UK Chart (peak #46).

June 19
MARCH VIOLETS: Third John Peel session broadcast (Radio One).
SISTERS OF MERCY: Record second John Peel session: 'Walk Away'/'Emma'/'Poison Door'/'No Time To Cry'.

June 23
THE CURE: LP *The Top* enters US Chart (peak #1).

July 7
THE CRAMPS: Single 'Smell Of Female' enters Independent Chart (peak #4).
SIOUXSIE & THE BANSHEES: LP *Hyaena* enters US Chart (peak #157).
X MAL DEUTSCHLAND: LP *Tocsin* enters Independent Chart (peak #1).
X MAL DEUTSCHLAND: LP *Tocsin* enters UK Chart (peak #).

July 12
THE CULT: Record first Richard Skinner session: 'Ghost Dance'/'Bad Medicine Waltz'/ 'Resurrection Joe'/'Go West'.

July 13
SISTERS OF MERCY: Second John Peel session broadcast (Radio One).

July 14
PLAY DEAD: Single 'Isobel' enters Independent Chart (peak #9).
RED LORRY YELLOW LORRY: Single 'Monkeys On Juice' enters Independent Chart (peak #3).

July 15
LORDS OF THE NEW CHURCH: Savoy, London.
SEX GANG CHILDREN: Single 'Dietsche' enters Independent Chart (peak #15).

July 28
SKELETAL FAMILY: Single 'So Sure' enters Independent Chart (peak #2).

August
DEATH IN JUNE: Release single 'The Calling'.
FLESH FOR LULU: Release single 'Restless'.

August 1
THE CULT: US live debut supported by Psi-Com (Perry Farrell, pre-Jane's Addiction).

August 4
MARCH VIOLETS: Single 'Walk Into The Sun' enters Independent Chart (peak #1).

August 11
AUSGANG: Single 'Solid Glass Spine' enters Independent Chart (peak #28).
THEATRE OF HATE: Compilation LP *Revolution* enters Independent Chart (peak #1).

August 18
THEATRE OF HATE: LP *Revolution* enters UK Chart (peak #67).

August 25
ALIEN SEX FIEND: Record second John Peel session: 'In God We Trust'/'EST – Trip To The Moon'/'Boneshaker Baby'.
DEATH IN JUNE: LP *She Said Destroy* enters Independent Chart (peak #13).
THE CURE: UK TV *Rock Around The Clock*.

September
BONE ORCHARD: release single 'Jack'.

September 1
ALIEN SEX FIEND: Single 'Deadandburied' enters Independent Chart (peak #4).

September 3
ALIEN SEX FIEND: Second John peel session broadcast (Radio One).

September 6
RED LORRY YELLOW LORRY: Record first Janice Long session: 'Sometimes'/'This Today'/ 'Head All Fire'/'Secret'.

September 8
SISTERS OF MERCY: Golden Summernight Festival, Germany.
THE CULT: LP *Dreamtime* enters UK Chart (peak #21).

September 11
THE CULT: Launch UK tour in Sheffield.

September 15
SKELETAL FAMILY: LP *Burning Oil* enters Independent Chart (peak #1).

SKELETAL FAMILY: Record second John Peel session: 'Far And Near'/'Hands On The Clock'/'Move'/'No Chance'.
SISTERS OF MERCY: York Racecourse.

September 27
RED LORRY YELLOW LORRY: First Janice Long session broadcast (Radio One).

September 30
THE CURE: Open Far Eastern tour.

October
FLESH FOR LULU: Release LP *Flesh For Lulu*.
FURYO: Release single 'Legacy (Andante)'.
THE CURE: Open North American tour. Drummer Andy Anderson replaced by Vince Ely (ex-Psychedelic Furs).

October 3
TONES ON TAIL: US debut at Channel, Boston.

October 4
SISTERS OF MERCY, SKELETAL FAMILY: Launch Black Planet UK tour in Edinburgh.

October 8
SKELETAL FAMILY: Second John Peel session broadcast (Radio One).

October 20
SISTERS OF MERCY: Single 'Walk Away' enters UK Chart (peak #45).

October 21
FLESH FOR LULU: Record first Janice Long session: 'Black Tattoo'/'Cat Burglar'/'Peace And Love'/'Endless Sleep'.

October 22
THE CURE: Launch North American tour at Commodore Ballroom, Vancouver BC.

October 27
SIOUXSIE & THE BANSHEES: EP *The Thorn* enters UK Chart (peak #47).
THE CURE: Release live LP *Concert* and limited edition rarities *Curiosity* (compilation).

November 3
DALI'S CAR: Single 'The Judgement Is The Mirror' enters UK Chart (peak #66).
THE CURE: Live LP *Concert* enters UK Chart (peak #26).

November 6
FLESH FOR LULU: First Janice Long session broadcast (Radio One).

November 7
THE CURE: Minneapolis. Boris Williams replaces Vince Ely.

November 9
DALI'S CAR: Release LP *The Waking Hour*.
TONES ON TAIL: Release single 'Christian Says'.

November 10
PLAY DEAD: Single 'Propaganda (19 Mix)' enters Independent Chart (peak #17).

November 13
DALI'S CAR: UK TV *Old Grey Whistle Test*: 'His Box'.

November 17
ALIEN SEX FIEND: Single 'EST (Trip To The Moon)' enters Independent Chart (peak #3).

MARCH VIOLETS: LP *Natural History* enters Independent Chart (peak #3).
PLAY DEAD: Single 'Conspiracy' enters Independent Chart (peak #18).

November 18
LORDS OF THE NEW CHURCH: Lyceum, London.

November 25
THE CULT, PLAY DEAD: Lyceum, London.

December
BAUHAUS: Release live video *Archive*.
THE CULT: UK TV *Old Grey Whistle Test*.

December 1
DALI'S CAR: LP *The Waking Hour* enters UK Chart (peak #).
ALIEN SEX FIEND: LP *Acid Bath* enters Independent Chart (peak #4).
RED LORRY YELLOW LORRY: Single 'Hollow Eyes' enters Independent Chart (peak #6).

December 8
BONE ORCHARD: LP *Jack* enters Independent Chart (peak #18).

December 13-14
THE CULT: Wembley Arena supporting Big Country.

December 22
THE CULT: Single 'Resurrection Joe' enters UK Chart (peak #74).

1985
SPECIMEN: Release single 'Sharp Teeth'.

January 25
TONES ON TAIL: Release EP *Tones On Tail* (compilation).

February
THE CURE: Phil Thornally quits band. Replaced by returning Simon Gallup.
DEATH IN JUNE: Release LP *Nada*.

February 9
RED LORRY YELLOW LORRY: LP *Talk About The Weather* enters Independent Chart (peak #3).

February 16
AND ALSO THE TREES: EP *A Room Lives In Lucy* enters Independent Chart (peak #30).

March
DAVID J: Release LP *Crocodile Tears & The Velvet Cosh*.
DEATH IN JUNE: release single 'Born Again'.

March 6
SKELETAL FAMILY: Record first Janice Long session: 'Waltz'/'Mixed Feelings'/'Trees'/'Watch Me'.

March 9
PLAY DEAD: Single 'Sacrosanct' enters Independent Chart (peak #4).
SISTERS OF MERCY: Launch 'Tune In Turn On Burn Out' UK tour in Glasgow.
SISTERS OF MERCY: Single 'No Time To Cry' enters UK Chart (peak #63).
SKELETAL FAMILY: Single 'Promised Land' enters Independent Chart (peak #2).

March 19
SKELETAL FAMILY: First Janice Long session broadcast (Radio One).

March 23
ALIEN SEX FIEND: Reissued single 'Ignore The Machine' enters Independent Chart (peak #22).
SISTERS OF MERCY: LP *First & Last & Always* enters UK Chart (peak #14).

April 1
SISTERS OF MERCY: Brighton – Gary Marx's final show with the band.

April 2
SISTERS OF MERCY: UK TV *Old Grey Whistle Test*: 'Marian'/'First And Last And Always'.

April 6
RED LORRY YELLOW LORRY: Single 'Chance' enters Independent Chart (peak #11).

April 13
BIRTHDAY PARTY: Live LP *It's Still Living* enters Independent Chart (peak #19).
SPECIMEN: Single 'Sharp Teeth' enters Independent Chart (peak #22).

April 21
NICO: Ronnie Scotts, London with John Cale.

April 24
SPECIMEN: Underground, Croydon.

April 27
LORDS OF THE NEW CHURCH: LP *Method To Our Madness* enters US Chart (peak #158).

April 30
X-MAL DEUTSCHLAND: Record fourth John Peel session: 'Polarlicht'/'Der Wind'/'Jahr um Jahr'/ 'Autumn'.

May
THE CULT: European tour.

May 11
THE BATFISH BOYS: Single 'Swamp Liquor' enters Independent Chart (peak #22).
MARCH VIOLETS: Single 'Deep' enters Independent Chart (peak #2).

May 12
FLESH FOR LULU: Clarendon, London.

May 13
X-MAL DEUTSCHLAND: Fourth John Peel session broadcast (Radio One).

May 17
LOVE & ROCKETS: Release single 'Ball Of Confusion'.

May 18
FLESH FOR LULU: EP *Blue Sisters Swing* enters Independent Chart (peak #6).
LORDS OF THE NEW CHURCH: Single 'Like A Virgin' enters Independent Chart (peak #2).
VIRGIN PRUNES: Compilation LP *Over The Rainbow* enters Independent Chart (peak #22).

May 25
SKELETAL FAMILY: LP *Futile Combat* enters Independent Chart (peak #7).
THE CULT: Single '(She Sells) Sanctuary' enters UK Chart (peak #15).

May 28
THE ROSE OF AVALANCHE: Record first John Peel session: 'Goddess'/'1,0 Landscapes'/ 'Gimme Some Lovin''/'Rise To The Groove'.

June
THE CURE: New line-up debuts in Barcelona, Spain.
BONE ORCHARD: Release single 'Princess Epilepsy'.

June 1
BLOOD AND ROSES: Single 'Some Like It Hot' enters Independent Chart (peak #16).

June 8
GENE LOVES JEZEBEL: Single 'Cow' enters Independent Chart (peak #9).

June 12
THE ROSE OF AVALANCHE: First John Peel session broadcast (Radio One).

June 15
PLAY DEAD: LP *Into The Fire* enters Independent Chart (peak #19).

June 16
THE CULT: Record first Janice Long session: 'Spiritwalker'/'Big Neon Glitter'/'Revolution'/'All Souls Avenue'.

June 18
SISTERS OF MERCY: Altamont – A Festival of Remembrance at the Royal Albert Hall, London.

June 26
THE CULT: First Janice Long session broadcast. (Radio One).

July
ALL ABOUT EVE: Release single 'D For Desire'.
DANSE SOCIETY: Release single 'Say It Again'.
THE BATFISH BOYS: Release LP *The Gods Hate Kansas*.

July 10
GENE LOVES JEZEBEL: Launch North American tour.

July 20
ALIEN SEX FIEND: LP *Liquid Head In Tokyo* enters Independent Chart (peak #7).

July 27
THE CURE: Single 'In Between Days' enters UK Chart (peak #15).

July 30
THE CURE: Record sixth John Peel session: 'The Exploding Boy'/'Six Different Ways'/ 'Screw'/'Sinking'.

August
THE CURE: Release LP *The Head In The Door*.
FIELDS OF THE NEPHILIM: Release EP *Burning The Fields*.

August 7
THE CURE: Sixth John Peel session broadcast (Radio One).

August 10
ROSE OF AVALANCHE: Single 'LA Rain' enters Independent Chart (peak #10).

August 22
SEX GANG CHILDREN: *Re-enter The Abyss (The 19 Remixes)* enters Independent Chart (peak #22).

September
THE CURE: Release single 'Close To Me'.

THE CULT: Japanese tour.

September 3
FIELDS OF THE NEPHILIM, CHRISTIAN DEATH: 1 Club, London.

September 7
THE CURE: LP *The Head On The Door* enters UK Chart (peak #7).

September 8
THE CURE: Open UK tour at St Austell Colisseum.

September 13
LOVE & ROCKETS: Release single 'If There's A Heaven Above'.

September 14
ALIEN SEX FIEND: Single 'Maximum Security Twilight Zone' enters Independent Chart (peak #6).
NICO: Compilation LP *The Blue Angel* enters Independent Chart (peak #27).

September 21
SKELETAL FAMILY: Markethalle, Hamburg. Andrew Eldritch and Wayne Hussey join them on stage.
THE CURE: Single 'Close To Me' enters UK Chart (peak #24).

September 26
LOVE & ROCKETS: Live debut opens North American tour at Spit, Boston.

September 28
THE CURE: Open North American tour.
RED LORRY YELLOW LORRY: Single 'Spinning Round' enters Independent Chart (peak #9).

October
THE CULT: UK tour.

October 5
THE CULT: Single 'Rain' enters UK Chart (peak #17).
THE CURE: LP *The Head On The Door* enters US Chart (peak #59).

October 11
LOVE & ROCKETS: Release LP *Seventh Dream Of Teenage Heaven*.
PETER MURPHY: Solo debut on compilation LP *One Pound Ninety Nine*: 'The Light Pours Out Of Me'.

October 12
ALIEN SEX FIEND: LP *Maximum Security* enters Independent Chart (peak #5).
PLAY DEAD: Single 'This Side Of Heaven' enters Independent Chart (peak #5).

October 19
ROSE OF AVALANCHE: Single 'Goddess' enters Independent Chart (peak #16).

October 26
SIOUXSIE & THE BANSHEES: Single 'Cities In Dust' enters UK Chart (peak #21).
THE CULT: LP *Love* enters UK Chart (peak #4).

November
BONE ORCHARD: release LP *Penthouse Poultry*.

November 1
THE CURE: Radio City Music Hall, New York.

November 2
FLESH FOR LULU: Single 'Baby Hurricane' enters Independent Chart (peak #8).

November 9
FLESH FOR LULU: LP *Big Fun City* enters Independent Chart (peak #10).
THE CRAMPS: Single 'Can Your Pussy Do The Dog' enters UK Chart (peak #68).
THE CRAMPS: Single 'Can Your Pussy Do The Dog' enters Independent Chart (peak #1).
X MAL DEUTSCHLAND: Single 'Sequenz' enters Independent Chart (peak #5).

November 10
SKELETAL FAMILY: Record second Janice Long session: 'What Goes Up'/'Restless'/'Split Him In Two'/'The Wizard'.

November 15
BAUHAUS: Release LP *19-* (compilation).
PETER MURPHY: Release single 'Final Solution'.

November 19
THE CURE: UK TV *Old Grey Whistle Test* broadcasts part of MENCAP gig from Camden Palace.

November 20
LOVE & ROCKETS: Open second North American tour at Kennel Club, Philadelphia.

November 23
PLAY DEAD: LP *Company Of Justice* enters Independent Chart (peak #3).

November 25
SKELETAL FAMILY: Second Janice Long session broadcast (Radio One).

November 30
BAUHAUS: Compilation LP *19-* enters UK Chart (peak #36).
THE CULT: Single 'Revolution' enters UK Chart (peak #30).

December
BIRTHDAY PARTY: Release compilation LP *A Collection: Best & Rarest*.
RED LORRY YELLOW LORRY: Mick Brown departs for THE MISSION.
THE CURE: French tour.

December 6
THE CULT: New York Ritz.

December 14
GENE LOVES JEZEBEL: Single 'Desire' enters Independent Chart (peak #4).

December 15
MARCH VIOLETS: Record first Janice Long session: 'Close To The Heart'/'South Country'/'High Times'/'Avalanche Of Love'.

December 28
DEATH IN JUNE: Single 'And Murder Love' enters Independent Chart (peak #22).
LORDS OF THE NEW CHURCH: Compilation LP *Killer Lords* enters Independent Chart (peak #22).
THE CULT: LP *Love* enters US Chart (peak #).
THEATRE OF HATE: Live LP *Original Sin Live* enters Independent Chart (peak #12).

1986

SPECIMEN: Now a virtual Ollie Wisdom solo project, release Canadian single 'Indestructible'.

January 13
MARCH VIOLETS: First Janice Long session broadcast (Radio One).

January 19
WAYNE HUSSEY & CRAIG ADAMS BAND: Record first Janice Long session: 'Sacrilege'/ 'And The Dance Goes On'/'Severina'/'Like A Hurricane'.

January 20
THE SISTERHOOD (Eldritch): Release single 'Giving Ground'.

January 20
THE SISTERHOOD (Hussey, Adams) Live debut at Alice In Wonderland, London.

January 28
SIOUXSIE & THE BANSHEES: Record fifth John Peel session: 'Candy Man'/'Cannons'/ 'Lands End'.

February
DANSE SOCIETY: Release single 'Hold On'.
PLAY DEAD: Release compilation LP *In The Beginning: The 19 Singles*.
THE CULT, THE SISTERHOOD (Hussey/Adams). European tour.

February 1
IN TWO A CIRCLE: Single 'Rise' enters Independent Chart (peak #5).
THE SISTERHOOD: Single 'Giving Ground' enters Independent Chart (peak #1).

February 2
FIELDS OF THE NEPHILIM: Dingwalls, London.

February 3
SIOUXSIE & THE BANSHEES: Fifth John Peel session broadcast (Radio One).
WAYNE HUSSEY & CRAIG ADAMS BAND: First Janice Long session broadcast (Radio One).

February 15
THE CURE: Single 'In Between Days' enters US Chart (peak #).
X MAL DEUTSCHLAND: Single 'Incubus Succubus II' enters Independent Chart (peak #29).

February 19
THE CRAMPS: Session broadcast on John Peel Show (Radio One): 'What's Inside A Girl'/ 'Cornfed Dame'/'Give Me A Woman'.

February 23
THE CULT: Record second Janice Long session: 'Love Removal Machine'/'Conquistador'/'King Contrary Man'/'Electric Circus'.

February 27
THE SISTERHOOD become THE MISSION onstage at the Electric Ballroom, London.

March
SKELETAL FAMILY: Release single 'Restless'.
THE CULT: Launch North American tour in Ontario, Canada.

March 1
THE CRAMPS: LP *A Date With Elvis* enters Independent Chart (peak #1).
ROSE OF AVALANCHE: LP *First Avalanche* enters Independent Chart (peak #3).
THE CRAMPS: LP *A Date With Elvis* enters UK Chart (peak #34).

March 4
THE CULT: Second Janice Long session broadcast (Radio One).

March 5
THE ROSE OF AVALANCHE: Record first Janice Long session: 'Velveteen'/'A Srick In The Works'/ 'Too Many Castles'/'Never Another Sunset'.

March 8
SIOUXSIE & THE BANSHEES: Single 'Candyman' enters UK Chart (peak #34).

March 11
THE ROSE OF AVALANCHE: First Janice Long session broadcast (Radio One).

March 12
THE CRAMPS: Session broadcast on Janice Long show (Radio One): 'Hot Pearl Snatch'/'Hot Pool Of Woman Need'/'How Far Can Too Far Go'/'Oloa From Hell'.

March 15
RED LORRY YELLOW LORRY: LP *Paint Your Wagon* enters Independent Chart (peak #1).

March 29
GENE LOVES JEZEBEL: Single 'Sweetest Thing' enters UK Chart (peak #75).

April 6
GHOST DANCE: Record first Janice Long session: 'Last Train'/'Can The Can'/'Only The Broken Hearted'/'River Of No Return'.

April 13
GENE LOVES JEZEBEL: Launch North American tour in Washington DC.

April 16
GHOST DANCE: First Janice Long session broadcast (Radio One).

April 25
THE CURE: Royal Albert Hall, London (Greenpeace benefit).

April 26
SIOUXSIE & THE BANSHEES: LP *Tinderbox* enters UK Chart (peak #13).

May
THE CURE: Release LP *Standing On The Beach* (compilation)
PLAY DEAD: release single 'Burning Down'.
THE BATFISH BOYS: Release EP *Crocodile Tears*.

May 3
ALL ABOUT EVE: Single 'In The Clouds' enters Independent Chart (peak #31).
THE CURE: Single 'Boys Don't Cry ' enters UK Chart (peak #22).

May 10
GHOST DANCE: Single 'River Of No Return' enters Independent Chart (peak #16).
CHATSHOW: Single 'Red Skies' enters Independent Chart (peak #32).
ROSE OF AVALANCHE: Single 'Too Many Castles In The Sky' enters Independent Chart (peak #8).

May 16
THE CURE: Pink Pop Festival, Holland.

May 17
ALIEN SEX FIEND: Single 'I Walk The Line' enters Independent Chart (peak #12).
THE CRAMPS: Single 'What's Inside A Girl' enters Independent Chart (peak #2).

May 22
PETER MURPHY: Live debut opens Italian tour in Bologna.

May 24
LOVE & ROCKETS: UK live debut, University, Warwick.
RED LORRY YELLOW LORRY: Single 'Walking On Your Hands' enters Independent Chart (peak #21).
SIOUXSIE & THE BANSHEES: LP *Tinderbox* enters US Chart (peak #).
THE MISSION: Launch Expedition I UK tour at QMU, Glasgow.

May 25
LOVE & ROCKETS: London Marquee.

May 30
LOVE & ROCKETS: Open third North American tour in Santa Clara CA.

May 31
THE CURE: Compilation LP *Standing On A Beach* enters UK Chart (peak #4).
THE MISSION: Single 'Serpent's Kiss' enters Independent Chart (peak #2).

June
AND ALSO THE TREES: Release LP *Virus Meadow*.

June 2
LOVE & ROCKETS: Release single 'Kundalini Express'.

June 7
PETER MURPHY: Release LP *Should The World Fail To Fall Apart*.

June 14
SKELETAL FAMILY: Record third Janice Long session: 'Just A Minute'/'Now'/'[Big Love]'/'Put It On Brown'.
THE CRAMPS: Single 'Kismiax' enters Independent Chart (peak #15).
GENE LOVES JEZEBEL: Single 'Heartache' enters UK Chart (peak #71).
THE CURE: Compilation LP *Standing On A Beach* enters US Chart (peak #48).
THE MISSION: Single 'Serpent's Kiss' enters UK Chart (peak #70).

June 16
PETER MURPHY: Release single 'Blue Heart'.

June 21
THE CURE: Glastonbury Festival.

June 24
SKELETAL FAMILY: Third Janice Long session broadcast (Radio One).

June 28
THE CULT: Brixton Academy.

July
PLAY DEAD: Release compilation LP *The Singles*.
THE CURE: North American tour.

July 5
PETER MURPHY: UK live debut at Royal Court Theatre, Liverpool.

VIRGIN PRUNES: Single 'Love Lasts Forever' enters Independent Chart (peak #18).

July 6
THE CURE: Open North American tour at Great Woods Centre, Mansfield, MA.

July 7
THE MISSION: Sign with Phonogram.

July 12
CHRISTIAN DEATH: LP *Atrocities* enters Independent Chart (peak #17).
PLAY DEAD: Compilation LP *The Singles* – enters Independent Chart (peak #16).

July 19
VIRGIN PRUNES: LP *The Moon Looked Down And Laughed* enters Independent Chart (peak #5).

July 26
PETER MURPHY: LP *Should The World Fail To Fall Apart* enters UK Chart (peak #).
THE MISSION: Single 'Garden Of Delight' enters Independent Chart (peak #1).
THE MISSION: Single 'Garden Of Delight' enters UK Chart (peak #49).
THE SISTERHOOD: LP *Gift* enters Independent Chart (peak #2).

August
THE CURE: European festival tour.
ALIEN SEX FIEND: Release single 'Get Into It'.
DANSE SOCIETY INTERNATIONAL: Release LP *Looking Through*.
PLAY DEAD: Release live LP *Caught From Behind*.
SKELETAL FAMILY: Release single 'Just A Minute'.

August 2
GHOST DANCE: Single 'Heart Full Of Soul' enters Independent Chart (peak #4).

August 22
THE MISSION, MARCH VIOLETS: Reading Festival.

September
ROSE OF AVALANCHE: Release LP *Always There*.
X MAL DEUTSCHLAND: Release single 'Matador'.

September 8
LOVE & ROCKETS: Release single 'Yin & Yang'.

September 14
X-MAL DEUTSCHLAND: Record first Janice Long session: 'Ozean'/'If Only'/'Sicklemoon'/'Eisengrave'.

September 15
LOVE & ROCKETS: Release LP *Express*.

September 19
GENE LOVES JEZEBEL: Launch North American tour in Phoenix AZ.

September 24
THE MISSION: Record first Janice Long session: 'Wasteland'/'Shelter From The Storm'/'Tomorrow Never Knows'/'Wishing Well'.
X-MAL DEUTSCHLAND: First Janice Long session broadcast (Radio One).

September 27
LOVE & ROCKETS: First UK tour opens at Sheffield Leadmill.

October
GENE LOVES JEZEBEL: Release single 'Desire'.
SKELETAL FAMILY: Release compilation LP *Ghosts*.

October 6
THE MISSION: First Janice Long session broadcast (Radio One).

October 11
FIELDS OF THE NEPHILIM: Single 'Power' enters Independent Chart (peak #24).
ROSE OF AVALANCHE: Single 'Velveteen' enters Independent Chart (peak #9).

October 13
PETER MURPHY: Release single 'Tale Of The Tongue'.

October 16
PETER MURPHY: Opens UK tour at University, Brighton.

October 18
GHOST DANCE: Single 'Grip Of Love' enters Independent Chart (peak #19).
GENE LOVES JEZEBEL: LP *Discover* enters US Chart (peak #155).
LOVE & ROCKETS Open North American tour at Moore Theatre, Seattle.
THE MISSION: Single 'Stay With Me' enters UK Chart (peak #30).

October 28
THE MISSION: UK leg of World Crusade tour launched at Rock City, Nottingham.

November
BRIGANDAGE: Release LP *Pretty Little Thing*.
FLESH FOR LULU: Release single 'Idol'.
VIRGIN PRUNES: release single 'Don't Look Back'.

November 1
ALIEN SEX FIEND: Single 'Smells Like Shit' enters Independent Chart (peak #7).
LOVE AND ROCKETS: LP *Express* enters US Chart (peak #72).
RED LORRY YELLOW LORRY: Single 'Cut Down' enters Independent Chart (peak #6).

November 7
BIRTHDAY PARTY: Death of Tracy Pew.

November 8
PETER MURPHY: Plays secret gig at Flag, London, as Bela Lugosi Returns.
THE BATFISH BOYS: LP *Head* enters Independent Chart (peak #16).

November 22
ALIEN SEX FIEND: LP *It* enters Independent Chart (peak #7).
THE MISSION: LP *God's Own Medicine* enters UK Chart (peak #14).

December 3
THE BATFISH BOYS: Single 'Justine' enters Independent Chart (peak #16).

December 13
JOY DIVISION: EP *The Peel Session* enters Independent Chart (peak #4).

December 20
INTO A CIRCLE: Single 'Inside Out' enters Independent Chart (peak #12).

December 27
X MAL DEUTSCHLAND: EP *The Peel Session* enters Independent Chart (peak #29).

1987

January 11
SIOUXSIE & THE BANSHEES: Record first Janice Long session: 'Shooting Sun'/'Song From The Edge'/'Little Johnny Jewel'/'Something Blue'.

January 16
THE MISSION: UK TV debut *The Tube*: 'Wasteland'.

January 17
SIOUXSIE & THE BANSHEES: Single 'This Wheel's On Fire' enters UK Chart (peak #14).
THE MISSION: Single 'Wasteland' enters UK Chart (peak #11).

February
X MAL DEUTSCHLAND: Release single 'Sickle Moon'.

February 2
PETER MURPHY: Release single 'Should The World Fail To Fall Apart'.
SIOUXSIE & THE BANSHEES: First Janice Long session broadcast (Radio One).

February 10
PETER MURPHY: US live debut at Paradise, Boston.

February 12
ALIEN SEX FIEND: Single 'Hurricane Fighter Plane' enters Independent Chart (peak #12).

February 14
SIOUXSIE & THE BANSHEES: EP *The Peel Sessions* enters Independent Chart (peak #6).

February 21
BIRTHDAY PARTY: EP *The Peel Session* enters Independent Chart (peak #7).

February 28
THE CULT: Single 'Love Removal Machine' enters UK Chart (peak #18).

March
THE CURE: South American tour opens in Buenos Aires.
FLESH FOR LULU: Release single 'Siamese Twins'.
PLAY DEAD: Release live LP *The Final Epitaph*.
THE CULT: UK tour.
X MAL DEUTSCHLAND: release LP *Viva*.

March 7
THE MISSION: LP *God's Own Medicine* enters US Chart (peak #18).

March 8
LOVE & ROCKETS: Release single 'No New Tale To Tell'.

March 14
ROSE OF AVALANCHE: Single 'Always There' enters Independent Chart (peak #3).
SIOUXSIE & THE BANSHEES: LP *Through The Looking Glass* enters UK Chart (peak #15).
THE MISSION: Single 'Severina' enters UK Chart (peak #25).

March 18
THE MISSION: UK leg of World Crusade II tour launched at Sheffield City Hall.

March 19
THE MISSION: ALL ABOUT EVE (JULIANNE REGAN): UK TV *Top Of The Pops*: 'Severina'.

March 28
SIOUXSIE & THE BANSHEES: Single 'The Passenger' enters UK Chart (peak #41).

April 4
FIELDS OF THE NEPHILIM: Single 'Preacher Man" enters Independent Chart (peak #2)
THE BATFISH BOYS: Single 'Bomb Song' enters Independent Chart (peak #18).

April 10
THE CURE: Release single 'Why Can't I Be You'.

April 11
SIOUXSIE & THE BANSHEES: LP *Through The Looking Glass* enters US Chart (peak #1).
THE CULT: Launch North American tour in Philadelphia, supporting Billy Idol.

April 18
THE CULT: LP *Electric* enters UK Chart (peak #4).
THE CURE: Single 'Why Can't I Be You' enters UK Chart (peak #21).

April 23
THE CURE: Premier concert movie *The Cure In Orange*.

April 24
THE MISSION: The Ritz, New York City.

April 25
ALL ABOUT EVE: Single 'Our Summer' enters Independent Chart (peak #2).
THE CULT: LP *Electric* enters US Chart (peak #38).

May
AND ALSO THE TREES: Release compilation LP *A Retrospective 19-19*.
AND ALSO THE TREES: Release live LP *The Night Of The 24th*.
ROSE OF AVALANCHE: Release compilation LP *Rose Of Avalanche*.
VIRGIN PRUNES: release live LP *The Hidden Lie*.

May 2
THE CULT: Single 'L'il Devil' enters UK Chart (peak #11).

May 9
THE LORRIES (ex-RED LORRY YELLOW LORRY) Single 'Crawling Mantras' enters Independent Chart (peak #3).

May 15
THE MISSION: Los Angeles – Craig Adams quits during North American tour. Returns following tour.

May 22
THE CURE: Release LP *Kiss Me Kiss Me Kiss Me*.

May 23
FIELDS OF THE NEPHILIM: LP *Dawnrazor* enters Independent Chart (peak #1

May 30
FIELDS OF THE NEPHILIM: LP *Dawnrazor* enters UK Chart (peak #62).

June
THE CURE: Release single 'Breathe'.
AND ALSO THE TREES: Release single 'The Critical Distance'.
THE CULT: Launch headlining North American tour, supported by Guns n'Roses.

June 6
DEATH IN JUNE: Single 'To Drown A Rose' enters Independent Chart (peak #18).
THE CRAMPS: Live LP *Rockin'n'Reelin...* enters Independent Chart (peak #4).
THE CURE: LP *Kiss Me Kiss Me Kiss Me* enters UK Chart (peak #6).

June 20
THE CURE: LP *Kiss Me Kiss Me Kiss Me* enters US Chart (peak #35).
THE CURE: Single 'Why Can't I Be You' enters US Chart (peak #54).

June 27
ALIEN SEX FIEND: Single 'The Impossible Mission' enters Independent Chart (peak #11).

July
FLESH FOR LULU: Release single 'Postcards From Paradise'.

July 1
THE MISSION: Leeds Elland Road, supporting U2.

July 4
FIELDS OF THE NEPHILIM: EP *Burning The Fields* enters Independent Chart (peak #2)
THE CURE: Single 'Catch' enters UK Chart (peak #27).
THE MISSION: Compilation LP *The First Chapter* enters UK Chart (peak #35).

July 11
ALL ABOUT EVE: Single 'Flowers In Our Hair' enters Independent Chart (peak #1).

July 14-15
THE CURE: Headline two nights at Inglewood Forum, CA.

July 19
GENE LOVES JEZEBEL: LP *Discover* enters UK Chart (peak #32).

July 25
SALVATION: LP *Diamonds Are Forever* enters Independent Chart (peak #9).
SIOUXSIE & THE BANSHEES: Single 'Song From The Edge Of The World' enters UK Chart (peak #59).

August
(DANCE) SOCIETY: Release single 'Saturn Girl'.

August 1
THE MISSION: Edinburgh, supporting U2.

August 5
ALL ABOUT EVE: Record first Janice Long session: 'Every Angel'/'Wild Hearted Woman'/'In The Meadow'/'Martha's Harbour'.

August 10
GENE LOVES JEZEBEL: Launch North American tour in Minneapolis.

August 11
THE CULT: Single 'Wild Flower' enters UK Chart (peak #24).

271

August 15
GHOST DANCE: EP *A Word To The Wise* enters Independent Chart (peak #4).

August 26
ALL ABOUT EVE: First Janice Long session broadcast (Radio One).

September
THE CURE: Release single 'Just Like Heaven'.

September 5
GENE LOVES JEZEBEL: Single 'The Motion Of Love' enters UK Chart (peak #56).

September 9
LOVE & ROCKETS: Release LP *Earth Sun Moon*.

September 12
INTO A CIRCLE: Single 'Forever' enters Independent Chart (peak #8).

September 26
ALIEN SEX FIEND: Single 'Here Cum Germs' enters Independent Chart (peak #14).
DEATH IN JUNE: LP *Oh, How We Laughed* enters Independent Chart (peak #26).

October 3
SISTERS OF MERCY: 'This Corrosion' enters UK Chart (peak #7).

October 6
LOVE & ROCKETS: Release single 'The Light'.

October 7
LOVE & ROCKETS: Open UK tour.

October 10
ALIEN SEX FIEND: LP *Here Cum Germs* enters Independent Chart (peak #22).
DEATH IN JUNE: *Brown Book* enters Independent Chart (peak #24).
CHRISTIAN DEATH: Single box set enters Independent Chart (peak #49).
THE CURE: Single 'Just Like Heaven' enters US Chart (peak #40).

October 14
GHOST DANCE: Record second Janice Long session: 'Born To Be Your Slave'/'I Will Wait'/'Dr Love'/'If Only You Were Here Now'.

October 17
FIELDS OF THE NEPHILIM: Single 'Blue Water' enters Independent Chart (peak #1).
THE CURE: Single 'Just Like Heaven' enters UK Chart (peak #29).

October 22
THE CURE: Open European tour in Oslo. Roger O'Donnell makes live debut with band.

October 24
FIELDS OF THE NEPHILIM: LP *Return To Gehenna* enters Independent Chart (peak #15).
FIELDS OF THE NEPHILIM: Single 'Blue Water' enters UK Chart (peak #75).
GENE LOVES JEZEBEL: LP *House Of Dolls* enters UK Chart (peak #).
JOY DIVISION: EP *The Peel Session* enters Independent Chart (peak #3).

October 28
GHOST DANCE: Second Janice Long session broadcast (Radio One).

October 31
ALL ABOUT EVE: Single 'In The Clouds' enters UK Chart (peak #47).
LOVE AND ROCKETS: LP *Earth Sun Moon* enters US Chart (peak #64).

November
AND ALSO THE TREES: Release single 'Shaletown'.

November 7
LOVE & ROCKETS: Open North American tour at Stoney Brook, Long Island.

November 12
THE CURE: Release video *The Cure In Orange*.

November 14
GENE LOVES JEZEBEL: LP *House Of Dolls* enters US Chart (peak #18).

November 21
FIELDS OF THE NEPHILIM: Complete UK tour at the Astoria, London.

November 28
RED LORRY YELLOW LORRY: Single 'Open Up' enters Independent Chart (peak #6).
SISTERS OF MERCY: LP *Floodland* enters UK Chart (peak #9).

December 5
GENE LOVES JEZEBEL: Single 'Gorgeous' enters UK Chart (peak #68).

December 7-9
THE CURE: Wembley Arena.

December 12
ALIEN SEX FIEND: Single 'Stuff The Turkey' enters Independent Chart (peak #14).
FLESH FOR LULU: LP *Long Live The New Flesh* enters US Chart (peak #).

1988

January
GENE LOVES JEZEBEL: Unreleased single 'Every Door'.
THE BATFISH BOYS: Release single 'Purple Dust'.
TONES ON TAIL: Release *Night Music* compilation.
VIRGIN PRUNES: Release LP *Heresie*.

January 23
ALL ABOUT EVE: Single 'Wild Hearted Woman' enters UK Chart (peak #33).
GENE LOVES JEZEBEL, FLESH FOR LULU: Launch North American tour in Washington DC.

February
THE MISSION: Launch North American tour.

February 6
GENE LOVES JEZEBEL: Single 'The Motion Of Love' enters US Chart (peak #).
RED LORRY YELLOW LORRY: Compilation LP *Smashed Hits Album* enters Independent Chart (peak #10).
SISTERS OF MERCY: LP *Floodland* enters US Chart (peak #11).

February 13
THE MISSION: Single 'Tower Of Strength' enters UK Chart (peak #12).

February 15
PETER MURPHY: Releases single 'All Night Long'.

February 20
THE CURE: Single 'Hot Hot Hot!!!' enters UK Chart (peak #45).

February 23
FIELDS OF THE NEPHILIM: Cat Club, New York City, supported by White Zombie.

February 27
ALL ABOUT EVE: LP *All About Eve* enters UK Chart (peak #7).
SISTERS OF MERCY: 'Dominion' enters UK Chart (peak #13).

March
ALIEN SEX FIEND: Release compilation LP *All Our Yesterdaze*.
THE MISSION, ALL ABOUT EVE, GHOST DANCE: One week residency at Astoria, London.
THE MISSION, RED LORRY YELLOW LORRY: Launch UK tour.

March 5
THE CURE: Single 'Hot Hot Hot!!!' enters US Chart (peak #65).

March 12
GHOST DANCE: Compilation LP *Gathering Dust* enters Independent Chart (peak #10).
THE MISSION: LP *Children* enters UK Chart (peak #2).

March 21
PETER MURPHY: Release LP *Love Hysteria*.

March 22
PETER MURPHY: Opens three night residency at La Locomotive, Paris.

March 27
PETER MURPHY: Sadlers Wells Theatre, London.

April
GENE LOVES JEZEBEL: US single 'Suspicion'.

April 2
INTO A CIRCLE: Single 'Evergreen' enters Independent Chart (peak #5).

April 5
THE MISSION: Launch European tour in Bourgen, France. US and Sth American gigs follow.

April 9
ALL ABOUT EVE: Single 'Every Angel' enters UK Chart (peak #30).
RED LORRY YELLOW LORRY: Single 'Nothing Wrong' enters Independent Chart (peak #5).

April 13
RED LORRY YELLOW LORRY: Record first Liz Kershaw radio session: 'Big Stick'/'Hands Off Me'/'The Rise'/'Chance'.

April 14
LOVE & ROCKETS: Open North American tour at Warner Theatre, Washington DC.

April 18
PETER MURPHY: Release single 'Indigo Eyes'.

April 19
RED LORRY YELLOW LORRY: First Liz Kershaw session broadcast (Radio One).

April 21
PETER MURPHY: Opens North American tour at Paradise, Boston.

April 23
THE MISSION: Single 'Beyond The Pale' enters UK Chart (peak #32).

April 30
THE MISSION: LP *Children* enters US Chart (peak #126).

May
AND ALSO THE TREES: release LP *The Millpond Years*.
AND ALSO THE TREES: Release single 'The House Of The Heart'.
SEX GANG CHILDREN: Release live LP *Nightland USA 19*.

May 7
ROSE OF AVALANCHE: LP *In Rock* enters Independent Chart (peak #10).

May 11
BRIGANDAGE: Release compilation LP *Brigandage*.

May 14
PETER MURPHY: LP *Love Hysteria* enters US Chart (peak #135).

May 21
THE CURE: EP *The Peel Session* enters Independent Chart (peak #7).

May 25
PETER MURPHY: Town & Country Club, London.

May 28
RED LORRY YELLOW LORRY: LP *Nothing Wrong* enters Independent Chart (peak #3).

May 30
LOVE & ROCKETS: Release single 'Mirror People'.

June 4
FIELDS OF THE NEPHILIM: Single 'Moonchild' enters Independent Chart (peak #1).
FIELDS OF THE NEPHILIM: Single 'Moonchild' enters UK Chart (peak #28).

June 6
LOVE & ROCKETS: Release Bubblemen single 'The Bubblemen Are Coming'.

June 7
PETER MURPHY: Opens Japanese tour at Fukoka, Osaka.

June 11
INTO A CIRCLE: LP *Assassins* enters Independent Chart (peak #7).

June 18
JOY DIVISION: Reissued single 'Atmosphere' enters Independent Chart (peak #2).
JOY DIVISION: Reissued single 'Atmosphere' enters UK Chart (peak #34).
SISTERS OF MERCY: Single 'Lucretia My Reflection' enters UK Chart (peak #20).

June 19
LOVE & ROCKETS: Dominion Theatre, London.

June 26
LOVE & ROCKETS: European tour opens at Sardines, Oslo.

July 2
CHRISTIAN DEATH: Single 'Church Of No Return' enters Independent Chart (peak #6).

July 23
JOY DIVISION: Compilation LP *Substance 17-* enters Independent Chart (peak #1).
JOY DIVISION: Compilation LP *Substance 17-* enters UK Chart (peak #7).

July 30
ALL ABOUT EVE: Single 'Martha's Harbour' enters UK Chart (peak #10).
SIOUXSIE & THE BANSHEES: Single 'Peek-A-Boo' enters UK Chart (peak #16).

August
FIELDS OF THE NEPHILIM: Release compilation LP *Return To Gehenna*.

August 12
PETER MURPHY: Opens North American tour at California Theatre, San Diego.

August 15
LOVE & ROCKETS: Release single 'Lazy'.

August 20
SALVATION: Single 'Sunshine Superman' enters Independent Chart (peak #12).

September 17
FIELDS OF THE NEPHILIM: LP *The Nephilim* enters Independent Chart (peak #2).
FIELDS OF THE NEPHILIM: LP *The Nephilim* enters UK Chart (peak #14).
SIOUXSIE & THE BANSHEES: LP *Peep Show* enters UK Chart (peak #20).

September 21
THE MISSION: Record first Liz Kershaw session: 'In The Grip Of Disease'/'Belief'/ 'Deliverance'/'Kingdom Come'.

September 28
THE MISSION: First Liz Kershaw session broadcast (Radio One).

October
ALIEN SEX FIEND: Release LP *Another Planet*.
ALIEN SEX FIEND: Release single: 'Bun Ho!'.
FLESH FOR LULU: Release single 'I Go Crazy'.

October 1
RED LORRY YELLOW LORRY: Single 'Only Dreaming' enters Independent Chart (peak #9).
SIOUXSIE & THE BANSHEES: LP *Peepshow* enters US Chart (peak #68).

October 8
SIOUXSIE & THE BANSHEES: Single 'Killing Jar' enters UK Chart (peak #41).

October 15
SIOUXSIE & THE BANSHEES: Single 'Peek A Boo' enters US Chart (peak #53).

November
ROSE OF AVALANCHE: release live LP *Live At The Town & Country*.
THE MISSION: Release single 'Kingdom Come'.

November 5
BIRTHDAY PARTY: EP *The Peel Session Vol 2* enters Independent Chart (peak #11).

November 12
ALL ABOUT EVE: Single 'What Kind Of Fool' enters UK Chart (peak #29).

November 19
CHRISTIAN DEATH: Single 'What's The Verdict' enters Independent Chart (peak #11).

November 22
DAWN AFTER DARK: Single 'The Groove' enters Independent Chart (peak #17).

November 25
THE MISSION: Launch UK stadium tour.

December 3
SIOUXSIE & THE BANSHEES: Single 'The Last Beat Of My Heart' enters UK Chart (peak #44).

December 24
CHRISTIAN DEATH: LP *Sex & Drugs & Jesus Christ* enters Independent Chart (peak #10).
ROSE OF AVALANCHE: Single 'The World Is Ours' enters Independent Chart (peak #8).

1989

January 3
LOVE & ROCKETS: Release single 'Motorcycle'.

February
SIOUXSIE & THE BANSHEES: EP *The Peel Sessions Volume 2*.
THE CULT: Launch North American tour supporting Metallica.
THE CURE: Lol Tolhurst departs.
X MAL DEUTSCHLAND: release LP *Devils*.

March
ALIEN SEX FIEND: Release single 'Haunted House'.

March 4
ROSE OF AVALANCHE: Single 'Never Another Sunset' enters Independent Chart (peak #19).

April
AND ALSO THE TREES: Release single 'Lady D'Arbanville'.

April 1
ROSE OF AVALANCHE: LP *Never Another Sunset* enters Independent Chart (peak #10).
THE CULT: Single 'Fire Woman' enters UK Chart (peak #15).

April 22
THE CULT: LP *Sonic Temple* enters UK Chart (peak #3).
THE CULT: LP *Sonic Temple* enters US Chart (peak #10).
THE CURE: Single 'Lullaby' enters UK Chart (peak #5).

April 29
THE MISSION: Benefit for Hillsborough disaster.

April 30
THE MISSION: Benefit for Lockerbie air disaster.

May
THE CURE, THE MISSION: European festival tour (three dates).

May 5
FIELDS OF THE NEPHILIM: London Marquee – secret gig launching UK tour.

May 13
THE CURE: LP *Disintegration* enters UK Chart (peak #3).
THE CURE: Single 'Fascination Street' enters US Chart (peak #46).

May 20
LOVE & ROCKETS: Single 'So Alive' enters US Chart (peak #3).
LOVE AND ROCKETS: LP *Love And Rockets* enters US Chart (peak #14).
SALVATION: Single 'All And More' enters Independent Chart (peak #18).
THE CURE: LP *Disintegration* enters US Chart (peak #12).

May 27
FIELDS OF THE NEPHILIM: Single 'Psychonaut' enters Independent Chart (peak #2).
FIELDS OF THE NEPHILIM: Single 'Psychonaut' enters UK Chart (peak #35).
THE CULT: Single 'Fire Woman' enters US Chart (peak #46).

June 17
GHOST DANCE: Single 'Down To The Wire' enters UK Chart (peak #66).

June 22
LOVE & ROCKETS: Open North American tour at Tupperware Auditorium, Kissimmee.

July 8
THE CULT: Single 'Edie (Ciao Baby)' enters UK Chart (peak #32).

July 10
BAUHAUS: Release *Swing The Heartache* (BBC anthology).

July 31
LOVE & ROCKETS: UK release single 'So Alive'.

August
THE CURE: Launch North American tour at Giants Stadium, NJ

August 12
THE CURE: Single 'Love Song' enters US Chart (peak #2).

August 29
JAMES RAY GANGWAR: Live debut at Camden Palace, London.

September
ALIEN SEX FIEND: Release live LP *Too Much Acid?*.
GHOST DANCE: release LP *Stop The World*.
GHOST DANCE: Release single 'Celebrate'.
LOVE & ROCKETS: Release LP *Love & Rockets*.
THE BATFISH BOYS: Release LP *The Batfish Brew*.

September 2
RED LORRY YELLOW LORRY: Single 'Temptation' enters Independent Chart (peak #13).
THE CURE: Single 'Love Song' enters UK Chart (peak #18).

September 6
THE CULT, THE CURE: MTV Music Awards.

September 23
LOVE & ROCKETS: Single 'No Big Deal' enters US Chart (peak #).

September 30
ALL ABOUT EVE: Single 'Road To Your Soul' enters UK Chart (peak #37).
THE CULT: Single 'Edie (Ciao Baby)' enters US Chart (peak #).

October
AND ALSO THE TREES: Release LP *Farewell To The Shade*.
JAMES RAY GANGWAR, GHOST DANCE: Two shows in London, Leeds.
LOVE & ROCKETS: Release *The Haunted Fishtank* video compilation.

October 7
RED LORRY YELLOW LORRY: LP *Blow* enters Independent Chart (peak #6).

October 14
THE CREATURES: Single 'Standing There' enters UK Chart (peak #53).

October 23
LOVE & ROCKETS: UK release single 'No Big Deal'.

October 28
ALL ABOUT EVE: LP *Scarlet & Other Stories* enters UK Chart (peak #9).

November
THE CREATURES: LP *Boomerang*.

November 18
THE CULT: Single 'Sun King' enters UK Chart (peak #39).

December
THE BATFISH BOYS: Release single 'Another One Bites The Dust'.
THE CULT: Launch headlining North American tour.

December 2
THE CURE: Single 'Lullaby' enters US Chart (peak #74).

December 16
ALL ABOUT EVE: Single 'December' enters UK Chart (peak #34).

1990

January
FLESH FOR LULU: Release single 'Time And Space'.

January 9
THE CULT: Launch North American tour in Tempe, AZ.

January 13
THE MISSION: Single 'Butterfly On A Wheel' enters UK Chart (peak #12).

January 22
JAMES RAY GANGWAR: Fulham Greyhound show filmed.

January 31
PETER MURPHY: Opens Asian tour in Tel Aviv.

February
THE CURE: 'Lullabye' video awarded Best Video at BPI awards.
FLESH FOR LULU: Release LP *Plastic Fantastic*.
THE CREATURES: Single 'Fury Eyes'.
THE MISSION: Video *Waves Upon The Sand* released.

275

February 3
PETER MURPHY: LP *Deep* enters US Chart (peak #44).

February 10
THE MISSION: UK radio *Saturday Sequence*: 'Butterfly On A Wheel'/'Bird Of Passage'.
THE CRAMPS: Single 'Bikini Girls With Machine Guns' enters UK Chart (peak #35).

February 17
THE MISSION: LP *Carved In Sand* enters UK Chart (peak #7).

February 18
THE CURE: Win Best Video ('Lullaby') at BRITS.

February 24
THE CRAMPS: LP *Stay Sick!* enters UK Chart (peak #62).

March 1
THE MISSION: Launch Deliverance UK tour.

March 6
PETER MURPHY: Opens North American tour at Mesa Amphitheatre, Phoenix.

March 10
THE CULT: Single 'Sweet Soul Sister' enters UK Chart (peak #42).
THE MISSION: Single 'Deliverance' enters UK Chart (peak #27).

March 17
THE MISSION: LP *Carved In Sand* enters US Chart (peak #11).

March 24
PETER MURPHY: Single 'Cuts You Up' enters US Chart; peaks at #55.
PETER MURPHY: Single 'Cuts You Up' enters US Chart (peak #55)

March 31
THE CURE: Single 'Pictures Of You' enters UK Chart (peak #24).

April
PETER MURPHY: Single 'Cuts You Up' enters US Modern Rock chart; peaks at #1.

April 17
PETER MURPHY: UK release single 'Cuts You Up'.

April 20
THE MISSION: Launch North American tour in Montreal.

April 21
THE CURE: Single 'Pictures Of You' enters US Chart (peak #71).
THE MISSION: Simon Hinkler quits band.

April 28
ALL ABOUT EVE: Single 'Scarlet' enters UK Chart (peak #34).

May 7
DAVID J: Releases single 'I'll Be Your Chauffeur'.

May 14
PETER MURPHY: Releases LP *Deep*.

May 17
PETER MURPHY: Town & Country Club, London.

June 2
THE MISSION: Single 'Into The Blue' enters UK Chart (peak #32).

June 18
DAVID J: Releases LP *Songs From Another Season*.

June 24
THE CURE: Glastonbury Festival.

July 5
PETER MURPHY: Opens North American tour in Indianapolis.

August
AND ALSO THE TREES: Release compilation *12-inch Box Set*.

August 4
FIELDS OF THE NEPHILIM: Single 'For Her Light' enters UK Chart (peak #54).

August 18
GENE LOVES JEZEBEL: LP *Kiss Of Life* enters US Chart (peak #123).
GENE LOVES JEZEBEL: Single 'Jealous' enters US Chart (peak #68).

August 23
GENE LOVES JEZEBEL: Launch North American tour supporting Billy Idol.

August 23
THE MISSION: Launch Mexican tour. Asia follows.

September
ALIEN SEX FIEND: Release single 'Now I'm Feeling Zombiefied'.
JOY DIVISION: release LP *Complete Peel Sessions*.

September 1
THE CURE: Make four hour pirate radio broadcast to London.

September 4
DAVID J: First US solo tour opens in Los Angeles.

September 22
PETER MURPHY: Opens European tour in Lisbon.

September 29
THE CURE: Single 'Never Enough' enters UK Chart (peak #13).

October
ALIEN SEX FIEND: Release LP *Curse*.
ROSE OF AVALANCHE: Release LP *String'a'Beads*.

October 6
FIELDS OF THE NEPHILIM: LP *Elizium* enters UK Chart (peak #22).

October 6-7
THE CULT: Gathering Of The Tribes festivals.

October 13
SISTERS OF MERCY: Single 'More' enters UK Chart (peak #14).

October 20
SISTERS OF MERCY: Launch Irish tour in Drogheda.

November
GENE LOVES JEZEBEL: Launch North American club tour.

November 2
SISTERS OF MERCY: LP *Vision Thing* enters
UK Chart (peak #11).
THE MISSION: LP *Grains Of Sand* enters UK
Chart (peak #28).

November 3
THE CURE: Single 'Close To Me (Remix)' enters
UK Chart (peak #13).
THE CURE: Single 'Never Enough' enters US
Chart (peak #72).

November 8
SISTERS OF MERCY: Launch tour of Yugoslavia.

November 17
THE CURE: LP *Mixed Up* enters UK Chart
(peak #8).
THE CURE: LP *Mixed Up* enters US Chart
(peak #14).
THE MISSION: Single 'Hands Across The
Ocean' enters UK Chart (peak #28).

November 24
FIELDS OF THE NEPHILIM: Single 'Sumerland
(Dreamed)' enters UK Chart (peak #37).

November 24,26
SISTERS OF MERCY: Wembley Arena.

November 26
THE MISSION: As METAL GURUS, release
'Merry Xmas Everybody'.

December
GENE LOVES JEZEBEL: Release single
'Tangled Up In You'.

December 1
SISTERS OF MERCY: LP *Vision Thing* enters
US Chart (peak #136).

December 22
SISTERS OF MERCY: Single 'Dr Jeep' enters
UK Chart (peak #37).

1991

January 19
THE CURE: Great British Music Weekend, Wembley.
THE CURE: Single 'Close To me (Remix)' enters
US Chart (peak #).

February
ALL ABOUT EVE: Release live LP *Thirteen*.

February 10
THE CURE: Perform at the BRITS.

February 11
DANIEL ASH: Release LP *Coming Down*.

February 16-17
SISTERS OF MERCY: Fan club shows in Leeds.

February 26
SISTERS OF MERCY: Launch European tour.

March 9
DANIEL ASH: LP *Coming Down* enters US
Chart (peak #19).

March 25
SISTERS OF MERCY: Launch North American
tour at Waterloo University, Canada.

April
GENE LOVES JEZEBEL: Launch North
American tour.

April 6
FIELDS OF THE NEPHILIM: Live LP *Earth
Inferno* enters UK Chart (peak #39).
THE CURE: Live LP *Entreat* enters UK Chart
(peak #10).

April 28
GENE LOVES JEZEBEL: SISTERS OF MERCY:
Irvine, CA.

April 28-30
FIELDS OF THE NEPHILIM: Farewell concerts
at the Town & Country Club, London.

April 30
SISTERS OF MERCY: Launch European tour in
Wrocklaw, Poland.

May 25
SIOUXSIE & THE BANSHEES: Single 'Kiss
Them For Me' enters UK Chart (peak #32).

June 1
THE MISSION: London Finsbury Park.

June 15
ALL ABOUT EVE: Single 'Farewell Mr Sorrow'
enters UK Chart (peak #36).

June 22
SIOUXSIE & THE BANSHEES: LP *Superstition*
enters UK Chart (peak #25).

June 25
DANIEL ASH: Release single 'Walk This Way'.

June 29
SIOUXSIE & THE BANSHEES: LP *Superstition*
enters US Chart (peak #65).

July 13
SIOUXSIE & THE BANSHEES: Single
'Shadowtime' enters UK Chart (peak #57).

August
AND ALSO THE TREES: Release single 'The
Pear Tree'.

August 10
ALL ABOUT EVE: Single 'Strange Way' enters
UK Chart (peak #50).

August 17
SIOUXSIE & THE BANSHEES: Single 'Kiss
Them For Me' enters US Chart (peak #23).

August 19
THE CURE: Release *Assemblage* box set.

September
FLESH FOR LULU: Release live video *Live
From London*.

September 7
ALL ABOUT EVE: LP *Touched By Jesus* enters
UK Chart (peak #17).

September 14
THE CULT: Single 'Wild Hearted Son' enters
UK Chart (peak #40).

October 5
THE CULT: LP *Ceremony* enters UK Chart (peak
#9).

October 12
THE CULT: LP *Ceremony* enters US Chart (peak
#25).

October 19
ALL ABOUT EVE: Single 'The Dreamer' enters UK Chart (peak #41).

November
ROSE OF AVALANCHE: Release LP *ICE*.

November 22
THE CULT: UK tour opens at Birmingham NEC.

December
SEX GANG CHILDREN: Release compilation LP *The Hungry Years*.

December 5
THE CURE: US TV Pay Per View concert.

December 30
THE CULT: Launch North American tour in Hamilton, ONT.

December 31
THE CULT: Maple Leaf Gardens, Toronto.

1992

February 5
SISTERS OF MERCY: Vanburgh College, York.

February 29
THE CULT: Kick Out The Jams festival, Detroit MI.

March
ALIEN SEX FIEND: Release LP *Open Head Surgery*.

March 28
THE CURE: Single 'High' enters UK Chart (peak #8).

April 4
THE CURE: Single 'High' enters US Chart (peak #42).

April 10
THE CURE: Launch series of 10 Cure Party Nights at Portsmouth Pier.

April 11
THE CURE: Single 'High (Remix)' enters UK Chart (peak #44).

April 21
PETER MURPHY: Releases LP *Holy Smoke*.

April 22
PETER MURPHY: US TV *Dennis Miller Show*: 'The Sweetest Drop'/'Cuts You Up'.

April 25
THE MISSION: Single 'Never Again' enters UK Chart (peak #34).

May 2
PETER MURPHY: LP *Holy Smoke* enters US Chart (peak #18).
SISTERS OF MERCY: Single 'Temple Of Love ' enters UK Chart (peak #3).
THE CURE: LP *Wish* enters UK Chart (peak #1).

May 7
THEATRE OF HATE, SEX GANG CHILDREN, THE CULT: Death of Nigel Preston.

May 9
SISTERS OF MERCY: Compilation LP *Some Girls Wander By Mistake* enters UK Chart (peak #5).
THE CURE: LP *Wish* enters US Chart (peak #2).

May 14
THE CURE: Launch North American tour (first in three years) at Civic Centre, Providence.
THE CURE: Launch North American tour in Providence.

May 23
THE CURE: Single 'Friday I'm In Love' enters UK Chart (peak #6).

June
AND ALSO THE TREES: Release LP *Green Is The Sea*.
FIELDS OF THE NEPHILIM: Release live LP *BBC Radio 1 In Concert*.
PLAY DEAD: Release compilation LP *Resurrection*.

June 5
PETER MURPHY: Opens North American tour at Riviera, Chicago.

June 6
THE CULT: Cult In The Park festival, Finsbury Park, London.

June 13
THE CURE: Single 'Friday I'm In Love' enters US Chart (peak #18)

June 20
THE MISSION: Single 'Like A Child Again' enters UK Chart (peak #30).

July
ANDI SEX GANG/SEX GANG CHILDREN: Release LP *Blind*.

July 4
THE MISSION: LP *Masque* enters UK Chart (peak #23).

July 15
PETER MURPHY: Single 'Hit Song'.

July 25
SIOUXSIE & THE BANSHEES: Single 'Face To Face' enters UK Chart (peak #21).

August
BAUHAUS: Release live LP *Rest In Peace* (final show)
RUBICON: Release single 'Watch Without Pain'.

August 17-19
THE CURE: Sydney Entertainment Centre, Sydney, Australia.

September
DAVID J: US only release LP *Urban Urbane*.
RED LORRY YELLOW LORRY: Release LP *Blasting Off*.

September 1
BIRTHDAY PARTY: Partial reunion during Nick Cave & The Bad Seeds' show at the Town & Country, London.

September 9
THE CURE: 'Friday I'm In Love' wins Best International Video at MTV Awards.

September 21
THE CURE: Launch European tour.

October
BIRTHDAY PARTY: Release compilation LP *Hits*.
RUBICON: Release LP *What Starts, Ends*.
RUBICON: Release single 'Crazed'.

October 10
ALL ABOUT EVE: EP *Phased* enters UK Chart (peak #38).

October 17
SIOUXSIE & THE BANSHEES: Compilation LP *Twice Upon A Time* enters UK Chart (peak #26).
THE CURE: Single 'A Letter To Elise' enters UK Chart (peak #28).
THE MISSION: Single 'Shades Of Green' enters UK Chart (peak #49).

November
ALL ABOUT EVE: Release compilation LP *Winter Words*.
THE MISSION: Craig Adams quits band.

November 7
ALL ABOUT EVE: LP *Ultraviolet* enters UK Chart (peak #46).

November 16
DAVID J: Opens North American tour in Atlanta.

November 18
THE CURE: Launch UK tour.

November 28
ALL ABOUT EVE: Single 'Some Finer Day' enters UK Chart (peak #57).

1993

January 30
THE CULT: Single '(She Sells) Sanctuary (Remix)' enters UK Chart (peak #15).

February
ALIEN SEX FIEND: Release LP *Altered States Of America*.

February 13
THE CULT: compilation LP *Pure Cult* enters UK Chart (peak #1).

February 22
DANIEL ASH: Solo live debut at Mercury Café, Denver opens North American tour.

March
RUBICON: Release single 'Before My Eyes'.

March 22
DANIEL ASH: Release single 'Get Out Of Control'.

April
GENE LOVES JEZEBEL: Launch North American tour.

April 26
DANIEL ASH: release LP *Foolish Thing Desire*.

May
GENE LOVES JEZEBEL: Release single 'Jospehina'.
THE CULT: Craig Adams confirmed as member.
SEX GANG CHILDREN: Release LP *Medea*.

May 6
DANIEL ASH: UK solo debut at Underworld, London.

May 29-30
THE CULT: Milton Keynes National Bowl, supporting Guns n'Roses.

June
AND ALSO THE TREES: Release compilation LP *From Horizon To Horizon 19-19*.
GENE LOVES JEZEBEL: Release LP *Heavenly Bodies*.

June 13
THE CURE: XFM Radio Festival, Finsbury Park.

July
FIELDS OF THE NEPHILIM: release compilation LP *Revelations*.
THE MISSION: Live BBC LP *No Snow No Show For The Eskimo*.
SEX GANG CHILDREN: Release compilation LP *Dieche*.
PLAY DEAD: Release compilation LP *The First Flower*.

August 21
THE MISSION, ANDREW ELDRITCH, RED LORRY YELLOW LORRY: 'Off The Street' benefit at Leeds Town & Country Club

August 28
SISTERS OF MERCY: Single 'Under The Gun' enters UK Chart (peak #19).

September
MARCH VIOLETS: Release compilation LP *The Botanic Verses*.

September 4
SISTERS OF MERCY: Compilation LP *A Slight Case Of Over-bombing* enters UK Chart (peak #14).

September 7
THE MISSION: Launch Club Mission tour of Europe.

September 25
THE CURE: Live LP *Show* enters UK Chart (peak #29).

October
ALIEN SEX FIEND: Release live LP *The Legendary Batcave Tapes*.

October 4-9
THE MISSION: Tour ends with six consecutive shows around London clubs.

October 9
THE CURE: Live LP *Show* enters US Chart (peak #42).

October 25
ALL ABOUT EVE: Release live LP *BBC Radio 1 In Concert*.

November 6
THE CURE: Live LP *Paris* enters UK Chart (peak #56).

November 13
THE CURE: Live LP *Paris* enters US Chart (peak #118).

December
AND ALSO THE TREES: Release LP *The Klaxon*.
MICHAEL ASTON/EDITH GROVE: Release LP *Edith Grove*.

1994

January 8
THE MISSION: Single 'Tower Of Strength (Remix)' enters UK Chart (peak #33.

February
RED LORRY YELLOW LORRY: Release compilation LP *The Singles 19*.
THE MISSION: Compilation LP *Sum & Substance* enters UK Chart (peak #49).

February 15
THE CULT: Launch North American tour in Seattle WA.

March
SKELETAL FAMILY: Release compilation *The Singles Plus 19*.

March 26
THE MISSION: Single 'Afterglow' enters UK Chart (peak #53).

April 11
THE CURE: MTV Unplugged.

May
THE MISSION: European tour.

June
RED LORRY YELLOW LORRY: Release US compilation LP *Generation: The Best Of*.

June 26
THE MISSION: Release compilation LP *Salad Daze* (BBC sessions).

June 27
LOVE & ROCKETS: Release single 'This Heaven'.

July
ALIEN SEX FIEND: Release single 'Inferno'.

August
ALIEN SEX FIEND: Release US compilation LP *Drive My Rocket*.

August 20
SIOUXSIE & THE BANSHEES: Single 'Interlude' enters UK Chart (peak #25).

September 5
LOVE & ROCKETS: Release single 'Body And Soul'.

September 26
LOVE & ROCKETS: Release LP *Hot Trip To Heaven*.

October
ALIEN SEX FIEND: Release LP *Inferno*.
THE MISSION: Release single 'Raising Cain'.

October 8
THE CULT: Single 'Coming Down' enters UK Chart (peak #50).

October 29
THE CULT: LP *The Cult* enters US Chart (peak #69).

1995

January 7
SIOUXSIE & THE BANSHEES: Single 'Oh Baby' enters UK Chart (peak #34).
THE CULT: Single 'Star' enters UK Chart (peak #65).

January 22
THE CULT: Big Day Out, Melbourne, Australia.

February
THE MISSION: UK tour.

February 4
THE MISSION: Single 'Swoon' enters UK Chart (peak #73).

February 18
SIOUXSIE & THE BANSHEES: Single 'Stargazer' enters UK Chart (peak #64).

February 25
THE MISSION: LP *Neverland* enters UK Chart (peak #58) as band launches UK tour in Norwich.

March 4
SIOUXSIE & THE BANSHEES: LP *The Rapture* enters US Chart (peak #127).

April
RUBICON: Release LP *Room 11*.
RUBICON: Release single 'Insatiable'.
THE MISSION: European tour.

April 3
PETER MURPHY: Release single 'The Scarlet Thing In You'.

April 10
PETER MURPHY: Release LP *Cascade*.

April 11
LOVE & ROCKETS: Fire at studio delays completion of new LP.

May
ANDI SEX GANG: Release LP *Western Songs For Children*.

June
ALIEN SEX FIEND: Release US compilation LP *I'm Her Frankenstein*.

June
JOY DIVISION: Release compilation LP *Permanent*.

June 17
JOY DIVISION: Single 'Love Will Tear Us Apart (Remix)' enters UK Chart (peak #19).

June 25
THE CURE: Glastonbury festival.

July 7
PETER MURPHY: North American tour opens at Roseland Theatre, Portland.

July 19
THE MISSION: Wayne Hussey and Mark Thwaite launch acoustic tour of South Africa.

September
GENE LOVES JEZEBEL: Release US compilation LP *From The Mouths Of Babes*.

September 12
MICHAEL ASTON: Release LP *Why Me, Why Now, Why This*.

September 20
PETER MURPHY: Opens Iberian tour in Lisbon.

October
ALIEN SEX FIEND: Release compilation *The Singles 19-19*.

November
GENE LOVES JEZEBEL: Release live LP *In The Afterglow*.

1996

January
LOVE & ROCKETS: Release single 'Glittering Darkness'.

February
BAUHAUS: Tribute LP *The Passion Of Covers* issued in USA.
ALIEN SEX FIEND: Release single 'Evolution'.
HOLY BARBARIANS: First live shows in LA.
MARCH VIOLETS: Release single 'Turn To The Sky'.

March
NEFILIM: Release LP *Zoon*.
NEFILIM: Release single 'Penetration'.
DAVID J/ALAN MOORE: Release LP *The Moon & Serpent Grand Egyptian Theatre Of Marvels*.

March 17
LOVE & ROCKETS: North American tour opens in Palo Alto.

March 19
LOVE & ROCKETS: US only release of LP *Sweet FA*.

April
GIGANTIC: Release LP *Disenchanted*.

April 6
LOVE & ROCKETS: Single 'Sweet Love Hangover' enters US Airplay chart.
LOVE AND ROCKETS: LP *Sweet FA* enters US Chart (peak #172).

May 4
THE CURE: Single 'The 13th' enters UK Chart (peak #15).

May 11
LOVE & ROCKETS: Second North American tour opens in Pensacola, Florida.

May 11
THE CURE: Single 'The 13th' enters US Chart (peak #44).
THE CURE: US network TV debut, *Saturday Night Live*.

May 25
THE CURE: LP *Wild Mood Swings* enters US Chart (peak #12).

June 15
THE MISSION: Compilation LP *Blue* enters UK Chart (peak #73).

June 28
THE MISSION: Launch final tour, European festivals.

June 29
THE CURE: Single 'Mint Car' enters UK Chart (peak #31).

July 2
THE CURE: Launch North American tour (first in four years) at Centrum Centre, Worcester, MA.

July 6
THE MISSION: Farewell concert at Nottingham Rock City. (The band will actually play its last show at the Doctor festival in Escallere on 13th July.)

July 8
THE CURE: Launch North American tour at Continental Airlines Arena, E Rutherford, NJ.

July 19
SISTERS OF MERCY: Launch *Roadkill/Goldkill* European tour in Leeds.

July 20
THE CURE: Single 'Mint Car' enters US Chart (peak #58).

August
AND ALSO THE TREES: Release LP *Angelfish*.
HOLY BARBARIANS: Release LP *Cream*.

PETER MURPHY/LOVE & ROCKETS: Dropped by Beggars Banquet.

November 5
THE CULT: Release US compilation LP *High Octane Cult*.

December 4
THE CURE: UK tour.

December 14
THE CURE: Single 'Gone' enters UK Chart (peak #60).

1997

January 9
THE CURE: Robert Smith performs at David Bowie Birthday Concert, NYC.

February
JAMES RAY: Release LP *Psychodalek*.

March
ALIEN SEX FIEND: Release LP *Nocturnal Emissions*.
VIRGIN PRUNES: Release LP *Greatest Hits*.

March 28
SISTERS OF MERCY: Cancel one-off show in Birmingham.

April
GENE LOVES JEZEBEL: Launch North American reunion tour.

June 3
SISTERS OF MERCY: Launch *Distance Over Time* European tour.

June 13
THE CURE: Radio Show Festival, Shoreline Amphitheatre, CA.

June 14
THE CURE: Irvine Meadows Amphitheatre, CA.

July
SPECIMEN: Release compilation album *Azoic*.
SPECIMEN: Release US compilation *Wet Warm Cling Film Red Velvet Crush*.

August
ALIEN SEX FIEND: Release single 'On A Mission'.

October 31
THE CURE: Irving Plaza, New York.

November 15
THE CURE: Compilation LP *Galore – The Singles 19-* enters US Chart (peak #32).

November 29
THE CURE: Launch North American tour at Tower Theatre, Philadelphia.
THE CURE: Single 'Wrong Number' enters UK Chart (peak #62).

December 16-17
THE CURE: Shepherds Bush Empire, London.

1998

January
JOY DIVISION: release box set *Heart And Soul*.
VIRGIN PRUNES: Release compilation LP *Sons Find Devils*.

January 14
SISTERS OF MERCY: Launch *Event Horizon* European/North American tour.

February
ALIEN SEX FIEND: Release compilation *Wardance Of The Alien Sex Fiend*.

February 18
THE CURE: Robert Smith battles Barbra Streisand in episode of *South Park*.

March
SEX GANG CHILDREN: Release compilation LP *Welcome To My World*.

June
THE CREATURES: Release single 'Sad Cunt'.

August
THE CREATURES: Release EP *Eraser Cuts*.
PETER MURPHY: Release EP *Recall*.

August 22
THE CURE: Bizarre festival, Cologne, Germany.

August 25
JAY ASTON: Release LP *Unpopular Songs*.

September 20
THE CULT: Billy Duffy forms Coloursound with Mike Peters (ex-Alarm).

October
GENE LOVES JEZEBEL: Release US remix LP *Desire: Greatest Hits remixed*, including remix by THE MISSION.
THE CREATURES: Release single '2nd Floor'.

November
ALIEN SEX FIEND: Release single 'Tarot'.

1999

March 23
GENE LOVES JEZEBEL: Release LP *VII*.

March 27
THE CREATURES: Single 'Say' enters UK Chart (peak #72).

April
SEX GANG CHILDREN: Release compilation LP *Shout and Scream*.

July 17
THE CULT: Launch North American tour in Seattle WA.

August 3
GENE LOVES JEZEBEL (MICHAEL ASTON): Release LP *Love Lies Bleeding*.

September
SEX GANG CHILDREN: Release LP *Veil*.
SKELETAL FAMILY: Release compilation LP *The Singles Plus 1983-85*.

September 7
GENE LOVES JEZEBEL: Release compilation LP *Voodoo Dollies*.

September 14
GENE LOVES JEZEBEL: Release live LP *Live In Voodoo City*.

September 23
SISTERS OF MERCY: Launch *To The Planet Edge* North American tour.

October
THE MISSION, GENE LOVES JEZEBEL: Launch North American tour.

SEX GANG CHILDREN: Release compilation LP *Pop Up*.

October 16
THE MISSION, GENE LOVES JEZEBEL: Launch North American tour in Boston MA.

November
SEX GANG CHILDREN: Release compilation LP *Hungry Years*.

November 7
THE MISSION: Release rerecorded hits collection *Resurrection*.

December
ANDI SEX GANG/MICK ROSSI: Release LP *Gabriel and the Golden Horn*.

2000

February
THE MISSION: Release compilation *Tower Of Strength*.
PETER MURPHY: North American tour.

February 17
THE CURE: Launch North American tour at Hollywood Palace.

February 22
PETER MURPHY: Release compilation LP *Wild Birds 1985-1995*.

March 4
THE CURE: LP *Bloodflowers* enters US Chart (peak #16).

March 6
FIELDS OF THE NEPHILIM: Woodstage Festival, Germany.

April
ANDI SEX GANG: Release LP *Faithfull Covers*.

May
ANDI SEX GANG: Release LP *Last Of England*.

May 4
THE CURE: Launch European tour in Milan, Italy.

May 18
THE CURE: Launch North American tour in Atlanta GA.

June
SEX GANG CHILDREN: Release compilation LP *Anthology*.

June 6
THE CULT: Release compilation LP *The Singles 1984-95*.

August 8
ALL ABOUT EVE: Release first of two volumes of live LP *Fairy Light Nights*.

August 12
SISTERS OF MERCY: Launch *Trip The Light Fantastic* European tour at the M'era Luna Festival, Germany.

August 13
FIELDS OF THE NEPHILIM: M'era Luna festival, Germany.

September
SEX GANG CHILDREN: Release *The Dark*

Archives, compilation including unreleased second album.

September 21
IAN ASTBURY: Release LP *Spirit/Light/Speed*.

September 26
THE MISSION: Release live LP *Ever After: Live*.

October
SEX GANG CHILDREN: Release compilation LP *Demonstration!*.
SEX GANG CHILDREN: Release compilation LP *The Dark Archives Volume 1*.

October 21
THE CULT: Appear at House Of Blues' *When Bands Attack* festival in Chula Vista CA.

November 21
THE CULT: Release box set *Rare Cult*.

2001

January
SEX GANG CHILDREN: Release compilation LP *Empyre and Fall*.

February
SEX GANG CHILDREN: Release LP *The Wrath Of God*.
SEX GANG CHILDREN: Release compilation LP *The Legends Collection*.

February 16
SISTERS OF MERCY: Launch *Exxile Of Euphoria* 20th anniversary tour at York University.

March
THE CULT: Launch North American tour.
GENE LOVES JEZEBEL (MICHAEL ASTON): Release LP *Giving Up The Ghost*.

May
SEX GANG CHILDREN: Release LP *Helter Skelter*.
DANSE SOCIETY: Release compilation LP *Seduction: The Society Collection*.

June 8
FIELDS OF THE NEPHILIM: Three European festival dates cancelled.

June 23
THE CULT: LP *Beyond Good And Evil* enters US Chart (peak #37).

July
FIELDS OF THE NEPHILIM: Release compilation LP *From Here To Gehenna*.

July 31
PETER MURPHY: Release live LP *Alive Just For Love*.

September
LAST RITES release LP *Guided By Light*.
PLAY DEAD: Release LP *Company Of Justice*.

November
THE MISSION: Release LP *Aura*.
SEX GANG CHILDREN: Release compilation LP *Fall: The Complete Singles*.
SKELETAL FAMILY: Release compilation LP *The Promised Land*.

November 13
THE CURE: Release compilation LP/DVD *Greatest Hits*.

2002

February 19
ALL ABOUT EVE: Release LP *Live & Electric at Union* Chapel.

March
THE MISSION: Release single 'Shine Like The Stars.'
DANIEL ASH: Release LP *Daniel Ash*.
GENE LOVES JEZEBEL: Release live LP *Live At Nottingham* (1985 recording).

April
GENE LOVES JEZEBEL: Release live LP *Accept No Substitute*.

April 19
THE MISSION: Launch South American leg of the AurA TourA tour.

April 23
PETER MURPHY: Release LP *Dust*.

April 24
THE MISSION: Four dates into the South American tour, Craig Adams quits band. Hussey completes tour alone.

April 27
SIOUXSIE & THE BANSHEES: Reformed band appear at the Coachella festival.

July 15
THE MISSION: Wayne Hussey launches solo tour of Europe/UK.

July 27
THE CURE: Hyde Park, London.

August 10
SISTERS OF MERCY: M'era Luna festival, Germany.

Other Titles available from Helter Skelter

Coming Soon

Psychedelic Furs: Beautiful Chaos
by Dave Thompson £12.99
Psychedelic Furs were the ultimate post-punk band – combining the chaos and vocal rasp of the Sex Pistols with a Bowie-esque glamour. The Furs hit the big time when John Hughes wrote a movie based on their early single "Pretty in Pink". Poised to join U2 and Simple Minds in the premier league, they withdrew behind their shades, remaining a cult act, but one with a hugely devoted following.

Steve Marriott: The Definitive Biography
by Paolo Hewitt and John Hellier £18.99
Marriott was the prime mover behind 60s chart-toppers The Small Faces. Longing to be treated as a serious musician he formed Humble Pie with Peter Frampton, where his blistering rock 'n' blues guitar playing soon saw him take centre stage in the US live favourites. After years in seclusion, Marriott's plans for a comeback in 1991 were tragically cut short when he died in a housefire. He continues to be a key influence for generations of musicians from Paul Weller to Oasis and Blur.

Pink Floyd: A Saucerful of Secrets
by Nicholas Schaffner £14.99
Long overdue reissue of the authoritative and detailed account of one of the most important and popular bands in rock history. From the psychedelic explorations of the Syd Barrett-era to 70s superstardom with *Dark Side of the Moon*, and on to triumph of *The Wall*, before internecine strife tore the group apart. Schaffner's definitive history also covers the improbable return of Pink Floyd without Roger Waters, and the hugely successful Momentary Lapse of Reason album and tour.

The Big Wheel
by Bruce Thomas £10.99
Thomas was bassist with Elvis Costello at the height of his success. Though names are never named, *The Big Wheel* paints a vivid and hilarious picture of life touring with Costello and co, sharing your life 24-7 with a moody egotistical singer, a crazed drummer and a host of hangers-on. Costello sacked Thomas on its initial publication.
"A top notch anecdotalist who can time a twist to make you laugh out loud." *Q*

Hit Men: Powerbrokers and Fast Money Inside The Music Business
By Fredric Dannen £14.99
Hit Men exposes the seamy and sleazy dealings of America's glitziest record companies: payola, corruption, drugs, Mafia involvement, and excess.
"So heavily awash with cocaine, corruption and unethical behaviour that it makes the occasional examples of chart-rigging and playlist tampering in Britain during the same period seem charmingly inept." *The Guardian.*

I'm With The Band: Confessions of A Groupie
By Pamela Des Barres £12.99
Frank and engaging memoir of affairs with Keith Moon, Noel Redding and Jim Morrison, travels with Led Zeppelin as Jimmy Page's girlfriend, and friendships with Robert Plant, Gram Parsons, and Frank Zappa.
"Miss Pamela, the most beautiful and famous of the groupies. Her memoir of her life with rock stars is funny, bittersweet, and tender-hearted." Stephen Davis, author of *Hammer of the Gods*

Bob Dylan: Like The Night (Revisited)
by CP Lee £9.99
Fully revised and updated B-format edition of the hugely acclaimed document of Dylan's pivotal 1966 show at the Manchester Free Trade Hall where fans called him Judas for turning his back on folk music in favour of rock 'n' roll.

Marillion: Separated Out
by Jon Collins £14.99
From the chart hit days of Fish and "Kayleigh" to the Steve Hogarth incarnation, Marillion have continued to make groundbreaking rock music. Collins tells the full story, drawing on interviews with band members, associates, and the experiences of some of the band's most dedicated fans.

Marc Bolan and T Rex: A Chronology
by Cliff McLenahan £13.99
Bolan was the ultimate glam-rock icon; beautiful, elfin, outrageously dressed and capable of hammering out impossibly catchy teen rock hits such as "Telegram Sam", and "Get It On". With their pounding guitars and three chord anthems T Rex paved the way for hard rock and punk rock.

Back to the Beach: A Brian Wilson and the Beach Boys Reader
Ed Kingsley Abbott £12.99
Revised and expanded edition of the Beach Boys compendium *Mojo* magazine deemed an "essential purchase." This collection includes all of the best articles, interviews and reviews from the Beach Boys' four decades of music, including definitive pieces by Timothy White, Nick Kent and David Leaf. New material reflects on the tragic death of Carl Wilson and documents the rejuvenated Brian's return to the boards. "Rivetting!" **** Q "An essential purchase." *Mojo*

Harmony in My Head
The Original Buzzcock Steve Diggle's Rock 'n' Roll Odyssey
by Steve Diggle and Terry Rawlings £14.99
First-hand account of the punk wars from guitarist and one half of the songwriting duo that gave the world three chord punk-pop classics like "Ever Fallen In Love" and "Promises". Diggle dishes the dirt on punk contemporaries like The Sex Pistols, The Clash and The Jam, as well as sharing poignant memories of his friendship with Kurt Cobain, on whose last ever tour, The Buzzcocks were support act.

Serge Gainsbourg: A Fistful of Gitanes
by Sylvie Simmons £9.99
Rock press legend Simmons' hugely acclaimed biography of the French genius.
"I would recommend *A Fistful of Gitanes* [as summer reading] which is a highly entertaining biography of the French singer-songwriter and all-round scallywag" – JG Ballard
"A wonderful introduction to one of the most overlooked songwriters of the 20th century" (Number 3, top music books of 2001) *The Times*
"The most intriguing music-biz biography of the year" *The Independent*
"Wonderful. Serge would have been so happy" – Jane Birkin

Blues: The British Connection
by Bob Brunning £14.99
Former Fleetwood Mac member Bob Brunning's classic account of the impact of Blues in Britain, from its beginnings as the underground music of 50s teenagers like Mick Jagger, Keith Richards and Eric Clapton, to the explosion in the 60s, right through to the vibrant scene of the present day.
'An invaluable reference book and an engaging personal memoir' – Charles Shaar Murray

On The Road With Bob Dylan
by Larry Sloman £12.99
In 1975, as Bob Dylan emerged from 8 years of seclusion, he dreamed of putting together a travelling music show that would trek across the country like a psychedelic carnival. The dream became a reality, and *On The Road With Bob Dylan* is the ultimate behind-the-scenes look at what happened. When Dylan and the Rolling Thunder Revue took to the streets of America, Larry "Ratso" Sloman was with them every step of the way.
"The War and Peace of Rock and Roll." – Bob Dylan

Currently Available from Helter Skelter

Gram Parsons: God's Own Singer
By Jason Walker £12.99
Brand new biography of the man who pushed The Byrds into country-rock territory on *Sweethearts of The Rodeo*, and quit to form the Flying Burrito Brothers. Gram lived hard, drank hard, took every drug going and somehow invented country rock, paving the way for Crosby, Stills & Nash, The Eagles and Neil Young. Parsons' second solo LP, *Grievous Angel*, is a haunting masterpiece of country soul. By the time it was released, he had been dead for 4 months. He was 26 years old.
"Walker has done an admirable job in taking us as clos   e to the heart and soul of Gram Parsons as any author could." **** *Uncut* book of the month

Ashley Hutchings: The Guvnor and the Rise of Folk Rock – Fairport Convention, Steeleye Span and the Albion Band
by Geoff Wall and Brian Hinton £14.99
As founder of Fairport Convention and Steeleye Span, Ashley Hutchings is the pivotal figure in the history of folk rock. This book draws on hundreds of hours of interviews with Hutchings and other folk-rock artists and paints a vivid picture of the scene that also produced Sandy Denny, Richard Thompson, Nick Drake, John Martyn and Al Stewart.

Al Stewart: True Life Adventures of a Folk Troubadour
by Neville Judd £25.00
Authorised biography of the Scottish folk hero behind US Top Ten hit "Year of The Cat". This is a vivid insider's account of the pivotal 60s London coffee house scene that kickstarted the careers of a host of folkies including

Paul Simon – with whom Al shared a flat in 1965 – as well as the wry memoir of a 60s folk star's tribulations as he becomes a chart-topping star in the US in the 70s. Highly limited hardcover edition!

Rainbow Rising: The Story of Ritchie Blackmore's Rainbow
by Roy Davies £14.99
Blackmore led rock behemoths Deep Purple to international, multi-platinum, mega-stardom. He quite in '75, to form Rainbow, one of the great live bands, with Ronnie James Dio and enjoyed a string of acclaimed albums and hit singles, including "All Night Long" and "Since You've Been Gone" before the egos of the key players caused the whole thing to implode. A great rock 'n' roll tale.

ISIS: A Bob Dylan Anthology
Ed Derek Barker £14.99
Expertly compiled selection of rare articles which trace the evolution of rock's greatest talent. From Bob's earliest days in New York City to the more recent legs of the Never Ending Tour, and his new highly acclaimed album, Love and Theft, the ISIS archive has exclusive interview material – often rare or previously unpublished – with many of the key players in Dylan's career: his parents, friends, musicians and other collaborators.

The Beach Boys' Pet Sounds: The Greatest Album of the Twentieth Century
by Kingsley Abbott £11.95
Pet Sounds is the 1966 album that saw The Beach Boys graduate from lightweight pop like "Surfin' USA", et al, into a vehicle for the mature compositional genius of Brian Wilson. The album was hugely influential, not least on The Beatles. This full story of the album's background, its composition and recording, its contemporary reception and its enduring legacy.

King Crimson: In The Court of King Crimson
by Sid Smith £14.99
King Crimson's 1969 masterpiece *In The Court Of The Crimson King*, was a huge U.S. chart hit. The band followed it with 40 further albums of consistently challenging, distinctive and innovative music. Drawing on hours of new interviews, and encouraged by Crimson supremo Robert Fripp, the author traces the band's turbulent history year by year, track by track.

A Journey Through America with the Rolling Stones
by Robert Greenfield UK Price £9.99
Featuring a new foreword by Ian Rankin
This is the definitive account of their legendary '72 tour. "Filled with finely-rendered detail ... a fascinating tale of times we shall never see again" *Mojo*

Razor Edge: Bob Dylan and The Never-ending Tour
by Andrew Muir £12.99
Respected Dylan expert Andrew Muir documents the ups and downs of this unprecedented trek, and finds time to tell the story of his own curious meeting with Dylan. Muir also tries to get to grips with what exactly it all means – both for Dylan and for the Bobcats: dedicated Dylan followers, like himself, who trade tapes of every show and regularly cross the globe to catch up with the latest leg of The Never Ending Tour.

Calling Out Around the World: A Motown Reader
Edited by Kingsley Abbott £13.99
With a foreword by Martha Reeves, this is a unique collection of articles which tell the story of the rise of a black company in a white industry, and its talented stable of artists, musicians, writers and producers. Included are rare interviews with key figures such as Berry Gordy, Marvin Gaye, Smokey Robinson and Florence Ballard as well as reference sources for collectors and several specially commissioned pieces.

I've Been Everywhere: A Johnny Cash Chronicle
by Peter Lewry £14.99
A complete chronological illustrated diary of Johnny Cash's concerts, TV appearances, record releases, recording sessions and other milestones. From his early days with Sam Phillips in Memphis to international stardom, the wilderness years of the mid-sixties, and on to his legendary prison concerts and his recent creative resurgence with the hugely successful 2000 release, *American Recording III: Solitary Man*.

Sandy Denny: No More Sad Refrains
by Clinton Heylin £13.99
Paperback edition of the highly acclaimed biography of the greatest female singer-songwriter this country has ever produced.

Emerson Lake and Palmer: The Show That Never Ends
by George Forrester, Martin Hanson and Frank Askew £14.00
Drawing on years of research, the authors have produced a gripping and fascinating document of the prog-rock supergroup who remain one of the great rock bands of the seventies.

Animal Tracks: The Story of The Animals
by Sean Egan £12.99
Sean Egan has enjoyed full access to surviving Animals and associates and has produced a compelling portrait of a truly distinctive band of survivors.

Like a Bullet of Light: The Films of Bob Dylan
by CP Lee £12.99
In studying in-depth an often overlooked part of Dylan's oeuvre.

Rock's Wild Things: The Troggs Files
by Alan Clayson and Jacqueline Ryan £12.99
Respected rock writer Alan Clayson has had full access to the band and traces their history from 60s Andover rock roots to 90s covers, collaborations and corn circles. Also features the full transcript of the legendary "Troggs Tapes."

Waiting for the Man: The Story of Drugs and Popular Music
by Harry Shapiro UK £12.99
Fully revised edition of the classic story of two intertwining billion dollar industries.
  "Wise and witty." *The Guardian*

Dylan's Daemon Lover: The Tangled Tale of a 450-Year Old Pop Ballad
by Clinton Heylin UK £12.00
Written as a detective story, Heylin unearths the mystery of why Dylan knew enough to return "The House Carpenter" to its 16th century source.

Get Back: The Beatles' Let It Be Disaster
by Doug Sulpy & Ray Schweighardt UK price £12.99
No-holds barred account of the power struggles, the bickering, and the bitterness that led to the break-up of the greatest band in the history of rock 'n' roll.
  "One of the most poignant Beatles books ever." *Mojo*

XTC: Song Stories – The Exclusive & Authorised Story
by XTC and Neville Farmer £12.99
"A cheerful celebration of the minutiae surrounding XTC's music with the band's musical passion intact ... high in setting-the-record-straight anecdotes. Superbright, funny, commanding." *Mojo*

Born in the USA: Bruce Springsteen and the American Tradition
by Jim Cullen £9.99
"Cullen has written an excellent treatise expressing exactly how and why Springsteen translated his uneducated hicktown American-ness into music and stories that touched hearts and souls around the world." *Q****

Bob Dylan
by Anthony Scaduto £10.99
The first and best biography of Dylan. "The best book ever written on Dylan" *Record Collector* "Now in a welcome reprint it's a real treat to read the still-classic Bobography". *Q*****

Firefly Publishing: An Association between Helter Skelter and SAF

Coming Soon from Firefly Publishing:

The Nirvana Recording Sessions
by Rob Jovanovic £14.99
Drawing on years of research, and interviews with many who worked with the band, the author has documented details of every Nirvana recording, from early rehearsals, to the In Utero sessions. A fascinating account of the creative process of one of the great bands.

Marty Balin: Full Flight – A Tale of Airplanes and Starships
by Marty Balin & Bob Yehling £20
Marty Balin founded Jefferson Airplane – which he fronted as the male half of American rock's greatest vocalist duo – Marty Balin & Grace Slick. A key figure at Woodstock, Monterey and famously beaten up onstage by Hell's Angels at Altamont, Balin wrote many of the band's key songs. He also took Airplane's successor, Jefferson Starship, to the top of the 1970s singles and albums charts with self-penned hits like "Miracles." Balin left Airplane with 17 scrapbooks containing memorabilia and photos of the band's history, which form the basis for this heavily illustrated book.

The Music of George Harrison: While My Guitar Gently Weeps
by Simon Leng £18.99
Often in Lennon and McCartney's shadow, Harrison's music can stand on its own merits. Santana biographer Leng takes a studied, track by track, look at both Harrison's contribution to The Beatles, and the solo work that started with the release in 1970 of his epic masterpiece *All Things Must Pass*. "Here Comes The Sun", "Something" – which Sinatra covered and saw as the perfect love song – "All Things Must Pass" and "While My Guitar Gently Weeps" are just a few of Harrison's classic songs.
Originally planned as a celebration of Harrison's music, this is now sadly a commemoration.

Mail Order

All Helter Skelter, Firefly and SAF titles are available by mail order from the world famous Helter Skelter bookshop.
You can either phone or fax your order to Helter Skelter on the following numbers:

Telephone: +44 (0)20 7836 1151 or Fax: +44 (0)20 7240 9880
Office hours: Mon-Fri 10:00am – 7:00pm,
Sat: 10:00am – 6:00pm, Sun: closed.

Postage prices per book worldwide are as follows:

UK & Channel Islands	£1.50
Europe & Eire (air)	£2.95
USA, Canada (air)	£7.50
Australasia, Far East (air)	£9.00
Overseas (surface)	£2.50

You can also write enclosing a cheque, International Money Order, or registered cash. Please include postage. DO NOT send cash. DO NOT send foreign currency, or cheques drawn on an overseas bank. Send to:

Helter Skelter Bookshop,
4 Denmark Street, London, WC2H 8LL, United Kingdom.
If you are in London come and visit us, and browse the titles in person!!

Email: helter@skelter.demon.co.uk
Website: http://www.skelter.demon.co.uk